HENRY MARTYN KIEFFER, D. D.
From a Portrait by Marie Constantin.

Some of the First Settlers of "The Forks of the Delaware" and Their Descendants

*Being a Translation from the German
of the Record Books of the
First Reformed Church of Easton, Pennsylvania
from 1760 to 1852*

Translated by the
Rev. Henry Martyn Kieffer, D.D.
Pastor of the Church
Author of The Recollections of a Drummer Boy, College
Chapel Sermons, The Old Sullivan Road, Etc.

Together with an Historical Introduction

In Commemoration of the
One Hundred and Fifty-Seventh Anniversary
of the Founding of the Congregation
1745-1902

HERITAGE BOOKS
2007

HERITAGE BOOKS
AN IMPRINT OF HERITAGE BOOKS, INC.

Books, CDs, and more—Worldwide

For our listing of thousands of titles see our website
at
www.HeritageBooks.com

A Facsimile Reprint
Published 2007 by
HERITAGE BOOKS, INC.
Publishing Division
65 East Main Street
Westminster, Maryland 21157-5026

Copyright © 1902 Henry Martyn Kieffer

Copyright © 1995 Heritage Books, Inc.

— Publisher's Notice —
In reprints such as this, it is often not possible to remove blemishes from the original. We feel the contents of this book warrant its reissue despite these blemishes and hope you will agree and read it with pleasure.

International Standard Book Number: 978-0-7884-0313-2

PREFATORY NOTE.

The First Reformed Church of Easton was founded during the earliest period of the settlement at "The Forks of the Delaware," and has been identified with the borough and city of Easton throughout their entire history. The church building which the congregation at present occupies was erected in 1776. It is the only public building in Easton remaining from the days of the Revolution, and for nearly half a century after its erection was the only church building in the town. Its record books, which possess the rare distinction of being continuous and unbroken for nearly a century and a half, are contemporaneous in their origin with the early beginnings of the settlement, and contain information of greatest value to the many thousands of the descendents of "The First Settlers of the Forks of the Delaware"; for the settlement having from the first been prevailingly German, nearly every family in the community, at some time or other in its history, left some trace of itself in the records of this old German Reformed Church. For genealogical purposes it is believed that this publication will prove of great value to many people. On a moderate estimate there are nearly, or quite, 20,000 names recorded in this book. The descendants of the people for whom these names stand, though scattered far and wide, will here find material for their family history which is simply invaluable.

CONTENTS.

The Forks of the Delaware.. 1
The First German Settlers... 5
The Old Church Record-books 11
The Indian Treaty in the Church, January 30, 1777......... 20
The Organization of the Congregation, and the Building of
    the Church 34
Recent History 61
The Old Organ and its Successors....................................... 70
The Change in the Name of the Church............................. 72
The Chime of Bells... 75
Church Records.. 77
    Title Page of Church Book... 77
    Baptisms 81
Book Second 277
    Title Page...277
    Deaths and Burials..278
        Easton 283
        Greenwich ("Gruenitz").....................................284
        Dryland..285
        Mount Bethel...285
        Easton 286
        Dryland..289
        Plainfield..291
        Mount Bethel 293
        Easton, Plaenfield, Mount Bethel and Dryland......294
Marriages 343
The Church at Dryland...400
The Congregation at Plainfield...401
Conclusion 403

ILLUSTRATIONS.

Henry Martyn Kieffer, D.D............................Frontispiece
Watermarks in Church Books...................................12–14
The First Reformed Church, Easton, Pa......................... 1
Interior of the First Reformed Church at the Centennial, 1876... 34
Interior of the First Reformed Church, 1902 73
Inscription in the Old Schlatter Bible............................ 40
The Schlatter Bible, and the Old Communion Set, bearing date, 1746.. 48
Fac-simile of a Page of the Old Church Record................. 80
The Deed Granted by the Penns, 1802........................... 90
Rev. Thomas Pomp..135
Bernard G. Wolff, D.D..160
J. H. A. Bomberger, D.D.......................................209
John Beck, D.D...273
Thomas Conrad Porter, D.D., LL.D............................305
A Confirmation Service in the Olden Time.....................360

THE FIRST REFORMED CHURCH, EASTON, PA.

THE FIRST REFORMED CHURCH
OF EASTON, PENNA.

THE FORKS OF THE DELAWARE.

WHAT is now known as "The City of Easton" was originally called "The Forks of the Delaware." By this name it was designated by the Indians themselves, long before the appearance of the white man at this most beautiful and romantic spot, and though the white man gave it a new name, the Indian to the latest generation clung tenaciously to the title given by his fathers to the place where the Lehigh River empties its waters into the greater Delaware. To the Colonial and Continental authorities seeking a council with the original proprietors of the soil, Teedyuscung, the Great King of the Delawares, said — "I will treat with you nowhere else than at the Forks of the Delaware."

If we are curious to know how this original name of the place was exchanged for that which the city now bears, we are told that when the first settlers established themselves here, about the year 1739, the territory of Northampton County was a part of Bucks, and that when the new county was surveyed and the town established by the authority of Thomas Penn, it was directed by him that the County should be called Northampton and the town Easton. The town was thus named in honor of the house of Lord Pomfret in England, Thomas Penn having married the daughter of Lord Pomfret.

Who was the first adventurous white man to set foot on this most beautiful and romantic spot, or who first drew up his canoe on the pebble-covered tongue of land that originally extended far out between the Delaware and Lehigh rivers at their intersection, no one can tell; but as one stands on what remains of "The Point," as it was once called, and looks about him at the high hills and bold bluffs, on all sides shutting him in, he may imagine the wild and romantic scene that must have presented itself to the eye of the first white discoverer of "The Forks of the Delaware." High hills on all sides round frowned down, covered with dark and primeval forests; no house or human habitation was anywhere to be seen; no sign of civilized man anywhere appeared. Here the dusky children of the forest were the only inhabitants—and comparatively few they were in numbers who dwelt permanently in this wild and rugged region; for "The Forks of the Delaware" was rather a mere meeting place for the Indians than aught else — a place in which "to light the council fire" rather than a place of permanent dwelling. Better lands for the building of towns and the cultivation of the soil could be found elsewhere than amongst these high hills. The more powerful Iroquois had their habitation in the Genesee valley in western New York; the Lenni-Lenape dwelt eastward along the Delaware, the Delawares northward in the Minnisink region — but nowhere could a council fire be so well lighted as where the two great rivers joined their waters with the mighty hills as witnesses of their union. And to these council fires, long before the advent of the white man, the Indians came down the Lehigh from the west in their light birch-bark canoes, or down the Delaware from the north, holding here their conferences of peace or war, trade or barter,

The Forks of the Delaware.

at the well-known and far-famed "Forks of the Delaware."

For centuries they had held undisputed possession of this charming spot, when the first white man, crossing the sands of New Jersey or descending the hills of the Lehigh, penetrated to this favorite Indian rendezvous. What his name or what his experience we know not, but we are told that one David Martin in 1739 built the first house at "The Point," as the intersection of the two rivers was then called —a log cabin, rude enough no doubt, but comfortable, and long celebrated as the scene of very important transactions between civilized and savage man. Here David Martin established his ferry, carrying the adventurous trader or the occasional traveller across either the Lehigh or the Delaware in his rowboat, for a reasonable consideration. The inquiry may naturally arise concerning the necessity for a ferry at a time when the white population was so sparse. Its existence at a date so early may perhaps be explained by the fact that when the town of Easton was duly laid out in 1750 by William Parsons a considerable population had already gathered on the New Jersey side of the river opposite, Thomas Penn in 1752 expressing some fear that what is now Phillipsburg might prove a dangerous rival to Easton, and suggesting that it might be prudent to secure all the land possible on the Jersey side of the river. At all events, Martin's ferry seems to have proved a profitable investment both to its original founder and his successors.

For it did not always remain a mere Ferry House, but was at an early date enlarged into a hotel, kept at first by one Nathaniel Vernon, and in his day it became the celebrated scene of many important Indian treaties, all of which were held here until the erection of the church on Third

Street, which afforded larger and better accommodations. These treaties were attended by certain very celebrated persons on the white man's side—by the Governor of New Jersey and his staff, by the Governor of Pennsylvania and his staff, by William Parsons and Conrad Weiser and other eminent people; and on the part of the Indians, powerful chieftains representing at times as many as eighteen or nineteen distinct tribes here assembled—amongst whom the representatives of the powerful Six Nations held first place, though Teedyuscung, King of the Delawares, in his cocked-hat covered with lace, and arrayed in his broadcloth coat cut in the height of the French fashion, must always have been a commanding figure. These conferences often lasted for two or three weeks at a time, and upon them the destiny of empires depended. What grand speaking must have been done on that historic point of land by these dusky warriors, and what scenes of revelry were there witnessed when the Council broke up in peace, and "the lock and chain were taken off the cask of rum," to the terror of the white inhabitants and the wild joy of the savage lovers of the white man's fire water, who believed, as an experienced chief once declared, that "In every barrel of rum there were a thousand songs and fifty fights."

The great historic interest which clusters about this spot should, we think, induce the wealthy citizens of Easton to purchase "The Point" and transform it into a neat and well kept public park, in which there should be a suitable monument commemorating the great events which there occurred in Colonial times. A granite statue of an Indian, in full warrior costume, holding the pipe of peace in his hand; or a suitable memorial to William Parsons, the father of Easton; or both combined, might well mark and beautify the point of land, visible from all our railroads, which originally gave the name to "The Forks of the Delaware."

THE FIRST GERMAN SETTLERS.

IT is evident that from a very early period in the history of the settlement at "The Forks of the Delaware," German immigrants bore a very important, if not a very conspicuous part. Certainly they constituted, at a very early date, the major portion of the population. It is true indeed that they do not figure very largely or prominently in the early annals and records of events, but in the early history of Easton, as in that of many other sections of Pennsylvania, this is to be accounted for largely by the circumstance that the Germans, though often constituting the bulk of the population, were not acquainted with the English language. The English language necessarily had the preference in a colony of England; it was the only language employed in the courts of justice, in the Councils of the Province, and in all correspondence with the mother country. Such being the case, our German ancestors were of necessity excluded from office-bearing in the affairs of state to a large extent, and in all public transactions in the early period of the colony have therefore left a trace of themselves entirely disproportionate to either their numbers or their importance in the true life and development of the State. They were perforce constrained to leave to others the pleasing task of writing the history which they were helping so largely to make. Besides this, it is to be remembered that the German is constitutionally modest and retiring. He does not possess the disposition of some other nationalities to push and elbow his way to the front, preferring rather to sit quietly and bide his time. So true are these facts that it has been well said that "the Pennsylvania-German Society will, to a very large extent, compel the history of the great Commonwealth of Pennsylvania to be rewritten."

We cull a few facts from which it may well appear that the Germans were a very important factor at an early day in the history of Easton.[1] "In a letter dated December 8, 1752, six months after the first sessions of the Court, William Parsons says that there were then eleven families living in the town (probably about fifty men, women and children); and in the histories of Northampton County and Lehigh Valley we have a list of these families and their callings — William Parsons, Clerk of Courts, etc.; Lewis Gordon, lawyer; Henry Alshouse, carpenter; Abram Berlin, smith; Nathaniel Vernon, ferryman; William Craig and John Anderson, tavern-keepers; Paul Miller, tavern-keeper; Ernest Becker, baker; Anthony Esser, butcher; John Finley, mason; Myer Hart, shopkeeper."

The first church and school-house was erected in Easton by the agency largely of the German settlers. In the year 1746 the Rev. Michael Schlatter came to this country from Switzerland and Holland, to visit the scattered people of the Reformed faith in the provinces of Pennsylvania, Maryland and Virginia. In 1751 he returned to Europe to report to the Synods of South and North Holland which had sent him forth. To the churches in Holland as well as in England he appealed for help for the destitute settlers in this new land, and on his return to America in 1752 he brought with him very substantial tokens of the interest of Christian people in these German settlers, in the shape of numerous bibles and a very considerable amount of money for the establishment of

[1] Condit's "History of Easton," p. 15.

churches and schools. Of these bibles. one is still in the possession of the " First Reformed Church of Easton." And as for the schools—it is recorded that, in order to make effectual Easton's portion of the Schlatter School Fund, on the 31st day of July, 1755, the following "do hereby engage and agree to and with William Parsons, James Martin, Peter Trexler, Esqr., John Lefebre, Lewis Gordon and Peter Kichline, deputy trustees, mentioned and appointed by the trustees general of the said charitable scheme, that each of us will pay the sum of money, and do and perform the work, labor, and service, in building and erecting a school-house, which may occasionally be made use of as a Church for any Protestant Minister, to our names hereunto respectively set down and affixed "—

"William Smith, in behalf of the Proprietor and Trustees— £30; William Parsons, £5; Nicolas Scull, £3; Nathaniel Vernon, £3; Peter Kichline, £2; Christian Rinker, £1; Jacob Bachman, £1; Jacob Miner, £1; Adam Yohe, £1; Lewis Knaus, 10s; Lewis Klotz, 10s; Henry Becker, 7s; George Michael Schurtz, 15s; John Levitz, 15s; Anthony Esser, 15s; George Reichart, 15s; John Wagle (Nagle?) £1; George Ernest Becker, £1; John Rinker, 10s; N. N. 7s; Daniel Gies, 5s; Jeremiah C. Russell, £1; Paul Miller, £1.5s; John Fricker, £1.6s; Meyer Hart, 20 lb. nails; Paul Reeser, 1,000 shingles: Jacob Minor, 12 days work; Stephen Horn, 1 week's work; Henry Alshouse, 5 days work; John Finley, 6 days work; John Nicholas Reeder, 6 days work; Bartholomew Hoffman, 5 days mason's work; Robert Miller, 4 days work; John Henry Bush, 5 days carpenters work; Jacob Krotz, 5 days carpenters work; James Fuller, 5 days stone digging; John Chapman, 3 days cutting stone; Henry Rinker, 30 bushels lime; Henry Bush and John Weidman, 30 wagons stone and digging; Thomas Harris, 50 sash lights."

The above list tells its own tale concerning the German

element of the population of "The Forks of the Delaware" more than twenty years before the signing of the Declaration of Independence. The Germans were relatively numerous, but they were neither wealthy nor conspicuous. They were making history—or helping largely to make it—but they were not much employed in recording it; they could handle a pick, a shovel or an axe—and they knew well how to handle a gun, too, as we shall shortly see—but not being masters of the language of "the powers that be," they were not expert in making reports of things done. They were at a disadvantage, evidently; but on the whole and in the long run, history is just.

Not only did the Germans lead the way in the religious and educational interests of the new community; they were equally zealous in things patriotic. In 1763 the first military company was formed in Easton for defence against the Indians, the following being the agreement by which the members bound themselves to service—

"Wee, the undernamed subscribers, doo hereby joyntly and severally agree that Jacob Arndt Esquire shall be our captain for three months from the date of these presence, and Be allwise Ready to obey him when he sees ocation to call us together in pursuing the Indians, or helping any of us that shall be in distress by the Indians. Each person to find arms and powder and lead at our own cost and have noe pay. Each person to find himself in all necessarys: to which articl, covenant and agreement, Wee Bind ourselves in the Penal sum of Five pounds, Lawful monies of Pensilvania, to be laid out for arms and ammunition for the use of the Company, unless the person soe Neglecting to obeay shall Show a lawfull Reason. Given under our hands this 13th day of October 1763."

This document was signed by the following persons who constituted the Muster Roll of Easton's first military

The First German Settlers.

company. The predominance of German names is apparent:

Jacob Arndt	Elias Shook	Christian Gress
John Sandy	Michael Sheund	Jacob Hartzell
Philip Odenwelder	Melchior Young	M. Lawall
John Jaeger	Jacob Grouse	Matthias Pfeiffer
Jacob Reichardt	Valentine Sandy	M. Owen Arndt
Jerry Leidy	William Bonstein	Matthew Rownig
Michael Butz	Elias Bender	Peter Seip
Christian Smith	Richard Richards	Christopher Hahn
Paul J. Ebbel	Garrett Moore	Christopher Sienteog
Adam Hay	Henry Raddler	John Painter
John Miller	Philip Mann	Robert Townsend.
P. J. Mann	James Bunston	

In the year 1828 a certain Mrs. Anne Royall, "a notorious newspaper satirist and novelist," made a journey in a stage coach from Philadelphia to Easton, an account of which is to be found in a volume in the library of the State Historical Society, entitled "Mrs. Royall's Pennsylvania, or Travels Continued in the United States, 1829."[1] In her account of this visit to Northampton County she says that Easton "contains one court house, one county house, one jail, one market house, four churches, two banks, one public library, seven merchant mills, one academy, nine store houses for flour, etc., four oil mills, two sawmills, two breweries, one distillery — and four thousand inhabitants. . . . Easton is settled by Germans, though the most of them use the English language, and are well educated. The professional men, particularly, are greatly superior to those of New York and not inferior to (if they do not excel) those of any other town. There is a plain, unmoved intelligence about them, similar to the people of the

---
[1] An account of her visit to Northampton County, published by Mr. Ethan Allen Weaver in the Easton *Free Press*, 1902.

Western States. . . . It would seem that good sense, good size, good manners and hospitality, which once distinguished Philadelphia, had fled for shelter to this part of the state. The people remind me of the French, particularly the young men and women, being very fond of music and dancing. You hear the violin and the piano forte of an evening almost in every home." She dwells at length on the various enterprises and public improvements at Easton—the bridges over the Lehigh and the Delaware, and especially upon the Lehigh Canal, over which the Lehigh coal is transported from Mauch Chunk to Philadelphia. This canal, she tells us, cost $800,000 and has fifty locks. "And these are the ignorant Germans! I begin to think these ignorant Germans have a little sound sense, and a great deal of wealth and judgment, with all their ignorance."

In the very valuable "History of the Lehigh Valley" we read that "In 1752 when the County of Northampton was laid out, there were nearly 6,000 inhabitants, of whom 600 were Scotch-Irish, in Allen and Mount Bethel Townships, 300 Dutch (Hollanders) in Smithfield, and the rest Germans. In some of the townships there is not an English name to be found on the assessment list."

We would certainly not withhold any honor or credit from the people of any nationality—English, Irish, Scotch or French—who bore a part in the early settlement of "The Forks of the Delaware," but neither do we think that the patient labors of the silent Germans should be overlooked by the writers of the history of Easton.

THE OLD CHURCH RECORD-BOOKS.

OF these there are three, two of which are devoted to the record, chiefly, of baptisms and marriages, the other to that of deaths, burials and marriages. Two of these books were evidently purchased about the same time, viz., about the year 1766. This we know from the fact that the first entries are in the handwriting of the second pastor of the congregation, the Rev. Frederick L. Henop, who became the pastor in 1766. There are indeed certain entries of an earlier date, pertaining to the ministerial acts of the first pastor, Rev. Mr. Weyberg, who became pastor in 1763 and remained only six months; but it is evident, both from the handwriting and from explicit statements to that effect, that these entries were made not by Rev. Mr. Weyberg but by Rev. Mr. Henop, who transcribed some of the records of Mr. Weyberg's brief pastorate into the church book from scattered memoranda left by him on his departure.

From this circumstance we are warranted in the belief that these church books were first used about the year 1766. The two are of the same size, quality of paper, and general appearance, except that the one is bound in hog skin, the other in sheep.

These books are noteworthy as containing three distinct water-marks, which are herewith given, representing Britannia with her sceptre in hand and accompanied by the inevitable British lion grasping the thunderbolts of power. The smaller one carries the crown and initials of Georgius Rex — King George the third.

The preservation of these books through so many years in fairly good condition is something to be grateful for, especially when one remembers that in the early days of

Easton's history there were no fire-proof safes in which they might be kept, and efforts at protection against fire were yet in their infancy. Indeed, one object the author

had in undertaking the work of translating and publishing these records was that they might be secured for all time against the danger of destruction by fire. Once published and distributed, in families and public libraries, it was felt, while fire might destroy some of the copies, it could never destroy all.

An examination of these books shows that, unfortunately, no list of the membership of the church was kept from the beginning. The record of births and baptisms, marriages and funerals, along with certain other matters was, however, carefully kept, albeit in handwriting occa-

sionally crabbed even to provocation. In the earlier years the handwriting was something marvellous, and from beginning to end was embarrassed by a singular admixture of the English way of writing. This English tendency in the script increases as the years go by, and in the latter days of Father Pomp held almost an even chance with the German — the records being made indifferently in German or English, apparently as the mood held the scribe. And not only this, but what is even more puzzling at times is the way in which letters in the same word are formed, now after the rule of the one language, and again after that of the other. Though, on the whole, these records were well kept and clearly written, the ink showing as

black at times as the day it left the nib of the quill with which the writing was done. However, it is provoking how occasionally the family name — the very name that is most important of all — was so very indistinctly and uncertainly written that the author has been obliged to spend many hours with magnifying glass in hand trying to decipher the uncertain inscription, it being so very distressing that the very thing you most want is the very thing that is so obscure, while what concerns you little is so very plain.

Faithful these dear old scribes were, however, and honest as the day was long. Though English and German and Latin be mixed, and family names sometimes spelled with a small letter instead of a capital, yet every essential of a good, clear and reliable record is here. Variations there are in the spelling of family names, indeed, the same pen often failing to write the same name twice consecutively in the same way—yet this is always likely to happen. Whether, for example, it be *Ehrig*, *Erig*, *Ehrich*, *Erich*, or some other form, will probably not prevent the family of the *Ihries* from recognizing their ancestors and ancestresses. But it is to be feared that if this work should ever fall into the hands of a family by the active name of *Jumper*, the members thereof will hardly know their Colonial ancestor under the very odd way in which his name is spelled in this book — *Tschumper*. But alas! the scribe sometimes spelled a name phonetically, and wrote it down in the book just as it sounded to the ear, leaving matters to a more critical period for disentanglement; and the letter j being always a difficult task for the German tongue, nothing better could be done for it than honor it with the combined sound of t, s, c and h.

The most remarkable case of this kind gave the translator a world of trouble. Here was a family name, plainly written *Mokelerei*. It was indeed a strange name. One hesitated to put it down, lest nobody want it, or even own it. But there was no getting around it; there it was, and so down it went as it was written—*Mokelerei*. And what fine family, think you, hides behind that odd-looking name? After much study and careful consideration of the matter, the translator ventures the opinion that *McCleary* is the family name intended. These old German scribes do not appear to have been familiar with the method and manner of writing Scotch names, the Mc's and Mac's being quite beyond them, as is shown in this record by the name "*Mecdaniel.*" When therefore a man by the name of McCleary presented himself for marriage or the baptism of his child, the good German pastor could do nothing better than simply write the name in the book as it sounded to his ear, and there it stands to this day—"*Mokelerei.*"

From the fact that at a very early day there were English and Scotch people here at the settlement of "The Forks of the Delaware," it has been argued that there must have been an English Church established here at an early period. It is very doubtful. No trace of any English Church in Easton, in any regular way, can be found prior to the year 1800, the records of the Presbyterian Church beginning 1811. That an English Church could have once existed here and become entirely extinct, leaving no trace of itself, is hardly possible. Where the English portion of the community attended services we know not, but that many of them brought their children to the Germans for baptism, and that not a few of them were married by the German pastors, these following records abundantly show. Prior to 1813 one notices the following names, taken at random from these pages:

White	Junkin	Todden
Ward	Burnsides	Howell

Berry	McClurey	Muhallon
Fitz-Randolph	Davis	Ralston
Falkinson	Winter	Jackson
Searles	Schooly	Green
Moore	Osburn	Townsend
Carey	Hillyard	Force
Ross	Ayer	Clemens
Seagreaves	Clifton	Saylor
Gaston	Burke	Philips
Gray	Potter	McDaniel
Barnes	Hayden	Lumerson
Marks	Depu	Sitgreaves
Patterson	Longerson	Reeder
Palmer	Magrann	Taylor, etc.

One notices here the inscription of certain names famous in the history of Pennsylvania, or of the country at large. Here is the name of George Taylor, one of the signers of the Declaration; the name of Robert Traill, very prominent in the early days of the settlement; the name of George Wolf, Governor of Pennsylvania; the name of Andrew Horatio Reeder, the first Governor of Kansas. Sometimes these honorable and distinguished men were present at the communion; sometimes they figured either as principals or subjects at a baptism; but it is to their everlasting honor that they despised not the Church of Jesus Christ, even though its services were conducted in an unknown tongue.

One cannot help the reflection, indeed, as he turns over the pages of these old church books, that one of the incidental blessings of membership in the Christian Church is the preservation of the name and the memory of its members. Here are the names of many thousands of people, long since dead and gone, and the best and most certain trace that can, in most instances, be found of them one must look for in the church books. Connection with the Church of Jesus Christ immortalizes. "The memory of the just is blessed, but the name of the wicked shall rot."

It has been the aim of the translator to preserve, as far as possible, especially in the earlier years, the old time phraseology of the record and the German method of spelling the Christian or baptismal names. There seems in this period to have been a painful paucity of first names, the majority of the children receiving but one name apiece, usually *Johannes* if it were a boy, and *Anna Maria*, *Catharina*, or *Elisabetha* if a girl; and often, the longer the child's name the shorter his life. Boys and girls appear for baptism with remarkable regard for the parity of the sexes, and most of them are baptized on Sunday, and very soon after they are born, thus showing the high regard in which the sacrament of baptism was held.

The attention of the reader is called to these records as showing the lamentable death rate prevailing amongst children a hundred years ago. The writer casts his eye over two pages of his manuscript, taken at random and counts on the one page twelve deaths of children out of a total of twenty-six; and on another page, eighteen out of thirty—that is to say, out of thirty deaths eighteen were children.

This rate is kept up regularly for many years, and contrasts most painfully with the record of deaths made by the pastor of the church at the present time. Few children die now — many children died then. The present pastor attends the funerals of two or three children in a year to those of fifteen or twenty adults—a hundred years ago the chances were that at least one half the deaths were those of children. This fact speaks loudly in praise of modern methods of sanitation, acquaintance with the laws of hygiene, and the increased number and efficiency of the men of the medical profession. In those early days physicians were few and far between; people knew very little about the laws of health; warm clothing in the severe winter was scarce and dear, and well-warmed houses unknown. Verily, it was a struggle for existence, and the weakest went to the wall; the hard conditions of pioneer life caused this "Slaughter of the Innocents," and many a Rachael " wept for her children and would not be comforted because they were not."

THE INDIAN TREATY IN THE CHURCH, JANUARY 30, 1777.

AS has been said in a former chapter, "The Forks of the Delaware" was a famous place for holding treaties with the Indians. Not only during the Revolution but long before, in the old Colonial times, when Pennsylvania was yet a British possession and governed by the proprietaries of the English Crown, the Indians manifested a steady preference for this romantic spot as a most agreeable place in which to "light the council fire." Hither on numerous occasions the red-men came from great distances to meet the palefaces, their conferences lasting sometimes for several weeks. The Indians seem to have been fond of these meetings, and to have multiplied reasons for holding them as frequently as possible, urging the necessity of such conferences when the Council or Congress could scarcely see the need for them. And no wonder. The red-man knew that these treaties furnished him an excellent opportunity of testing the liberality of his white brothers who had many strange things to give which the Indian dearly loved, and which he could obtain nowhere else — glass beads, silver jewelry and ornaments, guns and powder and lead, axes, blanket and kettles, and other things too numerous to mention, to say nothing of the rum which, alas! the Indian fondly expected at all these meetings.

Prior to the building of the Reformed Church, during a period of not less than forty years, numerous treaties were here made, the meetings being always held at "Vernon's Tavern" at "The Point." At such times

Easton was full of Indians, not less than five hundred being present on one occasion, representing nineteen distinct and separate tribes. But after the erection of the church in 1776 it was thought well to hold the treaty within the walls of that building, because it was the largest and most commodious edifice in the town. The writer has been at some pains to gather all the information possible concerning this treaty of 1777, having carefully examined the early "Journals of Congress," and the "Minutes of the Council of Safety," as given in "The Colonial Records," and believes that for the first time there is here published a connected record of all the documents pertaining to that important event in our local history. Thus we read in the "Journals of Congress," Vol. III., page 36:

"WHEREAS Congress are informed that certain tribes of Indians living in the back parts of the country, near the waters of the Susquehanna who are within the Confederacy and under the protection of The Six Nations, the friends and allies of the United States, are, upon motives friendly and peaceable, now on their way to Easton in the State of Pennsylvania, and whereas such may be the poor and necessitous circumstances of these Indians as to demand the attention of Congress—

"*Resolved*, That the Committee of Congress at Philadelphia deliver to George Walton and George Taylor, Esquires, or either of them, 1000 dollars: who are directed therewith to purchase such presents as may be suitable for the said Indians: and that one or both of them repair forthwith to Easton, and in the name of this Congress inform the said Indians that, although in the opinion of Congress, it is altogether improper for them to kindle a Council Fire at that place, as they have already done the same at Albany where, by their Commissioners, they hold their Councils and communicate every matter of importance to their good friends, The Six Nations and their allies, of which these tribes are a part; yet, in regard to the good and peaceable conduct of these nations, and in consideration of their wants, which this Congress are much inclined to relieve, and also in token of their friendship for them, as well as for all other Indians who are at peace with these United States, they, the said George Walton and George Taylor, Esquires, are directed to deliver these presents to them, and that they are to signify at the same time to the said Indians that this Congress have an entire confidence that the same peaceable and friendly conduct will be observed by them which they have hitherto regarded.

"*Ordered*, That the said Messieurs Walton and Taylor be furnished a copy of the foregoing resolution for their direction."

Next in order we read in "The Colonial Records," Vol. XI., page 96, in the "Minutes of the Council of Safety" as follows:

"January 20, 1777. *Resolved*, That Col. Dean and Col. Bull be appointed to attend the Treaty to be held with the Indians at Easton, Monday next, on behalf of this Council: when they are to advise and concur with the Committee of Assembly and Congress in all such measures as they shall think proper, to preserve peace and harmony with the Indian nations."

From the same Minutes under date of the day following we learn that the following additional action was taken:

"January 21, 1777. *Resolved* that Mr Thomas Payne be appointed Secretary to the Commissioners for the Indian Treaty to be held at Easton on Monday next."

That the five commissioners so far named might not appear at the treaty empty-handed, and well knowing the great expectations of the Indians, the Committee of Public Safety gave specific directions as to the kind and number of presents to be provided for the occasion. For, on page 108, Vol. XI., Colonial Records, it is stated that

"An order was sent to Hayman (Haman?) Levy to make up an assortment of articles fit for a Treaty with 70 Indians

The Indian Treaty in the Church.

(exclusive of women and children). He accordingly pack'd up the following Goods, for which a receipt was given by the Secretary.

>9,600 White Wampum.
>20,500 Black Wampum.
>30 Moons.
>30 Hair Pipes of Conk Shell.
>6 Pair Arm bands.
>12 Gordiots.
>100 Broaches.
>37 Pair Ear-Bobs.

All of silver, which with 15 Camp Kettles were this day forwarded to Cols. Bull and Deane, Commissioners on the part of this Council at Easton."

The wampum probably consisted of beads of glass, white or black, the white being the wampum proper, the Indians making them of the interior parts of shells strung on threads. "Wampum was highly esteemed amongst the American aborigines, being used as currency amongst them, and worn also in necklaces, bracelets, belts, scabbards, etc. Three of the dark, or six of the white passed for one English penny. Wampum was woven into belts of various patterns, into which dates, treaties and national events were 'talked.'"

The white and black beads were used for the purpose of making treaty belts. These were often made on the spot by the Indian women who were present, being probably brought along for this purpose. Thus, at the treaty held at Easton in 1756, in the month of July, at which council Teedyuscung, the King of the Delawares, was present, we read that Conrad Weiser, the Indian Interpreter, said that "The French gave great quantities of wampum to their Indians, and on matters of consequence these belts were several fathoms long, and very wide. The secretary was ordered to bring all the wampum he had into the Council, viz., fifteen strings and seven belts; a parcel of new black wampum, amounting to seven thousand; and having no new white wampum, nor any proper belt to give in return for Teedyuscung's peace belts, a messenger was sent to Bethlehem and he returned with five thousand; upon which the Indian women were employed to make a belt a fathom long (6 feet) and sixteen beads wide, in the center of which was to be the figure of a man, meaning the Governor of Pennsylvania, and on each side five other figures, meaning the Ten Nations mentioned by Teedyuscung. . . . The new belt not being finished during the sessions of the Council, the Governor explained the proposed figure to the chiefs, and desired the women might finish it on rainy days, or resting on their journey, which was promised."

What the "Moons" were, and the "Hair Pipes of Conk Shell," and the "Gordiots," the reader can ascertain by guessing, or by further inquiry, as the mood may chance to hold him. These gaudy baubles no doubt caught the eye and held the admiration of the poor Indians to a degree unimaginable by us, and contributed largely to the importance of the treaty.

In what way "Messieurs" Walton and Taylor and Payne reached the scene of the Council we know not, but evidently Colonel John Bull, true to his English name and moved by his American instincts, lost no time in setting forth from Philadelphia for Easton, a journey on horseback of some eighty miles in extent, as we learn by consulting the "Penna. Archives," 1776-7, page 201, from a letter written by this gentleman to the Council from Norriton in Montgomery County.

The Indian Treaty in the Church. 25

COL. JOHN BULL TO THE COUNCIL, 1777.

Sir: We have left the Council without any instructions and Whether we are to have any, or who shall give them, Congress, Council of Safety or Assembly, I will not undertake to say, but when I waited upon Mr Robert Morris, he informed me that they had wrote to Congress, and that if any answer arrived In time it aught to be sent forward to Eastown. I take the liberty of Communicating a few hints which I think aught to be attended to unless we are instructed to the Contrary. If we find them well disposed, we shall try to cultivate a good understanding with them, and Likewise Lay the Ground-work of a Great Treaty next Summer, at such time and Place as may Suit them best, but I think under our Circumstances Something Bestowed in that way to Continue the friendship of the Indians may be of infinite advantage, under our present struggle, and at the same time it will be Necessary to assure them of our own Sufficiency and Strength in Carrying on this war against our Enemies, how farr it will be Prudent or Practicable to Explain the Cause thereof I have not yet fully Deliberated upon.

I am, Sir, with Due Respect,
Your Verry Hu'ble Serv't
JOHN BULL.

NORRITON Jan. 26 1777, 8 oclock A. M
Directed to the Hon! THOMAS WHARTON Esq.
Pres. Council Safety.

Two days later he reached Easton after a long and tiresome two days' journey on horseback, having Col. Dean for his traveling companion in all probability, although that fact is not mentioned. At once upon his arrival he writes the following letter, to keep the Council well informed as to the progress of the treaty :

Sir—We are just arrived at Eastown, where we found about the same number of Indians we expected and Tolerably well Disposed, though much in want of Every Necessary, one article in Particular, Vist: about fifteen Camp Kettles not of the largest size. The Bearer of this comes Express with two horses on purpose to bring them up. Please to let Mr Howel Dispatch him immediately, as it will be absolutely Necessary they should be here before we make a Distribution of the goods. We this morning heard by a Gent^n from head-quarters which he left two days ago that Forts Independence and Washington are realy taken. If you have anything New pray send it.

I am, Sir, with Due Respect
Your Hub^l Servt
JOHN BULL

EASTOWN Jan. 28th 1777 9 oclock A. M.

N. B. Please to send the Medals which Mr Syng promised to send to the Council, if they are come to hand—if not, send the Messenger without them as they are not of so much consequence.

Directed to HON. THOS. WHARTON ESQR.
Pres. of Ye Council of Safety.

The worthy Colonel, despite his British cognomen, is evidently a thorough American patriot, and believes in early rising and in losing no time in pressing matters to an issue. He is evidently a good Commissioner, and keeps an eye on the chief and salient features of the occasion, being more concerned for the camp-kettles for the Indians than for the medals for himself and his fellow Commissioners. Or, were those medals intended for the Indians? Who knows? But no matter. Let them go, if need be, but send on by all means the fifteen camp-kettles, a very necessary and highly valuable present to the poor Indian who, alas! has not the knowledge how to make them. He can bring down the deer with his rifle, or the wild turkey with his bow and arrow, but how to make a camp-kettle is quite beyond him. For that he is dependent on the white man; he will give a

The Indian Treaty in the Church.

hundred acres, or a thousand if hard pressed, for one camp-kettle, poor son of Nature!

Though apparently quite eager for the conference to open, the Colonel is perforce compelled to await, as patiently as he can, the arrival of the Congressional representatives on the Commission, "Messieurs" Taylor and Walton, who did not reach Easton until the day following the date of the above letter. Whether Payne had accompanied Dean and Bull, or traveled in company with Taylor and Walton, we have no means of knowing. The following letter gives us some information concerning the opening of the Treaty—and much we wish it gave us more.

EASTON, Jan. 31 1777

Sir—The delegates from Congress, Colls. Taylor and Walton arrived on Wednesday, ye 29th, and yesterday, ye 30th, we opened the Treaty. When the Indians Delivered Two Strings, Three Belts, and about half their Talk, they having Three belts more to deliver this day, the Indians seem to be inclined to act the Wise Part with Respect to the present Dispute, if they are to be relied on they mean to be Neuter. We have already Learnt their good Intentions and Great Expectations in receiving Presents. However I think we have full as much with us as will satisfy them, we have not a word of news here, more Soldiers Returning from than are going to the Camp, I hope that is not the case in Philadelphia. I am, Sir,

With Comp* to my Brethren,
Your Hub¹ Servt,
JOHN BULL.

Directed to HON. THOS. WHARTON ESQR.
Pres. Council of Safety.

From "The History of Northampton County," by I. D. Rupp (1845), we learn that Colonels Lawry and Cunningham were also present at this Treaty, having been duly appointed by the Assembly of the State of Pennsylvania.

From the same source we also learn that the following Indian chiefs were present. Let their names be preserved!

Kayugas—Taasquah, or King Charles.
Senecas—Tawanah, or The Big Tree.
Munsies—Mytakawha, or Walking on Foot; Kaknah, or Standing by a Tree.
Nantikokes—Amatincka, or Raising Anything Up.
Kanois—Wilaknko, or King Last Night.
Interpreter, Thomas Green, a Mohawk.

The journals of Congress show that on June 13, 1777, the Auditor General reported due Abraham Berlin, chairman of the Committee of Northampton County, "for the amount of his account of sundries supplied the Indians by order of the Commissioners at the Conference held at Easton, $1,410.48."

The "State Archives" contain the following account of

"THE EXPENCE OF THE INGENS."

To 1 Gall. of spiritts	£2	4	0
To 1 Bottel	0	1	0
To 2 wine Decanters	0	12	6
To 18 Gall. of Sider 2-8	2	8	0
To 11 Gall. Sider J. C., 8-0	4	8	0
To 7 Boles Tody	1	1	0
To 4 Dobel Boles Do	1	4	0
To 15 Nithes and Days hay for one horse	2	5	0
To 11 Do	1	13	0
8 Do	1	4	0
7 Do	1	1	0
	£18	1	6
2 Nithes hay	0	4	0
	£18	5	6

Received Fb'y 18th, 1777, of Jas. Dean, the within acc't in full, for Isaac Sidman. HENRY FULLERT.

The Indian Treaty in the Church.   29

No one can possibly more regret than the writer the unfortunate lack of any more specific information concerning this treaty. A careful search of all the published records fails to yield anything further. A respectful request to the Librarian of Congress at Washington elicits only the information that " we have not been able to find any record of the proceedings of the conference with the Indians at Easton, Penna., in 1777." Conway, in his life of Thomas Paine, says that Paine was appointed by the Council of Safety in Philadelphia Secretary to the Commission sent by Congress to treat with the Indians at Easton. The Commissioners, with a thousand dollars' worth of presents, met the Indian chiefs in the German Reformed Church (built 1776) and, as they reported to Congress, ' after shaking hands, drinking rum, while the organ played, we proceeded to business.' The report was no doubt written by Paine, who for his services was paid 300 pounds by the Pennsylvania Assembly. . . . I have written to the Commissioner of Indian Affairs, asking if the records are to be found in the Archives of that Department. When he replies I will transmit the information to you." All of which is properly signed by the Chief Bibliographer of the Congressional Library — but the Commissioner of Indian Affairs has not yet been heard from, and quite likely will not be. The Commission must evidently have made a report to Congress, and that report must be somewhere — but where? The report in question must evidently be the authority for the statement so frequently made, in " Conway's Life of Thomas Paine," in the " History of the Lehigh Valley," and in the following sketch of the Reformed Church of Easton written by Dr. John Beck, that " the Commissioners met the Indians in the German Reformed Church of Easton, and after shaking hands and drinking rum together, during which time the organ was played, they proceeded to business."

In the absence of any further information one is left to imagine the scene — the high commissioners of Congress in their best new Continental uniforms taking their places in front of the pulpit (which was then on the east side of the church), and the seventy Indians arrayed in their feathers and war-paint slowly filing in and bestowing themselves in the aisles or pews, or where best they might. The solemn tones of the organ are heard, the handshaking begins, the rum is passed round, and the treaty duly opened. Through an interpreter sworn to interpret truly, the Commissioners make an address, conveying the good will of Congress as expressed in the generous donation of gifts adroitly displayed on the chancel floor, demanding in return the support of the Indian tribes, or at least their neutrality, in the struggle in which they, the said Congress and people of the United States, are engaged with their enemies. The speaker reminds the Indians in the usual manner :

"Brothers—You have been faithful in your leagues with us: your hearts have been clean, and you have preserved our Great Chain of Friendship and Brotherhood from spots or rust, or if there were any, you have been careful to wipe them away. Your leagues with our fathers are in writing on record, that our Children and our Children's Children may have them in everlasting remembrance. And we know that you preserve the memory of these things amongst you by telling them to your Children and they again to the next generation, so that they remain stamped on your minds never to be forgot, while the creeks and rivers run, and while the Sun, Moon and Stars endure.

"Brothers—You know well how our enemies, once our friends and brothers, but now our friends and brothers no more,

The Indian Treaty in the Church.

for their friendship was in the mouth and not in the heart, have tried to take away our lands from us which our fathers purchased of your fathers many moons ago, and have sent armies across the Great Waters to make us their slaves. With our brave soldiers we will fight them, and be free, doing as you do when your enemies come upon you to take away your lands and drive you from your homes. They shall be beaten off, and driven out of our Country, and there shall be here but one great, strong and powerful Nation of white men, from the rising to the setting Sun, the friends and protectors of our brothers, the Indians. We wish you to speak with your people at home to make a new League and Chain of Brotherhood with our people, and that every Link in the Chain be kept bright and clean : and that if you wish not to fight for us against our enemies, you remain at home and sit still and look on, for why should your blood be shed in this quarrel, and be in peace on your own lands, until we have driven our enemies away, as we will surely do, and when we have finished this friendly Treaty with you, we have a present for you, from the Congress and people of The United States, which you shall carry with you home, and show to your friends, as a pledge of our good-will and brotherhood, and in token of the enduring Chain of Friendship between us and you."

Saying which the speaker sat down, and the Indians made a peculiar sound of approval beyond our power here to reproduce; after which Taasquah, or King Charles, one of the great chiefs of the Kayugas, arose, and, with the assistance of other Indians of lesser note, laid down three bundles of dressed deer skins, and presented two strings of wampum and three belts, saying :

"That their friends and brothers, coming from the great Council with kind hearts and good words, had spoken well: that they were highly pleased that they had been so kindly received, and that they were very willing and desirous that there may be more frequent opportunities of conferring and discussing with their brethren, so that the Chain may be kept bright and without rust or spot, and that only good may be in the heart. Also, that they well understood that the Great King beyond the water had not treated his children in this land well, and that this is the reason for the present war, in which they will not engage one way or the other, until they have taken counsel of their brethren at Albany, when the great Council-Fire is again lighted, which will be soon, and that meanwhile they will be at peace with the Congress and people of the United States: in token and pledge of which peaceful sentiments they present these strings and belts of wampum."

Whereupon the Indians all gave their peculiar and indescribable sound of assent and ratification which nothing short of a phonograph could ever hope to reproduce.

The translation and interpretation of these addresses into the language of the different tribes represented occupied so much time that the better part of the day was consumed in the process, and in the accompanying ceremonies; so that the Council adjourned to meet the next day; when the treaty was concluded, much after the same fashion, the conclusion thereof being accompanied by the distribution of the gifts provided, and above enumerated, to the great delight of the Indians, in whose eyes ornaments of silver had an especial value. Warm clothing should have been more acceptable to them at that bitter season of the year, and in view of the long journey of more than three hundred miles before them on their way home to the lakes of western New York, for the snow was deep on the ground and the cold intense, even in Easton, and much more so amongst the Pocono mountains beyond the Blue Ridge which they must cross. One can only wonder how or where they were lodged during their stay in the town. In all probability they erected their wigwams at the foot of

The Indian Treaty in the Church.   33

Mount Jefferson, or under the lee of some of the other mighty hills of the "Forks of the Delaware" which would shield them against the cold blasts of the north wind, and the abundant forests on the sides of these hills furnished ample fuel for the great fires of their camp. The people of the town, numbering at that time about four or five hundred souls, breathed more easily after the excitement of this great gathering, when they saw the camp break up, and the Indians, single file and in long line, taking their way over the Bushkill and up Chestnut Hill, making for the Wind Gap in the Blue Mountains and the far-away settlements on the Susquehanna, or in the Genesee country, whence they had come. No doubt the poor squaws carried the camp-kettles, so precious in the eyes of these poor children of nature, and no doubt each camp-kettle was well loaded before it was strapped on the back; but happy indeed was each dark-skinned daughter of the forest if the cruel burden on the back was counter-balanced by the shining presence of a silver band about the arm or a pair of glittering "ear-bobs" in the ears — the marvellous gift of the pale-faced friend and brother.

The chief object of this treaty, viz., To detach the powerful confederacy of the Six Nations from the British, or at least to secure their neutrality, does not seem to have been secured; for in the following year, on July 3, 1778, the great and awful massacre at Wyoming occurred.

THE ORGANIZATION OF THE CONGREGATION, AND THE BUILDING OF THE CHURCH.

IN the effort to account for the origin of the Reformed Church in Easton, the writer cannot do the subject greater justice than by here inserting the following *"Historical sketch of the origin and growth of the Third Street Reformed Congregation, and of the founding of its Church building, prepared and read at its Centennial Celebration in the Church, July 4, 1876.*—This admirable sketch was prepared by the late Rev. Dr. John Beck, at that time the pastor of the congregation, and is remarkable alike for simplicity of style and lucid statement of facts.

AN HISTORICAL SKETCH OF THE ORIGIN AND GROWTH OF THE THIRD STREET REFORMED CONGREGATION, AND OF THE FOUNDING OF ITS CHURCH BUILDING, PREPARED AND READ AT ITS CENTENNIAL CELEBRATION, IN THE CHURCH, JULY 4TH, 1876.

BY REV. JOHN BECK, D.D., PASTOR.

The ancient Jews were required by divine command to celebrate a year of jubilee, at the expiration of every fifty years of their history. God designed thereby to impress upon their minds the great truth that their existence as a nation, their time, their property, and all the blessings and events of providence, were from His hand and under His

INTERIOR OF THE FIRST REFORMED CHURCH AT THE CENTENNIAL, 1876.

The Organization of the Congregation. 35

omnipotent control. This divine command appointing this great festival seems to have fully harmonized with a sentiment which existed in the hearts of the people, and no one of the many festivals observed by the Jews was celebrated with more spirit and display than characterized the observance of the year of jubilee. The return of the year was not only hailed throughout the land with the sound of trumpets, which echoed and reëchoed from every hill and valley, throughout the whole year, but great gladness of heart and general manifestation of joy and rejoicing marked the conduct of the people.

Twice the period of time embraced in a Jewish jubilee anniversary festival has passed in our national history. One hundred years ago to-day the foundations of our existence as a nation were laid broad and deep in the principles of liberty, justice and equality, by the Declaration of Independence; and we, as a nation, are this year celebrating our centennial anniversary—our centennial jubilee. By a happy coincidence, this year is also the centennial year of the founding of this church building in which we are now assembled. In view of this fact, and for other reasons, it was thought meet and right, by the consistory of this congregation, to anticipate by several months the real date of the founding of this church, and to combine the centennial celebration both of the founding of this church and the founding of our national government on this day, and to make the services both religious and patriotic in their character.

The patriotic part of the services has been committed to hands fully competent to perform it in a manner worthy of the day and of the occasion. The especial duty assigned to me is to present an historical sketch of the origin and growth of this congregation and of the founding of this church, which I now, without further preface, proceed to discharge.

Historians tell us that the beginnings of the history of all tribes and nations is enshrouded in more or less mist and obscurity. Whether this is true, as a general fact, I am not competent to affirm, but I can testify, after much labor and research, that the beginning of the history of this Reformed tribe of Israel in Easton is enveloped in mist and obscurity so dense that it is utterly impossible to discover it. It most certainly had a beginning, or it would not now be existing; but when and how this beginning took place no annals nor records tell, and we can only trace it faintly and approximately by inference and conjecture.

Immigration from Germany, whence came originally by far the largest portion of the fathers and founders of the (German) Reformed Church in the United States, began to flow into the province of Pennsylvania as early as 1681. The main stream of this immigration, however, seems to have begun to flow about the year 1720, and was composed chiefly of families from the Palatinate, a beautiful and fertile country on the Rhine. These immigrants were chiefly fugitives from political tyranny and religious persecution in their native land, and came hither, not only to better their temporal condition, but mainly to find a home and a place—a sanctuary and a refuge—in this new country, where they might worship God according to the faith and customs of their fathers, without suffering persecution and martyrdom either from King or Pope.

Many of these early German immigrants of the Reformed Church found a new home for themselves in what was Bucks County, and afterwards Northampton County, which at that time not only included what is now called Northampton County, but also what is now Lehigh, Car-

The Organization of the Congregation. 37

bon, Monroe, Pike, Wayne, and Susquehanna, and parts of Wyoming, Luzerne, Schuylkill, Bradford and Columbia.

From 1725 to 1740 there was another great influx of Germans of various religious opinions, more than 1,000 families of which settled in Northampton County. In 1752 the population of the county numbered between 5,000 and 6,000 persons, not including the Indians, who were numerous, and of these 5,000 or 6,000 inhabitants 800 are reported as inhabiting the "Forks of the Delaware," which included what is now Easton, and several of the surrounding townships; Easton proper containing at this time but eleven families—about 40 men, women and children. In 1763 it contained a population numbering about 250, the most of whom are reported to have been Germans, of the Reformed or Lutheran confessions.

These Germans, we have said, were immigrants for conscience' sake. They fled from home and country for the sake of their religion. Many of them are said to have been "truly pious, and though not able to bring their ministers, brought with them their catechisms, hymn-books, and other devotional books, and, in some cases, also pious schoolmasters." This being the religious character of these first German settlers of Easton, it is not surprising to find a movement inaugurated here so early as 1755 to raise money by subscription to erect a building to be used as a schoolhouse, and also "to be used occasionally as a church for any Protestant minister." This movement was successful, and in 1755 a log building was erected on the northeast corner of what is now Church and Sitgreaves streets, as I have learned from reliable authority, and was used both for school and church purposes. Here we have, then, so far as I have been able to discover after much research, the first building erected in Easton for church uses; and there is no doubt in my mind that in this log building, erected in 1755, our German Reformed forefathers first worshipped God after the faith and order of the (German) Reformed Church, and I have no more doubt that the worship was conducted, not by a minister, but either by some pious schoolmaster or other layman. In these early years ministers of any denomination were very few in number in the province of Pennsylvania. Consequently pious members of our church were compelled to depend upon themselves for religious edification, and rather than forego all religious services, they accepted these from the schoolmasters, who, by singing, reading, prayers and sermons, made up for the people as best they could the want of regular church ministrations. I make the statement that members of the German Reformed Church in Easton in these early days, between 1740 and 1760, had their religious and church wants provided for in this way; first, because it is legitimate to infer from their religious character and their religious training in the fatherland, and especially from the fact that most of them were exiles for conscience' sake, that they would make the best provision possible to supply their religious and church wants; and secondly, as I have not been able to find, in all the records and histories which I have been able to consult, that a regular Reformed minister of the gospel was located in Easton before 1760, it is equally legitimate to infer that the worship of the congregation was conducted by some pious schoolmaster or other layman, especially as this was done at this early day at other places. Moreover, I think the records and circumstances will warrant us to speak of an organized congregation as existing between the years 1745 and 1750. There is no record anywhere of the place

The Organization of the Congregation.

and date of the organization of a congregation; but, nevertheless, we have found several records, and a few well-authenticated facts, which point to this period as that during which the heretofore scattered members of the German Reformed Church of Easton and vicinity were organized into a church.

1. Rev. Michael Schlatter was sent by the Synod of Holland, in 1746, to this country for the purpose of visiting and gathering together the scattered members of our church, to organize congregations, and to be over them as a superintendent or bishop. He spent the years from 1747 to 1750 in serving the Race Street Reformed congregation, in Philadelphia, and in visiting the congregations in the interior of the State, and in Maryland and Virginia, to acquaint himself with their numbers and conditions, and to give them such services and aid as was in his power. In 1750 he was appointed by the Synod to visit Europe, especially Holland, Switzerland and the Palatinate, for the purpose of presenting to the Reformed people of those countries the sad state of the religious destitution existing among their brethren in this country and to solicit aid in their behalf. Having arrived in Holland, he drew up and published an appeal, in which, among other things, he mentions the congregations in Pennsylvania which he had visited during the years 1747 and 1750. Among these is mentioned the congregation at the Forks of the Delaware, by which name Easton was known at that time. Now, if Schlatter visited Easton some time between 1747 and 1750, he either found a congregation already organized, or if not, he very probably organized one then, for to do such work was one of the objects held in view by him in all his missionary journeys.

2. Another proof that this congregation was organized

at some time between 1745 and 1750 is furnished by this old German bible here lying before us. On the fly leaf of this venerable book is inscribed this record in German and Latin, which we translate into English as follows: "Biblia Sacra, or the Holy Bible, presented by Mr. Michael Schlatter, V. D. M. [Minister of the Word of God], and Inspector of the Liberties at Philadelphia, to Reformed Church and Congregation at I[E]aston, with the earnest request that the Elders and Deacons, and their successors, be properly concerned, that this Bible continue to be used by the Church at its public divine worship. Glory to God alone in the Highest. Glory alone to God." From this inscription it appears, first, that Rev. Michael Schlatter presented this Bible to this congregation when he was pastor of the church in Philadelphia; secondly, that when he presented it there was existing a congregation with elders and deacons.

Now it is known, from the life of Schlatter, that he ceased to be pastor of the congregation in Philadelphia in 1755, consequently he must have presented this bible in that year or at an earlier date, probably not long after his return from Europe, which occurred in 1752. These facts prove, we think, that this congregation was organized at some date between 1745 and 1750, and it is probable that its organization was effected by Schlatter himself—this bible being a gift in remembrance of that fact.

To pass now to the examination of what may be considered more certain data and facts of history as these are presented in the preserved records of the congregation, we would remark that the earliest of these records are not only without any proper authentication, but are very incomplete and disconnected.

The record bearing the oldest date is that of a baptism,

INSCRIPTION IN THE OLD SCHLATTER BIBLE.

The Organization of the Congregation. 41

and is as follows: " Anno 1760, September 28th, was born a son, and was baptised November 5th. He received the name of Ludwig. His sponsors were Philip Gress and Anna Margaret, his wife. His parents were Ludwig Knauss and Elizabeth his wife." But it must be remarked in regard to this record, that it stands isolated and alone in the book, and that it is evidently in the handwriting of Rev. John William Ingold, who was not pastor of the congregation until 1775. He may, perhaps, have learned of this baptism and recorded it some years after it took place. A similar isolated and detached record, or rather memorandum, is to the effect that the Coetus, or Synod, met in Easton in 1768. The imperfect character of these early records is evident also from this fact, that the name of the first regular pastor of the congregation is mentioned only incidentally in them, and that we must go to Dr. Harbaugh's " Lives of the Fathers of the Reformed Church " to learn more about him and his connection with the congregation.

The first regular pastor was Rev. Dr. Casper Deitrich Weyberg, and who, Dr. Harbaugh says, took charge of the congregation at Easton in the early part of the year 1763.

The church records make only incidental allusion to him in this way: There are nine baptisms recorded as having taken place in 1763. The person who makes this record — evidently not Dr. Weyberg himself, most probably Rev. Frederick L. Henop, as the handwriting shows — says that these names were left behind by Dr. Weyberg on slips of paper; but whether they are the names of the parents, the sponsors, or the children who were baptized, the writer was not able to tell.

At this time, 1763, Easton, in connection with Greenwich, N. J., Dryland and Plainfield, constituted a pastoral charge. These congregations seem to have been served in an irregular way before this time by some self-appointed preachers. But in 1763, as said, Rev. Dr. Weyberg became the first regular pastor of the charge, with the approval of Synod. The congregation in Easton had at this time no place of worship. "For want of more suitable accommodations, it is said, he preached in the then newly erected court house, and in the country around, in barns, or wherever room could be found to shelter the assembly." He was, however, pastor of the congregation only for six months, when he was called to Philadelphia. After the departure of Dr. Weyberg there followed a vacancy, which continued until the beginning of 1766, when Rev. Frederick L. Henop became pastor of the congregation. We cannot pass Dr. Weyberg, though his ministry in Easton was very brief, without mentioning an incident which occurred during his ministry in Philadelphia, and which illustrates his character as a patriot as well as a minister of the Gospel: "He took a warm interest in the war of the Revolution. He had quite a fancy for mingling, in some way or other, in the warlike struggles of the times. He stood out prominently as a patriot, and is said to have acted for a time in the capacity of chaplain. At the time when the British held possession of Philadelphia he preached to the Hessians, who thronged to hear him in great crowds. He boldly asserted the justice of the American cause, and bore down with such energy upon the wickedness of the oppressors that the British began to feel the effects of his fearless appeals in the daily desertions of their Hessian mercenaries. In order to put a stop to his preaching they threatened his life, and threw him into prison, from which, however, he was soon liberated. It is confidently affirmed that the Hessians would, in all

The Organization of the Congregation. 43

probability, to a man have left the British service if the old father had not been silenced."

He seems to have commenced the records of baptisms performed by him February 23, 1766, and continued it until October 8, 1769 — a period of about three years and eight months. Then he resigned and removed to Frederick, Maryland. The record of his baptisms is the only thing that remains to tell that he was pastor of the congregation, and we would not even be certain of that fact were it not for the very brief notice of him in Harbaugh's " Lives of the Fathers, etc." Rev. Henop was succeeded, in 1769, by Rev. Pithan, of whom it is said that he was conditionally received into Coetus, or Synod, and located on trial in Easton, Dryland, Plainfield and Greenwich. At the next meeting of the Synod, in 1770, complaints were made against him of drunkenness; but on his confessing his faults and promising to do better, he was permitted to preach in his charge a while longer. He did not, however, hold by his promise long, and in 1771 he, with some difficulty, was compelled to resign and remove.

Thus again in 1771 the congregation became vacant and remained so until 1776.

It was during this vacancy that the congregation, in union with St. John's Lutheran Congregation, began to take measures for the erection of a church.

From Rev. Henop's hand we have the first record of the existence of a consistory and the names thereof. It bears the date of 1768, and states that the elders were Ludwig Knauss and Philip Odenwelder; deacons, John Gettert and Henry Schneider. This consistory record is then interrupted and is not resumed until January 5, 1777, and is then continued annually until 1795, when a chasm occurs which extends to 1808. Among the names of members of the consistory from 1777 to 1795 we find the following: Elders — Philip Achenbach, John Simon, John Deichman, George Ernst Becker, Jacob Shumaker, Michael Gress, John Nicholas Troxel, John Best, Peter Lattig, Jacob Scheib and Michael Odenwelder; Deacons — Nicholas Kemmerer, Michael Fraes, John Young, Leonhard Walsch, Henry Hahn, Henry Winter, Christian Butz, Frederick Barthold, Christopher Meixel and Jacob Keller.

As we have seen, the Reformed congregation began to worship in the then newly erected court house in 1763. We have not been able to learn from any records or history that it worshipped in any other place until this building was erected. St. John's Lutheran congregation had worshipped from 1763 in the second story of a stone building on South Third street. But these congregations now felt the need of having a more permanent and suitable place of worship, and they joined together to secure this for themselves.

Honorable John Penn, of Stoke Pogeis, in the County of Bucks, in the Kingdom of Great Britain, and Honorable Richard Penn, of Queen Ann Street West, in the Parish of St. Mary Le Bone, in the County of Middlesex, in the Kingdom of Great Britain, who were descendants and heirs of William Penn, and proprietaries of Pennsylvania, donated to the two congregations (for the nominal sum of ten dollars, lawful money of the United States), three parcels of ground, one of which was that on which this building now stands. This grant was confirmed and conveyed by deed November 27, 1800, to Peter Snyder, Nicholas Troxell and Nicholas Kern, Trustees for the German Reformed Congregation, and Jacob Weygand, William Roup and Conrad Bittenbender, Trustees for German Lutheran Congregation, of Easton, for the nomi-

The Organization of the Congregation. 45

nal sum of ten dollars, lawful money of the United States.

The joint congregations having thus come into possession of an eligible location, proceeded to build the church within the original walls of which we are now assembled. The cornerstone was laid June 8, 1775, and the church was consecrated to the service of the Triune God, November 17, 1776. The internal arrangement and appearance was originally somewhat different from what they are at present. Of the church consecrated in 1776 only these four walls remain — the vestibule and steeple being additions, which were made in 1832–3. The internal arrangement was somewhat as follows, as I have been able to gather it from persons still living who frequently worshipped in it: The entrance to the church was by three doors, one of which was on Church street, behind the present pulpit, and the two others on Third street. The pews were arranged lengthwise on the Third street side, facing east; on the north side facing south, and on the south side facing north, cut by aisles running north and south, east and west. The galleries ran along the north, south and west sides of the church, to which access was had by two stairways, the one ascending from the southwest corner and the other from the northwest corner of the building. The organ was on the west side gallery, and was built in 1775 by Dannaker. The pulpit was on the east side of the building, and was of the wine-glass or goblet style, having a large sounding board over it. Beneath the pulpit was an altar (the one before us here to-day), which was surrounded by a railing. The ceiling was dome shape in form, was ornamented with figures in oil, and still exists above the present ceiling. The pews were of the high-backed, narrow-seated style, not made either to lounge or sleep in, but to keep their occupants upright and awake as worshippers always ought to be.

Let us try to picture to ourselves a service held in those early days. We will suppose the congregation assembled. The first thing that strikes our view, as we look over it, is the fact that the sexes are separated from each other, the women occupying the pews on the main floor of the building, surrounded on the north and south sides by a small fringe of men, for protection rather than ornament, perhaps. On each side of the pulpit was a long pew, running parallel with the wall, in one of which sat the venerable elders, and in the other the deacons of the congregation.

Another thing that strikes our view, is the plain, the very plain and simple dress of the worshippers. We see no silks, and broadcloths, no gay ribbons or flowers, for those were the days of the Revolution and of continental money. Instead, the men for the most part are clad in plain homespun and linsey wolsey, some even being in their shirt sleeves, if the weather is warm; the women clothed in large part with the same plain material — the workmanship of their own looms and hands — a few, it may be, in calico, or other equally inexpensive material. Their bonnets were made of black silk or gingham and pasteboard, and of a shape so as to cover the face, and so protect it not only from the hot sun and rude wind, but also from the ruder gaze of impertinent curiosity — a style of female headgear very unlike that prevalent at the present day, which seems to be made to adorn the back of the head and expose, not protect, the face or the modesty of the wearer.

On the galleries are the young men and maidens, who are kept in becoming order by the vigilant sexton, who makes his presence as often felt and heard, by sharp raps, as seen, by the eye.

The Organization of the Congregation. 47

While the organist is playing a solemn voluntary, the minister enters. He proceeds with slow step to the chancel, when, amid deep silence, he offers a silent prayer, which also every devout worshipper offers when they entered their pew. A solemn awe and reverence seems to pervade the whole audience, as if the divine presence was felt by all, as the minister gives out the first hymn, which, under the leadership of the organist and chorister, is sung, not by the choir, but by the whole congregation, who sing their psalms, and hymns, and spiritual songs with spirit and with understanding. Then follows the reading of the Holy Scriptures, which is listened to as if it were, as it truly is, the Word of God, and when, at the close of this, the minister thanks God for his Holy Word, and says, "let us pray," the whole congregation rises, and, with folded hands and bowed heads, enters, as it were, with the minister, into the holy place where God hears and answers prayer. After prayer, another hymn is sung with equal spirit, during which the minister leaves the altar and ascends the pulpit. When he rises to preach all eyes are fixed eagerly upon him, as upon one whom they regard as being more than an ordinary man, as being indeed an embassador of Christ and steward of the mystery, who in Christ's stead was beseeching them to become reconciled to God. After the sermon follows a short prayer, invoking the blessing of God upon His Word, another hymn, with doxology and benediction, then a few moments more of silent prayer, and while the organ sounds forth a voluntary in full harmony with the preceding service, the congregation departs, carrying with it the solemn, strengthening feeling that it has been in the house of God, at the gates of heaven.

But to return to our history. Diligent research has

failed to give us the names of the architect of the building, the building committee of the Reformed Congregation, or the cost of the building. From still living witnesses we have learned that the mason work was done by Mr. Philip Meixell, grandfather of the late Charles Meixell, Esq. It is said that he received his pay for his work in continental money,[1] which when he came to use it several years after, had depreciated so much in value that for the whole of it he was only able to buy a bag of wheat or ten bushels of potatoes.

From the original size, materials and general internal arrangements and appointments of the building, we are warranted to infer that it must have cost what was then a large amount of money; and when we consider the then social state of the community, the limited pecuniary means of the wealthiest, the uncertain political state of the country, the building was not only a worthy monument of the piety and liberality of the fathers who built it, but also a speaking witness of their courage and faith.

[1] "During the summer of 1780 this wretched 'Continental' currency fell into contempt. As Washington said—'It took a wagon-load of money to buy a wagon-load of provisions.' At the end of the year 1778, the paper dollar was worth sixteen cents in the northern states, and twelve cents in the south. Early in 1780 its value had fallen to two cents, and before the end of the year it took ten paper dollars to make a cent. In October Indian corn sold wholesale in Boston for $150 a bushel, butter was $12 a pound, tea $90, sugar $10, beef $8, coffee $12, and a barrel of flour cost $1,575. Samuel Adams paid $2,000 for a hat, and a suit of clothes. The money soon ceased to circulate, debts could not be collected and there was a general prostration of credit. To say that a thing was 'not worth a Continental' became the strongest possible expression of contempt.' We need not wonder that the good and worthy man, who laid the foundations of our chuch building, received only ten bushels of potatoes or wheat as others say, for his work. But we are sure that what he lacked in Continental money was somehow made up to him in a better currency."

THE SCHLATTER BIBLE, AND THE OLD COMMUNION SET, BEARING DATE, 1746.

The Organization of the Congregation. 49

The vacancy that occurred in the pastorate of the congregation by the removal of Rev. Pithan, in 1771, was not supplied until 1776. Some time during the first half of this year (probably June or July), Rev. William Ingold became pastor, and though the records are silent on the point, yet being pastor at the time, it is reasonable to conclude that he took part in the consecration of the church, November 17, 1776, in connection with Rev. Christian Striet, who was then pastor of St. John's Lutheran congregation, Rev. Schwarbach, of the Lutheran Church, also assisting. His first baptismal record bears the date of August 25, 1776, and he continues this record uninterruptedly and carefully to February 14, 1786. From these records of baptism it is reasonable to infer that he was pastor of the congregation for a continued period of about ten years. Dr. Harbaugh, however, in his "Lives of the Fathers of the Reformed Church," Vol. II., p. 399, presents a somewhat different account of his connection with this congregation. He says that "Rev. Ingold came to Easton in 1776, but failing to give satisfaction and win the confidence of the congregation; and, moreover, the congregation being small and not able to support him, he remained but a short time. Afterwards [he does not say how long afterwards] he returned to Easton, where he labored for nearly ten years (with poor success)." If this statement is correct (and there is the record of a baptism bearing the date of April 30, 1775, evidently in Ingold's handwriting), then he must have been here the first time in 1775, but only for a short time, and afterwards returned in 1776 and remained here until 1786. He makes one record of special interest, which we here translate from the German, viz., "Easton, November 23, 1776, the following young persons were confirmed, in the presence of the congregation, on the Saturday after the Sunday on which the church was consecrated: Ludwig Knauss, aged 15 years; Frederick Gebhart, 16 years; Peter Riebel, 14 years; Frederick Hess, 16 years; John Jacob Everig, 16 years; Frederick Lerch, of Saucon, 17 years; Jacob Oberle, of Saucon, 17 years; Elizabeth Denler, 15 years; Magdalene Beker, 16 years; Susannah Kachline, 15 years; Elizabeth Drumheller, 16 years; Christina Meixell, 17 years; Rosina Odenwelder, 15 years; Margaret Best, 16 years; Christina Busch, 15 years; Elizabeth Odenwelder, 13 years; Elizabeth Hess (married), 18 years; Anna Hess, 16 years; Elizabeth Ewing, 17 years; Susannah Laer, 17 Elizabeth Laer, 16 years; Magdalene Meixel, 16 years; Elizabeth Gress, 16 years; Anna Margaret Ewing, 14 years; Anna Maria Lerch, of Saucon, 15 years, and Susan Elizabeth Laubach, of Saucon, 16 years — altogether 26." Some of these names are still borne by present members of this congregation.

The congregation was not permitted to worship continuously and uninterruptedly on alternate Sundays in this building after it was consecrated and during the pastorate of Rev. Ingold. On the 20th of January, 1777, Hons. George Taylor and George Walton, Commissioners appointed by Congress to be present and preside at the Indian treaty to be holden in Easton, met the Indians in this church, and, according to the report which they made to Congress, "after the shaking of hands and drinking of rum, during which time the organ was played, they proceeded to business."

Again, during the war of the Revolution, from 1776 to 1780, the church, which was then one of the two largest buildings in Easton — the court house being the other — was frequently used as a hospital and was often crowded with sick and wounded soldiers, during which time the congregation was compelled to worship elsewhere, if at all. The congregation in connection with St. John's Lutheran congregation, in these early days also labored under another oppressive burden in the shape of a church debt of four hundred pounds — an ecclesiastical evil which still afflicts churches. In 1794 the Trustees of the two congregations petitioned the Legislature to permit Mr. Hellick to collect the amount of the debt throughout the State by subscription, which was granted, and we hope he succeeded in soon collecting the money.

Rev. Ingold was succeeded, after an interval of but a few months, by Rev. Lebrecht Frederick Hermann, D.D., who became pastor of the congregation, in connection with the congregations at Plainfield, Dryland and Greenwich, in the fall of 1786. Dr. Hermann was a man of ability and culture, having studied six years in the celebrated school connected with the Orphans' Home at Halle, in Germany, and then took a course of three years in theology in the university of that city. The labors of the charge were too severe for his strength, and, after serving the congregations only about four years, he resigned October, 1790, giving as a reason for doing so that he feared the consequences upon his health of the excessive labors which the charge devolved upon him.

It was during the ministry of Dr. Hermann that the first recorded donation for charitable purposes was given to the congregation. It is thus recorded in the church book: "Anno, 1788, April 6th, Mrs. Catherine Opp, wife of Michael Opp, presented the Reformed Congregation with a gift of Five Pounds. This sum of Five Pounds shall be constantly invested, and the interest derived therefrom shall be used for the German education of a poor child of the congregation." Thus early was some regard had for the poor and destitute children (it may be orphans) of the congregation.

The removal of Dr. Hermann, was followed again by a vacancy, which continued until August, 1793, when Rev. Dr. Christian Ludwig Becker, father of the Rev. Dr. Jacob Christian Becker, and grandfather of Mr. Thomas H. Becker, at present an elder of this congregation, became pastor. Dr. Becker was a man of more than ordinary ability and of thorough education, having spent, with great diligence and application, more than twenty years in college and university before he entered upon the duties of the ministry. Moreover, he was a man of extraordinary eloquence, "and in preaching was frequently caught up into a most overwhelming overflow of impassioned eloquence and tender feeling. He would at times sway a congregation as a wind moves a forest of pines, so that the stoutest would bend to the power that breathed upon them." The congregation by whom he was much beloved, was permitted to enjoy the ministry of this gifted, eloquent and pious father only for a short time. After he had preached here eighteen months, "he received a call from Lancaster, Pa., which, after much reflection and considerable reluctance, he at length accepted, and removed from Easton, March, 1795."

Dr. Becker was succeeded by Rev. Thomas Pomp, the only son of Rev. Nicholas Pomp, who was one of the four missionaries sent to this country in 1760 by the Reformed Church of Holland. Father Pomp took charge of the congregation in July, 1796, and continued to be its pastor for more than half a century. As there are not a few members of the congregation still living who enjoyed the advantage of sitting under his ministry, I need only say

The Organization of the Congregation. 53

that he labored with untiring zeal, universal acceptance, and great success in the congregation, and in the other three associated with it, being so devoted to his holy work that he only ceased from it when compelled to do so by the infirmities of old age.

It was during the pastorate of Father Pomp that two great events occurred in the history of the congregation. The first was the remodeling and reconstruction of the church. Up to 1830 the church had been owned and occupied jointly by the Reformed and St. John's Lutheran congregations. In 1831 the Lutheran congregation separated from the Reformed, built a church for themselves and sold their interest in this church to this congregation for $1,600.

As soon as the congregation came into sole possession of the church it began to move in the direction of its reconstruction. At a meeting of the consistory, held May 23, 1831, committees were appointed to collect money to purchase the Lutheran interest in the church and to reconstruct it. At a congregational meeting held January 2, 1832, Peter Shnyder, Philip Odenwelder and Daniel W. Butz were appointed a committee to whom was intrusted the whole matter of reconstructing the church, and at a meeting held on the 21st of the same month (January) it was resolved to build the steeple on the north side of the church, the whole building being rough-casted, and the building committee were instructed to proceed at once to make contracts for lumber, etc. The contract for the work was given to Mr. Clark Lowry, and the building was reconstructed into its present form and all ready except the steeple, for consecration in November, 1832. Accordingly, on Sunday, the 25th of November, 1832, it was reconsecrated with appropriate service. The

Rev. Dr. Theodore L. Hoffeditz preached the dedicatory sermon, in German, in the morning; the Rev. Samuel Hess preached, in German, in the afternoon, and Rev. Dr. Bernhard C. Wolff, in English, in the evening. The services were continued during the following Monday, when Rev. Dr. Benjamin S. Schneck preached, in German, in the morning; Rev. B. C. Wolff, in English again, in the afternoon, and Rev. Dr. John Gray, of Easton, also in English, in the evening. The steeple was not finished until 1833. The whole cost of the reconstruction was about $25,000.

The other important event mentioned as having taken place during Father Pomp's ministry was the introduction of the English language into the services of the congregation. The German was the language in which the worship of the congregation was conducted from the beginning of its history, and continued to be so used until 1831. Then there seems to have existed in the congregation a want and demand for some services in English, which Father Pomp and the consistory sought to provide for by the adoption of the following resolution: "Inasmuch as the English language is becoming more and more prevalent in our country, so that it may be necessary to have English divine services, therefore, it is permitted to have English services on the alternate Sundays, or on the afternoon on which German services are held. Provided that, as the charter requires, the preacher who conducts in English services be a member of a German Reformed Synod of the United States, or at least must have his call to this congregation confirmed by this Synod." This action, while it indicated progress, was, all things considered, nothing less than revolutionary in its character, and especially the fact that Father Pomp not only did not resist the introduction of English into the service of the congregation, as many other pastors then did and still do, but was actually the chairman of the committee which offered the resolution making the change and cordially approved of its adoption. This conduct on his part speaks volumes for the liberal and self-sacrificing spirit which so signally characterized his whole relation to the congregation from the beginning to the end.

The way being thus opened for the introduction of English services, the congregation proceeded to supply its want in this regard, but did not succeed in doing so until December 12, 1832, when Rev. Dr. Bernard C. Wolff was elected " as assistant minister, to preach in the English language." The call, which in pursuance of this election was extended to Dr. Wolff, was accepted by him, and on Sunday, April 7, 1833, he preached his introductory sermon.

There never were, perhaps, two truer "yoke-fellows," as St. Paul phrases it, associated together in ministerial labor in the same congregation than Father Pomp and Dr. Wolff. Being in a large degree of similar disposition and temperament, amiable, kindly and easy to be entreated; and being actuated by the same lofty spirit of devotion to their holy work and self-sacrifice in its prosecution, they labored together in peace and harmony, to the great satisfaction and prosperity of the congregation, for a period of about twelve years.

In December, 1844, Dr. Wolff received a call from the Third Reformed Church in Baltimore, Md., which he felt constrained to accept. Accordingly he resigned his co-pastorate of this congregation and removed from it in February, 1845. The vacancy this made in the English co-pastorate (Father Pomp still continuing as senior German pastor) was supplied in April, 1845, by Rev. Dr. J. H. A. Bomberger accepting a call thereto. The work of building up the congregation in temporal and spiritual things continued to be carried forward with marked success by the two pastors now in charge. Being still of one heart, and one mind, and one purpose, they continued to coöperate, each in his sphere, not only without any friction or embarrassment, but with the most amicable spirit and in complete harmony.

It was about this time that one of the most pleasing episodes in Father Pomp's ministry in this congregation occurred. He now had been pastor of the congregation for fifty years. It was happily conceived that this fact was worthy of being commemorated in some special manner. The suggestion commended itself to the consistory, who, at a meeting held June 13, 1846, resolved that the semi-centennial anniversary of Father Pomp's pastorate be properly celebrated, and proceeded to make the necessary arrangements to do so. This celebration took place on Sunday, July 19, 1846, in this church, in the presence of a congregation which thronged the building. The services consisted of a brief statistical report of his labors for fifty years by Father Pomp, and a commemorative sermon by Rev. Henry Bibighaus, of Philadelphia, in German, in the morning; in the afternoon Rev. Dr. T. L. Hoffeditz and Rev. Dr. J. C. Becker deliver addresses, also in German, the latter presenting, in the name of the congregation, a beautifully bound copy of the Bible to Father Pomp, who was so overcome by his feelings that he could only respond in the melting language of tears; in the evening Rev. Dr. B. C. Wolff, former associate pastor, preached an appropriate sermon, of an historical character, in English. The whole occasion was one which was as gratify-

The Organization of the Congregation. 57

ing to him whom it was designed to honor as it was creditable to the congregation.

But now also shadows began to gather over the pathway of Father Pomp. Not only had old age, with its infirmities, almost imperceptibly crept upon him, but his naturally strong constitution and robust health commenced to suffer from his onerous labors in this and the associated congregations of Dryland and Plainfield. He now stood in his place as a tried veteran, whose spirit was still strong and willing, but whose flesh was weak, and growing weaker; and being no longer able physically to discharge the duties of his holy office to his own satisfaction, he retired from active service April 19, 1850, still retaining, however, his official relation as pastor, with salary. Four years later, in the early morning of April 22, 1852, death gently released him from all his earthly labors and trials, "in the eightieth year of his age, the sixtieth of his ministry, and the fifty-seventh of his pastorate in Easton."

During the latter part of Father Pomp's ministry, in 1846, the congregation fell heir to a legacy of $1,000, which had been bequeathed to it by Jacob Arndt, Esq., in 1833; the legacy not being available until after the death of his wife and brother Abraham.

When Father Pomp withdrew from active service a vacancy was made in the German pastorate. At the urgent request of the consistory, Dr. Bomberger, much against his will, consented to become a candidate therefor, and was unanimously elected. The services in the two languages were thus united in one person, and Dr. Bomberger became the sole pastor of the congregation, and continued to be such, officiating in both German and English languages, with great acceptance to the congregation and with encouraging success, until August, 1854, when, having accepted a call to the First Reformed Church of Philadelphia, he resigned and removed to that city.

A few facts which occurred during the time of Dr. Bomberger's pastorate are worthy of being noted here. In May, 1850, the congregation received a legacy of $500 from the estate of Mr. David Meixel, which was bequeathed by him on the condition that only the interest thereof be used " to repair and ornament the graveyard of the congregation."

In July of the same year The Female Benevolent Society of the congregation received a legacy of $5,000 from the estate of Peter Miller, Esq., the interest of which was to be used by them for the benefit of the poor of the congregation and of the Sunday-school. During the fall and winter of the same year the Session Room was built, and during the summer of 1852 the church was frescoed and gas was introduced into it.

During the fall and winter of 1852–3 the present parsonage was built, and thus a new home was provided for the pastors of the congregation, the old parsonage having been sold September 25, 1852.

Dr. Bomberger was succeeded in the pastorate of the congregation in September, 1854, by him who is still pastor of it, and the historian of the present occasion (Rev. John Beck). Leaving the estimate of his character and official work to others we will simply mention a few matters which have occurred within the time of his ministry, and which we deem deserving of record in this sketch.

In the summer of 1865 the church was repainted, cal cimined and somewhat repaired, and put into the condition and order in which it still is.

On July 19, 1869, the congregation received a legacy of ten shares of Phillipsburg Bank Stock from Anthony

The Organization of the Congregation. 59

Loudenburg, of Phillipsburg, N. J., to be used for the education of poor young men for the ministry of the Reformed Church.

By the death of the older members of the congregation, and by the prevalence of the English language in the community, the need for the use of the German in the public worship of the congregation grew less and less. At length, after much deliberation, many changes, and great tribulation, the German was entirely discontinued in the fall of 1871, and since then the public services of worship have been conducted exclusively in the English language.

This one statement more needs to be made to complete this hasty sketch. This church and congregation stood alone in this town and vicinity in 1776. Now one hundred years after, in 1876, at least six additional flourishing congregations are existing on the same territory, and this congregation is the mother of them all.

And now, as we bring this historical sketch to a close, many earnest thoughts and practical reflections press for utterance; but we will refrain from giving them record or expression at this time and on this occasion; neither would we tax your patience any longer. We crave your attention for but one thought more. These old walls, plain though they be, have been hallowed not only by special acts of consecration, but by the praise, and prayer, and worship of a century, and, to the eye of a reverent faith, are studded as thickly with the shining tokens and memorials of the divine presence and favor, vouchsafed to the fathers and children of more than three generations, as a dark night is studded with stars. How many faithful souls have been made meet within them by the word and the sacraments for an inheritance among the saints in light, eternity alone will disclose, and it is inspiring to believe that they, as a cloud of witnesses, are looking down upon us from the heavenly world as we are to-day engaged in these memorial services.

But it is not only these walls, with their hallowed associations, that we have inherited from the fathers and founders of this church. They have also transmitted to us and our keeping the more precious legacy of their faith and order, for the maintenance and defence of which they deemed no sacrifice too costly. If on to-day, throughout this broad, fair land, the recital of the heroic deeds of the fathers and founders of our civil order, and of the numberless temporal and political blessings bestowed upon us as a nation, will stir up in every patriotic heart feelings of profound gratitude, and kindle anew a flame of a holy devotion to the principles of liberty, justice and equality, then surely, inasmuch as spiritual blessings and privileges far transcend in value those which are temporal and civil, the recital thus imperfectly rendered of what the fathers and founders of this church and congregation did and suffered, the priceless spiritual blessings bestowed upon them and us, should not only awaken in our hearts feelings of gratitude to God, which should constrain us to call upon our souls and all the powers within us to praise and bless the Lord, but also impel us here to-day to register the old vow of a whole-soul devotion and love, with a new meaning: "If I forget thee, O Jerusalem, let my right hand forget her cunning. If I do not remember thee, let my tongue cleave to the roof of my mouth; if I prefer not Jerusalem above my chief joy."

RECENT HISTORY.

THE long pastorate of the Rev. Dr. John Beck, covering a period of more than a score of years, ended with his death, April 19, 1877. His death occurred suddenly, during the interval between his resignation as pastor and the date on which it was to take effect, and came as a shock to the congregation and community. His ministry for so many years had been characterized by scholarly ability, a patient and efficient fidelity to the welfare of the congregation. Of his ability as a scholar and writer the foregoing most valuable historical sketch is evidence which will long remain, and for which the future will be grateful.

Rev. Thomas C. Porter, D.D., was the next pastor, installed August 29, 1877. For a very considerable time he had held a prominent place in the Faculty of Lafayette College, and, though retaining his relations to the college, filled in a faithful, devoted manner a pastorate of seven years, during which time there were many accessions to the church, and an elegant organ, the largest in Easton, was purchased. In the early part of Dr. Porter's term the old volunteer choir was dispensed with and the modern innovation of salaried choristers introduced. Another feature was the inaugurating of early services at Christmas and Easter, which have constantly grown in favor, not only with the congregation, but the general public. Another change was that the high pulpit, built in 1832, was lowered, after being in use half a century. In 1884, Dr. Porter finding that advancing years prevented the double duties he had been performing since his installation, tendered his resignation, which was accepted with considerable regret by the consistory and congregation. In his closing sermon, Dr. Porter, after referring to the very pleasant and cordial relations which had existed between him and his flock, incidentally mentioned that it was twenty-three years previous that he first preached in the church. This was during the session of the Synod of the German Reformed Church, in 1861, when President Lincoln appointed September 26 as a day of fasting and prayer, and Dr. Porter was invited to preach the sermon before the Synod and the congregation. During the years 1867–69, when there were alternate services in German and English, Dr. Porter preached in English in the Session Room on those Sundays when Dr. Beck held services in German in the church proper.

The pastorate of the church having become vacant by the resignation of Rev. Dr. Porter, the Rev. H. M. Kieffer, pastor for eleven years of the church of the Ascension, Norristown, Pa., was called at a meeting of the congregation held on the evening of August 11, 1884. The newly elected pastor was duly installed on Thursday evening, October 30th, by a committee of East Pennsylvania Classis appointed for the purpose, consisting of the Rev. Dr. T. C. Porter, Rev. T. O. Stem and Rev. Dr. D. Y. Heisler, the latter preaching the installation sermon. The new pastor preached his introductory sermon the following Sunday morning, November 2, taking as his text, Philippians 1:2, "Grace be unto you, and peace, from God our Father and the Lord Jesus Christ."

In the early part of 1885, preparations were made for repairing the church building which had stood without any material change or improvement (with the exception of the lowering of the old pulpit and the purchase of a new pipe organ) since the year 1832. The old Third Street Church, so widely known in the community and throughout the Reformed denomination for its open-handed liberality, had generously assisted in the erection and improvement of many churches and in the relief and support of many poor and struggling congregations, meanwhile allowing its own house of worship to suffer from neglect and to present, with the passing years, a somewhat shabby appearance. Loth to affect any very material changes, least of all to alter the ancient and venerable appearance of the building, the congregation still felt that some steps must be taken toward repairing and improving the property.

Accordingly a committee was appointed by the consistory some time in March, 1885, composed of the following persons: Elders Jacob Rader, William Keller, Henry Young; Messrs. William H. Thompson, Thomas Rinek, Horace S. Bachman (the name of the pastor, Rev. H. M. Kieffer, was subsequently added), to devise a plan of repairs and ways and means of securing the needed funds. This committee having secured the services of an architect, John M. Stewart, of Easton, spent many days in the old church, examining walls, floors and timbers, and considering and discussing how best the changes might be made. A plan having at length been adopted, it was concluded to make no canvass of the congregation for the purpose of soliciting subscriptions in the usual way, but to prepare a printed circular, which should set forth the need of the repairs and appeal to the liberality of the people. The Sunday morning previous to the sending out of these circulars, viz., on June 21, 1885, the people were publicly advised from the pulpit of the intention of the committee, the pastor preaching a sermon upon the subject of "The Building of the Tabernacle." (Exodus xxxv, 20–22.)

In the course of a month, or thereabout, the sum of six thousand dollars was secured, the people manifesting a great readiness and cheerfulness in the work. This amount was at first thought sufficient for the changes and improvements contemplated, but it was soon found, as is usual in such cases, that more money would be needed.

The church building, as it was before the repairs were begun, presented an appearance somewhat different, both externally and internally, from what the beholder sees it to be at the present day, although the general features of the building remain unaltered. Prior to the repairs, the outer walls were of a pale yellow color. The steeple, as well as all the woodwork, was painted white, and had on it the dial of the town clock, some years ago removed to Zion's German Lutheran Church. The main entrance to the building was by a door on the Third street side, where the vestibule now is. The old woodwork, door posts and doors are there now. There was also another door on Third street, occupying the position of the upper window next Church street. Strictly speaking it was not a door, but served the purpose of both door and window. It has since been converted into a window. On Church street there were four windows, two downstairs and two upstairs, two on either side of the pulpit. These have been closed up. The entrance on the east, or parsonage side, was the same as now.

Internally the changes were more marked than on the exterior. Passing into the church, as it was before the repairs, one observed, as he entered the vestibule, two box stairways leading to the galleries. He noticed that the ceiling of the vestibule was low and somewhat cramped in appearance by the projection into it of an old "bellows gallery" used in former times for the organ, but since fallen into disuse except as a lumber room. Where the two large arches now are, two doors of ordinary size opened into the central part of the vestibule. The entrances from the vestibule into the audience room were located at the same places as now, except that the side doors have been moved further toward the wall and the inner jambs sloped where they were at right angles before. There were six rows of pews instead of four, as at present, with three aisles separating them, the central aisle being where it is now, and the side aisles not being along the walls but separated from them by a row or tier of short pews. The old pews, indeed, were all short, all being of the same length. They contained three, or at the most four, sittings. They were low in the back, narrow in the seat, and very close together, and were generally considered models of discomfort. After the fashion prevailing in old-time churches, the pews were box pews, being furnished with doors. The pews, as well as the galleries and woodwork generally, were painted a pure white, the walls being a plain gray color. The pulpit was a massive structure of mahogany. There was no recess, chancel rail or font. The windows were of ordinary or clear glass, and were furnished with "Venetian blinds." The posts under the galleries were heavy wooden affairs, which somewhat obstructed the view. These facts are here mentioned, somewhat hastily, it is true, as being of some possible interest in the future.

The changes and repairs were actually commenced on the 22d day of July, 1885. What they consisted of may, perhaps, be best seen by comparing the above statement with the present appearance of the building. It may, however, be well to mention in a general way that the repairs were chiefly as follows: pulpit recess on Church street; outer vestibule on Third street; changes and new stairways in inner vestibule; new doors from the vestibule to the main audience room; new floors upstairs and down; new pews, with upholstering; new gas fixtures; chancel rail; pulpit furniture; stained glass windows (nine of these, or all on the first floor, being memorial windows); frescoing all the walls; lowering the gallery fronts eight inches; rearranging the gallery entrances and floors; new pews in the galleries. The outer walls were repainted, the color being changed from a pale yellow to a stone gray. The roof was repaired; new spouting was put up; the ball and vane on the steeple taken down and regilded. It may be of interest to record that the old tin spouting had done constant service since 1832, that is for a period of fifty-three years; and that Mr. Lewis Heller (at present in the employ of Mr. Daniel Black), when he was a young man, made the old spouting, and had the singular fortune also, when he was an old man, to help make the new.

Nine memorial windows were erected to the memory of those who years ago or recently were active in the church work, and they are as follows:

By Mrs. John Eyerman, to the memory of James and Mary Black, her father and mother.

By Mrs. Mary Saylor, of Germantown, to the memory of Judge George Hess, her father.

By Mrs. Charles Santee, of Philadelphia, to the memory of Peter and Elizabeth Shnyder, her father and mother.

By. Mrs. William Lawall and her daughter Lillian, to the memory of William H. Lawall.

By Miss Mary Mixsell, Mrs. Major Wykoff, Mr. C. Jacob Mixsell, and Mrs. Dr. Lalor, to the memory of their father and mother, Charles W. and Mary K. Mixsell.

By Mrs. John Hutchinson, to the memory of her mother, Elizabeth Nicholas, and her family.

By the Sunday-schools of the congregation, to the memory of Rev. John Beck, D.D., former pastor of the church.

By private persons, to the memory of the Rev. Thomas Pomp and the Rev. Dr. Bernard Wolff, also former pastors of the church.

The entire cost of these repairs and memorial windows was about $12,000, and the work has been thoroughly done.

Willing minds gave their opinions; loving care for the ancient structure preserved it almost entirely intact; skillful hands directed the various changes, and earnest committeemen lent months of time to the tiresome, tedious, troublesome task. But at last the work was done, and the old walls without and within, save as to color, are the same. They still reëcho, though too faint for ear to discern, the stirring eloquence, the pathetic appeals, the solemn warnings, the tender solicitude of the pastors who have long ago lain down in their graves, sleeping a blessed sleep after a life of devotion to the holy work of saving souls; the anthems of to-day are reflected by the same boundaries that reverberated the plaintive melodies, the solemn hymns, and the grand old tunes of a hundred years ago.

On Sunday morning, February 21, 1886, the Rededicatory Services began at the usual hour of worship — 10.30 o'clock. The church was crowded to its utmost capacity, and had there been more seats there would have been numbers of people to occupy them. As the organist played a voluntary, the pastor, Rev. H. M. Kieffer, and the assisting clergymen, Rev. Dr. Thomas G. Apple,

68 The First Reformed Church of Easton, Pa.

President of Franklin and Marshall College, Lancaster; Rev. Dr. J. Spangler Kieffer, of the Reformed Church, Hagerstown, Md., brother of the pastor; Rev. Dr. Reily, President of the Allentown Female College; Rev. Thomas C. Porter, D.D., of Lafayette College, the recently esteemed pastor of the church; Rev. T. O. Stem, pastor of St. Mark's Reformed Church; Rev. D. Y. Heisler, D.D., pastor of Grace Reformed Church, all of Easton, entered and assumed places in the pulpit. It was an imposing scene. Dr. Apple occupied the principal seat in the alcove, with Rev. Dr. Kieffer on his left and Rev. Dr. Reily on his right. Dr. Porter occupied the seat at the reading desk; Rev. Stem opposite, while Dr. Heisler and Rev. H. M. Kieffer were seated near the foot of the pulpit steps. An anthem by the choir was followed by a prayer by Dr. Porter, who also read the scripture lesson and announced the hymn. The collection and anthem were next on the program, and then Dr. Apple arose and delivered his Rededicatory Sermon, taking his text from Psalms LXXXIV: 1, "How amiable are Thy tabernacles, O Lord of Hosts."

The sermon in the evening was preached by the Rev. Dr. J. Spangler Kieffer, of Hagerstown, Md., the brother of the pastor, taking for his text Colossians 1 : 10, "Increasing in the Knowledge of God."

For the above account of the recent history of the congregation we are indebted to the interesting sketch prepared by the editor of the Easton *Free Press*, Mr. C. N. Andrews, and afterward published in pamphlet form.

It may also be worthy of note here that a very worthy elder of the congregation, Colonel Peter Kichline commanded a company of troops from Easton during the Revolution, and with his men as sharpshooters rendered

Recent History. 69

most valiant service to Washington's forces at the disastrous battle of Long Island. They covered the retreat of the Continental forces, and saved the army from capture.

Colonel Kichline had taken much interest in the erection of the new church, but before it was completed he marched away with his men to Washington's camps, and saw it finished for the first time when, after the battle above named, he brought his sick and wounded men to Easton, and found a comfortable shelter for them in the new church building.

Another event of interest connected with this old church is the fact that, in October, 1779, when Sullivan's army returned from its long march against the Western Indians in the Genesee Country in New York State, and reached Easton in October of that year, Chaplain Evans of the New Hampshire Brigade, by special appointment, preached a sermon in the church to the soldiers of the expedition.

THE PASTORS OF THE CONGREGATION.

From the organization to 1763, irregular supplies.
1763, six months, Rev. Casper Dietrich Weyberg.

1763–66,	Vacant.
1766–69,	Rev. Frederick L. Henop.
1769–71,	Rev. Mr. Pithan.
1771–76,	Vacant.
1776–86,	Rev. William Ingold.
1786–90,	Rev. Lebrecht Frederick Hermann, D.D.
1790–93,	Vacant.
1793–95,	Rev. Dr. Jacob Christian Becker.
1796–1852,	Rev. Thomas Pomp.
1833–44,	Rev. Dr. Bernard C. Wolff.
1845–54,	Rev. Dr. J. H. A. Bomberger.
1854–77,	Rev. Dr. John Beck.
1877–84,	Rev. Dr. Thomas C. Porter.
1884–	Rev. Dr. Henry Martyn Kieffer.

THE OLD ORGAN AND ITS SUCCESSORS.

FOR the benefit of those who are to come after, some of whom will undoubtedly be grateful for the information here given, it may be well to give some account of the musical instruments used in this historic church. Some of the facts here given have been but very recently ascertained, and are known to few if any of the members of the congregation.

It may seem strange that, at such an early period in the history of the Forks of the Delaware, when the settlers were both poor and few in number, they should undertake the building of a church of such considerable proportions and involving such an outlay of money. But it must be remembered that these poor Germans were pious people. With them religion and the church were first. It is remarkable, also, that no sooner was the church built than an organ was purchased and duly installed in the organ loft. For the German loved music — music and religion were, to his mind inseparable, and a church without an organ was inconceivable.

So, no sooner was the church finished than the organ appeared, as we know from the fact that when the Indian Treaty was held in 1777, the organ was played during the friendly handshaking and rum-drinking, according to the record. The organ was built, we are informed, by one Dannaker, in 1775.

What has become of this organ? We were always under the impression that it had long since been consigned to the junk-shop or the ash-barrel, such being the fate, unfortunately, of many of our priceless antiquities. But, lo!

The Old Organ and its Successors. 71

while engaged in this writing I am informed that the church at Plainfield, once and for many years served by the pastors of the church in Easton, was about to hold a rededication of their church organ, which they had lately enlarged and improved; also, that the organ in question is the original instrument used in the Easton church, having been purchased by the Plainfield congregation in 1833. In connection with which statement I am asked to give the people of Plainfield any information I may possess concerning their old organ. "Who was the builder, and when was it built? Was it played at the Indian Treaty of 1777?" To which interrogatories a full and courteous response was given, with the request that it be read at the rededication of the venerable organ, now one hundred and twenty-five years old.

That was the original organ. It was sold to the Plainfield church in 1833, and a new organ purchased, which in its turn was in constant use for half a century, yielding its place about the year 1880 to the very excellent instrument now in use.

One can only regret the loss of some of these old things. May we not hope that some day the old organ may come back to this church? There is room for it in the Session Room, or Chapel — if indeed the Plainfield people will ever graciously part with it out of regard for the congregation to which it once belonged.

THE CHANGE IN THE NAME OF THE CHURCH.

THE original name of the congregation was "The German Reformed Congregation of Easton." By this name it was commonly and popularly known from the beginning of its history, and by this "name, style and title" it was legally and formally denominated in its original charter granted in the year 1808.

In the course of time, however, some change in the name of the congregation began to appear necessary. The reasons for such a change are herewith given:

I. The name "German" was no longer suitable: first, because this word was by due authority of the Synod dropped from the official and legal name of the denomination as a whole, which since 1866 was known as "The Reformed Church in the United States," and not "The German Reformed Church in the United States" as formerly. To retain the name, "German," for the congregation after it had been dropped by the denomination seemed incongruous.

Then, too, the congregation had long ceased to be German. From the date of its organization until the year 1833, when the first English pastor was installed, all the services of the church had been held in the German tongue. From that date onward the German began to decline and the English to strengthen, good old "Father Pomp," the German minister, saying to Dr. Wolff his English assistant — "you must increase but I must decrease." German services, however, still continued to be held, at first in the morning, afterward in the afternoon, until toward the close of the pastorate of the Rev. Dr. Beck. But the German

INTERIOR OF THE FIRST REFORMED CHURCH, 1902.

The Change in the Name of the Church.

services were but poorly attended, and were maintained for years merely out of a tender regard for the preferences of the older and declining portion of the congregation. In the course of time the old people who were attached to the German had almost entirely passed away, and German ceased to be used. This was in the year 1871. From that date onward all the services of the church were in the English tongue, and to continue calling the congregation " German " when it was no longer so, was plainly inappropriate and often misleading to the general public.

Furthermore — when this congregation was organized there was but this one Reformed church in Easton — since then four other Reformed churches having been established, the original name of the congregation ceased to be distinctive. And this difficulty was still further intensified by the establishment of a Dutch Reformed Church on Spring Garden Street. There being then *two* Reformed churches in Easton and in close proximity to each other, it became necessary to distinguish them, and so, for many years the congregation of which we are writing was popularly known as " The Third Street Reformed Church." This name it retained for more than thirty years, being known by one name in law and by another in common usage.

This state of things was plainly undesirable, and the necessity for a change became apparent. In order that the change of name might be made in a regular and formal manner, it was thought well to secure an amended charter from the Court of Northampton. A new charter was desirable, quite independently of the matter of the name; and this chiefly for the reason that the old charter was no longer suited, in many important respects, to the changed circumstances of the congregation. Accordingly, after due application regularly made, the Court of Northampton County did, on the eighth day of March in the year 1897 grant the congregation an amended charter whereby its name was changed to that which it presently bears — " The First Reformed Church of Easton."

THE CHIME OF BELLS.

THE Chime of Bells in the tower of the old church was erected during the opening days of the year 1902, in commemoration of the one hundred and fifty-seventh anniversary of the founding of the congregation. The erection of this chime of bells was the result of an address delivered to the congregation by the pastor, Rev. Dr. Kieffer, on Sunday, November 12, 1899, concerning the propriety of holding a jubilee service at some time in the near future in commemoration of the founding of the congregation about one hundred and fifty years ago. The pastor then suggested the placing of a chime in the tower as a suitable method of marking the sesqui-centennial milestone in the long history of the congregation, and dwelt at some length on the religious impressiveness of a chime of bells as being an undoubted source both of pleasure and profit to many people in a city like Easton, which so far has known no chime. After the service the matter was taken up by some of the people in a very enthusiastic manner, subscriptions for three bells being made on the spot—Miss Mary Alice Huber leading the way, followed by Mrs. Matilda Chidsey and Mrs. Thomas Rinek. Gradually all the bells were provided for, six being memorial bells, as named below; one was given by the citizens of Easton in recognition of the close relationship which existed between this old church and the town of Easton from the earliest times, and one by the congregation as a whole. These, together with the great bell weighing 2,000 pounds placed in the tower at the centennial 1876, make a complete chime of nine bells.

The old bell was removed from the tower by the Meneely Bell Company, during the month of September, 1901, and taken to their foundry at Troy, New York, for the purpose of having the other eight bells cast in harmony with it. In December following, very considerable changes were made in the tower to prepare a suitable foundation for the bells, old timbers being replaced by new, and other improvements made as will appear on inspection. Exclusive of the cost of these repairs, the chime, including the old bell, cost $6,000. The following is a schedule of the bells with the inscriptions and the names of the donors:

1. F, 2,000 lbs. The Centennial Bell — 1876.
2. G, 1,550 lbs. In Memory of the Pastor, Rev. Henry Martyn Kieffer, D.D. Presented by the congregation.
3. A, 1,000 lbs. In Memory of the First Church at "The Forks of the Delaware." Presented by the citizens of Easton.
4. B *flat*, 825 lbs. In Memory of James and Mary Black, and their children. Presented by the Daniel Black Estate.
5. C, 550 lbs. In Memory of Michael and Elizabeth Butz and their children. Presented by Mrs. Matilda Chidsey.
6. D, 425 lbs. In Memory of Mrs. Matilda Baker Fulmer. Presented by her son, Chester B. Fulmer.
7. E *flat*, 375 lbs. In Memory of Daniel Whitesell and Catharine his wife. Presented by Mrs. Catharine Whitesell.
8. E, 330 lbs. In Memory of Anthony Zuilch and his wife, Jane Morton, and their sons, Thomas Cumings, Samuel Morton, and Henry Bibighaus. Presented by the Zuilch family.
9. F, 280 lbs. In Memory of David and Deborah Huber. Presented by their daughter, Mary Alice Huber.

GLORIA IN EXCELSIS DEO.

CHURCH RECORDS.

TITLE PAGE OF THE OLD CHURCH BOOK.

"CHURCH BOOK

" *Of the congregation of the Evangelical Reformed in Easton, in which are recorded the names of persons baptized, the elders and deacons, and their successors, etc.*"

1768. December 18. The following were installed as officers of the congregation: *Elders*, Ludwig Knauss and Philip Odenwelder; *Deacons*, John Gettert and Henry Schneider.

[The above entry is in the handwriting of the Rev. Frederick L. Henop, who became pastor in 1766. The record of the elders and deacons is not resumed until the year 1777, during the pastorate of the Rev. John William Ingold, in whose handwriting we read as follows:]

Anno 1777. January 5. The following were installed as deacons or stewards of the alms: Philip Achenbach and Nicholas Kemmerer, Jr. The elders are Nicholas Kemmerer, Sr., and John Simon.

Anno 1778. January 18. Philip Achenbach and Nicholas Kemmerer, Jr., go out of office as deacons, and in their stead the following were set over the congregation as deacons: John Deigmann and Philip Odenwelder, Jr.

In addition to these there were set over the congregation February 1, 1778, as deacons: Nicholas Drachsel (Troxel) and Michael Fraes.

Anno 1779. April 2. John Simon as an elder, and John Deigman as a deacon, go out of office and in their places were chosen George Ernst Becker, elder; and in addition, as elder, Jacob Schuhmacher, and John Schuck as deacon.

1780. March 12. Philip Odenwelder goes out of office as deacon and in his stead was chosen, as deacon, Michael Odenwelder. Nicholas Drachsel also vacates the office of deacon ("als diaconus") and in his stead was chosen June 2, the same year, John Young.

1782. February 24. Nicholas Kemmerer, Sr., and George Ernest Becker go out of office as elders, and as stewards of the Alms ("almosen Pfleger"—deacons) John Schuck, John Young and Michael Fraes, and new elders and deacons were chosen, as follows: In addition to those that remain in office to the present time as Elders: Jacob Schumacher, Philipp Odenwelder, Sr., and as new, Philipp Achenbach and Michael Gress. In addition to those remaining in office as deacons, Michael Odenwelder, John Deigman; and as new, John Best and Leonhard Welsch.

Anno 1873. February 16. Instead of Philip Achenbach, elder, and John Deichman, deacon ("almosen Pfleger") their term of office having expired, the following were chosen: *Elder*, John Deichman; *Deacon*, Henry Hahn.

Anno 1784. February 13. Philip Odenwelder, Sr., goes out of office as elder; and as deacons, Michael Odenwelder, Leonard Welsch, and Henry Hahn; and in their stead the following were obligated and installed ("verpflichtet und vorgestellt worden" viz: *Elder*, Philip Odenwelder, Jr.; *Deacons*, Philip Wattring, Henry Winter, Christian Butz.

Anno 1787. February 27. [In a different handwriting, probably in that of Rev. Lebrecht Frederick Hermann, who became pastor 1786.] After a full settlement of their church accounts, the two deacons, Jeremiah Hess and Christian Butz went out of office, and in their places were chosen and installed Frederick Berthold and John Fenner.

Anno 1788. January 12. After a settlement of the church accounts, there went out of office Elder John Deichman, and Deacon Philip Wottering, and in their places were chosen and installed, as elder, John Nicholas Traxel, and as deacon, George Adam Geissle.

Church Records.

Anno 1788. At this time the elders and deacons of our congregation are as follows: *Elders*, Philip Odenwelder, Jr., John Best, Philip Gorel, John Nicholas Traxel; *Deacons*, Henry Winter, John Fenner, Frederick Barthold, George Adam Geishle.

Anno 1786. A list of the church council of the congregation at Easton, consisting of the following persons: *Elders*, John Deichman, Philip Chorel, Philip Odenwelder, Jr., John Best; *Deacons*, Philip Wotring, Henry Winter, Christian Butz, Jeremiah Hess.

A. D. 1787. After a full settlement of their church accounts, the two deacons, Jeremiah Hess and Christian Butz, went out of office, and in their stead were chosen and duly obligated the following: Frederick Barthold and John Fenner, deacons.

Anno Domini 1788. January 12. The term of office of John Deichman, as elder, and of Philip Wotring as deacon, having expired, and in their stead were placed over the Christian Congregation, and duly obligated, as elder, John Nicholas Traxel; and as deacon, George Adam Geissle.

Anno 1789. January 17. After a faithful rendering of the accounts of the alms, Elder John Best and Deacon Henry Winter, retired from the church council, and in their places were chosen and duly obligated, as elder, Peter Ladig, and as deacon, John Odenwelder.

Anno 1790. January 23. There were assembled at the residence of the minister, the elders, deacons and some of the members of the congregation, and after the customary church settlement had been submitted and duly signed, the two elders, Mr. Philip Odenwelder and Nicholas Troxel, and the two deacons, Mr. Fred. Barthold and John Fenner, laid down their office, and in their stead were chosen, and on the 21st of March duly presented to the Christian Congregation and installed in their office as follows: *Elders*, Michael Odenwelder, Lenhard Leydig; *Deacons*, Philip Moessinger, Jacob Scheib.

Anno 1793. A list of the Church Council in the Congregation at Easton, consisting of the following persons: *Elders*, Philip Chorel, Peter Ladig, Michael Odenwelder; *Deacons*, George Adam Geissle, John Odenwelder, Philip Moessinger, Jacob Scheib.

Anno 1793. October 6. In the stead of Elder Lenhard Leydig, deceased now for more than two years, Deacon Jacob Scheib was chosen as elder; and in his stead Christopher Mixsel was elected as deacon, and on the 27th of October were presented to the Christian Congregation and duly installed into their offices; as elder, Jacob Scheib, and as deacon, Christopher Mixsel.

1795. January 3. There were assembled in the minister's house the elders, deacons, treasurer and members of the church. After a faithful rendering of their accounts, there retired from office Peter Lattig, as elder, and John Odenwelder and George Adam Geissle, as deacons. In their stead there were chosen by the congregation on the 4th of January, and on the 18th duly installed, as elder, George Adam Geissle, and as deaco ns Christian Butz and Jacob Keller.

Anno 1788. April 6. Mrs. Catharine Opp, the wife of Michael Opp, presented the Reformed Congregation with a gift of five pounds. This sum of five pounds shall be constantly invested and the interest derived therefrom shall be used for the German education of a poor child of the congregation.

Anno 1789. January 17. After a creditable rendering of their accounts Elder John Best and Deacon Henry Winter go out of office, and in their stead Peter Ladig was chosen elder and John Odenwelder, deacon.

Anno 1790. November 10. The interest of the five pounds, up to this time, and in accordance with the wish of Catharine Opp, has been properly expended and applied, the truth of which statement is herewith attested by

F. HERMAN, V.D.M.

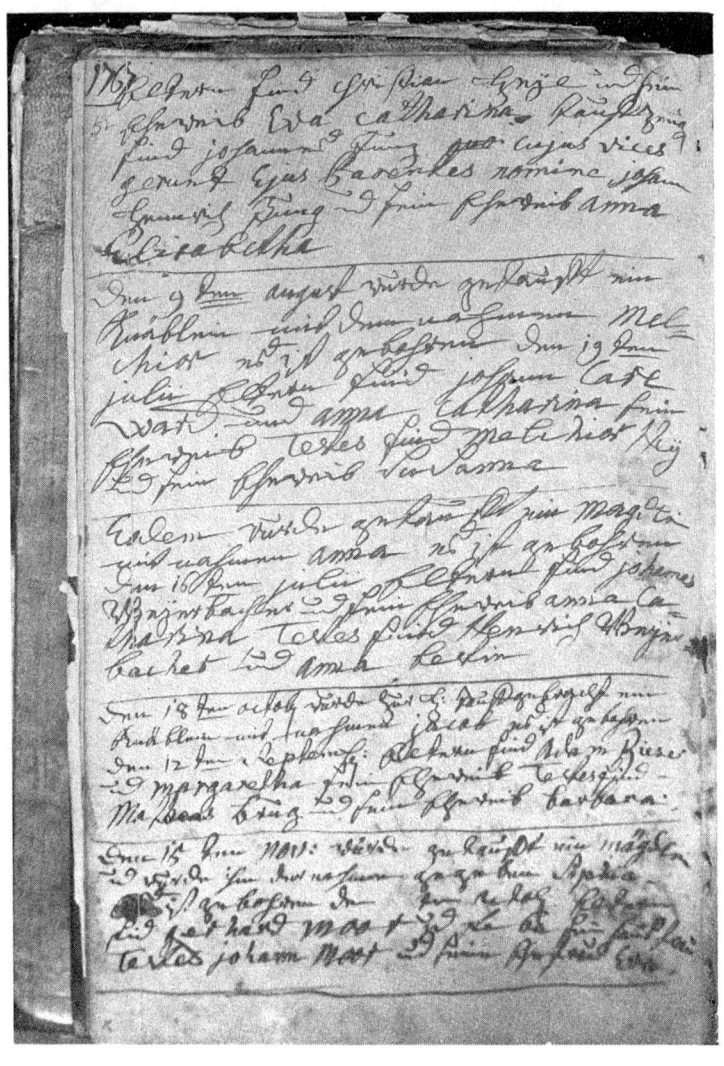

FAC-SIMILE OF A PAGE OF THE OLD CHURCH RECORD.

BAPTISMS.

Anno 1760. The 28th of February a son was born, and baptized the 5th of April in the same year. The child received the name of Ludwig. The Sponsors were Philip Gress(ie) and Anna Margaretha, *ejus uxor*. The parents were Ludwig Knauss and Elizabetha, *ejus uxor*.

The above entry stands alone, and is in the handwriting of the Rev. John William Ingold, who was not pastor of the congregation until 1776. It is thought that the above record may have been made by Rev. Mr. Ingold some years after the baptism of the child.

Then follows, in German handwriting that is exceedingly difficult to read, or rather to decipher:

"The Record of certain children who were baptized by the Rev. C. P. Weyberg, the evidence of which fact lies in the circumstance that the records were found in his handwriting in certain stray memoranda."

1763. June 12. A child of John Simon and Gertrude his wife. *Witnesses*, Mr. and Mrs. John Rieser. Child's name, John.

1763. June 12. A child of Michael Meyer and his wife Magdalena. *Witnesses*, George Kren (?) and Maria Barbara. Child's name, Maria Barbara.

1763. June 19. A child of Martin Lohr and his wife Elizabeth. *Witnesses*, Frederick Meixel, and his wife Anna. Name of the child, Abraham.

1763. August 9. A child of John Ries and his wife Sophia. *Witnesses*, parents. Child's name, John.

1763. August 9. A child of Ludwig Knaus and his wife Elizabetha. *Witnesses*, parents. Child's name, Anna Elizabetha.

1763. October 22. A child of Conrad Gressig (Gress?) and his wife Anna Margaretha. *Witnesses*, Friederich Meixel and Anna. Name of child, Anna.

1763. October 22. A child of Christopher Fox and his wife. *Witnesses*, Henry . . . and his wife Juliana. Child's name, Juliana Maria.

1763. April 17. A child of George Gangwer and his wife Anna Maria. *Witnesses*, Christian Menninger and Maria Catharina Gangewer. Child's name, John.

1763. April 17. A child of Carl Ward and his wife Anna Catharina. *Witnesses*, William Kehl and Maria Magdalena Kehl. Child's name Maria.

The above records, which are evidently in the handwriting of Rev. Fredenck L. Henop, who became pastor of the congregation in 1766, were made from memoranda left by Rev. Mr. Weyberg. The latter was the first regular pastor of the congregation, taking charge 1763, but remained only six months. This statement may make clear the following note which is entered immediately after the above records:

"These are the children whose names were found on slips of paper left behind by the Rev. Mr. Weyberg. It is indeed true that more names were on these slips, but inasmuch as one cannot tell whether they are the names of the parents, the sponsors, or the children, one did not wish to inscribe them, inasmuch as nothing should stand in this book but what one knows to be the truth."

Then follow six blank leaves — left blank perhaps in the hope that other records of the Church might be there inserted in proper place — and then follows the records of baptisms performed by the Rev. Frederick L. Henop, who became pastor at the date named above.

Church Records.

"The record of the children who were baptized in the congregation at Easton — to wit:

1766. February 23. A girl by the name of Susanna. *Parents*, George Fox and Elizabetha. *Sponsors*, Melchior Hay and his wife Susanna. The child was born Dec. 28, 1765.

1766. February 23. A girl was baptized, Susanna. *Parents*, Paul Rieser and his wife Maria Barbara. *Sponsors*, Melchior Hay and his wife Susanna. The child was born Jan. 28, 1766.

1766. April 22. A boy was baptized, John Philip. Born Jan. 5. *Parents*, Benedict and Anna Maria Butz. *Sponsors*, Philip Odenwelder and his wife.

1766. April 22. A boy, George Jacob. Born June 4, 1765. *Parents*, Michael Schmidt and Anna Maria. *Sponsors*, George Neuhart and Anna Maria Mann.

1766. May 4. A boy, John Peter. Born February 22. *Parents*, Peter (?) Ladig and Maria Elizabetha. *Sponsors*, Peter Schumacher and Mrs. Anna Maria Bruch.

1765. December 25. A girl, named Maria. Born November 21, 1765. *Parents*, William Hay and Catharine. *Sponsors*, Christian Best and Mrs. Maria Hess.

1766. August 10. A boy was brought to Holy Baptism. The name given him was John. Born July 15. *Parents* are John Schneider and Catharina Elizabetha. *Sponsors*, Conrad Ihrig and his wife Elizabetha.

1766. August 10. A boy, John Philip. Born July 5. *Parents*, Jacob Grub and his wife Elizabetha. *Sponsors*, John Philip Odenwelder and his wife Anna Maria.

1766. December 14. A girl was baptized Margaretha. Born August 23. *Parents*, Ephraim Blum and his wife Catharina. *Sponsors*, Peter Schneider and Mrs. Margaretha ——— (?).

1766. December 14. A girl was baptized and the name given her, Susanna. Born August 2. *Parents*, Peter Oehler and his wife Elizabetha. *Sponsors,* Melchior Hay and his wife Susanna.

1767. January 2. A boy was brought to Holy Baptism, to whom the name was given, John Gottfried. Born December 5, 1766. *Parents*, Matthew Miller and his wife Maria Barbara. *Sponsors*, Stephanus Horn and his wife Lunigunda.

1767. January 25. A girl named Maria Elizabetha. Born December 13, 1766. *Parents*, John William Hay and his wife Catharina. *Sponsors*, Frederick Frederick (?) and his wife Maria.

1767. January 25. A girl was baptized, Maria Margaretha. Born December 21, 1766. *Parents*, Peter Menich and his wife Sabilla. *Sponsors*, William Menich and his wife Margaretha.

1767. February 22. A boy was baptized, John Philip by name. Born February 13. *Parents*, Stephen Saam and his wife Susanna. *Sponsors*, Philip Odenwelder and Mrs. Elizabeth Arndt.

1767. March 22. A girl was baptized and the name given Sara Margaretha. Born February 16. *Parents*, Conrad Gress and Anna Margaretha, his wife. *Sponsors*, Balthazar Keel and Mrs. Sara Margaretha Doll (Dull).

1767. April 25. A boy was brought to Holy Baptism, named William. *Parents*, Henry Hess and his wife Margaretha. Born February 24. *Sponsors*, Mr. and Mrs. William Hess.

1767. April 25. A girl was baptized, named ——— (name not given). *Parents*, Anthony Asheier and his wife Sara. Born November 27, 1766. *Witnesses*, ——— (not given) Ebert and Mrs. Maria Dietz.

1767. March 25. A boy was baptized, named John Jacob. Born October 24, 1766. *Parents*, Andrew Kratz and his wife Barbara. *Sponsors*, John Jacob Kratz and Mrs. Elizabeth Butz.

Church Records. 85

1767. May 25. A girl was baptized named Elizabeth. *Parents*, ——— (first name wanting) Anberger and his wife Eva Maria. *Sponsors*, parents. (This entry is in pencil and almost illegible.)

1767. June 1. A girl was baptized, named Cecilia. Born April 17. *Parents*, Michael Butz and his wife Elizabetha. *Sponsors*, Adam Butz and his wife Anna Margaretha.

1767. June 1. A boy, John Michael. Born May 1. *Parents*, Adam Butz and his wife Anna Margaretha. *Sponsors*, Michael Butz and his wife Elizabeth. (Each "stood" for the child of the other.)

1767. June 7. A girl was baptized, named Anna Margaretha. Born October 5, 1766. *Parents*, John Maurer and his wife Maria Elizabeth. *Sponsors*, Jacob Maurer and Mrs. Catharina Maurer. (Here follow two words "Wilhelm mein," or Wilhelm Maun, probably meaning that Mrs. Catharine Maurer was the wife of William, not Jacob Maurer. Ed.)

1767. June 26. A girl was baptized, named Elizabetha Margaretha. Born May 3. *Parents*, John Yaeger and his wife Elizabetha. *Sponsors*, John Dengler and his wife Anna Margaretha.

1767. June 26. A boy named John. Born July 4. *Parents*, Christian Hay (Heyl?) and his wife Eva Catharina. *Sponsor*, John Young. In his stead, however, his parents carried the child in his name; that is, John Henry Young and his wife Anna Elizabetha. (A similar entry in German and Latin. Probably John Young was a child, or a minor, or too young to carry or hold the child at the baptism, and so his parents did it for him. Ed.)

1767. August 9. A boy was baptized, named Melchior. Born July 19. *Parents*, John Carl Ward, and his wife Anna Catharina. *Sponsors*, Melchior Hay and his wife Susanna.

1767. August 9. A girl was baptized, named Anna. Born July 16. *Parents*, John Betzerbacher and his wife Anna Catharina. *Sponsors*, Henry Betzerbacher and Anna Berlin.

The First Reformed Church of Easton, Pa.

1767. October 16. A boy was brought to Holy Baptism, named Jacob. Born September 12. *Parents*, Adam Rieser and his wife Margaretha. *Sponsors*, Matthew Brug (Bruch ?) and his wife Barbara.

1767. November 15. A girl was baptized, and the name given Sophia. Born (date wanting) October. *Parents*, Gerhard Moor and his wife Seba (?). *Sponsors*, John Moor and his wife Eva.

1767. November 29. A boy was baptized named Peter. Born (date wanting) September. *Parents*, Peter Schneider and Mrs. Anna Dietz. *Sponsors*, Abraham Bachman and Elizabetha ———.

1767. December 13. A girl was baptized, named Anna Maria. Born September 11. *Parents*, Michael Schmidt and his wife Catharina. *Sponsors*, Michael Schmidt and his wife Anna Barbara.

1767. December 13. A girl was baptized, named Sophia. Born (the entire date wanting). *Parents*, Daniel Lavare (Labarre?) and his wife Anna Margaretha. *Sponsors*, John Dietz (?) and his wife Sophia.

1767. December 13. A girl, named Sophia. *Parents*, William Hay and his wife Catharina. Born November 18. *Sponsors*, John Getthert and his wife Sophia.

1767. December 13. A boy named Frederick. Born April 3. *Parents*, Tobias Schall and his wife Anna. *Sponsors*, ——— Gewinner and his wife Catharine.

1767. December 27. A girl was baptized, and the name given was Catharina Maria. Born October 3, 1761. *Parents*, John Martin Ludwig and his wife Elizabetha. *Sponsor*, Mrs. Catharina Berlin.

1767. December 27. A girl was baptized, named Gertrude. Born January 3, 1763. *Parents*, John Martin Ludwig and his wife Elizabetha. *Sponsor*, Mrs. Gertrude Simon.

Church Records. 87

1767. December 27. A boy named John. Born March 23, 1766. *Parents*, John Martin Ludwig and his wife Elizabetha. *Sponsor*, John Spangenberg.

1767. December 27. A girl named Maria Elizabetha. Born June 24. *Parents*, Peter Holl (Hull?) and his wife Maria Elizabetha. *Sponsors*, Michael Butz and his wife Elizabetha.

1767. December 27. A girl named Christina. Born Oct. 22. *Parents*, Peter Ladich (Leidich, Leidy?) and his wife Maria Elizabetha. *Sponsors*, William Paulus (Paul) and his wife Margaretha.

1767. December 27. A boy named John. Born Oct. 9. *Parents*, Peter Oehler and his wife Elizabetha. *Sponsors*, John Simon and his wife Gertrude.

1768. January 31. A girl was baptized named Anna Margaretha. Born Nov. 17, 1767. *Parents*, Peter Trum and Margaretha Paulus. *Sponsors*, John Schneider and Catharine Elizabetha.

1768. January 31. A child was baptized named Christian. Born Dec. 26, 1767. *Parents*, Jacob Beisher and his wife Anna Elizabetha. *Sponsors*, Christian Best and Mrs. Elizabeth Brotzman.

1768. January 31. John Trum had a boy baptized named John. Born Dec. 13. *Parents*, John Trum and his wife Eva Margaretha. *Sponsors*, John Best and Mrs. Maria Hay.

1768. January 31. A girl named Elizabetha. Born Jan. 4. *Parents*, Jeremiah Koch and his wife Anna. *Sponsors*, John William Gramer (Kremer, Cramer?) and his wife Elizabetha.

1768. February 28. A boy was brought to Holy Baptism and the name given him was George Henry. Born Jan. 13. *Parents*, Adam Tuffart and his wife Susanna. *Sponsors*, George Heimrich and Mrs. Joanna Weygandt.

1768. February 28. A girl was baptized named Joanna Maria. Born November 23, 1767. *Parents*, George Becker and Catharina his wife. *Sponsor*, Mrs. Anna Maria Herr.

The First Reformed Church of Easton, Pa.

1768. March 13. A boy was baptized named John Henry. Born Jan. 23. *Parents*, Ephraim Blum and his wife Catharina. *Sponsor*, Henry Schneider.

1768. March 27. A girl was baptized and the name given, Barbara. *Parents*, Carl Heymer and his wife Anna Margaretha. *Sponsors*, Jacob Hembd and his wife Barbara. Born March 9.

1768. April 10. A girl was brought to Holy Baptism named Elizabetha. Born March 16. *Parents*, Adam Hay and his wife Anna Maria. *Sponsors*, Christopher Stecher and Mrs. Elizabeth Brotzmann.

1768. April 24. A boy was brought to Holy Baptism and the name given Jacob. Born December 13, 1767. *Parents*, Nicolas Kemmerer and his wife Juliana. *Sponsors*, Jacob Arndt and his wife Elizabetha.

1768. April 24. A boy who received the name John. Born December 11, 1767. *Parents*, George Neuhart and his wife Elizabetha. *Sponsors*, John Yaeger and his wife Elizabetha.

1768. April 24. A boy was brought to Holy Baptism named Henry. Born April 2. *Parents*, Henry Schneider and his wife Juliana. *Sponsors*, Ludwig Knauss and his wife Elizabetha.

1768. May 9. A boy was baptized with the name Ludwig. Born February 13. *Parents*, John Flori and his wife, Christiana. *Sponsors*, Ludwig Knauss and his wife Elizabetha.

1768. May 13. A boy was baptized, receiving the name Andrew Jacob. Born in the month of November, 1767. *Parents*, Philip Ruthstein and his wife Catharina. *Sponsors*, Andrew Jacob Nitaunier (?) and his wife Anna Catharina.

1768. June 5. A girl was brought to Holy Baptism, receiving the name Elizabeth. Born March 4. *Parents*, Ludwig Schaub and his wife Anna Margaret. *Sponsors*, Michael Yohe and Mrs. Elizabeth Kratz.

Church Records.

1768. June 19. A boy was baptized named Jacob. Born June 9. *Parents*, Michael Opp and his wife Catharine. *Sponsors*, Jacob Opp and his wife Anna Maria.

1768. August 28. A boy was baptized, receiving the name William. The day of his birth is unknown, but the child was apparently about two years old. His *parents* are William Niclac (Nicolas?). The name of the mother is likewise unknown who brought him to Holy Baptism. *Sponsor*, William Storm, Philip Storm's son.

1768. August 28. A boy who received the name Peter. Born July 30. *Parents*, Jacob Grub and his wife Elizabeth. *Sponsors*, Peter Oehler and his wife Elizabeth.

1768. September 11. A girl was baptized named Susanna. Born August 14. *Parents*, Peter Schneider and his wife Sara. *Sponsors*, Caspar Doll and his wife Margaret.

1768. September 11. A boy was baptized named Isaiah. Born November 13, 1767. *Parents*, James Johnston (?) and his wife, Christiana. *Sponsors*, Gerhard Moor and his wife Feba (Phoeba?).

1768. October 23. A girl was baptized, receiving the name Elizabeth Magdalena. Born September 18. *Parents*, Christopher Forre and his wife Elizabeth Magdalena. *Sponsors*, George Faust Becker and his wife, Helena.

1768. The 20th (No month given. Probably November.) A boy was baptized and the name given him, John Faust. Born October 17. *Parents*, John Dengler and his wife Anna Margaret. *Sponsors*, Faust Becker and his wife Helena.

1768. The 20th (No month given. Probably November.) A girl was baptized and named Juliana Barbara. Born October 23. *Parents*, Matthias Miller and his wife Maria Barbara. *Sponsors*, Henry Schneider and his wife Juliana Barbara.

1768. December 4. A girl was baptized named Magdalena. Born November 22. *Parents*, John Musch and his wife Anna Catharine. *Sponsors*, Parents.

1768. December 4. A boy was baptized named John Philip. Born November 17. *Parents*, Philip Schneider and his wife Elizabeth. *Sponsors*, Philip Groos and Mrs. Rosina Knecht.

1768. December 18. A girl was baptized named Anna Catharine. Born November 16. *Parents*, Samuel Pfeiffer and his wife Christina. *Sponsors*, Christian Pfeiffer and his wife Anna Catharine.

1768. December 18. A girl was baptized, name given Maria Barbara. Born August 29. *Parents*, John Best and his wife Maria Barbara. *Sponsors*, John Simon and his wife Gertrude.

1769. January 15. A boy was baptized, John Melchior. Born November 15, 1768. *Parents*, Melchior Hay and his wife Susanna. *Sponsors*, Melchior Stecher and his wife.

1769. February 12. A boy was baptized, and the name John Henry given. Born January 4. *Parents*, Henry Hess and his wife Margaret. *Sponsors*, Henry Schneider and his wife Juliana.

1769. February 12. A boy was baptized named Abraham. Born December 9, 1768. *Parents*, Michael Butz and his Maria Elizabeth. *Sponsors*, Abraham Kaemmerer and his wife Elizabeth.

1769. February 27. A boy was baptized named Jacob. Born February 4. *Parents*, Valentine Annewalt and his wife Anna Margaret. *Sponsors*, Jacob Wilhelm and Mrs. Rosina Hering.

1769. March 26. A girl was baptized named Gertrude. Born February 14. *Parents*, Nicholas Michel and his wife Catharine. *Sponsors*, John Auber and his wife Gertrude.

1769. April 9. A boy was baptized named John Henry. Born February 9, 1768. *Parents*, Jacob Abel and his wife Catharine. *Sponsors*, parents.

1769. April 9. A girl, named Catharine. Born 1769, *in the beginning of the year*. *Parents*, Jacob Werner and Elizabeth, his wife. *Sponsors*, Jacob Abel and his wife Catharine.

THE DEED GRANTED BY THE PENNS, 1802.

Church Records. 91

1769. April 23. A boy was baptized named John Philip, born the last week in February. *Parents*, Michael Kocher and his wife Catharine. *Sponsors*, Philip Storm and his wife Elizabeth.

1769. May 21. A girl was baptized named Susanna Christina. Born March 19. *Parents*, John Schneider and his wife Catharine Elizabeth. *Sponsors*, Christian Miller and Mrs Anna Christina Erich.

1769. May 21. A boy was baptized named Michael. Born March 31. *Parents*, Adam Sand and his wife Elizabeth Christina. *Sponsors*, Michael Lehn and his wife Barbara.

1769. June 4. A boy was baptized named John. Born May 6. *Parents*, Thomas Osterstock and his wife Maria Elizabeth. *Sponsors*, Nicholas Kirnser (?) and his wife Maria Elizabeth.

1769. June 18. A girl was baptized and named Maria Charlotte. Born April 27. *Parents*, Peter Menich and his wife Sibilla. *Sponsors*, Jacob Stein and Mrs. Charlotte Butz.

1769. July 16. A boy was baptized named Jeremiah. Born July 1. *Parents*, Jeremiah Koch and his wife Hanna. *Sponsors*, George William Raub and his wife Catharine.

1769. July 20. A boy was baptized named George Henry. Born July 11. *Parents*, George Newhard and his wife Magdalena. *Sponsors*, Henry Annewalt and his wife Catharine.

1769. August 13. A boy was baptized named Nicholas. Born June 20. *Parents*, Adam Butz and his wife Anna Margaret. *Sponsor*, Nicholas Rauch.

1769. August 13. A girl named Anna. Born May 22. *Parents*, William Hess and his wife Catharine. *Sponsors*, Christian Hess and Mrs. Anna Best.

1769. September 10. A boy was baptized, named Abraham. Born July 23. *Parents*, Frantz Hilliard and his wife, Christina. *Sponsors*, Adam Mann (?) and his wife.

1769. October 8. A girl was baptized with the name Elizabeth. Born September 14. *Parents*, Ephraim Blum and his wife, Catharine. *Sponsors*, John Henry Young and his wife Anna Elizabeth.

[Here the record of Rev. Frederick L. Henop ends. He was Pastor of the congregation from February 23, 1766, to October 8, 1769. Then begins the record of Rev. Mr. Pithan, who was Pastor from 1769–71.]

1769. November 30 (blurred, may be 3). A boy was baptized named John. Born November 1. *Parents*, Conrad Best and his wife. *Sponsors*, John Best and Mrs. Anna Best.

1769. November 19. A girl was baptized named Maria Elizabeth. Born October 27. *Parents*, George Leidi and his wife ———. *Sponsors*, Jacob Schumacher and Mrs. Maria Elizabeth Arendt (Arndt).

July 15. (No year given.) A boy was baptized. The day of his birth was the 11th of January. He received the name John Adam. *Parents*, Henry Busch and his wife, Anna Maria. *Sponsors*, John Adam Rieser and Mrs. Anna Maria Schauss.

[From this point onward to 1776 the records are in different handwriting, all very difficult to decipher. During this time the congregation was without a pastor.]

1771. April 22. A daughter was baptized, named Maria Margaret. *Parents*, John Van Nette and his wife. *Sponsors*, Jacob Dech and his wife Margaret.

(No date of this and the two following baptisms given. As the ink used and the handwriting are the same as above probably the baptisms are of the same date, April 22, 1771.)

A daughter named Maria. *Parents*, George Gieser and his wife Janette. *Sponsors*, parents ("Eltern Selbst").

A daughter named Elizabeth. *Parents*, Christian Fox and his wife Elizabeth. *Sponsors*, John Fox and Mrs. Elizabeth Mauer.

Church Records. 93

A daughter named Anna Margaret. *Parents*, Cornelius Daniel. *Sponsors*, Conrad Gress and Mrs. Margaret Gross.

January 14. (No year given. Perhaps 1772? In a different handwriting.) A boy was baptized named George Ernst. *Parents*, Adam Siffart and his wife Susanna. *Sponsors*, George Ernst Becker and his wife Margaret. Born May 16. (No year given.)

August 27. (No year given.) A girl, born July 23, was baptized. (No name of child recorded.) *Parents*, John Florin (Flori?) and his wife Christina. *Sponsors*, John Ries and his wife Sophia.

July 24. A son was born and received the name Conrad. *Parents*, Conrad Lion (?) and his wife Anna Magdalena. *Sponsors*, John Arndt and Maria the daughter of Conrad Hess.

April 27. (No year given. Different handwriting.) A boy was baptized named Abraham. *Parents*, Peter Monig and his wife Sibella. *Sponsors*, Abraham Breiter and his wife Sibella.

May 18. (No year.) A boy was baptized named Peter. *Parents*, John Simon and his wife Gertrude. *Sponsors*, Michael Gross and his wife.

June 16. (No year.) A boy was baptized, named John. *Parents*, Andrew Leidich and Mrs. Elizabeth Botzer. *Sponsors*, Jeremiah Koch and his wife Anna.

June 16. (No year.) A daughter named Elizabeth. *Parents*, John Hinnerlin and his wife Catharine. *Sponsors*, Michael Butz and his wife Maria Elizabeth.

September 12. (No year.) A boy was baptized, named Gerhard. *Parents*, Peter Breing (Breinig?) and his wife Catharine. *Sponsors*, Gerhard Mohr and his wife Phoeba. Born April 22, 1771.

September 30. (No year.) A daughter, born September 30, named Anna Elizabeth. *Parents*, Henry Schneider and his wife Juliana. *Sponsors*, Michael Odenwelder and Mrs. Margaret Becker.

September 30. (No year.) A daughter was baptized named Susanna. Born October 21. *Parents*, Philip Koch and his wife Elizabeth. *Sponsors*, Melchior Hay and his wife Susanna.

November 15. (No year.) A daughter was baptized, named Anna Catharine. Born October 29. *Parents*, Frederick Meier (Meyer?) and his wife Elizabeth. *Sponsors*, parents ("Eltern selbst").

December 12. (No year.) A boy was baptized, named John Conrad. *Parents*, William Hay and his wife Catharine. *Sponsors*, Conrad Hay and his wife Anna Maria. Born November 19.

May 24. (No year.) A boy was baptized, named John. *Parents*, Adam Butz and his wife Margaret. *Sponsors*, Nicholas Koenig.

May 24. (No year.) A daughter named, Juliana. *Parents*, Conrad Dorsheimer and his wife Christina. *Sponsors*, William Blatz and his wife Juliana. Born *the day before Easter, 1772*. (The above baptisms therefore belong, probably, to 1772?)

1772. June 16. A daughter was baptized. Born May 5. *Parents*, Gerhard Mohr and his wife Phoeba. *Sponsors*, John Mohr and his wife Eva Elizabeth.

1772. July 9. A daughter was baptized named Margaret. Born May 10. *Parents*, William Philips and his wife Catharine. *Sponsors*, Philip Platz and his wife Juliana.

1775. February 14. A son was baptized named Matthias. Born February 5, 1775. *Parents*, Matthias Miller and his wife, Maria Barbara. *Sponsors*, Matthias Stecher and Elizabeth Ihrich (Ihrie?)

1775. February 14. A daughter was baptized, and the name given Elizabeth. Born October 23, 1774. *Parents*, Peter Koechlein and his wife Catharine. *Sponsors*, parents.

Title Page of the Old Church Book. 95

1775. April 30. [This entry is in the handwriting of the Rev. Johann Wilhelm Ingold, who became pastor in 1776.] A daughter was born, and some time thereafter was baptized, receiving the name Anna Catharine. *Parents*, John Rebscher and his wife Elizabeth. *God Parents*, John Peter Ehrich (Ihrie?) and his wife Anna Catharine.

1775. March 6. Was born George, a son of John Nicholas Trauch and his wife Anna Margaret. The sponsors at the baptism were the grandparents, George Ernest Becker and his wife Magdalena.

1776. January 30. Was born John, a son of John Deichman and Elizabeth his wife. *Sponsors*, John Faust Dengler and his wife Margaret.

In the year 1776, and apparently in the spring of the year, the Rev. John William Ingold became pastor of the congregation, and continued in office for a period of ten years. His records are kept with exceeding care and most commendable clearness. The records are in the English characters for the most part, but here and there German characters are interspersed, the record thus showing the conflict of the two languages. Rev. Mr. Ingold's entries are made with good ink, and show as plainly as the day they were made. Each page is ruled into five columns, one each for " Parentes, Infantes, Nati, Baptizati and Comparentes "—these names indicating that Mr. Ingold was a good Latin scholar as well as a careful scribe.

96 The First Reformed Church of Easton, Pa.

John William Ingold, present pastor at Easton, in keeping with the rules of the Church, continues the record of the baptized children, in the Book of the Baptisms.

Parentes. Parents.	Infantes, Nati, Baptizati. Infants, Born, Baptized.	Comparentes. Godparents.
	Anno 1776.	
Adam Duffart et ejus uxor,[1] Susanna.	Philip, 4 April, 1776. 25 Aug., a. e.[2]	Philip Achenbach et Margaret, uxor.
Michael Walter et Anna Maria, uxor.	Catharine, 7 July, 1776. 22 April, a.e.	Jacob Bush et Anna Maria, ejus uxor.
John Mosch et Anna Catharine, uxor.	Christina, 25 Sept., 1776. 13 Oct., a. e.	Melchoir Young et Catharine, uxor ejus.
Jeremias Hess et Elizabeth, ejus uxor.	John, 20 Sept., 1776. 20 Oct., a. e.	Peter Hay and Elizabeth Hess, both single.
George Henry Kleinhaus et Anna Maria, uxor ejus.	Susanna, 3 Aug., 1776. 20 Oct., a. e.	John Vogt et Susanna, ejus uxor.
George Henry Gress et Eva Catharine, ejus uxor.	Anna Elizabeth, 21 Sept., 1776. 27 Oct., a. e.	Michael Gress et Anna Elizabeth, ejus uxor.
Jacob Heller et Susanna, ejus uxor.	Susanna, 15 Aug,, 1776. 4 Nov., a. e.	Adam Yohe et Christiana, ejus uxor.
John Kemmerer et Elizabeth, ejus uxor.	John Jacob, 1 Oct., 1776. 10 Nov., a. e.	Philip Jacob Kernt et Anna Maria, ejus uxor.
Christian Herzel et Anna Maria, ejus uxor.	Elizabeth, 6 Oct., 1776. 17 Nov., a. e.	Matthias Bruch et Anna Barbara, ejus uxor.
Nicholas Koch et Elizabeth, uxor.	John Jacob, 15 Oct. 1776. 24 Nov., a. e.	John Herzel et Anna Hess, both single.
Matthias Mueller et Maria Barbara, uxor.	Anna Catharine, 15 Nov., 1776. 1 Dec., a. e.	Catharine Horn, single.

[1] Ejus uxor—his wife. It has been thought well to let this Latin phrase stand throughout.
[2] The same year.

Parentes. Parents.	Infantes, Nati, Baptizati. Infants, Born, Baptized.	Comparentes. Godparents.
Michael Yohe et Anna Maria, ejus uxor.	Maria, 12 Oct., 1776. 1 Dec., a. e.	Abraham Berlin et Maria Hak, both single.
Andrew Riebel et Margaret, ejus uxor.	Peter, 7 Nov., 1776. 15 Dec., a. e.	Peter Weichant et Eva Young, both single.
Daniel Ellen et Catharine, ejus uxor.	John, 18 Dec., 1776. 22 Dec., a. e.	Peter Hay et Susanna Hay, both single.
Joseph Bernhard et Catharine, ejus uxor.	Esther, 9 Nov., 1776. 22 Dec.	Parents themselves.
Peter Kuechlein, Sr., et Catharine, ejus uxor.	Abraham, 10 Aug., 1776. 3 Sept., a. e.	Parents themselves.
Michael Kocher et Catharine, ejus uxor.	Anna Susanna, 2 Dec., 1776. 19 Jan., 1777.	Caspar Rippel et Susanna Rokel, both single.
Yost Kocher et Magdalena, uxor.	Maria Magdalena, 16 Nov., 1776. 26 Jan., 1777.	Henry Herzel et Christina Mann, both single.
John Rambach et Maria Catharine, uxor.	William, 15 Jan., 1777, "des abends." 26 Jan., a. e.	Parents themselves.
Philip Odenwelder et Anna Maria, uxor.	Anna Rosina, 31 Dec., 1776. 9 Feb., 1777.	John Yaeger et Anna Rosina Odenwelder, both single.
John Spangenberger et Elizabeth, ejus uxor.	Catharine, 17 Oct., 1776. 9 Feb., 1777.	Jacob Ries et Catharine Herster, both single.
Frederick Pfeiffer et Christina, uxor.	John Frederick, 16 Dec., 1776. 23 Feb., 1777.	Frederick Sehler et ejus uxor.
Adam Lechner et Magdalene, uxor.	Jacob, 25 Dec., 1776. 9 M'ch (1777).	Jacob Moser et Elizabeth Yaeger, both single.
Nicholas Kemmerer et Juliana, ejus uxor.	Philip, 3 March, 1777. 11 March, a. e.	Parents themselves.

Parentes. / Parents.	Infantes, Nati, Baptizati. / Infants, Born, Baptized.	Comparentes. / Godparents.
Frederick Boyer et Anna, uxor.	Anna Catharine, 5 Jan., 1777. 16 March, a. e.	Nicholas Michael et Catharine, ejus uxor.
Jacob Opp et Anna Maria, ejus uxor.	Catharine, 22 Aug., 1773. 30 March, 1777.	John William Ingold, pastor here, et Catharine Barbara, *uxor mea*.
Frederick Weidelich et Maria, uxor.	Dorothea Maria, 20 March, 1777. 23 March, a. e.	Jacob Likfeld et Dorothea Maria, ejus uxor.
John George Erndfried et Catharine Barbara, uxor.	Sara, 9 March, 1777. 6 April, a. e.	John Diwler et Sara Berlin, both single.
Andrew Raub et Magdalene, uxor.	John Jacob, 10 Feb., 1777. 6 April, a. e.	John Jacob Pitterbender et Eva Engle, both single.
John Schneyder et Catharine Elizabeth, uxor.	Maria, 19 Feb., 1777. 13 April, a. e.	George Stecher et Catharine, ejus uxor.
Philip Platz et Juliana, ejus uxor, of Phillipsburg.	Joseph, 4 March, 1777. 13 April, a. e.	Jacob Abel et Anna Maria, uxor ejus.
Philip Meixel et Magdalene, uxor.	John Philip, 9 March, 1777. 27 April, a. e.	Philip Zimmerman et Margaret King, both single.
William Keller et Magdalene, uxor.	William, 10 April, 1777. 27 April, a. e.	William Hess et Catharine, ejus uxor.
Philip Messinger et Susanna Elizabeth, uxor ejus.	Susan Elizabeth, 6 Jan., 1777. 4 May, a. e.	Jacob Abel et Elizabeth Ross, both single.
John Moser et Hanna, ejus uxor.	Susanna et Maria Magdalene, 3 Dec., 1775, 9 Dec., 1776. 8 May, 1777.	Bastian Moser et Susanna, ejus uxor. Andrew Moser et Maria Magdalene, ejus uxor.
John Best et Elizabeth, ejus uxor.	Andrew, 16 March, 1777. 11 May, a. e.	Andrew Uler et Anna, ejus uxor.

Church Records. 99

Parentes. / Parents.	Infantes, Nati, Baptizati. / Infants, Born, Baptized.	Comparentes. / Godparents.
Christian Holland et Susanna Margaret, uxor ejus.	Peter, 28 April, 1777. 21 May, a. e.	Peter Ehler et Elizabeth, ejus uxor.
John Rebscher et Elizabeth, ejus uxor.	Maria Elizabeth, 18 April, 1777. 19 May, a. e.	Henry Laux et Maria Elizabeth Menges, both single.
William Moritz et Anna Eva, ejus uxor.	Maria Catharine, 8 Dec., 1754. 8 June, 1777. N. B. After previous catechization.	Christian Holland et Susanna Margaret, ejus uxor.
Matthias Glaas et Eva Christina, uxor ejus.	John Matthew, 19 May, 1777. 5 June, a. e.	John Kless et Barbara, ejus uxor.
John Peter Feith et Barbara, ejus uxor.	John, 31 July, 1776. 22 June, 1777.	John George Somer et Anna Barbara, ejus uxor.
Abraham Berlin et Anna Maria, ejus uxor.	Abraham, 14 May, 1777. 6 July, a. e.	Abraham Berlin et Catharine, ejus uxor, the grandparents.
Nicholas Brotzman et Gertrude, ejus uxor.	Nicholas. 22 June, 1777. 20 July, a. e.	Nicholas Koch et Elizabeth, ejus uxor.
John Reutel et Carlotta, ejus uxor.	John, 16 April, 1777. 25 July, a. e.	George Hag et Rosina, ejus uxor.
John Odenwelder et Elizabeth, ejus uxor.	John, 11 June, 1777. 3 Aug., a. e.	John Best, et Elizabeth, ejus uxor.
Peter Fox et Margaret, ejus uxor.	John, 26 Nov., 1776. 3 Aug., 1777.	John Fox, et Elizabeth, ejus uxor.
John Schneyder et Anna Maria, ejus uxor.	Elizabeth, 9 May, 1777. 3 Aug., a. e.	John Morphy et Elizabeth, ejus uxor.

Parentes. Parents.	Infantes, Nati, Baptizati. Infants, Born, Baptized.	Comparentes. Godparents.
Michael Schmidt et Catharine, ejus uxor.	Anna Barbara, 1 Jan., 1777. 10 Aug., a. e.	Andrew Uler et Anna, ejus uxor.
John Messinger et Elizabeth, uxor.	Jacob, 28 Dec., 1776. 24 Aug., 1777.	Jacob Kuhn et Maria Wilhelm, both single.
Vallentin Beutelman et Maria Barbara, ejus uxor.	Henry, 1 July, 1777. 7 Sept., 1777.	William Henry Hentz et Margaret, ejus uxor.
George Walter et Barbara, uxor ejus.	John, 17 Aug., 1777. 7 Sept., 1777.	John Odenwelder et Elizabeth, ejus uxor.
Stephen Keler[1] et Catharine, ejus uxor.	John, 8 Aug., 1777. 7 Sept., 1777.	Gabriel Keler et Maria Elizabeth, ejus uxor.
Michael Wilhelm et Elizabeth, unmarried, but living together. The father is dead.	Maria, an illegitimate child, 26 April, 1176. 8 Sept., 1777.	John Young et Maria, uxor.
Jacob Schumacher et Elizabeth, uxor ejus.	Susanna, 2 Aug., 1777. 14 Sept., 1777.	John Arndt et Elizabeth, uxor ejus.
John William Ingold, Minister at this place, et Catharine Barbara, uxor mea.	Maria Catharine, 26 Aug., 1777. 18 Sept., 1777.	Jacob Opp et Anna Maria, uxor ejus.
Peter Rieser et Margaret, ejus uxor.	John Philip, 21 Aug., 1777. 21 Sept., 1777.	Philip Rieser et Margaret Butz, both single.
John Flori et Christina, uxor ejus.	John George, 4 July, 1777. 5 Oct., 1777.	John George Trumheller et Christina Ries (Rieser?), single.
William Petersen et Fronica (Veronica?), ejus uxor.	Jacob, 29 Aug., 1777. 19 Oct., 1777.	Jacob Klein et Philippina, ejus uxor.

[1] This name is written first Kehler, but erased and Keler substituted for it.

Church Records.

Parentes. Parents.	Infantes, Nati, Baptizati. Infants, Born, Baptized.	Comparentes. Godparents.
Henry Butz et Anna Eva, ejus uxor.	Elizabeth, 29 Sept., 1777. 26 Oct., 1777.	Michael Butz et Elizabeth, uxor, the grandparents.
John Hess et Magdalena, uxor.	John, 28 Sept., 1777. 26 Oct., 1777.	John Hess et Elizabeth Hess, both single.
John Rosenberger et Hannah, ejus uxor.	William, 23 July, 1777. 16 Nov., 1777.	Philip Achenbach.
John Papp et Anna Maria, uxor ejus.	Abraham, 22 Aug., 1777. 2 Dec., 1777.	Christian Mueller (Miller) et Maria, uxor ejus.
Peter Lattig et Elizabeth, ejus uxor.	Anna Maria, 23 Sept., 1777. 14 Dec., 1777.	Martin Rau et Anna Maria Sauberts, both single.
John Young et Anna Maria, uxor ejus.	Sara, 18 Dec., 1777. 25 Dec., 1777.	Peter Kuechlein, Junior, et Sara, ejus uxor.
John Nicolaus[1] Troxel et Anna Margaret.	John, 11 April, 1778. In June, 1778.	John Troxell et Elizabeth.
William Moebeck et Anna, uxor ejus.	Carolus, 14 Dec., 1777. 1 Jan., 1778.	Gottlieb Hepp, Junior, et Cathrine, uxor ejus.
Henry Hess et Margaret, ejus uxor.	Magdalena, 12 Sept., 1777. 4 Jan., 1778.	Frederick Hess et Magdalena Scholl, both single.
John Specht et Catharine, uxor ejus.	Maria, 5 Jan., 1778. 12 Jan., 1778.	Parentes ipsi (the parents themselves).
Jacob Pfeiffer et Maria, uxor ejus.	John Christian, 21 June, 1777. 16 Jan., 1778.	Christian Pfeiffer et Catharine, ejus uxor.
Adam Hay et Anna Maria, uxor ejus.	John Carl, 25 July, 1777. 18 Jan., 1778.	Melchior Hay et Margaret, ejus uxor.

[1] This entry is in a different handwriting and was evidently of a later date.

Parentes. Parents.	Infantes, Nati, Baptizati. Infants, Born, Baptized.	Comparentes. Godparents.
Robert Lewers et Maria, ejus uxor.	Sara, 22 April, 1777. 12 Feb., 1778.	Parentes ipsi.
Matthias Stecher et Christina, ejus uxor.	Barbara, 20 Dec., 1777. 13 Feb., 1778.	Cornelius Weichant et Barbara Stecher, both single.
Jacob Brotzman et Anna Maria, ejus uxor.	Jacob, 21 Dec., 1777. 22 Feb., 1778.	Nicholas Brotzman et Gertrude, ejus uxor.
Henry Gress et Eva Catharine, ejus uxor.	Susanna, 6 Jan., 1778. 22 Feb., 1778.	Michael Gress et Susanna Brotzman, both single.
Peter Erig et Anna Catharine, uxor.	Nicolaus, 24 June, 1776. 20 July, 1776.	John Nicolaus Scheuermann et Anna Elizabeth, ejus uxor.
Richard Mosten et Francisca, uxor ejus.	Richard, 17 Feb., 1778. 1 March, 1778.	John Andreas Sabel et Catharine Drachsel (Troxel), both single.
Philip Koch et Elizabeth, ejus uxor.	John William, 13 Feb., 1778. 1 March, 1778.	John William Hess et Catharine, uxor ejus.
Abraham Horn et Susanna, uxor ejus.	Abraham, 1 Feb., 1778. 8 March, 1778.	John Simon et Gertrude, uxor ejus.
Johannes Rambach et Maria Catharina, uxor ejus.	Maria Elizabeth, 1 Feb., 1778. 22 March, 1778.	Philip Grub et Maria Elizabeth Eweritz, both single.
Andreas Moser et Magdalena, ejus uxor.	Johann Jacob, 24 Feb., 1778. 22 March, 1778.	Jacob Biji (?) et Christina Meixel, both single.
Joh. George Horti et Eva, ejus uxor.	Andreas, 28 Sept., 1777. 29 March, 1778.	Andreas Riebel et Margaretha, ejus uxor.
John George Nicolaus et Magdalena, uxor.	Johann Georg, 24 Feb., 1778. 5 April, 1778.	George Ehrenfield et Catharine, uxor ejus.

Parentes. Parents.	Infantes, Nati, Baptizati. Infants, Born, Baptized.	Comparentes. Godparents.
Henry Laux et Maria Elizabeth, uxor.	Anna Maria, 15 Jan., 1778. 5 April, 1778.	Conrad Menges et Anna Maria, uxor ejus.
Caspar Riebel et Anna Regina, uxor ejus.	Johannes, 16 Dec., 1777. 19 April, 1778.	Johannes Rochel et Magdalena Becker, both single.
Dennes Dumi et Elizabeth Delphertz— not married.	Johannes, born out of wedlock, 22 March, 1778. 26 April, 1778.	Peter Erig et Anna Catharine, uxor ejus.
Valentine Sandel et Eva, uxor.	Susanna, 6 April, 1778. 10 May, 1778.	Adam Dophard et Susanna, uxor ejus.
Christian Mueller et Catharine, uxor ejus.	Isaac, 13 Feb., 1778. 10 May, 1778.	Michael Lawald et Sibilla, uxor ejus.
Michael Odenwaelder et Anna Margaretha, ejus uxor.	Catharina Elizabetha, 6 June, 1778. 28 June, 1778.	Michael Opp et Catharina Elizabetha, ejus uxor.
Friedeich Busch et Anna Maria, uxor.	Johannes, 30 March, 1778. 19 July, 1778.	Georg Walter et Barbara, uxor ejus.
John Yost, the reputed father, and Elizabeth Griesemer, the mother.	Anna Margaretha, illegitimate, 16 Feb., 1777. 16 Aug., 1778.	Anna Margaret Best, of the single estate.
Conrad Schekrer et Charlotta, uxor ejus.	Johann Heinrich, 6 Aug., 1778. 20 Sept., 1778.	Heinrich Butz et Eva, uxor.
Andreas Ribbel et Margaretha, uxor ejus.	Juliana Catharina, 28 Nov., 1778. 30 Dec., 1778.	Nicolaus Kemmerer, Jr., et Juliana Catharina.
	ANNO 1779.	
Georg Sax et Margaretha, uxor ejus.	Wilhelm, 30 Oct., 1778. 25 Jan., 1779.	Parentes ipsi.

Parentes. Parents.	Infantes, Nati, Baptizati. Infants, Born, Baptized.	Comparentes. Godparents.
Jacob Schaub et Elizabetha, uxor ejus.	Johann Michael, 27 Nov., 1778. 2 Feb., 1779.	Joh. Michael Schik et Anna Margaretha, uxor ejus.
Johannes Erig et Maria Magdalena, uxor ejus.	Elizabetha, 5 Feb., 1779. 1 March, 1779.	Andreas Grub et Elizabetha, uxor ejus, the grandparents.
Conrad Settel et Maria Magdalena, uxor ejus.	Catharina, 20 Jan., 1779. 28 March, 1779.	Michael Fraes et Gertruda, uxor ejus.
William Hess et Catharina, ejus uxor.	Johann Georg, 2 Dec., 1778. 4 April, 1779.	Johannes Frutschi et Elizabetha Hess, both single.
Nicholaus Koch et Elizabetha, uxor.	Abraham, 29 Jan., 1779. 11 April, 1779.	Nicolaus Brotzman et Gertruda, uxor ejus.
John Deichman et Elizabeth.	Elizabeth, 18 May, 1779. 1779.	Andreas Friedrich et Elizabeth Dengler.
Jacob Abel and Anna Maria, uxor.	Anna Margaretha, 27 Nov., 1788. 16 May, 1779.	Arnold Eberhard et Anna Margaretha, uxor.
Arnold Eberhard et Anna Margaretha, uxor.	Anna Maria, 10 April, 1778. 16 May, 1779.	Jacob Abel et Anna Maria, uxor ejus.
Leonhard Welsch et Maria Elizabeth, uxor ejus.	Christina Catharina, 21 April, 1779. 23 May, 1779.	Lorenz Schwartz et Christina Catharina Bauer, both single.
Johnnes Oberle et Elizabetha, uxor ejus.	Johann Rudolph, 16 May, 1779. 1 June, 1779.	Joh. Rudolph Oberle and Anna Margaretha, uxor, the grandparents.
Benedic Lutz et Anna Maria, uxor ejus.	Johann Michael, 6 April, 1779. 6 June, 1779.	Joh. Michael Odenwaelder et Margaretha, uxor ejus.
Johannes Deichman et Elizabetha, uxor ejus.	Johannes, 30 Jan., 1776. 8 Feb., 1776.	Joh. Yost Dengler et Anna Margaretha, uxor ejus.

Church Records.

Parentes. Parents.	Infantes, Nati, Baptizati. Infants, Born, Baptized.	Comparentes. Godparents.
	Elizabetha, 18 May, 1779. 6 June, 1779.	Andreas Friederich et Elizabeth Dengler, both single.
Casimir Hemb et Anna Catharina, uxor ejus.	Barbara, 13 June, 1778. 13 June, 1779.	Jacob Hemb et Barbara, uxor ejus.
Johannes Best et Elizabeth, uxor ejus.	Johannes, 8 April, 1779. 20 June, 1779.	Johannes Odenwaelder et Elizabetha, uxor ejus.
Jacob Butz et Maria, uxor ejus.	Michael Rawert, (Robert?) 9 Jan., 1779. 3 July, 1779.	Benjamin Siegel et Charlotta, uxor ejus.
Philip Achenbach et Anna Maria, uxor ejus.	Philip, 28 June, 1779. 1 Aug., 1779.	Conrad Ehrich et Maria Elizabetha, uxor ejus.
Philip Platz et Juliana, uxor ejus.	Georg, 30 Dec., 1778. 15 Aug., 1779.	Georg Haag et Rosina, uxor ejus.
Wilhelm Martin et Sara, uxor ejus.	Wilhelm, 7 June, 1779. 24 Aug., 1779.	Conrad Durschheimer et Christina, uxor ejus.
Henry Berntz et Maria, uxor ejus.	Waenki, 17 Jan., 1777. 24 Aug., 1779.	George Haag et Rosina, uxor.
	Elsi, 2 Oct., 1778. 24 Aug., 1779.	Gottlieb Hepp et Catharina, uxor ejus.
Michael Schmidt et Catharina, uxor ejus.	Elizabetha, 25 Feb., 1779. 26 Sept., 1779.	Parentes ipsi.
Johann Wilhelm Ingold, Pastor hujus loci, et Catharina Barbara, uxor mea.	Friderich Wilhelm, 6 Sept., 1779. 6 Oct., 1779.	The Rev. Friederich Delliker,[1] Preacher at New Germantown et Maria Barbara, uxor ejus.

---

[1] His name was originally De la Cour. He was no doubt a Huguenot. See Harbaugh's "Lives of the Fathers," Vol. II., p. 382.

106 *The First Reformed Church of Easton, Pa.*

Parentes. Parents.	Infantes, Nati, Baptizati. Infants, Born, Baptized.	Comparentes. Godparents.
Caspar Rippel et Anna Regina, uxor ejus.	Nicolaus, 1 Oct., 1779. 4 Oct., 1779.	Parentes ipsi.
Jacob Buss et Anna Maria, uxor ejus.	Anna Catharina, 27 Aug., 1779. 10 Oct., 1779.	Peter Hertz et Anna Catharina, uxor ejus.
Johannes Musch et Anna Catharnia, uxor ejus.	Johannes, 1 Oct., 1779. 10 Oct., 1779.	Parentes ipsi.
Johannes Odenwaelder et Elizabetha, uxor ejus.	Johann Philip, 30 Sept., 1779. 7 Nov., 1779.	Philip Odenwaelder et Susanna, uxor ejus, the grandparents.
Johannes Toepplin et Christina, uxor ejus.	Elizabetha, 30 Oct., 1779. 7 Nov., 1779.	Georg Hach et Rosina, uxor ejus.
Jacob Opp et Anna Maria, uxor ejus.	Sara, 5 Nov., 1779. 15 Nov., 1779.	Jacob Hoffmann et Maria Eva, uxor ejus, the grandparents.
Antoni Dechet et Catharina, uxor ejus.	Johann Henrich, 20 Aug., 1779. 12 Dec., 1779.	Georg Henrich Raub et Elizabeth Gress, both of the single estate.
Peter Lattig et Elizabeth, uxor ejus.	Johann Jacob, 30 Aug., 1779. 17 Oct., 1779.	Jacob Lattig et Elizabetha, uxor ejus.
Philip Wottring et Maria Elizabetha, uxor ejus.	Johann Jacob, 24 Nov., 1779. 12 Dec., 1779.	Simon Jacob Diel et Anna Elizabetha, uxor ejus.
	ANNO 1780.	
Henrich Schaus et Elizabetha, uxor ejus.	Johannes Anthon, 1 Dec., 1779. 16 Jan., 1780.	Johannes Anthon Ros et Maria Christina, uxor ejus, the grandparents.
Joseph Mimon et Anna Maria, uxor ejus.	Johannes, 10 Dec., 1772. 17 Jan., 1780.	Johann Georg Pitterbender et Catharine, uxor ejus.

Church Records.

Parentes. Parents.	Infantes, Nati, Baptizati. Infants, Born, Baptized.	Comparentes. Godparents.
	Elizabeth, 25 Jan., 1775, ut supra.	Mater ipsa, patre mortue.
Michael Fraes et Gertruda, uxor ejus.	Anna Catharina, 21 Nov., 1779. 17 Jan., 1780.	Abraham Arnd et Anna Maria, uxor ejus.
Daniel Lawar et Anna Margaretha, uxor.	Anna, 31 Oct., 1779. 7 Feb., 1780.	Ludwig Knaus et Anna Elizabetha Musch, both of the single estate.
Andreas Raub et Maria Magdalena, uxor.	Johannes, 28 Jan., 1780. 9 Feb., 1780.	Georg Raub et Barbara, uxor ejus, the grandparents.
Abraham Horn et Susanna, uxor ejus.	Catharina, 21 Dec., 1779. 20 Feb., 1780.	Melchior Hay et Margaretha, uxor ejus, the grandparents.
Jacob Schumacher et Elizabeth, uxor ejus.	Abraham, 10 Dec., 1779. 1 Jan., 1780.	Nicolaus Kemmerer et Juliana, uxor ejus.
Adam Rieser et Maria Eva, uxor ejus.	Eva Elizabetha, 24 Oct., 1779. 27 Feb., 1780.	Dieterich Sikmann et Elizabetha, uxor ejus.
Michael Odenwaelder et Anna Margaretha, uxor ejus.	Anna Catharina, 20 Dec., 1779. 20 Feb., 1780.	Michael Opp et Catharina, uxor ejus, the grandparents.
Johannes Weierbacher et Catharina, uxor ejus.	Johannes, 10 Jan., 1780. 13 March, 1780.	Christian Corell et Margaretha Best, both of the single state.
Georg Stecher et Elizabetha, uxor ejus.	Elizabetha, 1 Dec., 1779. 26 March, 1780.	Michael Messinger et Catharina Stoltz, both single.
Lorentz Schwartz et Catharina Christina, uxor ejus.	Maria Margaretha, 18 Feb., 1780. 26 March, 1780.	Michael Odenwaelder et Anna Margaretha, uxor ejus.

Parentes. Parents.	Infantes, Nati, Baptizati. Infants, Born, Baptized.	Comparentes. Godparents.
Frikrich Wagner et Catharina, uxor ejus.	Elizabetha, 4 Jan., 1780. 26 March, 1780.	Fridrich Kuhn et Anna, uxor ejus, the grandparents.
Michael Kocher et Anna Catharina, uxor ejus.	Anna Maria, 1 Jan., 1780. 26 March, 1780.	Balthasar Rokel et Elizabetha, the grandparents.
Michael Gress et Elizabetha, uxor ejus.	Elizabetha, 21 Feb., 1780. 26 March, 1780.	Elias Beutelmann, et Elizabetha Gress, both of the single estate.
Matthias Stecher et Christina, uxor ejus.	Johannes, 27 Jan., 1780. 9 April, 1780.	Johannes Schneyder et Catharina Elizabetha, uxor ejus, the grandparents.
Henrich Laux et Maria Elizabetha, uxor ejus.	Johann Henrich, 21 Feb., 1780. 23 April, 1780.	Joh. Nicolaus Scheuermann et Anna Catharina, uxor ejus.
Peter Hay et Barbara, uxor ejus.	Elizabetha, 7 March, 1780. 23 April, 1780.	Johannes Simon et Gertruda, uxor ejus, the grandparents.
Gebhard Dalli et Catharine, a negress —not married.	Gebhard, illegitimate, a mulatto. 12 Jan., 1780. 4 May, 1780.	Jacob Schumacher et Elizabetha, uxor ejus.
Yost Henrich Kocher et Maria Magdalena uxor ejus.	Joseph, 27 March, 1779. 6 May, 1780.	Philip Mann et Anna Magdalena, uxor ejus.
Wilhelm Hess et Catharina, uxor ejus,	Andreas, 6 Jan., 1780. 7 May, 1780.	Andreas Uler et Anna, uxor ejus.
Michael Raub et Maria Elizabetha, uxor ejus.	Georg Henrich, 26 Feb., 1780. 7 May, 1780.	Georg Henrich Raub et Maria Elizabetha Moyer, both single.
David Young et Elizabetha, uxor ejus.	David, 17 April, 1780. 7 May, 1780.	Jacob Likfeld et Dorothea, uxor ejus.

Church Records.

Parentes. Parents.	Infantes, Nati, Baptizati. Infants, Born, Baptized.	Comparentes. Godparents.
Nicolaus Brotzmann et Gertruda, uxor ejus.	Johann Friderich, 26 March, 1780. 13 May, 1780.	Johann Friderich Brotzmann et Margaretha, uxor ejus.
Jeremias Hess et Elizabetha, uxor ejus.	Magdalena, 23 March, 1780. 30 April, 1780.	Friederich Hess et Magdalena Scholl, both single.
Elias Hirte et Margaretha, uxor ejus.	Johann Georg, 31 March, 1780. 25 May, 1780.	Georg Schikli et Anna Maria, uxor ejus.
Philip Zimmerman et Anna Maria, uxor ejus.	Joseph, 23 May, 1780. 25 May, 1780.	Joseph Zimmerman et Elizabetha, uxor ejus,
Philip Odewaelder et Anna Maria, uxor ejus.	Johann Philip, 17 April, 1780. 28 May, 1780.	Philip Odewaelder, senior, et Susanna, uxor ejus, the grandparents.
Friederich Busch et Anna Maria, uxor ejus.	Johann Henrich, 31 Oct., 1779. 2 June, 1780.	Hennrich Busch, et Anna Maria, uxor ejus, the grandparents.
Johannes Albrecht et Maria Bender.	Johannes — "uneheliches." 18 Nov., 1779. 22 June, 1780.	Parentes.
Philip Koch et Elizabeth, uxor ejus.	Maria Elizabetha, 31 May, 1780. 25 June, 1780.	Philip Wottringet Elizabetha, uxor ejus.
Henrich Siklin et Rachel, uxor ejus.	Henrich, 17 May, 1780. 9 July, 1780.	Nicolaus Kemmerer et Juliana, uxor ejus.
Robbert Dann et Hanna, uxor ejus.	Johann Philip, 25 Dec., 1779. 20 Aug., 1780.	Philip Grub et Elizabeth, uxor ejus.
Belthasar Stiehl et Maria Christina, uxor ejus.	Johann Adam, 20 Aug., 1780. 17 Sept., 1780.	Adam Sand et Christina, uxor ejus.
Andreas Kuechlein et Elizabeth, uxor ejus.	Susanna, 29 Jan., 1781. 11 March, 1781.	Henrich Bernd et Susanna, uxor ejus.

Parentes. Parents.	Infantes, Nati, Baptizati. Infants, Born, Baptized.	Comparentes. Godparents.
Johannes Schuck[1] et Juliana, uxor ejus.	Eva, 7 Feb., 1781. 11 March, 1781.	Henrich Busch et Eva, uxor ejus.
John Nicolaus Troxel[1] et Anna Margaretha.	Michael, 6 Sept., 1781. — Oct., 1781.	John Herster et Margaretha.
Henrich Schaus et Elizabetha, uxor ejus.	Anna Maria, 16 Sept., 1781. 4 Nov., 1781.	Leonhard Welsch et Anna Elizabetha, uxor ejus.
Johannes Doebler et Christina, uxor ejus.	Johann Ludwig, 29 Sept., 1781. 18 Nov., 1781.	Joh. Ludwig Knaus et Margaretha Flori, both single.
Johannes Young et Maria, uxor ejus.	Johannes, 9 Oct., 1781. 11 Nov., 1781.	Johan Huerster et Fronica (Veronica?) Deicher, both single.
Philip Achenbach et Anna Maria, uxor ejus.	Daniel, 17 Oct., 1781. 18 Nov., 1781.	Adam Flori et Catharina, uxor ejus.
	ANNO 1782.	
Robertus Droehl et Elizabetha, uxor ejus.	Johann Georg, 11 Oct., 1781. 6 Jan., 1782.	Johann Georg Busch et Elizabeth Grotz, single persons.
Barbara Schneyder et Philip Secher, the reputed father.	Elizabetha, 16 Oct., 1781. 6 Jan., 1782.	Ludwig Knaus et Elizabetha, uxor ejus.
Nicholas Koch et Elizabetha, uxor.	Maria Magdalena, 16 Jan., 1782. 19 Jan., 1782.	Leonhard Hertzel et Maria Magdalena, the grandparents.
Joh. Wilhelm Hess et Catharina, uxor ejus.	Abraham, 18 April, 1781. 22 Jan., 1782.	Jeremias Hess et Elizabeth, uxor ejus.
Anna Maria Biseker et Daniel Messinger, the reputed father.	Jonathan, 18 Aug., 1781. 6 Feb., 1782.	Georg Schikli et Anna Maria, uxor ejus.
Philip Helick, schoolmaster at this place, et Eva, uxor ejus.	Philip Jacob, 15 Jan., 1782. 20 Feb., 1782.	Parentes ipsi.

[1] Entered by a different hand.

Church Records.

Parentes. Parents.	Infantes, Nati, Baptizati. Infants, Born, Baptized.	Comparentes. Godparents.
Hennrich Sichlin et Rachael, uxor ejus.	Johann Georg, 8 Dec., 1781. 24 Feb., 1782.	Joh. Georg Stecher et Elizabetha, uxor ejus.
Jeremias Hess et Elizabetha, uxor ejus.	Abraham, 10 Dec., 1781. 24 Feb., 1782.	Abraham Schumacher et Maria Keller, both single.
Leonard Welsch et Maria Elizabetha, uxor ejus.	Maria Catharina, 31 Jan., 1782. 24 Feb., 1782.	Philip Schlauch et Maria Catharina, uxor ejus.
Moritz Bischoff et Christina, uxor ejus.	Johannes, 4 Oct., 1781. 24 March, 1782.	Leonhard Osterstock et Anna Maria Busch, both single.
Jacob Weygant et Catharina, uxor ejus.	Gertraud, 15 Jan., 1782. 24 March, 1782.	Mrs. Gertrude Naul, the grandmother.
Johannes Best et Elizabetha, uxor ejus.	Johann Jacob, 15 Jan., 1782. 24 March, 1782.	Jacob Dech, et Christman, uxor ejus.
Johann Moser et Catharina, uxor ejus.	Rosina Eva, 23 Jan., 1782. 24 March, 1782.	Adam Schaeffer et Eva Moser, both single.
Johannes Ehrig et Maria Magdalena, uxor ejus.	Catharina, 2 Feb., 1782. 24 March, 1782.	Gottlieb Hipp et Catharina, uxor ejus.
Johann Odenwaelder et Elizabetha, uxor.	Bernhard, 22 Jan., 1782. 31 March, 1782.	Bernhard Mueller et Eva, uxor ejus.
Peter Lattig et Elizabetha, uxor ejus.	Rosina, 5 Nov., 1781. 31 March, 1782.	Joh. Georg Brug et Elizabetha, uxor ejus.
Wilhelm Keller et Magdalena, uxor ejus.	Jacob, 3 Jan., 1782. 31 March, 1782.	Jacob Drumheller et Elizabetha Hess, both single.
Conrad Menges et Maria, uxor.	Elizabetha, 18 Sept., 1781. 31 March, 1782.	Elizabetha Mueller.
	Mersi Simon, a woman, 29 years of age. 7 Apr., 1782.	Johann Simon et Gertrude, uxor ejus.

112 *The First Reformed Church of Easton, Pa.*

Parentes. Parents.	Infantes, Nati, Baptizati. Infants, Born, Baptized.	Comparentes. Godparents.
Antoni Dech et Catharina Elizabetha, uxor ejus.	Antonius, 1 Jan., 1782. 18 Apr., 1782.	Hennrich Gress et Catharina, uxor ejus.
Christian Butz et Magdalena, uxor.	Elizabetha, 28 Feb., 1782. 28 Apr., 1782.	Miss Elizabeth Butz, the grandmother.
Johannes Dophart et Catharina, uxor.	Elizabetha, 21 Jan., 1782. 9 May, 1782.	Michael Fraes et Gertraud, uxor ejus.
Christian Mueller, et Anna Maria, uxor.	Elizabetha, 6 Sept., 1781. 20 May, 1782.	Johannes Schneyder et Catharina Elizabetha, uxor ejus.
Peter Ehler et Elizabeth, uxor ejus.	Elizabetha, 25 May, 1770. 17 May, 1782.	Magaretha Arnold.
Peter Ehler et Anna Maria, uxor ejus.	Anna Maria, 2 Feb., 1782. 9 May, 1782.	Parentes ipsi.
Johannes Schuck et Juliana, uxor.	Sara, 18 May, 1782. 26 May, 1782.	Adam Dreisbach et Elizabetha Drachsel, both single.
Hennrich Fell et Elizabetha, uxor ejus.	Johannes, 16 Apr., 1782. 23 June, 1782.	Ludwig Schaub et Christina, uxor ejus.
Theophilus Schenen et Clementina, uxor.	Hennrich, 27 Oct., 1781. 7 July, 1782.	Parentes ipsi.
Andreas Kuechlien et Elizabetha, uxor ejus.	Peter, 6 July, 1782. 18 July, 1782.	Joh. Peter Kuechlein, senior, et Catharina, uxor ejus, the grandparents.
Jacob Schumacher et Elizabetha, uxor.	Anna Maria, 20 July, 1782. 18 Aug., 1782.	Jacob Arnd, Jr., et Elizabetha, uxor ejus.
Christopher Engel et Elizabetha, uxor ejus.	Susanna, 29 June, 1782. 18 Aug., 1782.	Johannes Young et Anna Maria, uxor ejus.
Jacob Fraunfelder et Anna Maria, uxor ejus.	Conrad, 8 Oct., 1872. 24 Nov., 1782.	Conrad Ehrig, senior, et Elizabetha, uxor ejus.

Church Records.

Parentes. Parents.	Infantes, Nati, Baptizati. Infants, Born, Baptized.	Comparentes. Godparents.
Henrich Deringer[1] et Catharina.	Ana Elizabeth, 7 March, 1771. 1781.	Conrad Rohn et Ana Elisabeth.
Peter Schneyder et Susanna, uxor ejus.	Elisabetha, 6 Aug., 1782. 12 Oct., 1782.	Parentes ipsi.
Michael Yohe et Anna Maria, exor ejus.	Michael, 25 July, 1782. 12 Oct., 1782.	Parentes ipsi.
Ludwig Rieger et Catharina, uxor ejus.	Maria Magdelena, 3 Feb., 1782. 7 April, 1782.	Dewald Drummheller et Maria Magdalena, uxor ejus.
	ANNO 1783.	
Johann Wilhelm Ingold, Pfarrer dahier, und Catharina Barbara, meine Ehe-frau.	Charlotta, 10 Jan., 1783. 10 Jan., 1783.	Wir Eltern, selbst.
Michael Gress et Elisabetha Margaretha, uxor.	Anna Maria, 2 Jan., 1783. 16 Feb., 1783.	Philip Odewaelder et Anna Maria, uxor.
Friederich Schaus et Eva Catharina, uxor.	Johannes—a young boy aged 14 years 10 months less 4 days. 20 Feb., 1783.	Ludwig Knaus, Sr.
Georg Hennrich Kleinhans et Anna Maria, uxor ejus.	Anna Catharina, 4 Oct., 1782. 16 March, 1783.	Isaac Schumacher et Catharina, uxor ejus.
Hennrich Winter et Hanna, uxor.	Hennrich, 20 Nov., 1782. 13 April, 1783.	Georg Wilhelm Raub et Catharina, uxor ejus.
Andreas Rippel et Margaretha, uxor.	Elisabetha, 14 Nov., 1782. 21 April, 1783.	Andreas Mueller et Elisabetha Mayer, both single.
Hennrich Fres et Maria, uxor.	Elisabetha, 9 March, 1783. 21 April, 1783.	Michael Fres et Gertruda, ejus uxor.

[1] Entered by a different hand.

114   The First Reformed Church of Easton, Pa.

Parentes. Parents.	Infantes, Nati, Baptizati. Infants, Born, Baptized.	Comparentes. Godparents.
Jacob Bachman et Catharina, uxor.	Catharine Hertzler—a married woman, aged 27 years. 26 April, 1783.	Melchoir Stecher et Catharina, uxor.
Ut supra.	Maria Mokelrei—a married woman aged 19 years. 26 April, 1783.	Ut supra.
Johann Arnd et Elisabetha, uxor.	Elisabetha, 13 Feb., 1783. 27 April, 1783.	Parentes ipsi.
Friederich Boyer et Anna, uxor.	Friederich, 20 Dec., 1782. 11 May, 1783.	Jacob Weyant et Catharina, uxor ejus.
John Deichman et Elisabeth.	Abraham, 7 Jan., 1782. 1782.	Abraham Lowar et Rosina.
Johannes Guennert et Elisabetha, uxor ejus.	Maria Magdalena, 6 March, 1783. 25 May, 1783.	Dewald Drumm-heller et Maria Magdalena, uxor.
Matthias Mueller et Maria Barbara, uxor.	Jacob, 27 April, 1783. 25 May, 1703.	Parentes ipsi.
Joh. Wilhelm Hess et Anna Catharina, uxor.	Wilhelm Henn-rich, 6 Dec., 1782. 8 June, 1783.	Josh. Wilhelm Frutschi et Anna Margaretha Wat-tring, both single.
Ulrich Hauser et Bar-bara, uxor.	Jacob, 7 June, 1783. 20 July, 1783.	Jacob Arnd, senior, et Elisa-betha, uxor ejus.
John Odewaelder et Elizabetha, uxor.	Catharina, 27 Oct., 1783. 21 Dec., 1783.	Hennrich Uhl et Eva Mueller, both single.
	Anno 1784.	
Adam Essig et Elisa-betha, uxor.	Christian, 25 Dec., 1783. 18 Jan., 1784.	Christian Butz et Magdalena, uxor ejus.

Church Records.

Parentes. Parents.	Infantes, Nati, Baptizati. Infants, Born, Baptized.	Comparentes. Godparents.
Peter Schneyder et Susanna, ejus uxor.	Susanna, 9 Dec., 1783. 18 Jan., 1784.	Parentes ipsi.
Lorentz Erb et Anna Maria, uxor.	Johannes, 14 Dec., 1783. 23 Oct., 1783.	Adam Dreisbach et Susanna, uxor ejus.
Daniel Reimer et Margaretha, uxor ejus.	Jacob, 10 Oct., 1783. 21 Oct., 1783.	Jacob Reimer, of the single state.
Daniel Reimer et Margaretha, uxor ejus.	Nicolaus, 4 Dec., 1781. 25 Dec., 1781.	Christian Best et Catharina, uxor ejus.
Friederich Berthold (?) et Elizabetha.	Susanna, 25 Nov., 1783. 1 Jan., 178 4.	Adam Driesbach et Susanna, uxor ejus, the grandparents.
Jeremias Hess, Elisabetha.	Anna, 6 Dec., 1783. 28 Dec., 1783.	Christian Hess et Anna, uxor ejus.
Peter Lattig, Elisabetha.	Anna Barbara, 26 March, 1784. Eodem die.	Mathias Bruch et Anna Barbara, uxor ejus.
Philip Odewaelder et Anna Maria.	Elisabetha, 9 April, 1784. 9 May, 1784.	Philip Lutz et Elisabetha Yaeger, both single.
Michael Gress et Elisabetha.	Johannes, 22 May, 1784. 18 July, 1784.	Johann Odewaelder et Elisabetha, uxor ejus.
Hennrich Fraes et Maria, uxor.	Jacob, 18 June, 1784. 15 Aug., 1784.	Jacob Weyand et Catharina, uxor.
Friedrich Hess et Maria, uxor ejus.	Jacob, 17 June, 1784. ut supra.	Jacob Keller et Elisabetha Hess, both single.
Johannes Hess et Magdalena, uxor ejus.	Maria Magdalena, 26 May, 1784. ut supra.	Friederich Hess et Maria, uxor ejus.
Johannes Ginnert et Elisabetha.	Elisabetha, 14 June, 1784. 29 Aug., 1784.	Michael Gress et Elisabetha, uxor ejus.

Parentes. Parents.	Infantes, Nati, Baptizati. Infants, Born, Baptized.	Comparentes. Godparents.
Jacob Zimmerman et Elisabetha.	Elisabetha, 10 June, 1784. 4 July, a. e.	Jacob Meyer et Elisabetha, uxor ejus.
Johannes Musch et Anna Catharina.	Anna Margaretha, 20 Sept., 1784. 26 Sept., a. e.	Parentes ipsi.

Anno 1785.

Parentes.	Infantes.	Comparentes.
Isaac Schuhmacher et Catharina.	Jacob, 7 Jan., 1785. 13 Feb., a. e.	Jacob Meuxel et Elisabeth Gress, both single.
Johannes Moser et Catharina.	Johannes, 9 Feb., 1785. 27 March, a. e.	Johannes Best et Elisabetha, uxor.
Lorentz Schwartz et Christina.	Jacob, 3 March, 1785. 24 April, a. e.	Jacob Arnd, Jr., et Elisabetha, uxor ejus.
Jacob Frauenfelder et Anna Maria.	Elisabetha, 10 Feb., 1785. 5 June, a. e.	George Rebscher, Elisabetha, uxor.
	Elisabetha Christina. 10 Feb., 1785. 5 June, a. e.	Adam Sand, Elisabetha Christina, uxor.
Georg Sewitz et Anna Maria.	Anna Maria, 4 May, 1785. 19 June, a. e.	Georg. Peter Kessler et Elisabetha Corell, both single.
John Nicolaus Traxel et Anna Margaretha.	Jacob, 15 March, 1784. April, 1784.	John Deichman et Elisabeth.
Hennrich Mueller et Maria Catharina.	Anna Catharina, 13 May, 1785. 31 July, a. e.	Peter Ihrig et Anna Catharina, uxor ejus.
Michael Fraess et Gertruda.	Elisabetha, 22 July, 1785. 28 Aug., a. e.	Hennrich Fraess et Maria, uxor ejus.
Jacob Schuhmacher et Elisabetha.	Catharina, 11 June, 1785. 14 Aug., a. e.	Israel Schuhmacher et Catharina, uxor.

Church Records.

Parentes. Parents.	Infantes, Nati, Baptizati. Infants, Born, Baptized.	Comparentes. Godparents.
Johann Schuck et Juliana Barbara.	Anna Rosina, 10 March, 1784. 11 April, 1784.	Abraham Lawar et Rosina, uxor ejus.
Andreas Raub et Magdalena.	Daniel, 30 Nov., 1784. 18 Jan., 1785.	Peter Seiler et Margaretha, uxor ejus.
John Arnd et Elisabetha, uxor ejus.	Jacob, 27 April, 1785. 5 June, 1785.	Parentes ipsi.
John Moklerei [1] et Maria, uxor ejus.	Anna, 4 Sept., 1784. 14 Aug., 1785.	Friederich Berthold et Elisabetha, uxor ejus.
	ANNO 1786.	
Ludwig Knaus, Jr., et Elisabetha, uxor ejus.	Johann, 29 Dec., 1785. 14 Jan., 1786.	Ludwig Knaus, Sr., et Elisabetha, uxor.
Isaac Sidmann (Sickmann?) et Elisabetha, uxor ejus.	Samuel, 11 March, 1785. 17 Jan., 1786.	The father et Christina Nungesser.
Jacob Grotz et Maria, uxor ejus.	Hennrich, 9 Jan., 1786. 26 Jan., 1786.	Parentes ipsi.
Lenhard Leidig [2] et Catharina, uxor ejus.	Georg, 15 Feb., 1785. 10 May, a. e.	"Die Eltern Selbst."
Johann Wilhelm Ingold, Pfarrer dahier, et Catharina Barbara, uxor mea.	Jacob, 17 Sept., 1785. 18 Sept., 1785.	Parentes ipsi.
Georg Messinger et Catharina, uxor ejus.	Catharina, 14 Oct., 1785. 28 Feb., 1786.	Parentes ipsi.
Johannes Schuck et Juliana, uxor ejus.	Christina, 29 Jan., 1786. 4 March, 1786.	Isaac Berlin et Maria, uxor.
Friederich Berthold et Elisabetha, uxor ejus.	Anna Maria, 13 Nov., 1785. 5 March, 1786.	Lorentz Erb et Anna Maria, uxor.

[1] Probably McCleary.
[2] In a different hand.

118 *The First Reformed Church of Easton, Pa.*

Parentes. Parents.	Infantes, Nati, Baptizati. Infants, Born, Baptized.	Comparentes. Godparents.
Wilhelm Hess et Catharina, uxor ejus.	Johann Paul, 26 Feb., 1784. 16 Oct., 1784.	Johannes Gotthard et Sophia, uxor.
Wilhelm Hess et Catharina, uxor ejus.	Jacob, 10 Nov., 1785. 9 March, 1786.	Jacob Kuhn et Elisabetha Yetz, both single.
Philip Wottring et Maria Elisabetha, uxor ejus.	Maria Elisabetha, 19 Jan., 1786. 12 March, 1786.	Johannes Best et Maria Elisabetha, uxor.
Anna Catharina Bender, the mother, Daniel Schneyder, the reputed father.	Anna Catharina, "Uneheliches," 14 Feb., 1786. 17 March, 1786.	Ludwig Schaub et Christina Margaretha, uxor.

Here the record in the handwriting of the Rev. Mr. Ingold ends.

The following seventeen entries are by a different hand, probably that of the next regular pastor, the Rev. Dr. Hermann, who became the pastor of the congregation, in connection with the congregations at Plainfield, Dryland and Greenwich, some time in the fall of the year 1786:

Parentes. Parents.	Infantes, Nati, Baptizati. Infants, Born, Baptized.	Comparentes. Godparents.
Peter Kuechlein, Jr., and Elisabetha.	Peter, 22 Feb., 1786. 19 March, 1786.	Parentes ipsi.
Jacob Seibel and Magdalena.	Eva, 6 Oct., 1785. 26 March, 1786.	Eva Seibel, the grandmother.
Christian Hertzel and Anna Maria.	Johan Jacob, 2 Dec., 1785. 30 March, 1786.	John Hertzel and Maria Bruch.
Nicholas Koch and Elisabetha.	Anna Christina, 1785? 10 Oct., (1786?). 17 April, 1786.	John Hertzel and Christina Heller

Church Records.

Parentes. Parents.	Infantes, Nati, Baptizati. Infants, Born, Baptized.	Comparentes. Godparents.
Abraham Berlin and Maria.	Johan Wilhelm, 28 Jan., 1783. 3 Aug., 1783.	Johan Wilhelm Ingold and Barbara —V. D. Minister.
Abraham Berlin and Maria.	Isaac, 9 July, 1779. 20 Aug., 1779.	Adam Haag and Elisabetha.
Henrich Schaus and Elisabetha.	Sara, 14 Oct., 1784. 25 Dec., 1784.	Lenhard Osterstock and Maria Busch.
Henrich Schaus and Elisabetha.	Henrich, 10 April, 1786. 5 May, 1786.	Mrs. Eva Catharina Schaus, the grandmother.
Adam Lehn and Maria.	Elisabetha, 24 April, 1786. 30 July, 1786.	Jacob Meixel and Maria.
Johan Odewaelder and Elisabetha.	Michael, 5 May, 1786. 4 Aug., 1786.	Michael Odenwaelder and Anna Margaretha.
Michael Gress and Elis. Margaretha.	Elisabetha Margaretha, 27 Aug., 1786. 22 Oct., 1786.	Michael Odenwaelder and Anna Margaretha.
Peter Schneider and Susanna.	Maria, 21 Aug., 1786. 8 Oct., 1786.	Parentes ipsi.
Johan Mokelerei and Maria.	Johannes, 11 July, 1786. 22 Oct., 1786.	Johan Schuck and Juliana.
Henrich Deringer and Catharina, uxor ejus.	Eva Margaretha, 3 March, 1784. 21 March, 1784. Johan Henrich, 6 Oct., 1786. 23 Oct., 1786.	Georg Lauerbach and Eva Margaretha Rohn. Henrich Goebel and Eva Margaretha Rohn.
John Nicolaus Traxel and Anna Margaretha.	Henrich, 17 March, 1786. April, a. e.	Michael Traxel and Juliana Mueller.
John Deichman and Elisabeth.	Georg Henrich, 29 Aug., 1785. 1785.	Georg Lauderbach and Margaretha Rohn.

The following children were baptized by the Rev. Lebrecht Friederich Hermann, the Pastor at the time.

Parentes. Parents.	Infantes, Nati, Baptizati. Infants, Born, Baptized.	Comparentes. Godparents.
	ANNO 1786.	
Peter Weygand and Margaretha, uxor ejus.	Jacob, 18 Nov., 1786. 20 Jan., 1787.	Jacob Zettel and Catharina, uxor ejus.
Jacob Ries and Christiana, uxor ejus.		
Valentin Steiner and Anna Catharina.	Abraham, 17 Dec., 1786. 28 Jan., 1787.	Michael Kocher and Catharina.
John Best and Elizabetha.	Elizabeth, 30 Jan., 1787. 7 March, 1787.	Benedict Lutz and Anna Margaretha.
George Drum and Catharina.	John Philip, 15 Feb., 1787. 7 March, 1787.	Anna Maria Best and Philip Wotring.
Frederick Wilhelm and Catharina.	Frederick, 11 Jan., 1784. 25 March, 1787. Michael, 11 July, 1786. 25 March, 1787.	Margaretha Wilhelm. Maria Wilhelm.
Michael Fraes and Gertrude.	Michael, 24 Feb., 1787. 8 April, 1787.	Henrich Fraes and Elizabetha.
Friederich Beyer and Anna.	Sara, 15 Nov., 1787. 8 April, 1787.	Johan Erdman and Sara.
Johan Arndt and Elizabetha.	Sara, 27 Feb., 1787. 8 April, 1787.	The parents.
Jacob Schumacher and Elizabetha.	Sara, 31 March, 1787. 15 May, 1787.	Ludwig Knauss and Elizabeth.
Jacob Schumacher and Eliz. Catharina.	Catharina, 7 April, 1787. 20 May, 1787.	Conrad Schumacher and Maria Meixel.

Church Records.

Parentes. Parents.	Infantes, Nati, Baptizati. Infants, Born, Baptized.	Comparentes. Godparents.
George Adam Geissle and Christina.	John, 6 April, 1787. 17 June, 1787.	George Lerch and Elizabeth.
Jacob Keller and Elizabeth.	Anna Christina, 7 May, 1787. 17 June, 1787.	Peter Lattig and Anna Christina Brotzman.
John Rambach and Maria.	Lenhard, 30 March, 1787. 15 July, 1787.	Peter Weygandt and Margaretha.
Lorenz Schwartz and Christina.	Catharina, 3 May, 1787. 15 July, 1787.	The parents.
Jacob Messinger and Maria.	Philip,[1] 24 March, 1787. 12 Aug., 1787. John,[1] 24 March, 1787. 12 Aug., 1787.	Philip Messinger and Susanna. Michael Messinger and Elizabetha.
Jacob Meixel and Elizabeth.	John, 19 July, 1787. 12 Aug., 1787.	The parents.
Moritz Bischof and Christina.	Anna Maria, 3 March, 1787. 18 Aug., 1787.	Anna Maria Busch.
Henrich Fres and Elizabeth.	John, 26 Sept., 1787. 27 Oct., 1787.	The parents.
Henrich Winter and Hannah.	Elizabeth, 8 Sept., 1787. 7 Nov., 1787.	Jacob Welsch and Elizabeth.
Jacob Seibel and Magdalena.	Margaret, 29 July, 1787. 11 Nov., 1787.	Eva Seipel, the grandmother.
Peter Kuechline, Jr., and Elizabeth.	——, ——, 1787.	The parents.
Johann Georg Dengler and Catharina.	Johannes, —— ——, 1787.	Andreas Kuechline and Elizabeth.

[1] Twins.

Parentes. Parents.	Infantes, Nati, Baptizati. Infants, Born, Baptized.	Comparentes. Godparents.
Christopher Schmid and Maria.	Elizabeth Margareth, 22 Sept., 1787. — Oct., 1787.	John Nicolaus Traxel and Anna Margaretha.
Lenhard Leidig and Catharina (twins).	Philip, Elizabeth, 10 Dec., 1787. 1 Jan., 1788.	The parents. Jacob Arndt and Elizabeth.
Jeremias Hess and Elizabeth.	Elizabeth, 10 Dec., 1787. 1 Jan., 1788.	Georg Klehans and Elizabeth.
Philip Fodredt (?) and Maria.	Sara, 19 Sept., 1787. 13 Jan., 1788.	Jacob Arndt and Elizabeth.
Georg Nulf and Susanna, uxor.	Anna Maria, 24 March, 1787. 3 Feb., 1788.	Andreas Stucker and Sara.
Andreas Stucker and Juliana, uxor.	Peter, 10 May, 1787. 3 Feb., 1788.	Martin Kind and Sara.
Johan Fenner and Joanna.	Jacob, 13 Jan., 1788. 6 Feb., 1788.	Jacob Sikman and Elizabeth, uxor.
Bernhard Sikman and Anna Margaretha.	Johan Jacob, 19 Jan., 1788. 10 Feb., 1788.	Jacob Boehler and Catharina Gorel.
Daniel Seiler and Maria.	Catharina, 5 Jan., 1788. 10 Feb., 1788.	Johan Meyer and Catharina.
Johan Steitinger and Christina.	Johan, 21 May, 1787. 10 Feb., 1788.	The parents.
Henrich Snyder and Catharina.	Henrich, 4 Feb., 1788. 13 Feb., 1788.	Lenhard Leidig and Maria Opp.
Ulrich Hauser and Barbara.	Georg, 25 Jan., 1788. 1 March, 1788.	Adam Stucker and Maria Magdalena.
Christian Gorrell and Catharina.	Johan, 12 Feb., 1788. 2 March, 1788.	Peter Keres and Barbara Kessler.

Church Records. 123

Parentes. Parents.	Infantes, Nati, Baptizati. Infants, Born, Baptized.	Comparentes. Godparents.
Peter Snyder and Susanna.	Margaretha, 28 Jan., 1788. 9 March, 1788.	The parents.
—— Walter.		Jacob Arndt and Elizabeth.
	6 March, 1788.	
Fried. Barthold and Elizabetha.	Elisabeth, 10 June, 1788. July, ——.	The parents.
Henry Schaus and his wife, Elisabeth.	Elisabeth, 1 Feb., 1788. 19 March, 1788.	The parents.
Peter Ladig and Elisabeth.	Sara, 27 Jan., 1788. 21 March, 1788.	Ludwig Knauss and Elisabeth.
Caspar Ritter and Catharina.	Isaac, 22 Feb., 1788. 3 April, 1788.	Michael Ritter and Salome.
Johann Eberhard and Susanna.	Susanna, 5 March, 1788. 3 April, 1788.	The child's mother.
Georg Putz and Catharina.	Elisabeth, 17 Jan., 1788. 6 April, 1788.	Philip Gorel and Maria.
Matthias Mueller and Maria Barbara.	Salome, 12 Jan., 1788. 6 April, 1788.	The parents.
William Hess and Catharina.		
Johannes Schuck and his wife, Juliana.	Johann Jacob, 31 May, 1788. 6 June, 1788.	Christopher Hertzel and his wife, Catharine.
—— Kunkel.	Johan, —— 10 July, 1788.	Johann Schuck and his wife, Juliana.
Michael Odenwaelder and his wife, Anna Margaretha.	Jacob, ——. 13 July, 1788.	Johan Odenwaelder and his wife, Elisabeth.

Parentes. Parents.	Infantes, Nati, Baptizati, Infants, Born, Baptized.	Comparentes. Godparents.
Wilhelm Keller and his wife, Magdalena.	Johan Joseph, 30 Nov., 1787. 13 July, 1788.	Johannes Hay and Maria Best, both single.
Friederich Barthold and his wife, Elisabeth.	Elisabeth, 10 July, 1788. 19 July, 1788.	Both parents.
Peter Hille and Elizabeth.	Johannes, 25 June, 1788. 18 Sept., 1788.	Johannes Flory and Christina.
Leb. Friederich Hermann et uxor mea, Maria.	Friderica Doris, 26 Aug., 1788. 21 Sept., 1788.	Daniel Feidt and Maria, the grandparents.
John Nicolaus Traxel and Anna Margaretha, uxor ejus.	Abraham, 8 Aug., 1788. 25 Sept., 1788.	Johan Schuck and Juliana.
Michael Butz and Catharina.	Elisabeth, 28 July, 1788. 21 Sept., 1788.	Elisabeth Moessiner, the child's grandmother.
John Kloemann and Magdalena.	Magdalena, 5 Jan., 1788. 7 Oct., 1788.	Anna Maria Opp.
Henrich Deringer and his wife, Catharina.	Johan, 20 Aug., 1788. 14 Oct., 1788.	Johan Stecher and Eva Margaretha Rohn.
John George Dengler and Catharina.	George, Date wanting. In Oct., 1788.	The father of the child.
Michael Gress and Elizabeth.	John Michael, 15 Aug., 1788. 2 Nov., 1788.	Michael Gress and Elizabeth, the grandparents.
Michael Butz and Catharina.	Elizabeth, 28 July, 1788. 2 Nov., 1788.	Ludwig Knauss and Elizabeth.
Jacob Frauenfelder and Maria.	Sara, 23 July, 1788. 30 Nov., 1788.	Valentine Uly and his wife, Christina.
George Adam Geissle and Christina.	Anna Maria, 22 Oct., 1788. 30 Nov., 1788.	Christian Hertzel and Anna Maria.

Church Records.

Parentes. Parents.	Infantes, Nati, Baptizati. Infants, Born, Baptized.	Comparentes. Godparents.
Philip Hasselbach and Rebecca.	Johannes, 14 Dec., 1788. 11 Jan., 1789.	John Deichman and Elizabeth.
G. Frederick Wagner and Catharina.	Johannes, 28 Nov., 1788. 19 Jan., 1789.	The parents.
George Lerch and Elizabeth.	Catharina, 2 Dec., 1788. 25 Jan., 1789.	Johan Zeller and Elizabeth.
Frederick Lerch and Elizabeth.	Johan Georg, 9 Jan., 1789. 14 Feb., 1789.	John George Roether and Anna Maria.
Peter Rippel and Maria.	Maria, 11 Jan., 1789. 17 Feb., 1789.	Adam Stucker and Anna Maria.
John Deichman and Elizabeth.	Catharina, 28 Feb., 1789. 21 March, 1789.	G. Frederick Wagner and Catharina.
Andrew Stucker and Juliana.	Rosina, 1 Jan., 1789. 19 March, 1789.	Martin Kind and Sara.
Michael Rippel and Elizabeth.	Elizabeth, 27 Oct., 1788. — Feb., 1789.	Andrew Rippel and Margaretha.
Peter Kuechlein and his wife Elizabeth.	Michael, No date given. In the month of March, 1789.	The parents.
Martin Kindt and Sara.	Simon, 28 Jan., 1789. In the month of March, 1789.	Andrew Stucker and Juliana.
John Best and Elizabeth.	Susanna, 8 Feb., 1789. Feb., 1789.	Andrew Uly and Anna.
Peter Ladig and Anna Christina.	Elizabeth, 21 March, 1789. April, 1789.	Peter Ladig and Elizabeth.
Jacob Keller and Elizabeth.	Jacob, March, 1789. 19 April, 1789.	Jacob Kratz and Maria.

Parentes. Parents.	Infantes, Nati, Baptizati. Infants, Born, Baptized.	Comparentes. Godparents.
Jacob Koehler and Anna Margaretha.	Anna Maria, 14 May, 1789. 15 May, 1789.	Anna Maria Catharina Rambach and Anna Marg. Koehler.
Abraham Laher and Susanna.	Samuel, 3 April, 1789. 20 May, 1789.	Henry Raup and his wife Elizabeth.
Philip Wotring and his wife.	Maria, Date wanting. 14 June, 1789.	Philip Wotring and his wife.
John Mokelera and Maria.	Maria, 12 Oct., 1788. Wanting.	Peter Richter and Elizabeth.
John and Maria Keil.	Elizabeth, 1 Feb., 1789. Wanting.	Nicol. Best and Elizabeth.
Conrad Schumacher and Maria.	Wanting. Wanting. Wanting.	John Meixel and Margaret Schumacher, both single.
John Arndt and Elizabeth.	John, Wanting. Wanting.	The parents.
Jacob Fraes and his wife Margaretha.	William, 9 July, 1789. Wanting.	Jacob Koemmerer and Maria Fraes.
Jacob Scheib and Maria Christina.	Jacob, 16 Aug., 1789. Wanting.	The parents.
Philip Dotterer and Maria.	Elizabeth, 30 Sept., 1789. Wanting.	The parents.
Wilhelm Hess and Catharina.	Tobias, Wanting. Wanting.	Tobias Scholl.
John Mennier and Maria.	Daniel, 2 June, 1789. 23 Aug., 1789.	Daniel Feidt and Maria.
Michael Butz and Catharina.	Maria, 10 July, 1789. 13 Oct., 1789.	Maria Butz and Philip Emrich.

Church Records. 127

Parentes. Parents.	Infantes, Nati, Baptizati. Infants, Born, Baptized.	Comparentes. Godparents.
Henry Fraes and Maria.	Henry, 26 Sept., 1789. 15 Nov., 1789.	The parents.
L. Frederick Herman and my wife Maria.	Joanna Maria Elizabeth, 16 Oct., 1789. 17 Nov., 1789.	John David Young, V.D.M., and Jacob Welsch and his wife Elizabeth.
Jacob Mexel and his wife Elizabeth.	Philip, 17 Sept., 1789. 13 Dec., 1789.	Philip Mexel and Magdalena, the child's grandparents.
Christoph Schmidt and his wife Maria.	Maria Barbara, 1 Nov., 1789. 13 Dec., 1789.	Peter Nungester and his wife.
—— Corel and his wife.	Wanting. Wanting. Wanting.	John Schuck and his wife Juliana.
Henry Shouse and Elizabeth.	Susanna, 24 Dec., 1789. 2 Feb., 1790.	The parents.
Matthias Eyerman and Hannah.	Elizabeth, 19 Nov., 1789. 8 Feb., 1790.	Lenhard Leydig and Elizabeth.
Henry Kern and Susanna.	Maria, 12 Oct., 1789. 7 March, 1790.	Michael Traxel and Rebecca Mueller.
Isaach Schumacher and Catharina.	Sara, 16 Feb., 1789. 21 March, 1790.	Johan Georg Meyer and Elizabeth Mexel, both single.
Christian Corell and Catharina.	Juliana, 23 Oct., 1789. 21 March, 1790.	John Schuck and Juliana.
Abr. Achenbach and Maria Catharina.	Maria Apelonia, 24 Dec., 1789. 4 April, 1790.	Christ. Wolf and Maria Aplona.
Georg Butz and Catharina.	Anna Maria, 28 Dec., 1789. 4 April, 1790.	Maria Butz and Daniel Heller.

Parentes. Parents.	Infantes, Nati, Baptizati. Infants, Born, Baptized.	Comparentes. Godparents.
Georg Moessinger and Catharina.	Susanna, 18 Sept., 1789. 4 April, 1790.	Philip Moessinger and Susanna.
Jacob Moessinger and Maria.	Isaac, 24 Aug., 1789. 2 May, 1790.	John Koehler and Margaret.
John Fenner and Hannah.	Peter, 30 March, 1790. 2 May, 1790.	Peter Werkhauser and Anna Margaret.
Peter Werkhauser and Anna Margaret.	Johannes, 15 Feb., 1790. 2 May, 1790.	John Fenner and Hannah.
Jacob Koechlein and Maria.	Peter, Wanting. 2 May, 1790.	Peter Ihrich and Elizabeth.
Peter Schneider and his wife Susanna.	Peter, Wanting. 24 April, 1790.	The parents.
Daniel Seler and Maria.	Anna Maria, 15 April, 1790. 24 May, 1790.	Michael Gress and Elizabeth.
Frederick Beyer and Anna.	Christina, 11 April, 1790. 11 July, 1790.	Valentine Weber and Christina.
John Georg Dengler and Catharina.	Jacob, Wanting. In the month of July, 1790.	The parents.
Matthias Mueller and Maria Barbara.	Peter, 14 June, 1790. 8 Aug., 1790.	The parents.
Jacob Ries and Christina.	Christina, Wanting. 8 Aug., 1790.	Conrad Schumacher and Maria.
Conrad Ihrig and Christina.	Maria Elizabeth, 1 July, 1790. 14 Aug., 1790.	Conrad Ihrig, Sr., and his wife.
Ludwig Knauss, Jr., and Elizabeth, his wife.	Elizabeth, 30 June, 1790. 22 Aug., 1790.	N. N. Schumacher, the child's grandmother.

Parentes. Parentes.	Infantes, Nati, Baptizati. Infants, Born, Baptized.	Comparentes. Godparents.
Abraham Bachman and his wife, Philipina.	Lorenz, 7 July, 1790. 17 Sept., 1790.	Christoph Hertzel and his wife Catharina.
Peter Rippel and Maria.	Jacob, 13 Sept., 1790. 17 Oct., 1790.	Jacob Arndt, Jr., and Elizabeth.
John Odenwaelder and Elizabeth Margaret.	Jacob, 12 Aug., 1790. ———, 1790.	Philip Odenwaelder and Anna Maria.
Nicolas Traxel and Margaret.	Peter, 23 Aug., 1790. ———, 1790.	Christoph Meixel and his wife Elizabeth.
Michael Odenwaelder and Margaretha.	Peter, 4 Oct., 1790. 7 Nov., 1790.	Jacob Opp and Maria Odenwaelder.
Henry Gern and Susanna.[1]	Henry, 2 Dec., 1790. 25 April, 1791.	The parents.
John Odenwaelder and Elizabeth Margaret.	Elizabeth, 10 Oct., 1791. 8 Nov., 1791.	Benedick Lutz and his wife Anna Maria.
Jacob Frauenfelder and Anna Maria.	Anna Margaretha, 1 Dec., 1791. 6 Jan., 1792.	Balthazar Schwarz and his wife Anna Margaretha.
Henry Doringer and Catharina.	Catharine, 29 May, 1791. Wanting.	The parents.
Conrad Ihrig and Christina.	George Washington, 26 Dec., 1791. 13 May, 1792.	Jacob Arndt, Jr., and Elizabeth.
Henry Shneyder and Catharina.	Samuel, 1 Feb., 1792. 13 May, 1792.	John Herster and Margaretha.
Michael Traxsell and Susanna.	Maria Catharina, 13 June, 1792. 24 June, 1792.	Catharina Keslinn.
John Christoph Schmidt and Anna Maria.	Catharina, 18 July, 1792. 2 Sept., 1792.	The parents.

[1] This and the next sixteen entries are in a different handwriting.

130   *The First Reformed Church of Easton, Pa.*

Parentes. Parents.	Infantes, Nati, Baptizati. Infants, Born, Baptized.	Comparentes. Godparents.
Nicholas Drachel and Margaretha.	Elizabetha, 17 Nov., 1792. 30 Nov., 1792.	Elizabeth Kuechlein and the child's father.
John Jacob Scheipp and Maria Christina.	John, 18 Nov., 1792. 26 Dec., 1792.	The parents.
Frederick Lerch and his wife Elizabeth.	Jonas, 26 Dec., 1792. 26 Dec., 1792.	John Wind and his wife Susanna.
Peter Lattig and his wife Christina.	Maria, 9 Dec., 1790. 8 March, 1791.	Philip Brotzman and his wife Maria Christina.
Peter Lattig and his wife Christina.	Jacob, 23 March, 1793. 23 April, 1793.	Jacob Brotzman and Susanna.
Christian Hertzel and his wife Anna Maria.	Samuel, 6 Sept., 1793. 26 Dec., 1793.	Peter Lattig and his wife.
Michael Troxel and his wife Susanna.	Elizabeth, 26 Oct., 1793. 14 Nov., 1793.	Christopher Meixel and his wife Elizabeth.
Henry Schause and Elizabeth.	Jacob, 2 Jan., 1794. 19 Jan., 1794.	The parents.
Christoph Meixel and his wife Elizabeth.	Wilhelm, 3 Aug., 1794.	The parents.

The following children were baptized by the Pastor, the Rev. Doctor Christian Ludwig Becker.

Parentes. Parents.	Infantes, Nati, Baptizati. Infants, Born, Baptized.	Comparentes. Godparents.
	Anno 1794.	
Henry Schneyder and his wife Catharina.	William, 25 May, 1794. 5 June, 1794.	John Schuck and his wife Juliana.
John Arndt and his wife Elizabeth.	Anna, 15 March, 1794. 6 June, 1794.	The parents.

Church Records.

Parentes. Parents.	Infantes, Nati, Baptizati. Infants, Born, Baptized.	Comparentes. Godparents.
John Odenwaelder and his wife Elizabeth.	Susanna, 13 Jan., 1794. 8 June, 1794.	Philip Odenwaelder, Sr., and his wife Catharina.
Wilhelm Laball and his wife Elizabeth.	George, 10 July, 1793. 10 June, 1794.	George Schnabel and his wife Margaret.
John George Schnabel and his wife Maria.	Elizabeth, 17 Feb. (1794?). 10 June, 1794.	Wilhelm Laball and his wife Elizabeth.
A son-in-law of Christian (?) Braun.	Jabob Meyer, of Dryland, 12 June, 1794,	was baptized and confirmed.
Bernhard Sickman and his wife Margaret.	Philip, 4 June, 1794. 29 June, 1794.	Susanna Correll and Martin Kind.
Michael Messinger and his wife Elizabeth.	Susanna, 20 March, 1794. 6 July, 1794.	Rosina Sieckman.
Richard Jacobs and his wife Elizabeth.	John, 20 March, 1794. 16 July, 1794.	Jacob Schumacher, and his wife Elizabeth.
Wilhelm Waied and his wife Susanna.	Samuel, 10 Feb., 1794. 5 July, 1794.	Margaret Eberhard.
Johann Yost Dilcher and his wife Anna Margaret.	Jacob, 15 July, 1794. 8 Sept., 1794.	Jacob Roadt and his wife Eva Margaretha.
Christian Ludewig. The reputed father (undecipherable).	Anna Maria, —— 1793. 16 Sept., 1794.	Mrs. Gloeckner.
	Abraham, adult. Mecdaniel. (McDaniel?) Wanting.	Baptized 17 Sept. Confirmed 27 Sept., 1794.
Abraham Seller and his wife Sophia.	Amalia, 1 Sept., 1794. 28 Sept., 1794.	The parents.
Jeremiah Best and his wife Elizabeth.	Anna Catharina, 16 Sept., 1794. 12 Oct., 1794.	Christian Best and his wife Catharina.

Parentes. Parents.	Infantes, Nati, Baptizati. Infants, Born, Baptized.	Comparentes. Godparents.
Andrew Kessler and his wife Catharina.	Samuel, 14 Sept., 1794. 12 Oct., 1794.	John Leidig and his wife Juliana.
Jeremiah Hess and his wife Elizabeth.	Rachael, 19 Oct., 1794. 5 Nov., 1794.	Peter Lattig and his wife Elizabeth.
Abraham Vogel and his wife Elizabeth.	Jacob, 14 Aug., 1794. 9 Nov., 1794	The parents.
	Abraham Hubler, 14 Nov., 1794.	Baptized and confirmed.
Christian Hertzel and his wife Anna Maria.	Anna Maria, 5 Oct., 1794. 20 Nov., 1794.	Philip Brotzman and his wife Christina.
	Christian Hackman, 22 Nov., 1794.	Baptized and confirmed.
Henry Doeringer and his wife Catharina.	Johann Conrad, 17 Sept., 1794. 1 Dec., 1794.	Conrad Rohn and Catharine Meier.
Theis (Matthias?) Laux (?) and his wife Margaretha.	Johann Matthias, 6 Sept., 1794. 7 Dec., 1794.	Benjamin Metz and Margaret —— (undecipherable).
Michael Traxel and his wife Susanna.	John, 22 Nov., 1794. 21 Dec., 1794.	John Leydig and his wife Juliana.
Peter Schneyder and his wife Susanna.	Joseph, 26 Oct., 1794. 21 Dec., 1794.	The parents.
Peter Dietz and his wife Anna Maria.	Anna Maria, 16 Oct., 1794. 26 Dec., 1794.	Jeremiah Best and his wife Elizabeth.
Friederich Lerch and his wife Elizabeth.	Elizabeth, 1 Nov., 1794. 26 Dec., 1794.	Georg Emrich and his wife Anna Margaretha.
	ANNO 1795.	
Michael Simon and his wife Maria.	John, 25 Sept., 1794. 1 Jan., 1795.	Simon Senior aud his wife.

Church Records. 133

Parentes. Parents.	Infantes, Nati, Baptizati. Infants, Born, Baptized.	Comparentes. Godparents.
Johann Georg Dengler and his wife Catharina.	Samuel, 19 Nov., 1794. 4 Jan., 1795.	Margaretha Eberhard.
Cornelius Weygand and his wife.	Catharina Elizabeth, 28 Dec., 1794. 14 Jan., 1795.	Mr. Brotzman and his wife Elizabeth.
Gebhard Barthold and his wife.	Carl, 16 Oct., 1794. 14 Jan., 1795.	The parents.
Jacob Schneider and his wife Catharina.	Catharina, 19 April, 1793. 28 April, 1793.	Ludewig Stecher and his wife Catharina.
Jacob Schneider and his wife Catharina.	Peter, 13 Jan., 1795. 31 Jan., 1795.	Peter Hilger and his wife Elizabeth.
Christian Corel and his wife Catharina.	Catharina, 17 Nov., 1794. 31 Jan., 1795.	Henry Reimer and his wife Catharina.
Georg Peter Kesler and his wife Elizabeth.	Susanna, 22 Nov., 1794. 31 Jan., 1795.	Susanna Corell.
Matthias Passinger and his wife Catha-	John, 6 Dec., 1794. 2 Feb., 1795.	John Yaeger and his wife Catharina.
Peter Kuechlein and his wife Elizabeth.	Susanna, 4 Jan., 1795. 10 Feb., 1795.	The parents.
John Schweitzer and his wife Magdalena.	Elizabeth, 19 Nov., 1794. 19 Feb., 1795.	Edward Freeman and his wife Susanna.
Friederich Baier and his wife Hanna (Anna?).	William, 19 Dec., 1794. 13 March, 1795.	The parents.
Peter Miller and his wife Maria Christina.	Peter, 1 Feb., 1795. 13 March, 1795.	Conrad Seibbel and his wife Catharina.
Conrad Seibel and his wife Catharina.	Johanna, 23 Aug., 1794. 13 March, 1795.	Jacob Scheib and his wife Maria Catharina.

134 *The First Reformed Church of Easton, Pa.*

Parentes. Parents.	Infantes, Nati, Baptizati. Infants, Born, Baptized.	Comparentes. Godparents.
Georg Adam Geisli (Yeisley?) and his wife Christina.	Jacob, 18 Jan., 1795. 15 March, 1795.	Peter Zeller and his wife Elizabeth.
Wilhelm Wotring and his wife Rosina.	Johann Wilhelm, 30 Dec., 1894. 15 March, 1795.	Philip Wotring and his wife Elizabeth.
John Krauss (?) and his wife Elizabeth.	Johannes, 12 Dec., 1794. 15 March, 1795.	John Flori and his wife Christina.
John Nicolas Traxel and his wife Margaretha.	Wilhelm, 23 Feb., 1795. 16 March, 1795.	Michael Traxel and his wife Susanna.
Philip Brotzman and his wife Christina.	Peter, 15 March, 1795. 16 March, 1795.	Peter Lattig and his wife Elizabeth.
Christoph Meixsel and his wife Elizabeth.	Juliana, 9 May, 1793. 25 May, ——.	John Schuck and his wife Juliana.
Christoph Meixsel and his wife Elizabeth.	Elizabeth, 7 May, 1795. 5 July, '92 (?).	Doctor Christian Ludwig Becker, Minister in Lancaster.
Christ. Engel (wife Elisabeth).	Wilhelm, 10 Sept., 1795. Wanting.	Christ. Meixel and consort.
Peter Meruny.	John Peter, 7 Oct., 1795. Wanting.	Parents.
Christian Heckman (?) and his wife Susanna.	Christian, 12 Oct., 1795. 23 Feb., 1796.	Georg Adam Yeisley and consort.
Fried. Hess and his wife Maria.	Maria Christina, 13 Nov., 1795. 28 Sept., 1796.	Philip Brotzman and consort.
Jacob Ries and Christina.	Anna Maria, 16 July, 1795. 27 March, 1796.	Adam Lehn and wife.

REV. THOMAS POMP.

Church Records.

A record of the children baptized by the Rev. Thomas Pomp, minister at Easton, begun in the year 1796.

Date of Baptism and name of Child.	Names of Parents and Sponsors.	Date of Birth.
Anna Maria, July 3, 1796.	[1] Nicolas Best and Rosina. Philip Odenwaelder and consort.	May 2, 1796.
Juliana, July 3, 1796.	Peter Kessler and Elizabeth. Adam Schuck and consort.	April 12, 1796.
Susanna, Aug. 27, 1796.	Michael Traxell and Susanna. Christoph. Engel and consort.	Aug. 13, 1796.
John, Oct. 9, 1796.	Michael Paulus and Christina. Parents.	May 26, 1796.
William, Oct. 9, 1796.	Andrew Kessler and Catarina. Christoph. Meixell and consort.	Aug. 17, 1796.
Philip, Sept. 25, 1796.	Philip Brotzman and Christina. Peter Lattig and consort.	Aug. 19, 1796.
Elizabeth, Sept. 25, 1796.	Thomas Richard and Susanna. Andrew Kieffer and Lattig (Lottie?).	Aug. 2, 1796.
Maria, Nov. 7, 1796.	Michael Simon and Maria. Parents.	June 26, 1796.
Henry, Nov. 5, 1796.	Jacob Seipel and Magdalena, parents.	July 7, 1796.
Elizabeth, Nov. 12, 1796.	Henry Reimer and Catarina. Peter Kessler and consort.	Sept. 11, 1796.

[1] The names of the parents are given *in the first line of each entry*, those of the sponsors in the second.

Date of Baptism and name of Child.	Names of Parents and Sponsors.	Date of Birth.
William, Dec. 4, 1796.	Thomas Sebring and Susanna, parents.	Sept. 13, 1796.
Carl, Dec. 12, 1796.	Ludwig Flory and Salome. John Flory and consort.	Oct. 30, 1796.
Anna, Dec. 26, 1796.	Peter Schnyder and Susanna, parents.	Oct. 28, 1796.
1797.		
Margaretha, March 25, 1796.	Peter Kuechlein and Anna Elizabeth, parents.	Feb. 26, 1797.
Anna Maria, Nov. 5, 1796.	Henry Doering and Catarina. Henry Laucks and consort.	Aug. 23, 1796.
John, Jan. 10, 1797.	Nicolas Franz (?) and Susanna. William Hudchins and consort.	Oct. 4, 1795.
John, Jan. 23, 1797.	John Leidig and Juliana, parents.	"Promised to find out the birthday," and probably forgot.
Johan George, Feb. 4, 1797.	Johan Sand and Magdalena. Johan George Correll and consort.	Dec. 18, 1796.
Margaretha, April 13, 1797.	Beint (?) Walter and Maria. Parents.	March 23, 1797.
Elizabeth, April 14, 1797.	Peter Miller and Maria. Elizabeth Miller.	Feb. 24, 1797.
Thersa, April 15, 1797.	Abraham Seller and Sophia. Parents.	March 13, 1797
Johan Peter, Jan. 20, 1797.	Peter Bab and Catarina. Parents.	Sept. 25, 1796.

Church Records. 137

Date of Baptism and name of Child.	Names of Parents and Sponsors.	Date of Birth.
Johannes, April 23, 1797.	William Woodringer and Rosina. Johan Brotzman and consort.	March 11, 1797.
Rachel, May 5, 1797.	Samuel Russell and Maria. Martin Kind and consort.	Sept. 29, 1796.
Johannes, May 5, 1797.	John Ward and Catarina. Wilhelm Lahr and Elizabeth Ward.	March 5, 1797.
Johannes, May 5, 1797.	Conrad Ward and Barbara. Martin Kind and consort.	March 17, 1797.
Johan. Jacob, May 6, 1797.	Matthias Weis and Christina. Jacob Conrad and consort.	Sept. 27, 1797.
Isaac, May 21, 1797.	John Richarts and Susanna. Philip Brotzman and consort.	March 2, 1797.
Samuel, June 12, 1797.	Jacob Yohe and Susanna. Parents.	May 2, 1797.
Henrietta, July 2, 1797.	Adam Schuck and Barbara. Parents.	May 2, 1797.
Susanna, Oct. 9, 1797.	Daniel Mandel and Margaret. Adam Hay.	July 2, 1797.
Anna Maria, Dec. 1, 1797.	Peter Seiler and Margaretha. Jacob Schumacher and consort.	Sept. 12, 1797.
Micha Samuel, Dec. 3, 1797.	Christoph Engel and Susanna. Michael Traxell and consort.	Oct. 26, 1797.

138   The First Reformed Church of Easton, Pa.

Date of Baptism and name of Child.	Names of Parents and Sponsors.	Date of Birth.
Joseph, Dec. 17, 1797.	Nic. Traxell and Margaretha. Adam Dreisbach and consort.	Oct. 6, 1797.
Carl, July 30, 1797.	Melchoir Hay and Elizabeth. Adam Hay and consort.	March 16, 1797.
Joseph, July 30, 1797.	John Hay and Maria. Adam Hay and consort.	July 5, 1797.
Anna, Sept. 15, 1797.	John Young and Maria. Parents.	March 17, 1797.
Maria, June 16, 1797.	George Stevens and Elizabeth. Andrew Hay and Catharine Stevens (single).	June 2, 1797.
Johannes, Aug. 27, 1797.	William Licht and Anna Christina. Jacob Rambach and Christ. Stecher.	June 27, 1797.
Judea, Aug. 27, 1797.	John Longerson and Elizabeth. John Fritz and consort.	May 16, 1797.
Sarah, Aug. 5, 1797.	Henry Schnyder and Catharina. Parents.	June 24, 1797.
William, Sept. 24, 1797.	Jacob Kaemmerer and Magdalena. Parents.	Aug. 10, 1797.
Margaretha, Aug. 13, 1797.	Peter Laddig and Christina, Jacob Laddig and Marg. Brotsman.	July 8, 1797.
Anna Maria, Aug. 13, 1797.	Philip Drumheller and Anna. Andrew Kieler and Anna Maria Riehl.	July 4, 1797.
Johan Peter, Sept. 10, 1797.	Jacob Seib and Susanna. Jacob Heller.	July 29, 1797.

Date of Baptism and name of Child.	Names of Parents and Sponsors.	Date of Birth.
Thomas, Oct. 7, 1797.	Frederick Lerch and Elizabeth. John Leidig and consort. To Mr. George Butz and his wife Susanna the following children were born.	Aug. 11, 1797.
Jesse,	Sponsors, Jacob Keller and consort.	March 29, 1795.
Samuel,	Sponsors, Peter Hertzel and consort.	Feb. 17, 1797.
Maria.	Sponsors, Frederick Hess and consort.	July 22, 1793.

1798.

Henry, Jan. 28, 1798.	Henry Abel and Anna Maria Catarina. Philip Gross and consort.	Oct. 13, 1797.
Samuel, Jan. 30, 1798.	Jacob Guth and Margaretha. John Eritt and consort.	Dec. 14, 1797.
Elizabeth, Feb. 1, 1798.	Andrew Hertz and Margaret. Christian Beck.	Dec. 9, 1797.
Johannes, Feb. 1, 1798.	Daniel Klaus (?) and Dorothea. William Jansan and consort.	Oct. 18, 1797.
Catharina, Feb. 13, 1798.	Michael Dech and Catharina. Catharina Sassaman.	Dec. 28, 1797.
Simon Jacob, April 6, 1798.	George Peter Kessler and Elizabeth. Henry Reimer and consort.	Dec. 24, 1797.
Peter, April 22, 1798.	John Sand and Maria Magd. Peter Kessler and consort.	Jan. 6, 1798.

140   *The First Reformed Church of Easton, Pa.*

Date of Baptism and name of Child.	Names of Parents and Sponsors.	Date of Birth.
John, April 22, 1798.	Moses Dieder (?) and Marg.	Nov. 9, 1797.
Philip, April 29, 1798.	George Messinger and Elizabeth. Philip Messinger and consort.	Feb. 5, 1798.
Maria, April 15, 1798.	Christian (undecipherable) and Elizabeth. Parents.	March 3, 1798.
Jacob, May 20, 1798.	John Leidig and Christina. Christian Hartzel and consort.	Nov. 12, 1797.
Susanna, May 20, 1798.	Christian Hackman and Susanna. Nicolas Yeisley and Susanna Hartzel.	March 28, 1798.
Daniel, May 20, 1798.	Jacob Frey and Agnes. Daniel Braun and Louisa, uxor ejus.	Feb. 5, 1798.
Sarah, March 29, 1798.	Peter Spenkler (Spangler?) and Anna Elizabeth. Christian Best and consort.	Dec. 11, 1797.
George William, May 22, 1798.	Andrew Raub and Catharina. George William Raub and consort.	About nine months old.
John George, May 5, 1798.	Philip Broeder and Christina, his wife.	March 12, 1798.
Jacob, June 17, 1798.	George Schmid and Elizabeth. Jacob Schmid and consort.	April 28, 179 8.
Anna Catarina, June 4, 1798.	Jacob Young and Elizabeth. Parents.	March 5, 1798.
Michael Samuel, July 9, 1798.	Michael Traxel and Susanna. Parents.	June 16, 1798.

Church Records. 141

Date of Baptism and name of Child.	Names of Parents and Sponsors.	Date of Birth.
Carl, July 13, 1798.	John Kerster and wife. Parents.	Jan. 20, 1798.
John, July 15, 1798.	Michael Sand and Maria. Frederick Wagner and Catarina Schiffer.	May 22, 1798.
Elizabeth, July 29, 1798.	Andrew Stocker and Maria. Parents.	May 24, 1798.
Daniel, Aug. 20, 1798.	George Schwartz and Margaret. Parents.	May 23, 1798.
John Jacob, Aug. 26, 1798.	John Dietz and Hanna. John Otto and consort.	July 25, 1798.
Elizabeth, Aug. 26, 1798.	William Yetzt and Maria. George —— and Sara.	July 19, 1798.
Andrew. Aug. 27, 1798.	Israel Lehn and Elizabeth. Abraham Lehn and consort.	June 19, 1798.
John, Sept. 9, 1798.	Benjamin Collman and Addy. Jacob Fraes.	June 4, 1798.
Joseph, Aug. 12, 1798.	John Ressly and Magdalena. Valentine Uhler and consort.	May 23, 1798.
John, Aug. 12, 1798.	Philip Brotzman and Christina. John Brotzman and consort.	June 8, 1798.
Lea, Aug. 12, 1798.	George Drumheller and Elizabeth. Jacob Sickman and consort.	June 6, 1798.
Henry, Aug. 15, 1798.	John Leidig and Juliana. John Troxel and Eva Shuck.	July 15, 1798.

Date of Baptism and name of Child.	Names of Parents and Sponsors.	Date of Birth.
Samuel, Sept. 9, 1798.	Frederick Gewinner and Anna Maria. Parents.	Aug. 16, 1798.
Juliana, Sept. 9, 1797.	Christian Winters and Margaret. Parents.	Oct. 24, 1797.
John, Sept. 12, 1797.	John Bender and Elizabeth. Parents.	Oct. 8, 1797.
Susanna, Aug. 30, 1798.	Thomas Hartman and Anna Maria. Parents.	June 18, 1798.
William, Sept. 2, 1798.	James Lucker and Maria. Parents.	Aug. 27, 1798.
Carl, Sept. 2, 1798.	George Traxel and Rosina. Nicolas Traxel and wife.	July 10, 1798.
John Jacob, Sept. 23, 1798.	John George Korrell and Susanna. Philip Korell and consort.	Aug. 26, 1798.
Elizabeth, Sept. 23, 1798.	John Rambach and Maria. Daniel Brown and consort.	July 29, 1798.
Rebecca, Oct. 8, 1798.	Samuel Coleman. William Janson and consort.	July 26, 1798.
Nicholas Peter, Jan. 28, 1798.	T. Pomp and Catharina. Parents.	Jan. 21, 1798.
John George, Oct. 17, 1798.	Tobias Moser and Christina, his wife. George Hertzel and consort.	Dec. 11, 1797.
Anna Maria, Oct. 21, 1798.	Michael Butz and Margaret. Jacob Kaemrer and consort.	Sept. 21, 1798.

Church Records. 143

Date of Baptism and name of Child.	Names of Parents and Sponsors.	Date of Birth.
John, Nov. 11, 1798.	Peter Ribbel and Maria.	Feb. 16, 1798.
Maria Catharina, Nov. 11, 1798.	George De (?) Binder and Maria Theresia, nata Vulcar.	Oct. 20, 1798.
Jeremiah, Oct. 11, 1798.	Jacob Ries and Christina.	Aug. 29, 1797.
Margaret, Oct. 11, 1798.	John Schaub and Elizabeth.	Aug. 11, 1798.
Elizabeth, Nov. 18, 1798.	Henry Schug and Elizabeth. Anna Maria Schug.	Sept. 22, 1798.
Simeon, Dec. 14, 1798.	Mathias Koenig and Eva Elizabeth. Parents.	Oct. 27, 1798.
John, (?) Dec. 16, 1798.	Thomas Richert and Susanna. John Jacob Lattig and Margaret Rill.	Oct. 12, 1798.
Maria, Dec. 25, 1798.	George Keller and Rachael Parents.	Nov. 21, 1798.
Henry, Dec. 27, 1798.	John Dietz and Elizabeth. Conrad Riesser and consort.	February 1, 1795.
Maria, Dec. 27, 1798.	John Dietz and Elizabeth. Henry Riesser and Susanna his wife.	February 29, 1793.
Andrew, Dec. 25, 1798.	Daniel Herster and Catarina. Anna Maria Herster.	Aug. 19, 1798.
Susanna, Dec. 25, 1798.	William Bernd (?) and Elizabeth. Abraham Horn and consort.	Sept. 20, 1798.
George, Dec. 30, 1798.	Michael Abel and Maria. George Koch and wife.	Aug. 1, 1798.

Date of Baptism and name of Child.	Names of Parents and Sponsors.	Date of Birth.
	ANNO 1799.	
Maria, January 8, 1799.	Peter Miller and Maria Christina. The parents.	Nov. 4,[1] a. p.
Anna, January 10, 1799.	Conrad Seibel and Catarina. Anna ———.	Nov. 7, a. p.
Jacob, January 13, 1799.	Nicolaus Best and Rosina. Christian Best and his wife.	Dec. 1, a. p.
Isaiah, Jan. 20, 1799.	Thomas Titius and Elizabeth. The grandmother, Maria Eva Riesser.	Dec. 19, a. p.
Deborah, Jan. 30, 1799.	John Wagener and Barbara. Maria Wagener.	Sept. 8, a. p.
Jacob, Feb. 4, 1799.	Frederick Herman and Catharina. Jacob Brug (?).	Dec. 21, a. p.
Maria, March 1, 1799.	Frederick Beyer and Hanna. The parents.	Oct. 24, a. p.
Elizabeth, March 15, 1799.	Christian Korrell and Catarina. Peter Stocker and consort.	Feb. 7, 1799.
Johann Philip, March 24, 1799.	Nicolaus Woodring and Catarina. Johann Philip Woodring and consort.	Jan. 29, 1799.
Elizabeth, April 21, 1799.	T. Pomp and Catharina. Elizabeth Pomp.	April 18, 1799.
Michael, May 5, 1799.	Moses Wilhelm and Susanna. Peter Ohlangst and Sarah Wilhelm.	March 27, 1799.

[1] The previous year.

Church Records.

Date of Baptism and name of Child.	Names of Parents and Sponsors.	Date of Birth.
Elizabeth, May 15, 1799.	John Wagner and Margaret. William Richard and Elizabeth.	March 5, 1799.
Sarah, May 19, 1799.	Jonathan Coleman and Elizabeth, Nicolaus Woodring and consort.	April 12, 1799.
Anna Maria, June 30, 1799.	John Hertzel and Elizabeth, Christian Hertzel and consort.	May 17, 1799.
John, Aug, 11, 1799.	Peter Brecht and Susanna. Adam Moyer and consort.	April 25, 1799.
Anna Maria, Aug. 11, 1799.	Jacob Kaemrer and Magdalena. David Kaemrer and consort.	May 29, 1799.
John, Aug. 11, 1799.	Nicolaus Yeisley and Sarah. Adam Yeisley and consort.	June 3, 1799.
Samuel, Aug. 25, 1799.	Peter Seiler and Margaret. The parents.	July 17, 1799.
George, Aug. 25, 1799.	John Schick and Jane. Abraham Miller and consort.	July 5, 1799.
Margaretha, Sept. 8, 1799.	Adam Seiler and Maria. Jacob Schumacher and consort.	Aug. 12, 1799.
Abraham, Sept. 22, 1799.	William Woodring and Rosina. Abraham Woodring and consort.	Aug. 8, 1799.
Sara, Oct. 5, 1799.	Nicolaus Dietz and Sophia.	July 22, 1799.

Date of Baptism and name of Child.	Names of Parents and Sponsors.	Date of Birth.
William Jefferson,	John Todden and Maria. Jacob Keller and his wife.	
Thomas McKeen, Aug. 2, 1799.	John Todden and Maria. Abraham Horn and his wife.	July 15, 1799. [1]
Catharina, Sept. 30, 1799.	Peter Stocker and Elizabeth. Christian Correll and his wife.	Sept. 4, 1799.
Elizabeth, Dec. 1, 1799.	Thomas Hay and Maria. John Odenwaelder and consort.	Oct. 24, 1799.
John, Aug. 11, 1799.	Nicolaus Yeisley and Sarah. Adam Yeisley and consort.	June 3, 1799.
George, Dec. 4, 1799.	George Messinger and Catharina. The parents.	Jan. 25, 1797.
Anna Maria, Dec. 4, 1799.	George Messinger and Catharine. The parents.	May 20, 1799.
Appelonia, Dec. 4, 1799.	Daniel Messinger and Phillippina. The parents.	Aug. 5, 1799.
John, Dec. 6, 1799.	Philip Drumheller and Anna. John Oberle and consort.	Oct. 21, 1799.
Peter, Oct. 27, 1799.	Henry Winters and Susanna. The parents.	Nov. 25, 1798.

[1] As only one birth date is given, probably twins.

Church Records.   147

Date of Baptism and name of Child.	Names of Parents and Sponsors.	Date of Birth.
	1800.	
John George, Jan. 5, 1800.	George Butz and Susanna. Jacob Lattig and Elizabeth Heil (?).	July 6, 1799.
Daniel, Feb. 4, 1800.	Peter Bab and Catharina. The parents.	Dec. 10, 1799.
Elizabeth, Feb. 10, 1800.	Philip Schmid and Dorothea. Christoph Schmid and consort.	Dec. 21, a. p.
Anna Maria, Feb. 10, 1800.	Abraham Schmid and Sibilla. John Schmid and consort.	Sept. 8, a. p.
Julia, April 5, 1800.	Michael Traxel and Susanna. The parents.	Feb. 23, 1800.
Peter, April 20, 1800.	John Fehr and Eva. Peter Hay and consort Barbara.	Dec. 19, 1799.
George, April 14, 1800.	Frederick Bruch and Catharina. George —— and Magdalena Sibele.	Feb. 28, 1800.
John, April 14, 1800.	Peter Rup and Barbara. John Rothrock and consort.	Feb. 20, 1800.
Daniel, April 20, 1800.	Nicolaus Traxel and Margaret. Daniel Herster and sort.	Dec. 4, a. p.
John, May 4, 1800.	Philip Schwartz and Anna. The parents.	About 9 months old.
Sara, June 2, 1800.	Henry Schuck and Elizabeth. Conrad Jumper and consort.	March 13, 1800.

Date of Baptism and name of Child.	Names of Parents and Sponsors.	Date of Birth.
John Philip, June 14, 1800.	John Meixel and Rebecca. Philip Meixel.	April 13, 1800.
David, Jan. 24, 1800.	Henry Abel and Maria. The parents.	Dec. 28, 1799.
Adam, June 28, 1800.	Adam Sand and Maria. Adam Wagner and consort.	May 16, 1800.
(Blurred), June 20, 1800.	Philip Scherer and Susanna. Jacob Ohnangst and consort.	May 29, 1800.
Susanna, June 29, 1800.	Frederick Grub and Maria. John Young and Susanna Schnader.	March 29, 1800.
Maria Magdalena, Aug. 10, 1800.	Nicolaus Woodring and Catharina. Adam Lehr and his wife.	July 3, 1800.
Elizabeth, Sept. 7, 1800.	Frederick Stein and Anna Margaretha. Elizabeth Beitelman.	April 7, 1800.
Anna Maria, Oct. 5, 1800.	Andrew Willauer and Elizabeth. William Willauer and consort, Elizabeth.	June 23, 1800.
Maria, Oct. 14, 1800.	Jacob Schug and Susanna. The parents.	Sept. 14, 1800.
Johann Philip, Nov. 2, 1800.	Abraham Woodring and Margaretha. Philip Woodring and Maria Elizabeth.	Sept. 13, 1800.
Mary, Nov. 16, 1800.	Michael Rosenberger and Margaretha. William Rosenberger and consort.	July 18, 1800.
Margaret, Nov. 16, 1800.	John Ressly and Magdalena. Henry Brug (?) and consort.	Aug. 7, 1800.

Church Records.

Date of Baptism and name of Child.	Names of Parents and Sponsors.	Date of Birth.
John, Nov. 16, 1800.	Michael Messinger and Elizabeth. John Resser.	April 27, 1800.
Anna, Sept. 29, 1800.	John George Correll and Susanna. Philip Correll and Maria Schug.	Aug. 4, 1800.
Margaret, Nov. 25, 1800.	Henry Reimer and Catharine. John Sand and wife.	Sept. 15, 1800.
Elizabeth, Nov. 23, 1800.	Adam Stocker and Barbara. Matthias Stecher and consort.	Oct. 24, 1800.
Jacob, Nov. 23, 1800.	John Sand and Magdalena. Peter Holland and consort.	Sept. 1, 1800.
George, Nov. 30, 1800.	Matthias Gross and Catharina. John Spangenberg and consort.	Oct. 26, 1800.
Elizabeth, Dec. 15, 1800.	Barnhart Walter and Anna Maria. Adam Wagner and Margaretha.	Aug. 19, 1800.
Hugh, Dec. 17, 1800.	Samuel Irvine and Maria Seyers, illegitimate. Elias Diedrich and Catharina.	June 12, 1797.
Michael, Dec. 25, 1800.	Michael Abel and his wife Maria. Nicholaus Koch and wife Elizabeth.	July 11, 1800.
	1798.	
Samuel, Jan. 27, 1799.	John Arndt and wife, Elizabeth. Parents.	Aug. 17, 1798.

150 *The First Reformed Church of Easton, Pa.*

Date of Baptism and name of Child.	Names of Parents and Sponsors.	Date of Birth.
Peter, Feb. 5, 1799.	Philip Messinger and wife, Margaretha. Parents.	Aug. 19, 1798.
	1801.	
Frederick, Jan. 2, 1801.	Ludwig Handshill (blurred) and Regina. Frederick Dofft and Salome.	Nov. 20, 1800.
John, Jan. 6, 1800.	Samuel Coleman and Maria. John Coleman and Sarah.	Sept. 12, 1800.
John, Jan. 11, 1800.	Christian Hackman and Susanna. John Brug and Rosina Catharina.	Sept. 16, a. p.
Nicolaus, Jan. 14, 1800.	Nicholaus Best and Rosina. Philip Odenwelder.	Dec. 28, 1800.
Elizabeth, Feb. 16, 1800.	Henry Fries and Elizabeth, The parents.	Aug. 13, a. p.
Sara, Feb. 11, 1800.	An illegitimate child, which David Beitelman and wife Margaretha promise to bring up in a Christian way.	
Catharina, February 22, 1801.	William Woodring and Rosina. Nicolaus Woodring and wife Catharina.	Jan. 3, 1801.
Elizabeth, March 22, 1801.	Philip Yaeger and Rosina. Philip Odenwaelder and Elizabeth.	Dec. 20, 1800.

Church Records. 151

Date of Baptism and name of Child.	Names of Parents and Sponsors.	Date of Birth.
Jacob, March 22, 1801.	Peter Seiler and wife Margaretha. Jacob Schumacher and wife Elizabeth.	Feb. 20, 1801.
Jacob, March 22, 1801.	William Yates and wife Maria. John George Bruch and Christina Laddig.	Jan. 17, 1801.
Aron, March 22, 1801.	Peter Schneyder and wife Susanna. The parents.	Jan. 12, 1801.
Christina, March 23, 1801.	Nicolaus Dietz and wife Sophia. The parents.	Jan. 23, 1801.
Susanna, March 24, 1801.	Melchior Hay and Elizabeth. Thomas Richart and consort.	Dec. 25, a. p.
Sara, April 3, 1800.	Michael Sand and Maria. Adam Sand and consort.	Feb. 12, 1801.
Elizabeth, April 3, 1801.	John Koch and wife Maria. Nicolaus Koch and wife Elizabeth.	Jan. 10, 1801.
Henry, April 4, 1801.	Philip Broeder and Christina. The parents.	June 14, 1800.
Christina, April 6, 1801.	John Schonz and Elizabeth. Philip Roth and Susanna, ejus uxor.	Aug. 15, a. p.
John, April 11, 1801.	Andrew Kesseler and Catharina. Christian Nicolaus.	May 3, 1800.
John, May 17, 1801.	George Traxel and Rosina. John Brotzman and consort.	April 10, 1801.

Date of Baptism and name of Child.	Names of Parents and Sponsors.	Date of Birth.
John, March 31, 1801.	John Hay and Maria. Philip Odenwaelder and wife Anna Maria.	April 9, 1801.
Elizabeth, May 31, 1801.	John Odenwaelder and wife Anna Margaret. John Odenwaelder and wife Elizabeth.	April 28, 1801.
Magdalena, June 14, 1801.	Jacob Kaemrer and wife Magdalena. Michael Butz and wife Margaretha.	April 2, 1801.
Elizabeth, June 22, 1801.	Benjamin Coleman and wife Addy. Leonhard Beitelman and wife Elizabeth.	Nov. 26, 1800.
John, June 28, 1801.	John Hertzel and wife Elizabeth. George Adam Yeisley and wife Christina.	May 27, 1801.
Susanna, July 13, 1801.	John Traxel and Elizabeth. Susanna Horn.	July 13, 1801.
Maria, Aug. 9, 1801.	John Gruber and wife Maria. Jacob Schnyder and wife Maria.	May 26, 1801.
Peter John, July 6, 1801.	Peter Gellman (?) and Elizabeth. The parents.	Dec. 20, 1800.
Margaret, Aug. 13, 1801.	Joseph Roessly and Anna Maria.	July 12, 1801.
Elizabeth, Oct. 4, 1801.	William Moritz and wife Catharina. George Reichurt and Rebecca Drittenburg.	Sept. 7, 1801.
(Undecipherable), Oct. 13, 1801.	Michael Paulus and Christina. The parents.	Aug. 6, 1800.

Date of Baptism and name of Child.	Names of Parents and Sponsors.	Date of Birth.
George, Oct. 18, 1801.	Henry Derr and wife Christina. George Hauch and Catharine Nicolaus.	Aug. 19, 1801.
Catharina, Oct. 29, 1801.	Jacob Koenig and wife Elizabeth. The parents.	Sept. 3, 1801.
Susanna, Nov. 1, 1802.	Jacob Schuesster and wife Maria. Susanna Beitelman.	April 15, 1802.[1]
John George, Nov. 17, 1801.	Peter Schwartz and wife Maria. The parents.	Oct. 10, 1801.
John Peter, Nov. 22, 1801.	John Frederick and Catharina. Peter Frederick and Susanna Conrad.	Oct. 4, 1801.
Anna Catharina, Nov. 29, 1801.	John Dietz and wife Hanna. James McDaunald and Catharine Wolf (?)	Sept. 24, 1801.
	1802.	
John, Jan. 24, 1802.	John Grotz and Catharina. John George Grotz and wife Maria.	Nov. 25, a. p.
Samuel, ——, 1802.	John Schick and wife Jane. The parents.	Jan. 6, 1801.

[1] So it stands on record. Evidently an error in the date.

A list of children who were baptized in the following years, namely 1798, 1799, 1800 and 1801.

Date of Baptism and name of Child.	Names of Parents and Sponsors.	Date of Birth.
	1798.	
Philip, March 1, 1798.	Christian Scheivley and wife Elizabeth. Philip —— and consort.	Jan 15, 1798.
Elizabeth, March 11, 1798.	Jacob Arner and wife Catharina. Abraham Gross and consort.	March 3, 1798.
Eliza, May 13, 1798.	John Philips and wife Hanna. Parents.	Feb. 4, 1798.
Elisha, Oct. 5, 1797.	Eseck Howell and wife Magdalena. Parents.	July 10, 1797.
	1799.	
William, March 17, 1799.	John Mayer and wife Margaretha. The parents.	Feb. 5, 1799.
Anthony, April 18, 1799.	Philip Beisher and wife Catharina. Joseph Beisher and wife Sarah.	Nov. 21, 1798.
Jacob, May 1, 1798.	Philip Hambert (?) and wife Catharina. Rudolph Schweitzer and wife Barbara.	Dec. 4, 1797.
Susanna, May 13, 1799.	Frederick Lerch and wife Elizabeth. Philip Wolff and wife Susanna.	March 27, 1799.
Simon, July 21, 1798.	Simon Schuchard and wife Barbara. The parents.	Sept. 11, 1798.

Church Records.

Date of Baptism and name of Child.	Names of Parents and Sponsors.	Date of Birth.
Elizabeth Maria, July 24, 1797.	Joseph Rosenberger and Fronica. The parents.	July 10, 1797.
John, Sept. 23, 1798.	Jacob Boyer and Christina. Jacob Winter.	Sept. 10, 1798.
David, May 12, 1799.	Peter Schneyder and wife Susanna. The parents.	March 13, 1799.
Alex'der Hamilton, Sept. 22, 1798.	Frederick Berthold and Elizabeth. Laurentz Erb and his wife.	March 11, 1798.
Catharina, Sept. 22, 1799.	Frederick Berthold and wife Elizabeth. Adam Dreisbach and his wife.	Sept. 22, 1799.

1800.

Susanna, Jan. 1, 1800.	Michael Simon and Maria. The parents.	July 28, 1799.
James Macky, Jan. 2, 1800.	William Rosenberger and Maria. Parents.	July 26, 1799.
Jacob, Jan. 9, 1800.	Michael Dech and Catharina. Jacob Dech and wife Elizabeth.	Nov. 12, 1799.
Karl, Jan. 26, 1800.	Henry Schneider and wife Catharina. Nicolaus Kern and wife Margaret Barbara.	Dec. 26, 1799.
Daniel, Jan. 19, 1801.	John Mulhallon and wife Sarah. Parents.	Dec. 29, 1797.
Thomas, Jan. 19, 1802.	John Mulhallon and Sarah. Parents.	Dec. 11, 1801.

Date of Baptism and name of Child.	Names of Parents and Sponsors.	Date of Birth.
Juliana, Feb. 24, 1800.	Peter Rippel and Maria. Andrew Stecker and his wife.	Nov. 26, 1799.
Hanna, March 21, 1800.	John Rambach and Maria. Michael Fraess and his wife.	March 17, 1799.
Henry, March 24, 1800.	Michael Messinger and Elizabeth. George Stecher and his wife.	June 2, 1799.
Andrew, March 24, 1800.	George Stecher, Jr., and Maria. Henry Young and Margaretha Stecher.	Dec. 2, 1799.
Christina, March 24, 1800.	John Stecher and Catharina. John Schweitzer and Christina Stecher.	Jan. 2, 1800.
Conrad, May 2, 1799.	Conrad Schuesster and Susanna Diehl, illegitimate. Adam Moyer and his wife Catharina.	Oct. 13, 1799.
Valentine, May 2, 1800.	Peter Moyer and wife, Maria Catharina. Adam Wagner and his wife Margaretha.	April 8, 1800.
Catharina, Feb. 4, 1799.	George Bruch and wife, Barbara. Abraham Beitelman and his wife.	Sept. 6, 1799.
Jefferson Kreider, May 30, 1799.	Adam Heckman and his wife Elizabeth. Conrad Kreider and Catharina.	March 14, 1799.
Elizabeth, June 16, 1799.	Jacob Keller and Elizabeth. Abraham Krotz and Maria Laddig.	May 10, 1799.

Date of Baptism and name of Child.	Names of Parents and Sponsors.	Date of Birth.
Catharina, June 16, 1799.	Joseph Richard and Elizabeth. Adam Yeisley and his wife.	April 14, 1800.
John, June 16, 1799.	Jacob Messinger and Margaretha. Michael Fraess and his wife.	March 20, 1799.
Sarah, June 16, 1798.	Robert Miller and Catharina. Jacob Keller and consort.	April 4, 1798.
Regina Christina, June 15, 1800.	Frederick Wagner and Catharina. Adam Heckman and wife Elizabeth.	May 2, 1800.
George, June 24, 1800.	John Eweritt (Ewart?) and wife Catharina. George Huth and Anna.	Feb. 27, 1800.
Elizabeth, July 13.	Isaac Schumacher and wife Elizabeth. Jacob Schumacher and his wife.	May 29, 1800.
Abraham, Aug. 20, 1799.	John Dietz and Hanna. Henry Schneyder and wife Catharina.	Dec. 13, 1799.
Levingston, Aug. 21, 1799.	James Ralston and Elizabeth Jackson. " *Uneheliches.*"	July 9, 1799.
Anna, Aug. 31, 1800.	Adam Schuck and Barbara. Parents.	June 16, 1800.
Liddia, Aug. 31, 1800.	The mother, Elizabeth Schuck. The grandmother.	Jan. 13, 1800.
Elizabeth, Aug. 29, 1800.	Benjamin Green and Elizabeth. Parents.	June 28, 1800.

158   *The First Reformed Church of Easton, Pa.*

Date of Baptism and name of Child.	Names of Parents and Sponsors.	Date of Birth.
Henry, Sept. 20, 1800.	Jacob Messinger and Maria. Philip Messinger and wife Margaretha.	April 18, 1800.
Maria, Oct. 12, 1800.	Richard Jacobs and Elizabeth. Anthony Kratzer and consort Elizabeth.	Sept. 16, 1800.
Catharina, Oct. 26, 1800.	Frederick Lerch and wife Elizabeth. John Stecher and wife Catharina.	Aug. 22, 1800.
Christina, Oct. 26, 1800.	Adam Willauer and wife Elizabeth. Frederick Lerch and wife Elizabeth.	Aug. 21, 1800.
John, Dec. 31, 1800.	Conrad Jumper and wife Magdalena. David Klein and Maria Kotz.	Nov. 12, 1800.
Elizabeth, Dec. 18, 1800.	Peter Lantz and wife Catharina. John Bruch and Elizabeth Scherer.	March 28, 1800.
(Wanting), Oct. 4, 1800.	Jacob Rosenberger and Margaret. Hanna Rosenberger.	Oct. 2, 1800.
Elizabeth Salome, April 27, 1802.	Joseph Townson and Margaret. Elizabeth Bartel.	April 24, 1802.
	1801.	
Henry, March 31, 1799.	James Lucker and Maria. John Schuck and wife Juliana.	Oct. 1, 1799.
Rosina, April 25, 1801.	John Odenwaelder and Elizabeth. Philip Yaeger and his wife.	Apr. 7, 1801.

Church Records. 159

Date of Baptism and name of Child.	Names of Parents and Sponsors.	Date of Birth.
Francis, May 31, 1800.	John Leidig and Juliana. George William Mueller and Catharina Herster.	Aug. 30, 1800.
Michael, May 2, 1801.	Bernhard Walter and Maria. Michael Odenwaelder and wife Margaretha.	March 25, 1801.
Maria, Sept. 15, 1801.	David Kaemrer and Anna. Susanna Kaemrer.	Sept. 17, 1801.
Juliana, Dec. 14, 1801.	Henry Schneyder and wife Catharina. Adam Heckman and wife Elizabeth.	Dec. 1, 1801.
Abraham Burr, Dec. 20, ———	Adam Heckman and wife Elizabeth. Abraham Horn and wife Susanna.	Wanting.
Thomas, Dec. 26, 1801.	Abraham Brotzman and wife Maria. Thomas Richard and wife Susannna.	Sept. 26, 1801.
Elizabeth, Dec. 27, 1801.	Michael Simon and wife Maria. The parents.	March 9, 1801.
Maria, Aug. 23, 1801.	Philip Brotzman and wife Christina. Abraham Hertzel and Maria Laddig.	June 3, 1801.
Elizabeth, Aug. 23, 1801.	Henry Kuhn and wife Maria. Maria Magdalena Gehres.	May 21, 1801.
Eliza, April 5, 1800.	Moses Davis and Mary. Nicolaus Kern and wife Barbara.	May 30, 1800.

The First Reformed Church of Easton, Pa.

Date of Baptism and name of Child.	Names of Parents and Sponsors.	Date of Birth.
Aaron, Nov. 15, 1801.	William Bernd and wife Elizabeth. George Schlauch and Susanna Yohe.	April 14, 1801.
Sophia, Dec. 12, 1801.	Abraham Forse and wife Hannah. Sophia Kurtz.	Dec. 1, 1801.
John, Date wanting.	John Simon and wife Susanna. The parents.	May 24, 1798.
Maria Magd., Date wanting.	John Simon and wife Susanna. Martin Frey and wife Maria Magdalena.	Aug. 23, 1800.
George, April 19, 1800.	George Doffard and wife Elizabeth. The parents.	April 1, 1800.
Susanna, April 5, 1801.	Philip Odenwaelder, Jr., and Elizabeth. Phil. Odenwaelder, Sr., and wife Anna Maria.	March 25, 1801.
Joseph, Aug. 30, 1801.	George Schwartz and wife Margaretha. The parents.	May 20, 1801.
	ANNO 1802.	
William, Jan. 7, 1802.	Peter Babb and his wife Catharina. The parents.	Nov. 30, 1801.
Elizabeth, Jan. 24, 1802.	John Richard and wife Susanna. Abraham Brotzman and Maria.	Oct. 31, 1801.
Susanna, Jan. 24, 1802.	Joseph Richard and wife Elizabeth. Abraham Hertzel and Christina Yeisley.	Nov. 30, 1801.
Alexander, Jan. 24, 1801.	Jacob Schick and wife Elizabeth. The parents.	Oct. 26, 1800.

BERNARD G. WOLFF, D.D.

Church Records.

Date of Baptism and name of Child.	Names of Parents and Sponsors.	Date of Birth.
Jacob, Jan. 24, 1801.	Adam Hauch and wife Rebecca. Jacob Schick and wife Elizabeth.	Dec. 23, 1801.
Henry, Feb. 24, 1801.	Jacob Schnabel and wife Elizabeth. Henry Arner and wife Catharina.	Dec. 24, 1801.
Peter, Feb. 25, 1801.	Philip Klaus and wife Christina. Lehnhart Beitelman and wife Elizabeth.	Sept. 19, 1801.
Sara, March 21, 1802.	Nicolaus Wudring and Catharina. Jacob Wudring and consort.	Jan. 19.
Suelly, March 21, 1802.	John Ramberg and Maria. Rudy Schwertzer and consort.	Sept. 30, a. p.
Judith, March 21.	Henry Schug and Elizabeth. Peter Schug and Maria Grotz.	Oct. 13, a. p.
Rudolf, April 11, 1802.	John Dech and wife Elizabeth. Rudolf Oberly and wife Barbara.	March 9, 1802.
Elizabeth, April 25, 1802.	John Young and Susanna. George Rieser and Susanna Fogel.	March 7, 1802.
Rachael Schardre, May 7, 1802.	John Transu and wife Barbara. The mother.	Nov. 17, 1801.
Sarah, Jan. 6, 1803.	Jacob Schuester and wife Elizabeth. Jacob Kaemrer and wife Magdalena.	March 6, 1802.

Date of Baptism and name of Child.	Names of Parents and Sponsors.	Date of Birth.
Mar. Magd., Jan. 6, 1802.	Frederick Stein and wife Anna Margaretha. Michael Boyer and Maria Magdalena Rapp.	Dec. 25, 1801.
Peter, June 6, 1802.	George Messinger and wife Elizabeth. The parent.	March 20, 1802.
Sarah, June 27, 1802.	Nicolaus Yeisley and wife Sarah. John Hertzler and Elizabeth.	May 7, 1802.
John, Aug. 7, 1802.	Adam Willauer and wife Elizabeth. John Knecht and wife Elizabeth.	March 1, 1802.
John, Aug. 7, 1802.	Michael Roseburry and wife Margaret. The parents.	March 16, 1802.
Jonathan, Aug. 10, 1802.	Andrew Willauer and Elizabeth. Andrew Stocker and consort.	June 12, 1802.
Maria, Sept. 5, 1802.	Andrew Kieffer and wife Elizabeth. Abraham Brotzman and wife Maria.	July 28, 1802.
Susanna, Sept. 5, 1802.	Henry Abel and wife Maria. Parents.	May 3, 1802.
Jacob, Sept. 5, 1802.	Michael Abel and wife Maria. Jacob Koch and Sarah Messinger.	Feb. 15, 1802.
Rosina, Sept. 5, 1802.	Isaac Schumacher and wife Catharina. John Lantz and Elizabeth Zimmerman.	July 12, 1802.

Church Records. 163

Date of Baptism and name of Child.	Names of Parents and Sponsors.	Date of Birth.
Daniel, Sept. 20, 1802.	Christian Butz and Maria. The parents.	Sept. 7, 1801.
Abraham, Oct. 3, 1802.	Gottfried Meixel and wife Hanna. Abraham Stein, Anna Keller.	Sept. 1, 1802.
David, Oct. 12, 1802.	David Kaemrer and wife Anna. Jacob Fraess and wife Susanna.	Sept. 15, 1802.
Margaretha, Oct. 12, 1802.	Michael Messinger and wife Elizabeth. Jacob Uhler and Margaretha Messinger.	June 17, 1802.
Isaac, Nov. 21, 1802.	Jacob Hertzel and Magdalena. John Hertzel et consort.	Oct. 25, 1802.
Cathrina, Nov. 25, 1802.	John Yeisley and Magdalena. Joseph Raesly.	Aug. 5, 1802.
Sara, Nov. 25, 1802.	Frederick Ziegler and Maria. Rudolph Schweitzer et consort.	Sept. 27, 1802.
Jacob, Nov. 28, 1802.	Abraham Woodring and wife Margaretha. Jacob Brotzman and wife Maria.	Sept. 10, 1802.
Susanna, Dec. 3, 1802.	William Winters and consort Elizabeth. The mother.	Aug. 29, 1802.
John Jacob, Dec. 4, 1802.	John Koch and Anna Maria. Nicholas Koch et consort.	Oct. 3, 1802.
Maria Eva, Dec. 4, 1802.	Peter Moser (?) and Catharina Moser. Eva Moser.	March 5, 1802.

The First Reformed Church of Easton, Pa.

Date of Baptism and name of Child.	Names of Parents and Sponsors.	Date of Birth.
Martin, Dec. 26, 1802.	David Losey and Maria. Martin Rau and his wife Fronica.	Feb. 14, 1802.
Christina, Jan. 19, 1803.	Philip Broeder and his wife Christina. The parents.	Dec. 3, 1802.

The following children were baptized:

Date of Baptism and name of Child.	Names of Parents and Sponsors.	Date of Birth.
	ANNO 1802.	
Lydia, March 9, 1802.	Christian Correl and Catharina. Susanna Correl.	Dec. 25, 1801.
Adam, March 17, 1802.	John Sand and wife Magdalena. Adam Sand and Maria.	Jan. 29, 1802.
Peter, April 23, 1802.	Peter Rippel and Maria. Adam Stocker and Barbara.	Feb. 2, 1802.
David, July 1, 1802.	Adam Schuck and Barbara. The parents.	April 2, 1802.
Margaretha, Aug. 29, 1802.	Philip Messinger and wife Margaretha. Jacob Rambach and Marg. Messinger.	Sept. 13, 1801.
Andrew, Sept. 30, 1802.	Frederick Lerch and wife Elizabeth. Valentine Uhler and wife Christina.	May 28, 1802.
Elizabeth, Sept. 30, 1802.	Valentine Uhler and wife Christina. Frederick Lerch and wife Elizabeth.	Aug. 11, 1802.
Charles, Oct. 24, 1802.	George Wolf and wife Maria. Lorentz Erb and wife Maria.	Jan. 1, 1800.

Church Records.   165

Date of Baptism and name of Child.	Names of Parents and Sponsors.	Date of Birth.
Lorentz Erb, Oct. 24, 1802.	Nathan Gulick and wife Elizabeth. Lorentz Erb and wife Maria.	Nov. 22, 1801.
Camilla, Nov. 14, 1802.	John Clemens and wife Maria. David Saylor and wife Elizabeth.	Aug. 21, 1802.
Samuel, Nov. 21, 1802.	William Ennes and Elizabeth. Elizabeth Arndt.	Sept. 8, 1802.
Sophia, Dec. 26, 1802.	William Wite (White?) and wife Susanna. Valentine Weber and wife Catharina.	Oct. 1, 1801.
William, Dec. 27, 1802.	John Philips and wife Hanna. The parents.	Aug. 17, 1799.
Sarah Ann, Dec. 27, 1802.	John Philips and wife Hanna. The parents.	Oct. 24, 1802.
Susanna, Dec. 27, 1802.	John Shoup and wife Elizabeth. The parents.	June 3, 1802.
	1803.	
John, Jan. 31, 1803.	Conrad Schumper and Magdalena. John Wagner and wife.	Dec. 15, 1802.
Catharina, Feb. 27, 1803.	Michael Butz and Catharina. John Mayer and consort.	Dec. 11, 1802.
Carl, March 2, 1803.	John Walter and Elizabeth. The parents.	Jan. 10, 1803.
Aaron, March 8, 1803.	Andrew Koechlein and Susanna. The parents.	Jan. 19, 1803.

Date of Baptism and name of Child.	Names of Parents and Sponsors.	Date of Birth.
Maria Elizabeth, March 20, 1803.	William Woodring and wife Rosina. Philip Woodring and wife Maria Elizabeth.	Feb. 9, 1803.
Sara, March 2, 1803.	Joseph Raesly and wife Anna Maria. John Adam Willauer and wife Elizabeth.	Feb. 2, 1803.
Peter, March 23, 1803.	Henry Reimer and wife Catharina. Peter Lantz and wife Catharina.	Sept. 21, 1802.
Catharina, April 13, 1803.	John Leidig and wife Juliana. Parents.	Sept. 28, 1802.
Susanna, May 15, 1803.	Jacob Kaemrer and wife Magdalena. The parents.	Feb. 13, 1803.
Kornilius (Cornelius), May 15, 1803.	Samuel Kohlman and wife Maria. John Oberly and wife Elizabeth.	Dec. 26, 1802.
Elizabeth, May 15, 1803.	Nicolaus Dietz and wife Sophia. The parents.	Dec. 25, 1802.
Margaretha, May 15, 1803.	John Fehr and wife Eva. Michael Bassler and Marg. ———.	Dec. 15, 1802.
Catharina, May 19, 1803.	Philip Appel and Susanna. Adam Stocker and consort.	Dec. 22, 1802.
John George, May 20, 1803.	Jacob Miller and Maria. George Fox (? blurred) and consort.	April 9, 1802.
Thomas, June 12, 1803.	George Peter Keller and wife Elizabeth. Philip Korrel and wife Elizabeth.	April 20, 1803.

Church Records. 167

Date of Baptism and name of Child.	Names of Parents and Sponsors.	Date of Birth.
John, June 12, 1803.	John Dietz and wife Hanna. The mother.	April 24, 1803.
Lydia, Jan. 26, 1803.	Jacob Fries and Susanna. Michael Fries and consort.	June 2, 1802.
Elizabeth, June 29, 1803.	John Mayer and Margaret. The parents.	May 25, 1803.
Carl, July 10, 1803.	George Reichert and Susanna. Peter Young and Susanna Eyerman.	March 17 (?), 1803.
Elizabeth, July 26, 1803.	Henry Keller and Susanna. Jacob Keller and his wife.	May 28, 1803.
Anna Magd., Aug. 18, 1803.	Thomas Osterstock and wife Catharina. Conrad Jumper and wife Magdalena.	March 11, 1802.
Elizabeth, April 10, 1803.	Jonathan Kohlman and wife Elizabeth. George Adam Yeisley and wife Christina.	Feb. 15, 1803.
Liddia, April 10, 1803.	Christian Metzger and wife Elizabeth. Elizabethet Mzger.	Jan. 17, 1803.
Elizabeth, April 10, 1803.	Philip Frantz and wife Elizabeth. Elizabeth Getter.	Feb. 17, 1803.
Samuel, April 10, 1803.	John Grub and wife Margaretha. Anthony Dech and wife Maria.	Jan. 30, 1803.
David, Sept. 3, 1803.	Matthias Schnabel and wife Catharina. The parents.	June 24, 1803.

Date of Baptism and name of Child.	Names of Parents and Sponsors.	Date of Birth.
Joseph, Sept. 11, 1803.	Henry Klaus and Elizabeth. George Kessler and Maria ——.	April 16, 1803.
Nansy, Sept. 11, 1803.	Jacob Gross and Elizabeth. Matthias Gross and Catharina Young.	June 30, 1803.
Frederick, Oct. 11, 1803.	Jacob Schaeffer and Elizabeth. Frederick Lerch and his wife.	July 5, 1803.
Jonas, Oct. 11, 1803.	John Sand and Magdalena. Conrad Jumper and consort.	Aug. 3, 1803.
Sarah, Oct. 11, 1803.	Bernhard Raub and Maria. Jacob Lattig and consort.	June 30, 1803.
William, Oct. 15, 1803.	Henry Schug and Elizabeth. Christian Metzger and consort.	July 13, 1803.
Abraham, Oct. 30, 1803.	Philip Brotzman and Christina. Abraham Brotzman and Maria, consort.	Aug. 24, 1803.
John, Oct. 31, 1803.	David Marks and Mary. The parents.	Nov. 26, 1802.
Samuel, Nov. 23, 1803.	Christian Kocher and wife Catharina. The parents.	Oct. 25, 1803.
George, Nov. 7, 1803.	George Traxel and Rosina. Maria Wolff.	Aug. 8, 1803.

Church Records.

Date of Baptism and name of Child.	Names of Parents and Sponsors.	Date of Birth.
George William, Nov. 20, 1803. "*Uneheliches.*"	The mother is Catharina Slauch. The grandparents, Philip Schlauch and his worthy wife, have assumed responsibility for the Christian nurture of this child.	Oct. 17, 1803.
Elizabeth, Dec. 4, 1803.	John Dietz and Elizabeth. Elias Scholl and his wife.	Aug. 5, 1803.
David, Dec. 11, 1803.	John Stem and Anna. The parents.	Oct. 23, 1803.
Jacob, Dec. 25, 1803.	John Rambach and wife Maria. Jacob Rambach and wife Elizabeth.	Sept. 16, 1803.
1804.		
Maria, Jan. 10, 1804.	Philip Correll and wife Elizabeth. Maria Correll, the grandmother.	Feb. 7, 1804.[1]
John, Jan. 30, 1804.	Abraham Schmid and Sabilla. Frederick Frutschie and his wife.	Nov. 9, 1803.
Abraham, March 8, 1804.	Conrad Frey and Elizabeth. Philip Klauss et consort.	Jan. 30, 1804.
Anna Marg., March 8, 1804.	Jacob Frauenfelder and wife Catharina. Margaretha Messinger.	Jan. 18, 1804.
John, March 8, 1804.	Thomas Richard and consort. Parents.	Nov. 18, 1803.

[1] Evidently an error in the date—but so it stands on record.

Date of Baptism and name of Child.	Names of Parents and Sponsors.	Date of Birth.
Margaret, April 23, 1804.	Abraham Stem and Charlotte. Conrad Yeisle and Magdalena Stem.	Feb. 25, 1804.
Peter, May 13, 1804.	Conrad Frauenfelder and wife Maria. Frederick Harendorf and Christina Frauenfelder.	March 24, 1804.
Catharina, May 13, 1804.	Jacob Best and wife Catharina. John Odenwaelder and wife Anna Marg.	Jan. 5, 1804.
Michael, May 22, 1804.	George Boyer and wife Anna. Michael Boyer and wife Margaretha.	March 26, 1804.
John, May 27, 1804.	Philip Odenwelder and wife Elizabeth. Nicolaus Koch and Elizabeth.	April 17, 1804.
Daniel, May 27, 1804.	James McDanill and wife Cathrina. John Otto and Susanna Adolf.	April 7, 1804.
Kezia, June 10, 1804.	Jacob Laddig and wife Sarah. The parents.	May 13, 1804.
Maria Magdalena, June 12, 1804.	Jacob Seibel and Maria Magdalena. Jacob Scheib and his wife.	Sept. 5, 1803.
Sara, June 24, 1804.	Michael Traxel and Susanna. The parents.	June 3, 1804.
Christina, July 4, 1804.	John Frey and wife Margaretha. Christina —— (name wanting).	April 7, 1804.

Church Records.

Date of Baptism and name of Child.	Names of Parents and Sponsors.	Date of Birth.
Sara, July 29, 1804.	Abraham Schmid and Barbara. The parents.	May 28, 1804.
Elias, Aug. 5, 1804.	The mother is Susanna Messinger, John Messinger's daughter. Mr. Samuel Ren and his good wife have obligated themselves for the Christian nurture of this child.	Wanting.
John, Aug. 15, 1804.	Nathaniel Marks and his wife Jane. Parents.	Sept. 29, 1803.
Leonhard, Aug. 21, 1804.	George Butz and Susanna. Leonhard Beytelman and consort.	Feb. 7, 1804.
Maria, Sept. 2, 1804.	John Odenwaelder, Jr., and Anna Marg. John Mueller and Sara.	July 27, 1804.
William, Sept. 25, 1804.	Adam Hauck and wife Rebecca. Parents.	Aug. 17, 1803.
Elizabeth, Oct. 28, 1804.	John Lantz and wife Hanna. Peter Lantz and wife Elizabeth.	Sept. 18, 1804.
William, Oct. 28, 1804.	Nicolaus Woodring and wife Catharina. William Woodring and wife Rosina.	Sept. 20, 1804.
Melchior, Dec. 7, 1804.	Melchoir Hay and Elizabeth. Peter Hay et uxor.	Oct. 14, 1804.
Peter, Dec. 9, 1804.	Michael Traxel and Catharina. Andrew Hay et uxor.	Sept. 1, 1804.

Date of Baptism and name of Child.	Names of Parents and Sponsors.	Date of Birth.
Isaac, Jan. 3, 1804.	Joseph Thomas and Margaret. George Scnabel and consort.	July 20, 1804.
Samuel, Nov. 20, 1804.	Peter Bop and Catharina. The parents.	Aug. 3, 1804.
	ANNO 1803.	
Maria, March 15, 1803.	Valentine Mutschler and wife Elizabeth. John Focht and wife Margaretha.	March 6, 1803.
John, March 15, 1803.	William Polen and Christina. Peter Winters.	July 22, 1802.
Elizabeth, March 15, 1802.	Catharina Winters. The grandfather.	Dec. 24, 1802.
Jacob, June 12, 1803.	Abraham Force and wife Hanna. George Barnet and Catharine Herster.	March 6, 1803.
Jacob, July 26, 1803.	Philip Odenwaelder and wife Elizabeth. John Odenwaelder and wife Elizabeth.	June 13, 1803.
Andrew, July 31, 1803.	Henry Stoflet and wife Abalona. Andrew and Juliana Stocker.	March 23, 1803.
Jacob, July 31, 1803.	Peter Reis and wife Susanna. Henry Eyerman and Maria Batt.	June 19, 1803.
Susanna, Sept. 11, 1803.	Henry Winters and wife Susanna. The parents.	Dec. 15, 1801.
Nancy, Sept. 11, 1803.	Henry Winters and wife Susanna. The parents.	March 19, 1803.

Church Records.   173

Date of Baptism and name of Child.	Names of Parents and Sponsors.	Date of Birth.
Sarah, Nov. 7, 1803.	John Simon and wife Susanna. The parents.	Feb. 25, 1802.
Christina, Nov. 7, 1803.	John Simon and wife Susanna. Jacob Sheip and wife Christina.	Oct. 14, 1803.
Anna, Nov. 22, 1803.	Peter Batt and wife Elizabeth. The parents.	Sept. 6, 1803.
Sarah Scott, Nov. 24, 1803.	John Mulhollon and wife Sarah. The mother.	July 1, 1803.
John George, Nov. 27, 1803.	John George Bruch and wife Anna Catharina. John George Bruch and Catharina Keder.	Nov. 3, 1803.
Christina, Nov. 27, 1803.	Henry Walter and wife Elizabeth. George Walter and wife Barbara.	Sept. 16, 1803.
Henry David, Dec. 11, 1803.	John Moritz and wife ———. Daniel Moritz and Maria Wolf.	Nov. 4, 1803.
John George, Jan. 1, 1804.	Christian Correl and wife Catharina. George Peter Kessler and wife Elizabeth.	Feb. 30, 1803.
Peter, Dec. 25, 1803.	John Hay and wife Maria. Peter Hay and wife Barbara.	Oct. 27, 1803.
Levi, Jan. 22, 1804.	Andrew Willauer and wife Elizabeth. Martin Frey and wife Maria Magdalena.	Sept. 31, 1803.
Lydia, Jan. 22, 1804.	Jeremiah Hess and wife Elizabeth. Conrad Hess and wife Elizabeth.	Nov. 9, 1803.

Date of Baptism and name of Child.	Names of Parents and Sponsors.	Date of Birth.
Elizabeth, Jan. 22, 1804.	Conrad Hess and wife Elizabeth. Adam Heckman and wife Elizabeth.	Dec. 15, 1803.
Samuel, Jan. 22, 1804.	William Fitz-Randolf and wife Susanna. Frederick Barthold and wife Elizabeth.	Oct. 24, 1803.
Samuel, Feb. 19, 1804.	Henry Siegraeves and wife Eva. The parents.	March 24, 1803.
Margaretha, March 12, 1803.	The mother is Susanna Rumseld. "*Uneheliches.*" Philip Messinger and wife Margaretha.	Feb. 26, 1803.
Margaretha, April 1, 1804.	Frederick Lerch and wife Elizabeth. Adam Willauer and wife Elizabeth.	Jan. 13, 1804.
Joseph, April 22, 1804.	Michael Sand and wife Maria. Conrad Tschumper[1] and wife Magdalena.	Feb. 14, 1804.
John Jacob, May 5, 1804.	Henry Raub and wife Anna Elizabeth. Adam Schenrer and wife Margaretha.	April 20, 1804.
Maria, June 25, 1804.	John Veidt and wife Catharina. John Young and wife Maria.	March 10, 1804.
Eliza, July 22, 1804.	Henry Schneyder and wife Catharina. The parents.	July 5, 1804.
Carl, July 29, 1804.	John Bruch and wife Catharina. Adam Stenger and wife Catharina.	June 13, 1804.

[1] Jumper! See elsewhere.

Church Records. 175

Date of Baptism and name of Child.	Names of Parents and Sponsors.	Date of Birth.
	ANNO 1805.	
Catherine, Feb. 3, 1805.	Adam Stocker and wife Barbara. Christian Stocker and consort.	Dec. 7, 1804.
Anna Maria, Feb. 9, 1805.	Henry Arnot and Cathrina. Michael Ritter and Maria Pauli.	Jan. 3, 1804.
	ANNO 1804.	
Anna, Aug. 12, 1804.	Andrew Koechlein and Susanna. The parents.	Jan. 26, 1804.
Joseph, Aug. 21, 1804.	George Sewitz and Elizabeth. George Sewitz and Maria.	Sept. 3, 1803.
Andrew, Nov. 11, 1804.	John Neigh and wife Catharina. The mother.	Nov. 22, 1804.
James, Nov. 11, 1804.	Peter Wilson and wife Maria. The parents.	Feb. 24, 1804.
John, Nov. 25, 1804.	Peter Voight and wife Margaretha. John and Margaretha Voight, of Greenwich.	Sept. 23, 1804.
Sarah, Dec. 25, 1804.	Jacob Nicolaus and wife Margaretha. Andrew and Sarah Vogel.	Oct. 27, 1804.

The First Reformed Church of Easton, Pa.

Anno 1805.

[A marginal note, in very fine handwriting, says as follows:]
John Henry Weiss, born April 4, 1804, to Jacob Conrad and consort John Weiss, born June 6, 1800, to John Weiss.

Maria Christina Weiss, born Feb. 21, 1802, to Christian Scheib.

The above children were baptized January 27, 1805.

Date of Baptism and name of Child.	Names of Parents and Sponsors.	Date of Birth.
Harriott, Jan. 6, 1805.	Peter Hauch and wife Margaretha. John Able and Caty Blaeckley.	July 15, 1804.
George Washington, Jan. 20, 1805.	George Wolf,[1] and wife Maria. Lorentz Erb and wife Maria.	Oct. 21, 1804.
Samuel Dickson, Jan. 20, 1805.	Nathan Gulick and wife Elizabeth. Lorentz Erb and wife Maria.	Dec. 13, 1804.
Marietta, Jan. 20, 1805.	Nathan Gulick and wife Elizabeth. Maria Wolf.	Oct. 2, 1803.
Charlotta, Jan. 20, 1805.	Frederick Barthold and wife Elizabeth. Lorentz Erb and Catharine Dreisbach.	March 11, 1804.

[1] Governor of Pennsylvania.

Church Records. 177

Name of Child and Date of Birth and Baptism.	Parents.	Sponsors.
	ANNO 1805.	
Isaiah Buss, Jan. 16, 1804. Jan. 27, 1805.	Abraham and Maria.	The parents.
Jacob Shick, Sept. 7, 1802. Feb. 6, 1805.	Jacob and Elizabeth.	The parents.
Charles Shick, Sept. 14, 1804. Feb. 6, 1805.	Jacob and Elizabeth.	The parents.
Nancy Howell, Feb. 4, 1804. Feb. 6, 1805.	Spencer and Mary.	The mother.
Molly Schister, Dec. 14, 1804. Feb. 12, 1805.	Catharina Roeder.	Peter Roeder and wife Elisabeth.
Joseph Koenig, Nov. 3, 1804. Feb. 12, 1805.	Adam and Catharina.	Isaac Kuhn and wife Elisabeth.
Philip Arndt, March 16, 1804. Feb. 12, 1805.	John and Elisabeth.	The parents.
Jacob Hackman, Nov. 12, 1804. Feb. 12, 1805.	Abraham and Salome.	John Simon and wife Susanna.
Jacob Yeisley, Nov. 25, 1804. Feb. 16, 1805.	Nicolaus and Sarah.	Jacob Lautz and Maria Richard.
Margaretha Kocher, Nov. 26, 1804. Feb. 16, 1805.	Henry and Maria.	John Kocher and Barbara Biesecker.
Thomas Shuck, Dec. 17, 1804. March 6, 1805.	Adam and Barbara.	The parents.
William Woodring, Feb. 3, 1805. April 12, 1805.	William and Rosina.	Philip Brotsman and wife Christina.
John Andrew Koch, Jan. 8 (1805). April 12, 1805.	John and Anna Maria.	George Braucker and wife Elisabeth.

178 The First Reformed Church of Easton, Pa.

Name of Child and Date of Birth and Baptism.	Parents.	Sponsors.
Elisabeth Kocher, Dec. 17, 1804. April 14, 1805.	Abraham and Susanna.	Antony Lerch and Elisabeth Edelman.
Catharina Messinger, Jan. 6 (1805). April 14, 1805.	Jacob and Anna Maria.	Jacob Frauenfeld and wife Catharina.
Lydia Kotz, Jan. 11, 1805. April 14, 1805.	Henry and wife Charity.	Philip Metzgar ―― ―― Kotz.
Elisabeth Schuman, March 19. April 14, 1805.	William and wife Christiana.	Frederick Huttendorf and Elisabeth Kreider.
Elisabeth Krotz, Jan. 19. April 14, 1805.	John and Catharina.	Peter Rippel and wife Margaretha.
Elisabeth Stemm, Jan. 13. April 15, 1805.	John and Anna.	The parents.
Catharine Beischer, Feb. 11, 1804. May 4, 1805.	Jacob and Catharina.	Molly Beischer.
Susanna Dieterich, Jan. 12, 1805. Apr. 29, 1805.	Jacob and Sarah.	The parents.
George Seipel, Feb. 8, 1805. May 12, 1805.	Jacob and Elisabeth.	George Seipel, Sr.
Philip Reimer, Dec. 29, 1804. June 15, 1805.	Henry and Catharina.	Philip Correll and wife Elisabeth.
Samuel Koleman, March 14, 1805. June 23, 1805.	Samuel and Maria.	John Oberly and Phoeby Coleman.
Elisabeth Schuesser, Feb. 19, 1805. June 23, 1805.	Jacob and Elisabeth.	The parents.
Matilda Meixsell, March 10, 1805. June 23, 1805.	Philip and wife Maria.	The father and the grandmother.

Church Records.

Name of Child and Date of Birth and Baptism.	Parents.	Sponsors.
Carl Sand, May 5, 1805. June 30, 1805.	John and Magdalena.	Christian Correll and wife Catharina.
William Leidich, Oct. 21, 1804. June 30, 1805.	John and Juliana.	The parents.
Sophia Gery, Jan. 2, 1805. June 30, 1805.	John and Christina.	John Leidich and wife Juliana.
George Schneyder, June 27, 1804. July 11, 1805.	William and Margaretha.	The parents.
David Haack, March 19, 1805. July 21, 1805.	Adam and wife Rebecca.	The parents.
Sarah Abel, May 12, 1805. July 21, 1805.	Henry and Maria.	Jacob Rambach and Sarah Messinger.
Catharina Bruch, Dec. 4, 1804. July 24, 1805.	Frederick and Catharina.	Adam Stenger and wife Catharina.
Margaretha Schumacher, June 27, 1805. Aug. 4.	Isaac and Catharina.	Jacob Schumacher and wife Elisabeth.
John Peter Lumerson, Feb. 1, 1805. June 30.	John and Elsie.	The parents.
Edward Hertzel, Jan. 18, 1805. Aug. 9.	Jacob and Catharina.	The parents.
Susanna Broeder, April 3, 1805. Aug. 9, 1805.	Philip and Christina.	The parents.
Lydia Kind, June 14, 1805. Aug. 14, 1805.	Isaac and Elisabeth.	Michael Messinger and wife Elisabeth.
Henry Kieffer, Oct. 28, 1804. Aug. 18, 1805.	John and Catharina.	The parents.

The First Reformed Church of Easton, Pa.

Name of Child and Date of Birth and Baptism.	Parents.	Sponsors.
Maria Anna Rinker, June 22, 1805. Aug. 18, 1805.	John and Sarah.	Jacob Sickman and wife Elisabeth.
Elisabeth Mechlin, July 2, 1805. Aug. 21, 1805.	John and Margaretha.	John Dech and wife Elisabeth.
Anna Thron, May 22, 1805. Aug. 21, 1805.	Matthias and Anna.	John Mechlin and wife Margaretha.
Elisabeth Abel, March 28, 1804. Aug. 22, 1805.	Michael and Maria.	The parents.
Hanna Keller, June 14, 1805. Aug. 19, 1805.	Henry and Susanna.	John Stemm and consort.
Peter Schneyder, Aug. 31, 1804. Aug. 30, 1805.	John and Catharina.	Abraham and wife Barbara.
Peter Hertzel, July 11, 1805. Sept. 1, 1805.	John and Elisabeth.	Andrew Kieffer and Elisabeth.
Maria Young, May 5, 1805. Sept. 1, 1805.	John and Susanna.	The parents.
John Reis, Aug. 2, 1805. Sept. 1, 1805.	Peter and Susanna.	The parents.
John Young, June 1, 1803. Date wanting.	John and Susanna.	Peter Young and Susanna Young.
John Boyer, Aug. 12, 1805. Oct. 2, 1805.	John and Catharina.	John Knecht and Margaretha.
Sarah, July 31, 1804. Oct. 8, 1805.	The mother, Rosina Schuck.	Maria Lucker.
Jesse Riegel, July 6, 1805. Oct. 8, 1805.	Benjamin and Hanna.	Abraham Vogel and wife Abbie.

Church Records. 181

Name of Child and Date of Birth and Baptism.	Parents.	Sponsors.
Susanna Schubb, July 18, 1805. Oct. 11, 1805.	Jacob and Maria.	Catharina Westerman.
Sarah Ettinger, Aug. 10, 1805. Oct. 21, 1805.	Henry and Eva.	The mother.
Peter Rieser, July 18, 1805. Oct. 21, 1805.	Peter and Maria.	The parents.
Andrew Ripple, Oct. 21, 1805. Baptized *eodem die*.	Peter and Margaretha.	Andrew Ripple and consort.
Sophia Schneyder, July 1, 1805. Oct. 27, 1805.	Henry and Catharine.	Jacob Schick and Elisabeth.
Philippina Kohlman, July 2, 1805. Oct. 27, 1805.	Jonathan and Elisabeth.	Andrew Moser and Philippina Kohlman.
Catharine Mueller, Oct. 4, 1805. Nov. 10, 1805.	Jacob and Maria.	Henry Geiding (?) and wife.
Philippina Uhler, Sept. 22, 1805. Nov. 18, 1805.	Jacob and Margaretha.	Abraham Messinger and Cath. Uhler.
Elizabeth Frees, Oct. 4, 1805. Nov. 21, 1805.	Jacob and Susanna.	John Kaemmerer and wife Elisabeth.
Magdalena Koenig, Sept. 27, 1805. Nov. 29, 1805.	Jacob and Elisabeth.	The parents.
Karl Koch, Sept. 29, 1805. Dec. 1, 1805.	Jacob and Elisabeth.	Nicolaus Koch and consort.
John Walter, July 31, 1805. Dec. 16, 1805.	John and Elisabeth.	The parents.
Joseph Trumheller, Nov. 13, 1805. Dec. 22, 1805.	Philip and Nancy.	Peter Jacoby and Elisabeth Rodenbach.

182 *The First Reformed Church of Easton, Pa.*

Name of Child and Date of Birth and Baptism.	Parents.	Sponsors.
John Frauenfelder, Oct. 14, 1805. Dec. 22, 1805.	Jacob and Catharina.	Jacob Frauenfelder and Anna Cath.
Liddiana Schuck, July 20, 1805. Dec. 22, 1805.	Henry and Elisabeth.	Philip Correl and wife Elisabeth.
ANNO 1806.		
Maria Heller, Nov. 8, 1805. Jan. 5, 1806.	Jacob and Susanna.	George Heller and Maria Schneyder.
William White, Oct. 28, 1805. Jan. 12, 1806.	William and Susanna.	John Nicolas, Jr., and wife Sarah.
Thos. Willauer, Sept. 17, 1805. Jan. 13, 1806.	Adam and Elisabeth.	Henry Werkhauser and wife Elisabeth.
Anna Catharina, Jan. 14, 1806. Feb. 2, 1806.	Margaret Withus (?).	Catharine Nicolaus.
Carl Ritter, Jan. 12, 1806. } ? Jan. 5, 1806. }	Michael and Margaretha.	Henry Arner and consort.
Maria Magd. Odenwaelder, Dec. 29, 1805. Feb. 16, 1806.	Philip and Elisabeth.	Bernd. Odenwaelder and Maria Magd. Koch.
Henry Forse, Jan. 10, 1806. March 1, 1806.	Abraham and Hanna.	The parents.
Charles Deshler, Feb. 27, 1806. March 1, 1806.	Adam and Debora.	The father.
Joh. George Raub, March 16, 1805. March 15, 1806.	Bernhart and Maria.	George William Raub and Catharina.
Jacob Frauenfelder, Dec. 20, 1805. March 16, 1806.	Conrad and Maria.	John Stecher and wife Catharina.
Sophia Schick, March 3, 1804. March 16, 1806.	John and Jane.	The parents.

Church Records. 183

Name of Child and Date of Birth and Baptism.	Parents.	Sponsors.
Sarah Schick, Jan. 31, 1806. March 16, 1806.	John and Jane.	The parents.
Elisabeth Koechlein, Feb. 16, 1806. March 30, 1806.	Andrew and Susanna.	Peter Koechlein and Catharina.
Susanna Mueller, Feb. 25, 1806. March 7, 1806.	Peter and Maria Christina.	Jacob Scheib and consort.
Maria Elis. Woodring, March 5, 1806. March 30, 1806.	Jacob and Elisabeth.	Philip Woodring and wife.
Joseph Sand, March 8, 1806. April 10, 1806.	Michael and Anna Maria.	The parents.
Susanna Wilhelmina Pomp, March 29, 1806. April 7, 1806.	Thomas and Catharina.	The father and Wilhelmina Mattes (?).
Samuel Snouer Schlough, Feb. 10, 1806. April 20, 1806.	George and Anne.	The parents.
James Davidson Winters, Feb. 19, 1806. Feb. 20, 1806.	Henry and Susan.	The parents.
Franz Schmidt, March 27, 1806. May 18, 1806.	Abraham and Barbara.	The parents.
Michael Hahn, March 14, 1806. April 27, 1806.	Hartman and Catharina.	Henry and Susanna Yaeger (?).
Jacob Labach, March 12, 1806. April 27, 1806.	Adam and Catharina.	Catharina Labach.
Elisabeth Dotterer, Oct. 26, 1802. June 1, 1806.	Henry and Nancy.	Elisabeth Young.

Name of Child and Date of Birth and Baptism.	Parents.	Sponsors.
Davis Henry Dotterer, Nov. 4, 1805. June 1, 1805 (1806?).	Henry and Nancy.	Elisabeth Dechart.
Daniel Odenwaelder, April 2, 1806. June 8, 1806.	Philip Junior and Elisabeth.	John and Margaret Odenwaelder.
Juliana Kaemrer, Feb. 12, 1806. June 8, 1806.	Jacob and Magdalena.	The parents.
George Flory Diets, March 27, 1806. June 8, 1806.	Nicolaus and Sophia.	The parents.
Rosina Woodring, June 10, 1806. July 20, 1806.	Abraham and Margaretha.	William Woodring and consort.
Markleir (?) Luckar, March 7, 1806. July 12, 1806.	James Luckar and wife Maria.	The parents.
Sophia Luckar, June 9, 1803. July 12, 1806.	James Luckar and wife Maria.	The parents.
John Luckar, Feb. 9, 1801. July 12, 1806.	James Luckar and wife Maria.	The parents.
Edward Traxsell, June 12, 1806. July 27, 1806.	Michael and Susanna.	The parents.
Carl Bishoph, June 3, 1806. Aug. 3, 1806.	John and Anna.	The parents.
Margaretha Wall, March 18, 1806. Aug. 3, 1806.	Daniel and Maria.	The parents.
John Barnett, March 12, 1806. July 20, 1806.	Thomas and Catharine.	Philip Schlough and wife Catharine.
Susanna Laddig, July 5, 1806. Aug. 3, 1806.	John Jacob and Sara.	The parents.

Church Records. 185

Name of Child and Date of Birth and Baptism.	Parents.	Sponsors.
William Traxsell, Dec. 6, 1802. Aug. 22, 1806.	John and Elisabeth.	The parents.
Lorentz Traxsell, Nov. 28, 1804. Aug. 22, 1806.	John and Elisabeth.	The parents.
Maria Traxsell, March 30, 1806. Aug. 10, 1806.	George and Rosina.	Michael Seip and consort.
Rachel Messinger, May 7, 1805. Aug. 24, 1806.	Philip and Margaretha.	Adam Stecher and wife Margaretha.
David Zerfass, June 8, 1806. Aug. 26, 1806.	John and Susanna.	Bernhard Arndt.
Christina Stocker, Aug. 8, 1806. Sept. 21, 1806.	Adam and Barbara.	Matthias Stecher and wife Elizabeth.
Lehnhard Beitelman, Aug. 15, 1806. Sept. 21, 1806.	Elias and Catharina.	David Beitelman and Margaretha.
John Mayer, Aug. 15, 1806. Sept. 21, 1806.	John and Margaretha.	The parents.
David McDannold, Aug. 15, 1806. Sept. 28, 1806.	James and Catharina.	Philip Heil and wife Susanna.
Peter Rippel, Aug. 10, 1806. Sept. 28, 1806.	Peter and Margaretha.	Peter Gross.
Carl Engel, July 19, 1806. Oct. 5, 1806.	Christopher and Susanna.	Henry Eyerman and Elisabeth Herster.
John Osterstock, Sept. 9, 1806. Oct. 12, 1806.	Abraham and Charlotte.	Peter and Rosina Osterstock.
Carl Reis, Aug. 20, 1806. Oct. 26, 1806.	John and Catharina.	Jacob Stocker and wife.

186   *The First Reformed Church of Easton, Pa.*

Name of Child and Date of Birth and Baptism.	Parents.	Sponsors.
Margaretha Zimmerman, March 31, 1806. Oct. 31, 1806.	Abraham and Nancy.	The parents.
John Schlough, Nov. 6, 1806. Nov. 10, 1806.	John and Susanna.	The parents.
Jacob Baeysher, Feb. 7, 1806. Nov. 18, 1806.	Jacob and Catharina.	John Wagner and wife Eva.
Ann Jane Justice, Oct. 6, 1805. Nov. 21, 1806.	Philip and Elisabeth.	The parents.
Margaretha Traxsell, Oct. 31, 1806. Nov. 23, 1806.	Michael and Catharina.	Carl Hay and Elisabeth Hay.
Maria Marg. Rees, Nov. 19, 1806. Nov. 25, 1806.	John and Maria.	Philip Zeller and wife Margaretha.
Harriott Eringer, Sept. 5, 1805. Nov. 25, 1806.	Frederick and Elisabeth.	The parents.
Julianna Zeller, Dec. 31, 1805. Nov. 25, 1806.	Jacob and Elisabeth.	The parents.
Robert Frytag Groves, May 9, 1806. Nov. 25, 1806.	Robert and Christiana Elisabeth.	Michael Frytag and the mother.
Susanna Weber, Sept. 17, 1805. Nov. 30, 1806.	William and Elizabeth.	Frederick Philip and Hanna Tschudi (?).
John Hay, Aug. 30, 1806. Dec. 7, 1806.	Melchior and Elisabeth.	John Seib and wife Catharina.
John Ettinger, Nov. 18, 1806. Dec. 16, 1806.	Henry and Eva.	Christian Correl and wife.
Sarah Holland, Oct. 22, 1806. Dec. 15, 1806.	Peter and Susanna.	Peter Kessler and wife.

Church Records. 187

Name of Child and Date of Birth and Baptism.	Parents.	Sponsors.
Carl Simon, Dec. 12, 1806. Dec. 18, 1806.	Michael and Maria.	Catharine Weygandt.
John Peter Kocher, July 23, 1806. Sept. 8, 1806.	Conrad and Elisabeth.	The parents.
Maria Lantz, Nov. 23, 1806. Dec. 25, 1806.	John and Hanna.	Abraham Hertzel and wife Christina.
Peter Raesly, Sept. 1, 1806. Dec. 28, 1806.	John and Magdalena.	Adam Sand and wife Maria.
Jacob Oehler, Dec. 1, 1806. Dec. 28, 1806.	Abraham and Maria.	The parents.
George Jumper, Nov. 7, 1806. Dec. 28, 1806.	Conrad and Magdalena.	Henry Raesly and Christina Hurtendorf.
Dibbe Shuck, Oct. 30, 1806. Dec. 28, 1806.	Peter and Susanna.	Michael Sand and Maria.
	Anno 1807.	
Juliana Stocker, Dec. 7, 1806. Jan. 11, 1807.	Daniel and Christina.	Juliana Stocker.
Jacob Shaeffer, Oct. 11, 1806. Jan. 18, 1807.	Jacob and Elisabeth.	Rudolph Schweitzer and wife Barbara.
Elias Shuman, Dec. 4, 1806. Jan. 25, 1807.	William and Christina.	The parents.
Robert Ennes, Oct. 21, 1806. Feb. 3, 1807.	Robert and Catharine.	The parents.
Maria Marks, Feb. 25, 1806. Feb. 9, 1807.	Nathaniel and Rachel.	The parents

Name of Child and Date of Birth and Baptism.	Parents.	Sponsors.
Maria Mill, Sept. 30, 1806. Feb. 9, 1807.	Jacob and Hannah.	Maria Persil.
Simon Kaemrer, Jan. 3, 1807. March 1, 1807.	David and Anna.	George Messinger and Elisabeth.
Samuel Traxsell, May 4, 1807 (?). March 1, 1807.	Jacob and Maria.	The parents.
Elisabeth Romig, Feb. 23, 1807. March 15, 1807.	Jacob and Rosina.	Andrew Stocker and wife Juliana.
Daniel Odenwaelder, Feb. 20, 1807. April 12, 1807.	John and Anna Margaret.	John Kind and Anna Margaretha.
Samuel Kocher, Nov. 8, 1806. April 12, 1807.	Conrad and Elizabeth.	The parents.
Christina Preice (?). Feb. 4, 1807. April 12, 1807.	Frederick and Maria.	Andrew Stocker.
Anna Kotz, Nov. 6, 1806. April 17, 1807.	Henry and Charity.	The parents.
Carl Abel, Aug. 8, 1806. April 21, 1807.	Michael and Maria.	Nicholas Koch and Elisabeth.
George Schweitzer, Nov. 22, 1806. April 21, 1807.	John and Margaretha.	George Stecher and wife.
George Rieser, Jan. 6, 1807. April 26, 1807.	Philip and Christina.	Rudolph Schweitzer and consort.
Christina Woodring, April 4, 1807. May 10, 1807.	John and Elisabeth.	Christina Laddig.
Edward Fitz-Randolph, May 6, 1807. May 10, 1807.	William and Susanna.	Edward Lacky and wife Maria.

Church Records.

Name of Child and Date of Birth and Baptism.	Parents.	Sponsors.
David Emig, Dec. 29, 1806. May 10, 1807.	George and Magdalena.	The parents.
Philippina Townson, March 5, 1807. May 14, 1807.	Joseph and Margaretha.	The parents.
Scharlotte Pentz, March 2, 1807. May 17, 1807.	Jacob and Rosina.	Andrew Hay and wife Elisabeth.
Catharina Hauch, Aug. 4, 1806. May 17, 1807.	Peter and Margaretha.	The parents.
Elisabeth Sitgreaves, April 4, 1807. May 17, 1807.	Henry and Eva.	Andrew Hay and wife Elisabeth.
Jesse Schuck, April 14, 1807. May 17, 1807.	Adam and Barbara.	The parents.
Thomas Palmer, April 6, 1807. May 17, 1807.	Daniel and Christina.	Henry Schuck and wife Elisabeth.
Michael Messinger, Dec. 31, 1805. May 18, 1807.	Michael and Elisabeth.	Michael Schwartz and consort.
Rebecca Weis, Feb. 28, 1806. May 25, 1807.	Matthias and Christina.	Rebecca Ludwig.
Catharina Metzger, Feb. 5, 1807. May 29, 1807.	Philip and Margaret.	Barbara Metzger.
David Walter, March 1, 1807. May 31, 1807.	George and Sarah.	Jacob Schumacher and consort.
Rosina Yeisley, May 1, 1807. June 7, 1807.	Nicholas and Sarah.	John Richard and wife Susanna.
Sarah Reimer, April 26, 1807. June 21, 1807.	Henry and Catharine.	Christina Correll and Catharine Correll.

Name of Child and Date of Birth and Baptism.	Parents.	Sponsors.
Maria Magd. Heller, April 16, 1807. June 28, 1807.	George and Susanna.	David Beitelman and wife Marg.
Rosina Stocker, June 16, 1807. June 28, 1807.	Andrew and Magdalena.	Adrew Stocker and Juliana.
Catharina Sacks, Nov. 6, 1806. July 3, 1807.	William and Catharine.	The parents.
David Heinlein, April 27, 1807. July 5, 1807.	George and Elisabeth.	John Best and wife Magdalena.
Catharine Klein, May 23, 1807. July 5, 1807.	David and Elisabeth.	The parents.
George Forse, July 11, 1807. July 16, 1807.	Abraham and Hanna.	The parents.
John Carl Meixsell, Jan. 6, 1807. July 19, 1807.	Christopher and Elisabeth.	John Bernd and wife Elena.
Susanna Frees, July 2, 1807. Aug. 2, 1807.	Jacob and Susanna.	Jacob Schnyder and wife Anna Maria.
Thomas Schuck Anthony, July 9, 1807. Aug. 16, 1807.	Henry and Sarah.	John Traxell and Elisabeth.
Christina Leidig, April 5, 1807. Aug. 16, 1807.	John and Juliana.	The parents.
Elisabeth Gery, Oct. 7, 1806. Aug. 16, 1807.	John and Christina.	Charles Hay and wife Elisabeth.
Henry Sperring Traxell. March, 1807. Aug. 16, 1807.	John and Elisabeth.	Henry Anthony and wife Sarah
Elisabeth Digeman, March 10, 1806. Aug. 23, 1807.	John and Rebecca.	The parents.

Church Records.

Name of Child and Date of Birth and Baptism.	Parents.	Sponsors.
John Peter Belles, March 23, 1807. Aug. 22, 1807.	Amos and Osina.	The parents.
Elisabeth Horn, July 23, 1807. Aug. 23, 1807.	John and Elisabeth.	The parents.
Susanna Woodring, July 27, 1807. Aug. 30, 1807.	William and Rosina.	The parents.
John Carl Seip, June 22, 1807. Aug. 30, 1807.	Jacob and Susan.	John Brotzman and wife Elisabeth.
Henry Schnyder, July 29, 1807. Aug. 30, 1807.	Henry and Catharine.	The parents.
Regina Heckman, Feb. 27, 1807. Aug. 30, 1807.	George and Maria.	Adam Heckman and wife Elisabeth.
Carl Biers, Aug. 6, 1807. Sept. 6, 1807.	George and Elisabeth.	Adam Wagner and wife Regina.
Mary Smith Dietz, Jan. 6, 1807. Sept. 6, 1807.	Peter and Christina.	The parents.
Daniel Wagoner Mixsell, Jan. 4, 1807. Sept. 14, 1807.	Philip and Maria.	The parents.
Daniel Wagoner Burk, April 22, 1807. Sept. 14, 1807.	Joseph and Susanna.	The parents.
Anna Mira Lucker, May 29, 1807. Sept. 22, 1807.	James and Maria.	Elisabeth Carey.
Elisabeth Platz, July 16, 1803. Feb. 18, 1807.	Thomas and (wanting).	The parents.
Philip Platz, Jan. 24, 1804. Feb. 18, 1807.	Thomas and (wanting).	The parents.

Name of Child and Date of Birth and Baptism.	Parents.	Sponsors.
Aaron Platz, Dec. 24, 1806. Feb. 18, 1807.	Thomas and (wanting).	The parents.
Charles Frey, Feb. 17, 1807. March 22, 1807.	Jacob and Maria.	The parents.
Charles, Jan. 19, 1807. Mar. 22, 1807.	Sarah Schiffer.	The grandfather, Conrad Schiffer, has obligated himself for the Christian nurture of this child.
Elisabeth, Feb. 2, 1809. March 4, 1809.	David Kaemmerer and Anna.	Christian Laabach and consort Elisabeth.
John Philip (?) Dodendorf, Aug. 15, 1807. Oct. 11, 1807.	John Andrew and Teresia.	Sarah Arndt.
Horace Erb Wolf, May 16, 1807. Oct. 11, 1807.	George and Maria.	Lawrence Erb.
Rachel Gulick, Sept. 26, 1807. Oct. 11, 1807.	Nathan and Elisabeth.	Maria Erb.
Simon Buss, June 29, 1807. Oct. 13, 1807.	Abraham and Maria.	The parents.
Abraham Hilliart, Jan. 27, 1807. Oct. 13, 1807.	Abraham and ———	Magdalena Kloeman.
Sarah Riegel, March 13, 1807. Oct. 13, 1807.	Benjamin and Anna.	John Reidenauer and wife Sarah.
John Hackman, Oct. 9, 1807. Oct. 23, 1807.	Jacob and Elisabeth.	Thomas Richard and wife Susanna.
Daniel Moser, March 20, 1807. Nov. 13, 1807.	Tobias and Christina.	Daniel Claus and wife Dorothea.

Church Records. 193

Name of Child and Date of Birth and Baptism.	Parents.	Sponsors.
Maria Anna Correll, Sept. 7, 1807. Nov. 15, 1807.	Henry and Elisabeth.	The parents.
John Serrels, June 24, 1807. Dec. 20, 1807.	James and Margaret.	Isaac Stine and Barbara Stofflet.
Sandy Shuck, Sept. 7, 1807. Nov. 22, 1807.	Henry and Elisabeth.	The parents.
ANNO 1808.		
John Morgan Ewing, Sept. 16, 1804. Jan. 3, 1808.	John and Magdalena.	The father.
Joseph Ewing, Feb. 20, 1807. Jan. 2, 1808.	John and Magdalena.	The father.
Andrew Horatio Reeder,[1] July 12, 1807. Jan. 10, 1808.	Absolom and Christina.	The parents.
Susanna Lerch, Dec. 30, 1807. Feb. 3, 1808.	Frederick and Elisabeth.	The parents.
Thomas Richard, Jan. 9, 1808. Feb. 8, 1808.	Thomas and Susan.	The parents.
William Stem, Jan. 11, 1808. Feb. 14, 1808.	Abraham and Charlotte.	John Otto and Elisabeth Hertzel.
Susanna Lerch, Jan. 26, 1808. March 5, 1808.	Anthony and Catharina.	Peter Dreisbach and wife Susanna.
Susanna Messinger, Jan. 27, 1808. March 6, 1808.	Michael and Elisabeth.	Henry Uhler and wife Hanna.

[1] Afterward the first Governor of Kansas.

Name of Child and Date of Birth and Baptism.	Parents.	Sponsors.
Elisabeth Odenwaelder, Jan. 16, 1808. March 10, 1808.	Philip and Elisabeth.	Henry Uhler and wife Hanna.
Maria Lerch, Feb. 26, 1808. March 13, 1808.	John and Regina.	Michael Messinger and Elisabeth Schweitzer.
George Schmidt, March 2, 1808. March 19, 1808.	Frans and Maria.	George Wagner (?) and Elisabeth Eichman.
George Butz, Jan. 10, 1808. March 13, 1808.	Michael and Margaretha.	Jacob Seipel and wife Elisabeth.
Susannah Edelman, Jan. 25, 1808. March 27, 1808.	Adam and Maria.	John Felix Lynn and wife Elisabeth.
Elisabeth Odenwaelder, March 18, 1808. May 8, 1808.	Bernhard and Sarah.	John Odenwaelder, Sr., and wife Elisabeth.
Maria Christ. Wagner, Feb. 25, 1808. May 8, 1808.	Matthias and Margaret.	Peter Miller and Maria Elisabeth.
Sophia Kaemmerer, Dec. 24, 1807. May 8, 1808.	Jacob and Magdalena.	The parents.
Juliana Hortendorf, April 10, 1808. May 8, 1808.	Frederick and Eva.	Jacob Katz and Christina Hortendorf.
Sarah Krotz, Feb. 1, 1808. May 8, 1808.	John and Catharina.	Isaac Krotz and wife Hanna.
Margaretha Messinger, June 22, 1807. May 8, 1808.	Jacob and Maria.	Jacob Schmidt and wife Elisabeth.
Carl Heller, Dec. 2, 1807. May 8, 1808.	(Wanting.)	(Wanting.)

Name of Child and Date of Birth and Baptism.	Parents.	Sponsors.
Maria Cath. Pomp, April 21, 1808. May 8, 1808.	Thomas and Maria Catharina.	The parents.
Cath. Werkhaeuser, March 29, 1808. May 11, 1808.	Jacob and Salome.	Henry Schuck and wife Elisabeth.
Elisabeth Messinger, May 27, 1804. May 11, 1808.	Michael and Elisabeth.	Valentine and wife Christina.
Carl Messinger, April 16, 1808. June 5, 1808.	Abraham and Margaret.	Fred. Schweitzer and Maria Messinger.
George Frauenfelder, Sept. 6, 1807. June 5, 1808.	Jacob and Catharina.	Elick Brown and wife Sarah.
Peter Frauenfelder, Jan. 4, 1808. June 5, 1808.	Conrad and Maria.	Henry Shuck and wife Elisabeth.
John Beitelman. March 2, 1808. June 5, 1808.	Lehnhart and Hannah.	John Sand and wife Molly.
Sophia Dietz, March 15, 1808. June 5, 1808.	Nicholas and Sophia.	The parents.
David Koenig, April 12, 1808. June 10, 1808.	Jacob and Elisabeth.	The parents.
John Appel, Feb. 23, 1808. June 10, 1808.	Andrew and Elisabeth.	John Nusbickel and Margaret Eckart.
Carl Broeder, March 17, 1808. June 24, 1808.	Philip and Christina.	The parents.
Andrew Koechlein, April 24, 1808. July 3, 1808.	Andrew and Susanna.	The parents.
Margaret Worman, Jan. 20, 1808. July 3, 1808.	John and Jane.	Cath. Sommer.

Name of Child and Date of Birth and Baptism.	Parents.	Sponsors.
Henry Bishoff, May 2, 1808. July 3, 1808.	John and Anna.	The parents.
Michael Schubert Miller. July 16, 1807. July 3, 1808.	John and Rachel.	Barbara Hemp.
Anna Oberly, Nov. 7, 1807. Dec. 25, 1807.	Rudolph and Barbara.	George Bayer and wife Anna.
Susanna Young, April 25, 1808. July 17, 1808.	John and Susanna.	The parents.
Catharine Herman, Jan. 10, 1808. Aug. 5, 1808.	Frederick and Catharine.	The parents.
Anna Maria Schwartz, Feb. 19, 1806. Aug. 13, 1807.	Michael and Barbara.	The mother.
Elias Messinger, Aug. 8, 1806. Aug. 13, 1808.	Jacob and Maria.	The mother.
Jacob Messinger, April 28, 1808. Aug. 13, 1808.	Jacob and Maria.	Jacob Werkhaeuser and wife Sarah.
Hannah, May 13, 1808. Aug. 23, 1808.	Hannah Dietz.	James McDaniel and wife Catharine.
Maria Anna Junker,[1] June 28, 1808. Aug. 21, 1808.	George and Elisabeth.	Godfrey Belling and wife Maria.
Rebecca Laddig, July 15, 1808. Aug. 28, 1808.	Jacob and Sarah.	The parents.
Cath. Marg. Schlauch, April 7, 1808. Aug. 28, 1808.	George and Anna.	Philip Schlauch and wife Maria Catharine.

[1] Yunker.

Name of Child and Date of Birth and Baptism.	Parents.	Sponsors.
Sarah Cath. Engel, July 21, 1808. Aug. 28, 1808.	Christoph and Susanna.	Christian Correll and wife Catharine.
Jacob Stemm, March 13, 1808. Aug. 28, 1808.	John and Anna.	Jacob Keller and wife Elisabeth.
Sarah Simon, March 24, 1808. Sept. 11, 1808.	Michael and Maria.	The parents.
Peter Diemer, March 9, 1807. Sept. 14, 1808.	Benjamin and Sarah.	Peter Saylor and wife Anna Marg.
Anna Maurer, July 21, 1808. Sept. 14, 1808.	Peter and Anna Marg.	Anna Uhler.
Jacob Leibert, Aug. 12, 1808. Sept. 18, 1808.	John and Magdalena.	Melchior Ettinger and wife Barbara.
David Traxsell, Aug. 17, 1808. Sept. 25, 1808.	George and Rosina.	The father and Cath. Sommer.
Christina Kleider, Aug. 17, 1808. Oct. 11, 1808.	Abraham and Elisabeth.	The parents.
William Fitz-Randolph, Aug. 6, 1808. Oct. 15, 1808.	William and Susanna.	Charlotte Fitz-Randolph.
Thomas Shnyder, Oct. 4, 1808. Oct. 18, 1808.	Henry and Catharine.	The parents.
Eve Cath. Depue, Sept. 24, 1808. Oct. 26, 1808.	Benjamin and Elisabeth.	Philip Trach and wife Eva.
Catharine Raesley, Sept. 28, 1808. Nov. 4, 1808.	Joseph and Anna Maria.	George Stecher and wife Catharine.
Paul Moser, Sept. 5, 1808. Nov. 13, 1808.	Paul and Maria.	Frans Stocker and Susan Deily.

The First Reformed Church of Easton, Pa.

Name of Child and Date of Birth and Baptism.	Parents.	Sponsors.
Dorothea Stocker, Oct. 31, 1808. Nov. 13, 1808.	Adam and Barbara.	George Stecher and Barbara Stofflet.
Charles Deschler Horn, July 22, 1808. Nov. 21, 1808.	Charles and Elisabeth.	Charles Deshler and Barbara Wagoner.
George W. Fraes,[1] June 3, 1808. Nov. 24, 1808.	Henry and Elisabeth.	The parents.
David Odenwaelder, Aug. 2, 1808. Nov. 25, 1808.	Philip and Elisabeth.	John Best, Jr., and wife Elisabeth.
John P. Moyer, Oct. 5, 1808. Dec. 5, 1808.	William and Anna Maria.	John Peter Saylor and wife Anna Marg.
Thomas Moser, Nov. 9, 1808. Dec. 20, 1808.	Andrew and Cath.	Thomas Nicum (?) and Elisabeth.
ANNO 1809.		
Susan Koechlein, Dec. 22, 1808. Jan. 7, 1809.	Peter and Catharine.	Andrew Koechlein and Elisabeth.
Adde Arner, Nov. 10, 1808. Jan. 24, 1809.	Henry and Catharine.	Joseph Sand (?) and Barb. Huber.
John Holland, Jan. 9, 1809. Feb. 9, 1809.	Peter and Susanna.	John Correll and Elisabeth Kessler.
Henry Hess, Nov. 12, 1808. Feb. 11, 1809.	Frederick and Catharine.	Henry Schaerer and wife Cath.
Abraham Shaerer, Jan. 28, 1809. Feb. 11, 1809.	Henry and Maria.	Abraham Schaerer and Sarah Hess.

[1] The first instance of an *initial* in the name.

Church Records.

Name of Child and Date of Birth and Baptism.	Parents.	Sponsors.
Anna Maria Hayden, April 17, 1806. Feb. 12, 1809.	Isaac and Margaretha.	Philip Schlauch and wife Catharine.
Anna Cath. Hayden, July 16, 1808. Feb. 12, 1809.	Isaac and Margaretha.	Philip Schlauch and wife Catharine.
George Gehry, Nov. 15, 1808. Feb. 19, 1809.	John and Christina.	John Gehry, Sr., and wife Christina.
Regina Knaus, Jan. 2, 1809. Feb. 19, 1809.	John and Regina.	The parents.
Anna Elis. Heckman. Feb. 3, 1809. Feb. 19, 1809.	John and Maria.	The parents.
Anna Maria Clifton, Dec. 18, 1808. Feb. 19, 1809.	John and Gertraut.	The parents.
Elisabeth Gruber, Dec. 18, 1808. Feb. 20, 1809.	Michael and Hanna.	John Gruber and Elisabeth.
Charles Richard, Dec. 29, 1808. Feb. 23, 1809.	Joseph and Elisabeth.	Thos. Richard and Susanna.
Simon Schaefer, Jan. 21, 1809. March 12, 1809.	Jacob and Elisabeth.	The parents.
John Jacob Burke, Nov. 13, 1808. March 12, 1809.	Joseph and Susan.	Father and Maria Opp.
Edmund Burke Meixsell, Dec. 30, 1808. March 12, 1809.	Philip and Maria.	Father and Maria Opp.
Catharina Stocker, Feb. 21, 1809. April 2, 1809.	Daniel and Christina.	Adam Stenger and wife Cath.
Adam Preis, March 14, 1809. Apr. 2, 1809.	Frederick and Maria.	Adam Stocker and wife Barbara.

The First Reformed Church of Easton, Pa.

Name of Child and Date of Birth and Baptism.	Parents.	Sponsors.
Nancy Romig, March 21, 1809. April 2, 1809.	Jacob and Rosina.	Christian Stocker and wife Cath.
Catharina, Feb. 17, 1809. Apr. 7, 1809.	Susanna Bachman.	John Miller and wife Rachael.
Abraham Miller, Nov. 21, 1808. April 7, 1809.	John and Rachael.	Barbara Hemp.
Sarah Weiberg, April 4, 1804. April 7, 1809.	Samuel and Rosina.	The parents.
Maria Magd. Weiberg, Jan. 12, 1806. April 7, 1809.	Samuel and Rosina.	The parents.
David Weiberg, Nov. 1, 1808. April 7, 1809.	Samuel and Rosina.	The parents.
John Lantz, March 18, 1809. April 9, 1809.	John and Hanna.	John Kress (?) and Marg.
Carl Walter, Nov. 3, 1808. April 15, 1809.	George and Sarah.	Jacob Odenwaelder and Maria Walter.
Peter Hay, March 15, 1809. May 4, 1809.	Melchior and Elisabeth.	Thomas Pomp and the parents.
Elisabeth Ayer, Aug. 31, 1808. May 7, 1809.	William and Catharina.	The parents.
John Peter Saylor, Jan. 19, 1809. May 7, 1809.	Peter and Anna Marg.	Peter Raub and Susan Lautz.
Joseph Hackman, Feb. 13, 1809. May 7, 1809.	Jacob and Elisabeth.	The parents.
Susanna Cath. Weizel, April 17, 1809. June 4, 1809.	Henry and Juliana.	Christian Correll and Catharina.

Church Records.

Name of Child and Date of Birth and Baptism.	Parents.	Sponsors.
Abraham Hornbeck, Nov. 2, 1808. June 28, 1809.	Henry and Diana.	The parents.
Maria Elis. Woodring, May 2, 1809. July 2, 1809.	Abraham and Margaret.	Philip Woodring and Maria Elisabeth.
Sarah Ann Kocher, June 1, 1809. July 2, 1809.	Henry and Maria.	John Pfeiffer and Sarah.
Margaretha Beitelman, June 20, 1809. Aug. 2, 1809.	Lehnhart and Hannah.	Abraham Messinger and Marg.
Elizabeth Willauer, May 30, 1809. Aug. 8, 1808.	Adam and Elisabeth.	Jonathon Knecht and Marg.
Hanna Snyder, May 12, 1807. Aug. 8, 1809.	John and Catharina.	Andrew Stocker and Juliana.
Philip Abel, Feb. 13, 1809. Aug. 13, 1809.	Michael and Maria.	Philip Odenwaelder and Elisabeth.
Jacob Brinker, June 13, 1809. Aug. 16, 1809.	George and Elisabeth.	The parents.
Elisabeth Sand, June 23, 1809. Aug. 16, 1809.	John and Magdalena.	Peter Correll and Maria Beck.
Sophia Schuck, June 22, 1809. Aug. 20, 1809.	Adam and Barbara.	The parents.
Abraham Mayer, Dec. 26, 1805. Sept. 1, 1809.	Peter and Salome.	The parents.
Liddia Mayer, April 1, 1808. Sept. 1, 1809.	Peter and Salome.	The parents.
David Coleman, May 4, 1809. Sept. 24, 1809.	Samuel and Maria.	John Seipel and wife Maria.

202   *The First Reformed Church of Easton, Pa.*

Name of Child and Date of Birth and Baptism.	Parents.	Sponsors.
Samuel Woodring, Aug. 4, 1809. Sept. 24, 1809.	William and Rosina.	Jacob Woodring and Elisabeth.
Margaretha Hillgart, Feb. 23, 1809. Oct. 10, 1809.	Abraham and Eva.	John Kocher and Susanna.
John Diemer, Aug. 27, 1809. Oct. 10, 1809.	Benj. and Sarah.	John Herzel and Elisabeth.
Benjamin Wagner, Sept. 15, 1809. Oct. 22, 1809.	George and Elisabeth.	Jacob Shoemacher and Elisabeth.
John Oberly, Sept. 9, 1809. Nov. 19, 1809.	John and Catharine.	John Dech and Elisabeth.
Henry Edward Lamb, Nov. 6, 1809. Dec. 3, 1809.	Abel and Susanna.	Henry Flemsing and Margaret.
Sarah Ann Coleman, Aug. 20, 1809. Dec. 23, 1809.	Jonathon and Elisabeth.	John Bishop and wife Anna.
Samuel Odenwaelder, Oct. 30, 1809. Dec. 25, 1809.	John and Anna Marg.	Philip Odenwaelder and wife Elisabeth.

ANNO 1810.

David Odenwaelder, Nov. 30, 1809. Jan. 14, 1810.	Bernhart and Sarah.	Philip Odenwaelder and Elisabeth.
Daniel Jacob Reis, Dec. 24, 1809. Jan. 14, 1810.	Peter and Susanna.	The parents.
Anna Maria Appel, Nov. 9, 1809. Jan. 14, 1810.	Andrew and Elisabeth.	The parents.
Maria Christina Seipel, Nov. 10, 1809. Jan. 28, 1810.	Henry and Sarah.	Peter Miller and wife Christina.

Church Records.

Name of Child and Date of Birth and Baptism.	Parents.	Sponsors.
William Young, May 16, 1809. Jan. 29, 1810.	Peter and Anna.	Jacob Babb and Marg. Young.
Anna Marg. Wolf, Dec. 7, 1809. Feb. 1, 1810.	George and Maria.	Frederick Barthold and Anna Maria Erb.
John Henry Gulick, July 20, 1809. Feb. 1, 1810.	Nathan and Elisabeth.	Frederick Barthold and Anna Maria Erb.
Sarah Scheierman, Dec. 1, 1809. Feb. 6, 1810.	Ludwig and Christina.	Abraham Beitelman and wife Catharina.
Christian Winter, Nov. 22, 1809. Feb. 11, 1810.	Henry and Catharine.	Jacob Fraes and wife Susanna.
Sarah Frauenfelder, Oct. 30, 1809. Feb. 11, 1810.	Jacob and Catharine.	Valentin Werkhaeuser and Sarah Messinger.
Rebecca Correll, Jan. 3, 1810. Feb. 11, 1810.	Philip and Elisabeth.	Joseph Heller and wife Marg.
George Adam Herzel, Nov. 20, 1809. Feb. 13, 1810.	Abraham and Christina.	Adam Bruch and Elisabeth Herzel.
George William Hauck, Jan. 15, 1810. Feb. 25, 1810.	George and Sarah.	George William Raub and wife Catharine.
Peter Snyder Schooly, Aug. 23, 1809. Feb. 25, 1810.	William and Margaret.	The parents.
Susanna Kutz, Feb. 18, 1810. March 6, 1810.	Abraham and Catharine.	The parents.
John Weis, Feb. 11, 1810. March 11, 1810.	Jacob and Elisabeth.	John Stem and wife Anna.
Juliana Emig, Feb. 3, 1809. March 11, 1810.	George and Magdalena.	The parents.

204 *The First Reformed Church of Easton, Pa.*

Name of Child and Date of Birth and Baptism.	Parents.	Sponsors.
Margaret Osburn, Nov. 16, 1808. March 22, 1810.	John and Rebecca.	The parents.
Sallande, Feb. 28, 1809. March 22, 1810.	Anna Belles.	Peter Snyder and wife Elisabeth.
Charles Davis, Dec. 8, 1809. March 31, 1810.	Thomas and Catharine.	The parents.
Elisabeth Seipel, Dec. 21, 1809. April 8, 1810.	John and Maria.	Jacob Scheip, Maria Christina.
John Belles, Sept. 17, 1809. April 8, 1810.	John and Elisabeth.	The parents.
Rebecca Ann Belles, Sept. 9, 1809. April 8, 1810.	Amos and Osina.	The parents.
Sarah Koch, Sept. 28, 1809. April 12, 1810.	John and Maria.	The parents.
Charlotta Messinger, Feb. 23, 1810. April 19, 1810.	Abraham and Margaretha.	John Kaemrer and Elisabeth.
Catharina Schweizer, Dec. 6, 1809. April 19, 1810.	John and Margaretha.	Anna Uhler.
Elisabeth Bruch, March 18, 1810. April 29, 1810.	John and Catharina.	Francis Stocker and Elisabeth Stenger.
Nicolaus Woodring, March 25, 1810. May 5, 1810.	Nicolaus and Catharina.	Philip Meixsell.
Susanna Klein, Feb. 28, 1810. May 6, 1810.	David and Elisabeth.	Isaac Messinger and Susanna.
Catharina Weizel, March 11, 1810. May 6, 1810.	Benjamin and Catharina.	Daniel Weizel and Catharina Schiffer.

Church Records.   205

Name of Child and Date of Birth and Baptism.	Parents.	Sponsors.
Anna Maria, Jan. 1, 1810. May 31, 1810.	Elisabeth Folmer.	Jacob Young and wife Margaret have obligated themselves for the Christian nurture of this child.
Sarah Drahn, Nov. 9, 1809. June 17, 1810.	Matthias and Anna.	Philip Pfeiffer and Catharina Bess.
John Michael Messinger, June 22, 1810.[1] June 17, 1810.	Philip and Margaret.	John Correll, Maria Obits.
Salome Obits, Aug. 5, 1809. June 17, 1810.	George and Magdalena.	Philip Messinger, Margaretha.
John Raesly, April 26, 1810. July 1, 1810.	Joseph and Maria.	David Kaemrer, Anna.
David Koenig, March 1, 1810. July 1, 1810.	Adam and Catharina.	Peter Maurer, Anna Margaretha.
Jacob Odenwaelder, May 27, 1810. July 1, 1810.	Philip and Elisabeth.	John Odenwaelder, Margaretha.
Michael Frauenfelder, April 9, 1810. July 1, 1810.	Conrad and Maria.	Jacob Jumper, Elisabeth Frauenfelder.
Susanna Schaefer, Apr. 9, 1810. July 1, 1810.	Jacob and Elisabeth.	The parents.
Susanna Wilhelmina Keller, March 14, 1810. July 1, 1810.	Jacob and Susanna.	The parents.
Abezina Butz, Jan. 20, 1810. July 1, 1810.	Jacob and Maria.	The parents.

[1] Evidently a mistake — but so the record stands.

206 *The First Reformed Church of Easton, Pa.*

Name of Child and Date of Birth and Baptism.	Parents.	Sponsors.
Susanna Dietz, April 5, 1810. July 15, 1810.	Nicolaus and Sophia.	The parents.
Marcus Lannes Burnsides, Dec. 16, 1809. July 23, 1810.	John M., and Eva.	John B. Miles and Susanna.
Peter McClury, April 5, 1810. July 23, 1810.	Anthony and Anna.	Christian Otto and Sophia Wesner.
Catharina Schick, Nov. 30, 1808. Aug. 8, 1810.	Jacob and Elisabeth.	The parents.
Samuel Mayer Eyer, July 25, 1810. Aug. 12, 1810.	John and Maria.	Adam Schuck and Barbara.
Sophia (?) Shnyder Young, Aug. 5, 1810. Aug. 16, 1810.	John and Susanna.	The father.
Elizabeth Weizel, July 24, 1810. Aug. 19, 1810.	Henry and Juliana.	John Correll and Elizabeth Lerch.
Sophia Stem, Feb. 26, 1810. Aug. 26, 1810.	Abraham and (S)Charlotta.	The parents.
George Wilhelm, July 14, 1805. Aug. 27, 1810.	(Wanting.)	George Wilhelm Sauerbeck.
Carl Schmidt Worman, April 1, 1808. Aug. 27, 1810.	Andreas and Maria.	George Schmidt and Elizabeth.
Susanna Worman, Aug. 23, 1810. Aug. 27, 1810.	Andreas and Maria.	George Schmidt and Eva Schmidt.
Maria Hackman, July 9, 1810. Sept. 5, 1810.	Jacob and Elisabeth.	Maria Brutsman.

Church Records. 207

Name of Child and Date of Birth and Baptism.	Parents.	Sponsors.
Peter Kind, May 17, 1810. Sept. 5, 1810.	Isaac and Elisabeth.	William Lerch and Maria Messinger
Daniel Bier, Aug. 10, 1810. Sept. 23, 1810.	George and Elisabeth.	Peter Wagner and Elisabeth.
Peter Mayer, Nov. 9, 1808. Sept. 23, 1810.	John and Margaretha.	Christina Marg. Schaup.
John Koechlein Young, Sept. 9, 1810. Sept. 23, 1810.	Peter and Anna.	John Young and Maria.
Elisabeth Uhler, Jan. 18, 1810. Oct. 7, 1810.	Jacob and Margaret.	Isaac Kind and Elisabeth.
William Walter, Sept. 5, 1810. Oct. 7, 1810.	Frederick and Elisabeth.	Elisabeth Schumacher.
James Serrels, July 29, 1809. Oct. 9, 1810.	James and Rebecca.	Maria Serrels.
John Worman, Oct. 9, 1810. Oct. 18, 1810.	John and Jane.	John Young and Susanna.
George Stocker, Sept. 6, 1810. Oct. 21, 1810.	Abraham and Elisabeth.	Rudolph Schweitzer and Barbara.
Henry Beitelman, June 22, 1810. Oct. 21, 1810.	Leonhard and Hannah.	Henry Schuck and Elisabeth.
Christian Junkin, Sept. 20, 1810. Oct. 21, 1810.	George and Elisabeth.	Adam Stocker and Barbara.
Elisabeth Rippel, Sept. 10, 1809. Oct. 15, 1810.	John and Susanna.	Conrad Hayn and Elisabeth Kessly.
Carl Messinger, May 18, 1810. Nov. 5, 1810.	Jacob and Anna Maria.	John Kohler and Barbara.

Name of Child and Date of Birth and Baptism.	Parents.	Sponsors.
Jacob Heil, Sept. 29, 1810. Nov. 18, 1810.	Philip and Susanna.	John Bess and Elisabeth.
Jacob Engel, Aug. 28, 1810. Nov. 29, 1810.	Christoph and Susanna.	Jacob Hauch and Maria Opp.
ANNO 1811.		
Daniel Woodring, Nov. 1, 1810. Jan. 1, 1811.	John and Elisabeth.	William Woodring and Rosina.
William Neigh, Sept. 17, 1809. Jan. 1, 1811.	Samuel and Catharine.	The parents.
Juliana Holland, Dec. 21, 1810. Jan. 6, 1811.	Peter and Susanna.	Philip Correll and Elisabeth.
Sabina Gertrude Simon, Nov. 29, 1810. Jan. 8, 1811.	Michael and Maria.	The parents.
Matilda Laddig, Oct. 17, 1810. Jan. 9, 1811.	Jacob and Sarah.	The parents.
Charles Gerey, Feb. 16, 1810. Jan. 13, 1811.	John and Christina.	John Gery, Sr., Christina.
Frid. Wilh. Heinrich Pomp, Dec. 23, 1810. Jan. 9, 1811.	Thomas and Catharina.	Fridrich Van der Sloot and Catharina.
Eliza Broeder, Nov. 11, 1810. Jan. 18, 1811.	Philip and Christina.	The parents.
Carl Appel, Jan. 21, 1811. Jan. 28, 1811.	Andrew and Elisabeth.	The parents.
Matilda White, Oct. 4, 1810. Feb. 2, 1811.	William and Susanna.	Conrad Bender and Susanna.

J. H. A. BOMBERGER, D. D.

Name of Child and Date of Birth and Baptism.	Parents.	Sponsors.
Anna Cath. Shnyder, Apr. 8, 1810. Feb. 4, 1811.	John and Catharine.	Ulric Knecht and Eva Elisabeth.
Anna Maria Levan, Jan. —, 1800. Feb. 4, 1811.	Susanna Willauer.	Ulric Knecht and his wife Eva Elisabeth have assumed responsibility for the Christian nurture of this child.
Rebecca Woodring, Jan. 9, 1811. Feb. 10, 1811.	Abraham and Margaret.	Jacob Woodring and Elisabeth.
Sarah Ann Ward, Sept. 13, 1807. (Wanting.)	Adam and Susanna.	Barbara Ward, the grandmother.
Susanna Koechlein. Dec. 29, 1810. Feb. 12, 1811.	Andrew and Susanna.	Andrew Koechlein and Elisabeth.
Jacob Metzger, Sept. 27, 1810. Feb. 24, 1811.	Philip and Margaret.	Jacob Frees and Susanna.
Elisabeth Claus, March 6, 1811. Apr. 4, 1811.	Daniel and Dorothea.	Philip Claus and Christina.
Anna Maria Hess, Feb. 3, 1811. Apr. 4, 1811.	George and Maria Margaret.	Henry Siegel, Anna Maria.
Elisabeth Hess, Dec. 3, 1810. Apr. 26, 1811.	Frederick and Catharine.	Maria Kratz.
John Jacob Stemm, March 6, 1811. May 4, 1811.	John and Anna.	Jacob Keller, Margaret Laubach.
Solomon Werkhaeuser, March 15, 1811. May 5, 1811.	Valentine and Sarah.	The parents.

Name of Child and Date of Birth and Baptism.	Parents.	Sponsors.
Herman Snyder Heckman, Nov. 26, 1810. May 5, 1811.	John and Maria.	The parents.
Daniel Herster Snyder. March 12, 1811. May 5, 1811.	Peter and Elisabeth.	The parents.
Mary Ann Odenwaelder, Oct. 8, 1811. May 19, 1811.	Philip and Elisabeth.	Jacob Keller, Susanna.
Elisa Maria Broeder, Dec. 13, 1810. May 23, 1811.	John and Elisabeth.	John Laddig (?), Maria Broeder.
Anna Maria Romig, Apr. 20, 1811. May 27, 1811.	Jacob and Rosina.	Peter Greber, Maria.
Liddia Frankenfeld, April 19, 1811. June 2, 1811.	George and Maria Magdalena.	Michael Abel and Maria.
Josua Bruch, March 19, 1811. June 2, 1811.	George and Catharine.	William Yates and Maria.
Diana Knecht, May 5, 1811. June 2, 1811.	Adam and Barbara.	Rudolph Schweitzer and Barbara.
Andrew Reesly, March 6, 1811. June 2, 1811.	Jacob and Elisabeth.	Andrew Koechlein and Susanna.
Theophilus Rees, March 15, 1811. June 2, 1811.	Philip and Mary.	The parents.
Jeremiah Traxsell, Feb. 16, 1811. June 2, 1811.	George and Rosina.	Henry Shnyder and Catharine.
Carl Kotz, April 10, 1811. June 16, 1811.	John and Rebecca.	Jacob Kotz and Maria Diemer.

Church Records.

Name of Child and Date of Birth and Baptism.	Parents.	Sponsors.
Edmund Bishoph, June 1, 1811. July 24, 1811.	John and Anna.	Henry Shnyder and Catharine.
Eliza Traxsell Dengler. April 27, 1811. July 21, 1811.	Jacob and Maria.	John Traxsell and Elisabeth.
Thomas Nicholas Traxsell, Dec. 5, 1810. July 21, 1811.	Michael and Catharine.	Jacob Osterstock and Hanna Hauch.
Maria Stocker, Jan. 24, 1811. July 28, 1811.	Daniel and Christina.	Andrew Stocker, Magdalena.
Elisabeth Koechlein, June 14, 1811. July 28, 1811.	Peter and Catharine.	John Deichman, Elisabeth.
John Keiper, June 2, 1811. Aug. 4, 1811.	Peter and Maria.	The parents.
John G. Moyer, May 10, 1811. Aug. 7, 1811.	William and Maria.	Jacob Zimmerman, Maria Elisabeth.
Lydia Mayer, May 27, 1810. Aug. 7, 1811.	John and Liddia.	Jacob Mayer, Elisabeth Mayer.
Susanna Seip, May 16, 1811. Aug. 11, 1811.	Jacob and Susanna.	John Eritt, Christina.
Benjamin Dietrich, March 21, 1811. Aug. 12, 1811.	Jacob and Salome.	The parents.
Susanna Rippel, Feb. 15, 1811. Aug. 25, 1811.	Peter and Margaret.	The parents.
Maria Messinger, June 22, 1811. Aug. 25, 1811.	Isaac and Susanna.	The parents.
Francis Philip Ennes, May 2, 1811. Aug. 27, 1811.	Robert and Catharine.	The parents.

Name of Child and Date of Birth and Baptism.	Parents.	Sponsors.
William Ward, Jan. 30, 1808. Sept. 1, 1811.	Adam and Susanna.	The parents.
William Riegel, Apr. 28, 1811. Sept. 7, 1811.	Benjamin and Hannah.	The parents.
Anna Maria Frees, Aug. 5, 1811. Sept. 10, 1811.	William and Maria.	Jacob Shnyder, Anna Maria.
Simon Koch, Aug. 1, 1811. Sept. 10, 1811.	Jacob and Elisabeth.	John Koch, Maria.
David Messinger, March 20, 1811. Sept. 14, 1811.	George and Elisabeth.	George Stecher, Catharine.
Maria Klein, July 23, 1811. Sept. 22, 1811.	David and Elisabeth.	John Reesly, Magdalena.
Anna Maria Schmidt, Aug. 29, 1811. Sept. 30, 1811.	Abraham and Barbara.	The parents.
Abbolina Bronce (?), May 31, 1811. Oct. 6, 1811.	Henry and Elisabeth.	The parents.
Carl Woodring, Sept. 21, 1811. Oct. 10, 1811.	William and Rosina.	John Woodring, Elisabeth.
Christina Lahr, Sept. 25, 1811. Oct. 18, 1811.	Samuel and Elisabeth.	Peter Hertzel, Christina.
William Berry, Dec. 26, 1811 (?). Feb. 26, 1811.	George and Susanna.	Christina Hertzel, Christina Maria.
John Miller, Aug. 29, 1811. Oct. 20, 1811.	William and Maria.	John Richard, Susannah.
Sarah Weiss, Aug. 17, 1811. Oct. 20, 1811.	Jacob and Elisabeth.	Solomon Weiss, Maria.

Name of Child and Date of Birth and Baptism.	Parents.	Sponsors.
Thomas Schweitzer, Aug. 22, 1811. Oct. 21, 1811.	Conrad and Catharine.	John Stecher, Catharine.
Sarah Butz, Aug. 19, 1810. Nov. 10, 1811.	Michael and Margaret.	The parents.
Marg. Elis. Fitz-Randolph, March 8. Nov. 16.	William and Susanna.	Mary Lacky and parents.
George Transue, Sept. 15, 1811. Nov. 17, 1811.	Abraham and Elisabeth.	Abraham Transue, Sophia.
John Folkinson, July 27, 1811. Nov. 19, 1811.	John and Magdalena Preis.	Adam Schuck, Barbara.
Mary Ann Sarrels, Aug. 18, 1811. Nov. 19, 1811.	James and Rebecca.	Philip Messinger, Margaret.
Hanna Janson, Aug. 31, 1811. Nov. 19, 1811.	Henry and Christina.	George Messinger, Elisabeth.
Anna Cath. Scheierman, Oct. 11, 1811. Dec. 11, 1811.	Peter and Susanna.	Peter Wagner, Elisabeth.

ANNO 1812.

Susanna Lamb, Dec. 23, 1811. Jan. 8, 1812.	Abel and Susanna.	Mathias Wagner, Margaret.
Elisabeth Wagner, Nov. 18, 1811. Jan. 8, 1812.	Matthias and Margaret.	Abel Lamb, Susanna.
Elisabeth Gruber, Jan. 9, 1812. Jan. 10, 1812.	John and Elisabeth.	Jeremiah Best, Elisabeth.
Joseph Pfaff, Oct. 5, 1811. Jan. 12, 1812.	John and Susanna.	Rudolph Schweitzer, Barbara.

Name of Child and Date of Birth and Baptism.	Parents.	Sponsors.
Maria Oberly, Nov. 28, 1811. Jan. 22, 1812.	John and Catharina.	Elisabeth Oberly.
Sarah Moore, Jan. 8, 1812. Jan. 23, 1812.	Robert and Mary.	The parents.
George Peter Obitz, Nov. 4, 1811. Feb. 2, 1812.	George and Magdalena.	Peter Correll, Catharine Mill.
Thos. Stenger, Jan. 4, 1812. Feb. 3, 1812.	Isaac and Susanna.	Adam Stenger, Catharine.
Aaron Shuch, Nov. 18, 1811. Feb. 5, 1812.	Henry and Elisabeth.	The parents.
Jacob Kessler, Aug. 12, 1811. Feb. 14, 1812.	William and Rosina.	Jacob Leppard, Elisabeth.
Louisa Kaemrer, Nov. 28, 1811. Feb. 21, 1812.	Jacob and Magdalena.	Jacob Seipel, Elisabeth.
Eli Diemer, Sept. 14, 1811. March 14, 1812.	Benjamin and Sarah.	The parents.
Maria Magd. Clauss, June 25, 1811. March 22, 1812.	Henry and Elisabeth.	John Rothrock, Maria.
Edward Carey, Sept. 14, 1811. April 2, 1812.	John and Christina.	John Ludwig, Hanna Hauck.
Jacob Messinger, March 11, 1812. May 6, 1812.	Abraham and Margaret.	Jacob Frees, Susanna.
Maria Reis,[1] March —, 1812. May 3, 1812.	Peter and Susanna.	The parents.
Jacob Ross, Jan. 30, 1812. May 6, 1812.	Joseph and Susanna.	The parents.

[1] Blurred by an ink-stain. Probably as given. See second entry, 1810.

Church Records. 215

Name of Child and Date of Birth and Baptism.	Parents.	Sponsors.
George Shuck, Sept. 11, 1811. May 20, 1812.	Peter and Susanna.	The parents.
Catharine Kutzler, March 15, 1812. May 21, 1812.	Christian and Susanna.	Jacob Shaefer, Elisabeth.
George Seagreaves, March 21, 1812. May 24, 1812.	Henry and Eva.	George Dengler, Margaret.
John David Brinker, Oct. 4, 1811. May 31, 1812.	George and Elisabeth.	The parents.
Jacob Sewitz, April 15, 1812. May 31, 1812.	David and Catharine.	Peter Greber, Maria.
Sarah Odenwaelder, April 8. May 31.	John and Anna Margaret.	Jacob Keller, Elisabeth Odenwaelder.
Susanna Hertzel, April 8. May 31.	Peter and Christina.	The parents.
Susanna Hackman, Dec. 28, 1811. May 31, 1812.	Jacob and Elisabeth.	The parents.
Elisabeth Frauenfelder, April 11, 1811. May 31, 1812.	Jacob and Catharine.	The parents.
John Jacob Hartman, Sept. 16, 1811. May 31, 1812.	Albert and Elisabeth.	George Young, Maria Osterstock.
Jacob Shaefer, Feb. 20, 1812. June 3, 1812.	Jacob and Elisabeth.	John Lerch, Rosina.
Elisabeth Gaston, May 19, 1812. June 21, 1812.	William and Liddia.	George Peter Kessler, Elisabeth.
William Augustus Wolf, May 23, 1812. June 21, 1812.	George and Maria.	George W. Raub, Catharine.

216 The First Reformed Church of Easton, Pa.

Name of Child and Date of Birth and Baptism.	Parents.	Sponsors.
Ann Erb Gulick, Oct. 2, 1811. June 21, 1812.	Nathan and Elisabeth.	Anna Erb.
Herman Peter Young, March 28, 1812. June 15, 1812.	John and Susanna.	The parents.
Mary Jane Gray, June 11, 1812. June 23, 1812.	William and Christina.	The parents.
Juliana Koch, May 20, 1812. June 28, 1812.	John and Maria.	John Koch, Maria.
Anna Maria Frauenfelder, March 28, 1812. June 28, 1812.	Conrad and Maria.	The parents.
George, Sept. 28, 1811. July 19, 1812.	Elisabeth Bachman.	John Brotzman, Elisabeth.
Catharine Miller, May 5, 1812. July 19, 1812.	John and Rachel.	The father and Barbara Hemp.
Mary Ann Barns, Nov. 28, 1811. July 19, 1812.	Steven and Nancy.	Polly Lucker.
John Butz, June 1, 1811. July 12, 1812.	David and Maria.	The parents.
David Seipel, April 16, 1812. July 12, 1812.	Henry and Sarah.	David Butz, Maria.
John Dietz, Feb. 14, 1812. July 26, 1812.	Nicholas and Sophia.	The parents.
Elisabeth Scheuerman, July 6, 1812. Aug. 1, 1812.	Ludwig and Christina.	John Eritt, Catharine.
Rebecca Gross, May 14, 1812. Aug. 2, 1812.	Daniel and Christina.	George Lerch, Elisabeth Gross.

Church Records. 217

Name of Child and Date of Birth and Baptism.	Parents.	Sponsors.
William Bruch, July 25, 1812. Aug. 16, 1812.	John and Catharina.	Adam Stenger, Catharina.
Daniel Lerch, July 4, 1812. Aug. 16, 1812.	Fridrich and Maria.	George Lerch, Maria Andre.
Samuel Willauer, Feb. 29, 1812. Aug. 20, 1812.	Adam and Elisabeth.	Henry Uhler, Hanna.
John Reesly, July 13, 1812. Aug. 30, 1812.	Jacob and Elisabeth.	John Reesly, Magdalena.
Edward Berndt, June 28, 1812. Aug. 30, 1812.	Tobias and Elisabeth.	Conrad Haas, Hanna.
Anna Maria Hertzel, June 26, 1812. Sept. 17, 1812.	Abraham and Christina.	Philip Brotzman, Christina.
Jacob Weis, Sept. 10, 1812. Sept. 18, 1812.	Jacob and Elisabeth.	Jacob Mayer, Susanna.
Elvina (?) Christina Dengler, June 28. Sept. 20.	Jacob and Maria.	John George Menner, Christina.
Carl Weitzel, June 15, 1812. Sept. 26, 1812.	Henry and Juliana.	Frederick Schweitzer, Catharina.
Sabina Salsich, Sept. 11, 1812. Oct. 13, 1812.	John and Maria.	John Broeder, Elisabeth.
David Marks, Jan. 11, 1812. Oct. 24, 1812.	Nathaniel and Rachel.	The parents.
Maria Ann Weiss, Oct. 20, 1812. Nov. 7, 1812.	Solomon and Maria.	Conrad Rieser, Christina.
Mary Ann Steinbach, Oct. 10, 1812. Nov. 22, 1812.	George and Maria.	Jacob Steinbach, Elisabeth.

Name of Child and Date of Birth and Baptism.	Parents.	Sponsors.
Catharina Koch, Aug. 26, 1812. Nov. 25, 1812.	Abraham and Maria.	John Koch, Maria.
John George Pfeiffer, Oct. 13, 1812. Nov. 29, 1812.	John and Sarah.	The parents.
Elisabeth Palmer, Aug. 22, 1812. Dec. 15, 1812.	Daniel and Christina.	The parents.
Catharina Stocker, Sept. 9, 1812. Dec. 20, 1812.	Abraham and Elisabeth.	Jacob Stocker, Maria Schweitzer.
Thomas Baumgarten, Born Oct. 30, 1812. Baptism wanting.	Godfried and Maria.	Adam Wagner, Regina.
Sarah Ann Wagner, Aug. 20, 1812. Dec. 20, 1812.	George and Elisabeth.	George Loesher, Elisabeth Kemrer.
Salome Messinger, Aug. 11, 1812. Dec. 25, 1812.	Jacob and Anna Maria.	George Obitz, Magdalena.
Christian Heller, Oct. 16, 1812. Dec. 25, 1812.	Jacob and Susanna.	The parents.
Thos. Washington Laddig, Oct. 16, 1812. Dec. 26, 1812.	Jacob and Sarah.	The parents.

Anno 1813.

Jacob M. Simons West, Dec. 13, 1812. Jan. 2, 1813.	George and Catharine.	Michael Simons, Margaret, or Maria.
Mary Ann Arner, Sept. 24, 1812. Jan. 3, 1813.	Henry and Catharine.	Jacob Bess, Catharine.

Church Records.

Name of Child and Date of Birth and Baptism.	Parents.	Sponsors.
Thos. William Knaus, Oct. 30, 1812. Jan. 3, 1813.	John and Regina.	The parents.
Juliana Heller, Dec. 28, 1812. Jan. 8, 1813.	George and Susanna.	The parents.
Conrad Kreider Heckman, Sept. 26, 1812. Jan. 9, 1813.	John and Maria.	The parents.
John George Correll, Dec. 15, 1812. Jan. 17, 1813.	Philip and Elisabeth.	Peter Koehler, Maria.
Margaret Elis. Leppart, Dec. 25, 1812. Jan. 17, 1813.	Jacob and Elisabeth.	Abel Lamb, Susanna.
Eleanora Burnsides, Jan. 27, 1812. Jan. 18, 1813.	John M. and Eva.	Henry Doering and the child's mother.
Sarah Stem, Oct. 16, 1812. Jan. 25, 1813.	Abraham and Scharlotte.	The parents.
Thomas Mill, Nov. 28, 1812. Jan. 31, 1813.	John and Anna Maria.	Philip Messinger, Margaret.
Benjamin Broeder, Nov. 12, 1812. Feb. 1, 1813.	John and Elisabeth.	John Schade, Christina Transue.
Sarah Quere, July 31, 1812. Feb. 9, 1813.	Daniel and Eva.	Susanna Quere.
Samuel Yeisley, Oct. 4, 1812. Feb. 23, 1812.	Nicholas and Sarah.	Jacob Reichard, Maria Hess.
Samuel Ecker, Dec. 25, 1812. March 18, 1813.	John and Sarah.	George Steckel, Maria.

Name of Child and Date of Birth and Baptism.	Parents.	Sponsors.
Margaret and Elisabeth Lumbert, (Wanting), 1812. (Wanting), 1813.	Charles and Ann.	The parents.
John Kraemer, Jan. 28, 1813. March 14, 1813.	William and Susanna.	Peter Jacoby, Maria.
Nancy Ross, Feb. 28, 1810. March 27, 1813.	John and Nancy.	The parents.
Easter Simelton Ross, Mathew Loury Ross, Feb. 24, 1812. March 27, 1813.	John and Abbe.	The parents.
Sarah Ann Hemsing, March 3, 1813. April 14, 1813.	Henry and Margaret.	Peter Nungesser, Barbara.
Isabella Beard, May 13, 1812. April 24, 1813.	David and Sarah.	The parents.
Daniel Transue, Feb. 25, 1813. April 25, 1813.	Isaac and Margaret.	Abraham Transue, Sophia.
Amalia Pomp, May 12, 1813. June 22, 1813.	Thomas and Catharine.	Jacob Wilhelm Dechant, Rebecca.
Elisabeth Bauers, June 17, 1812. May 13, 1813.	Henry and Maria.	The parents.
Christoph Hertzel, June 20, 1810. May 16, 1813.	Jacob and Catharine.	Christop Hertzel.
Elisabeth Hertzel, June 12, 1812. May 16, 1813.	Jacob and Catharine.	Christoph Meixsell, Elisabeth.
William Wagner, Feb. 2, 1813. May 5, 1813.	John and Margaret.	Philip Schmidt, Eva.
Maria Schweitzer, April 12, 1813. May 6, 1813.	Frederick and Catharine.	Rudolph Schweitzer, Barbara.

Church Records. 221

Name of Child and Date of Birth and Baptism.	Parents.	Sponsors.
Joseph Woodring, March 15, 1813. May 6, 1813.	John and Elisabeth.	William Miller, Maria.
Elisabeth Klein, March 28, 1813. May 6, 1813.	David and Elisabeth.	Peter Kiefer, Susanna Messinger.
Joseph Werkhaeuser, Dec. 23, 1812. May 6, 1813.	Valentine and Sarah.	Michael Messinger, Elisabeth Werkhaeuser.
John Stecher, April 15, 1813. June 13, 1813.	John and Catharine.	Melchoir Stecher, Maria Schweitzer.
Peter Kocher, May 3, 1813. July 4, 1813.	Jonas and Catharine.	Abraham Kocher, Susanna.
Maria Anna Young, Sept. 16, 1812. July 4, 1813.	Peter and Anna.	The parents.
John Dietz, May 13, 1813. July 11, 1813.	Nicholas and Maria.	The mother.
Samuel Shuck, May 13, 1813. July 19, 1813.	Adam and Barbara.	The parents.
Samuel Lerch, April 21, 1813. July 18, 1813.	John and Rosina.	Peter Keifer, Susanna Messinger.
Mary Ann Bess, May 25, 1813. July 25, 1813.	Jacob and Catharine.	John Bess, Elisabeth.
Andrew Kiefer, May 26, 1813. Aug. 1, 1813.	Andrew and Elisabeth.	John Bess, Magdalena.
William Henry Haas, April 12, 1813. Aug. 1, 1813.	Jacob and Barbara.	Henry Locher, Maria.
Edmund Jacob Horn, Dec. 16, 1811. Aug. 1, 1813.	John and Elisabeth.	The parents.

Name of Child and Date of Birth and Baptism.	Parents.	Sponsors.
Susanna Cath. Horn, May 16, 1813. Aug. 1, 1813.	John and Elisabeth.	The parents.
Elisabeth Walter, June 2, 1813. Aug. 3, 1813.	Lenhart and Sarah.	The parents.
Elisabeth Scherrer, June 20, 1813. Aug. 8, 1813.	Henry and Maria.	Jacob Keller, Elisabeth.
Alexander Jacob Krotz, March 13, 1813. Aug. 8, 1813.	Isaac and Hanna.	The parents.
Henry Conrad Schnyder, July 4, 1813. Aug. 8, 1813.	Samuel and Susanna.	The parents.
Elisabeth Jones, June 31, 1813. Aug. 11, 1813.	John and Maria.	Catharine Sommer.
Sarah Koch, May 13, 1813. Aug. 15, 1813.	Michael and Maria.	George Frankenfield, Maria Magdalena.
John Jacob Conrad Schlouch, May 23, 1813. Aug. 15, 1813.	John and Susanna.	John Sheip, Juliana Meixell.
Juliana Traxsell, July 17, 1808. Aug. 15, 1813.	Jacob and Maria.	The parents.
Aaron Traxsell, Nov. 16, 1810. Aug. 15, 1813.	Jacob and Maria.	The parents.
Sarah Ann Traxsell, Jan. 12, 1813. Aug. 15, 1813.	Jacob and Maria.	The parents.
Susanna Carey, March 23, 1813. Aug. 15, 1813.	George and Elisabeth.	John Carey, Christina.

Church Records. 223

Name of Child and Date of Birth and Baptism.	Parents.	Sponsors.
Martin Frey, June 9, 1813. Aug. 26, 1813.	Jacob and Margaret.	Martin Frey, Maria Magdalena.
Susanna Knecht, March 5, 1813. May 30, 1813.	Jacob and Maria.	John Riel, Susanna.
Frederick Lerch, July 29, 1813. Sept. 16, 1813.	Anthon and Catharine.	Frederick Lerch, Elisabeth.
Elisabeth Koch, June 11, 1813. Sept. 16, 1813.	Jacob and Elisabeth.	Philip Odenwaelder, Elisabeth.
Scharlotte Schuck, Aug. 10, 1813. Sept. 16, 1813.	Peter and Susanna.	The parents.
Rachael Berry, July 26, 1813. Sept. 26, 1813.	George and Susanna.	Christian Hertzell, Anna Maria.
Wilhelmina Simon, May 15, 1813. Sept. 26, 1813.	Michael and Maria.	The parents.
Elisabeth Traxsell, Dec. 24, 1812. Sept. 30, 1813.	Michael and Catharine.	Elisabeth Ecker.
Molly Keiper, Aug. 14, 1813. Oct. 10, 1813.	Peter and Maria.	The parents.
Molly Butz, Feb. 17, 1813. Oct. 10, 1813.	David and Maria.	The parents.
Phebe Hartendorf, May 15, 1813. Oct. 12, 1813.	Frederick and Eva.	The parents.
Jesse Coleman, Aug. 5, 1813. Oct. 12, 1813.	Samuel and Maria.	Jesse Scribner, Elisabeth.
Mary Ann Kaemrer, Aug. 27, 1813. Oct. 19, 1813.	Jacob and Magdalena.	Peter Ripple, Margaret.

Name of Child and Date of Birth and Baptism.	Parents.	Sponsors.
Daniel Seip, Aug. 14, 1813. Oct. 24, 1813.	Jacob and Susanna.	Melchior Hay, Elisabeth.
Maria Anna Sheip, Oct. 1, 1813. Oct. 24, 1813.	Jacob and Maria Magdalena.	Magdalena Haag.
Samuel Lerch, Sept. 21, 1813. Nov. 7, 1813.	George and Maria.	Samuel and Elisabeth Lerch.
Rebecca Moser, Aug. 21, 1813. Nov. 8, 1813.	Jacob and Magdalena.	John George Mosen, Susanna.
John S. Barnes, Sept. 12, 1813. Nov. 21, 1813.	Henry and Catharine.	John Snyder, Elsy.
Edmond Worman, April 21, 1813. Nov. 21, 1813.	John and Jane.	Henry Hemsing, Margaret.
Christina Traxsell, Sept. 5, 1813. Nov. 29, 1813.	John and Elisabeth.	The mother.
Mary Ann Lantz, Oct. 7, 1813. Nov. 30, 1813.	John and Hanna.	John Bess, Sr., Elisabeth.
Peter Frankenfield, Oct. 20, 1813. Dec. 1, 1813.	George and Maria Magdalena.	Philip Odenwaelder, Elisabeth.
John Yost Koechlein, Oct. 14, 1813. Dec. 6, 1813.	Peter and Catharine.	John Deichman, Susanna.
George Krotz, Sept. 11, 1813. Dec. 11, 1813.	Henry and Sarah.	Michael Stecher, Margaret Laddig.
Peter Woodring, Oct. 10, 1813. Dec. 19, 1813.	William and Rosina.	Jacob Brotzman, Catharine.
Anna Elis. Ackerman, Nov. 24, 1813. Dec. 26, 1813.	Jacob and Elisabeth.	Peter Koechlein, Maria.

Church Records.

Name of Child and Date of Birth and Baptism.	Parents.	Sponsors.
	ANNO 1814.	
Elisabeth Lantz, Oct. 20, 1813. Jan. 1, 1814.	Peter and Maria.	George Lerch, Elisabeth Lantz.
John Bishoph, Oct. 16, 1813. Jan 2, 1814.	John and Anna.	John Messinger, Catharine.
Jerome Robbins, March, 1813. Jan. 2, 1814.	William and Amy.	Peter Bishoph, Barbara.
Philippina Uhler, Dec. 25, 1813. Jan. 13, 1814.	Valentin and Elisabeth.	Catharine Uhler.
Samuel Stemm, Oct. 29, 1813. Jan. 16, 1814.	John and Anna.	Jacob Laddig, Maria Hess.
Elisabeth Brinker, Oct. 24, 1813. Jan. 16, 1814.	George and Elisabeth.	John Kocher, Susanna.
Hetty Sand, Sept. 22, 1813. Jan. 21, 1814.	Michael and Maria.	The parents.
Jonathon Koehler, Dec. 27, 1813. Jan. 21, 1814.	Lenhart and Catherine.	John Koehler, Barbara.
Rebecca Osburne, Oct. 12, 1813. Jan. 29, 1814.	John and Rebecca.	The parents.
William Henry Koch, Sept. 16, 1813. Jan. 30, 1814.	Henry and Maria.	John Seip, Catharine.
Elisabeth Ross, Nov. 26, 1813. Feb. 12, 1814.	Joseph and Susanna.	The parents.
Sabina Christina Weber, Feb. 9, 1814. Feb. 13, 1814.	George and Sarah.	Valentin Weber, Christina.

Name of Child and Date of Birth and Baptism.	Parents.	Sponsors.
George Heller, Dec. 23, 1813. Feb. 13, 1814.	George and Susanna.	Jacob Heller, Susanna.
Margaretha Eierman, Dec. 27, 1812. Jan. 21, 1813.	Henry and Elisabeth.	The parents.
Christoph. Meixsell, July 10, 1813. March 13, 1814.	Christoph. and Elisabeth.	Christoph. Engel, Susanna.
Susanna Luisa Nicholas, Jan. 21, 1814. March 13, 1814.	William and Elisabeth.	Christoph. Meixsell, Elisabeth.
Christian Odenwaelder, Jan. 24, 1814. March 13, 1814.	Philip and Elisabeth.	The parents.
Sabina Wagner, Feb. 16, 1814. March 31, 1814.	Mathias and Margaret.	The parents.
Thomas Weis, Oct. 30, 1813. Apr. 9, 1814.	Solomon and Maria.	Thomas Richard, Susanna.
Thomas N. Traxsell, April 28, 1813. April 9, 1814.	George and Rosina.	Anna Uhler.
Elisabeth Cath. Heller, Feb. 14. Apr. 10.	Christoph and Susanna.	Peter Lantz, Catharine.
Samuel Dean, Oct. 12, 1813. Apr. 11, 1814.	Samuel and Sarah.	John Ihrie, Catharine.
Jacob Koehler, Dec. 20, 1813. Apr. 11, 1814.	Peter and Magdalena.	John Koehler, Barbara.
John Keller, Jan. 14, 1814. Apr. 24, 1814.	Jacob and Elisabeth.	John Odenwaelder, Elisabeth.

Name of Child and Date of Birth and Baptism.	Parents.	Sponsors.
Mary Ann Slaytor, Jan. 26, 1814. May 8, 1814.	John and Sarah.	Susanna Miles.
John Schaefer, March 16, 1814. May 19, 1814.	Jacob and Elisabeth.	The parents.
Elisabeth Moser, March 11, 1814. May 22, 1814.	Jacob and Elisabeth.	Thos. Nickum, Elisabeth.
Catharine Hackman, March 18, 1814. May 22, 1814.	Jacob and Elisabeth.	The parents.
Sarah Odenwaelder, Feb. 28, 1814. May 22, 1814.	Bernhart and Sarah.	Frederick Boyer, Elisabeth.
Adam Hertzell, Feb. 2, 1814. May 22, 1814.	Peter and Christina.	The parents.
Thos. Peter Haack, April 14, 1814. Sept. 26, 1814.	Peter and Margaret.	John Miller, Elisabeth.
Matilda Salome Erich, March 5, 1814. May 22, 1814.	Conrad and Mary.	John Ward, Salome.
Samuel Willis McCarty, Feb. 8, 1814. May 23, 1814.	Samuel and Ann.	The parents.
John Schick, March 16, 1813. May 30, 1814.	John and Jane.	The parents.
Andrew Seiler Melech, Nov. 22, 1813. June 3, 1814.	Godfried and Anna.	The parents.
Henry Frauenfelder, May 14, 1814. June 8, 1814.	Conrad and Maria.	The parents.

Name of Child and Date of Birth and Baptism.	Parents.	Sponsors.
Matilda Tilton, Sept. 9, 1811. June 12, 1814.	Peter and Elisabeth.	Peter Rohn, Elisabeth.
Edward Daniel, March 25, 1814. June 12, 1814.	Adam and Catharine.	Frederick Frey, Elisabeth.
Mary Ann Dengler, May 9, 1813. June 16, 1814.	John and Catharine.	The father and Ann Sourbeck.
Samuel Schick, April 22, 1814. June 19, 1814.	Christian and Margaret.	Andrew Appel, Elisabeth.
Elisabeth Young, March 30, 1814. June 19, 1814.	Abraham and Elisabeth.	Elisabeth Schumacher.
Elisabeth Taylor, Dec. 17, 1813. June 19, 1814.	Peter and Margaret.	Elisabeth Moyer.
Thomas Dengler, Sept. 24, 1813. June 28, 1814.	Jacob and Maria.	John Dengler, Catharine.
Simon Walter, March 28, 1814. July 3, 1814.	Frederick and Elisabeth.	Maria Fox.
Elisabeth Hertzell, Apr. 12, 1814. July 3, 1814.	John and Elisabeth.	Joseph Richard, Elisabeth Hertzel.
Margaret Stein, May 15, 1814. July 4, 1814.	Jacob and Elisabeth.	Adam Scherer, Margaret.
Christiana Rees, Aug. 24, 1812. July 5, 1814.	Philip and Mary.	Jacob Rees, Christina.
Mary Ann Rees, May 4, 1814. July 5, 1814.	Philip and Mary.	Jacob Rees, Christina.
Anna Maria Wagner, May 25, 1814. July 17, 1814.	Adam and Regina.	Peter Wagner, Elisabeth.

Name of Child and Date of Birth and Baptism.	Parents.	Sponsors.
Robert Trail Horn, June 21, 1814. July 17, 1814.	Melchior and Isabella.	The parents.
Maria Krotz, Nov. 4, 1813. July 17, 1814.	John and Catharine.	Maria Krotz.
Susanna Schwartz, March 24, 1814. July 31, 1814.	Peter and Maria.	Christopher Raub, Elisabeth.
Simon Lerch, May 5, 1814. July 17, 1814.	Frederick and Anna Maria.	Frederick Lerch, Elisabeth.
Andrew Transue, June 28, 1814. July 31, 1814.	Abraham and Elisabeth.	Andrew Schmidt, Margaretha.
George William Musselman, May 5, 1814. Aug. 17, 1814.	Elias and Susanna.	William Raub, Christina Messinger.
John Riegel, Nov. 9, 1813. Sept. 3, 1814.	George and Catharine.	The parents.
Steven Barnes, Oct. 10, 1813. Sept. 11, 1814.	Steven and Anna.	Christoph Hertzell, Anna Barnes.
John Eberhart, Nov. 3, 1812. Sept. 11, 1814.	Peter and Susanna.	Catharina Dengler.
John Miller, April 5, 1814. Sept. 11, 1814.	John and Rachel.	The mother and Barbara Hemp.
Joseph Jacob Meixsell, July 1, 1814. Sept. 11, 1814.	Philip and Maria.	The parents.
John George Odenwaelder, Sept. 12, 1814. Sept. 17, 1814.	Peter and Feronica.	Michael Odenwaelder, Margaret.

Name of Child and Date of Birth and Baptism.	Parents.	Sponsors.
Peter Koechlein, Sept. 11, 1814. Sept. 21, 1814.	Peter and Anna Maria.	Peter Koechlein, Elisabeth.
Sarah Ann Werkhaeuser, May 31, 1814. Sept. 25, 1814.	Jacob and Salome.	Philip Lerch, Elisabeth Workhaeuser.
Samuel Salzich, April 3, 1814. Sept. 25, 1814.	John and Maria.	Philip Broeder, Christina.
Maria Ann Miller, Aug. 10, 1814. Sept. 28, 1814.	Henry and Elisabeth.	Peter Miller, Maria Christina.
William Carey, June 17, 1813. Oct. 2, 1814.	John and Christina.	Jacob Carey, Catharine.
(Wanting) Lesher, May 18, 1814. Oct. 9, 1814.	George and Elisabeth.	John Lesher, Susanna Helick.
Carl Jumper, Sept. 6, 1814. Oct. 9, 1814.	Jacob and Catharine.	Joseph Reesly, Anna Maria.
Anna Juliana Weis, March 28, 1814. Oct. 9, 1814.	Mathias and Christina.	John Schlauch, Susanna.
George Biers, Sept. 5, 1814. Oct. 15, 1814.	George and Elisabeth.	John Johnson, Susanna.
Sarah Kogen, Feb. 12, 1813. Oct. 31, 1814.	Henry and Elisabeth.	The parents.
Juliana Platz, March 31, 1812. Nov. 15, 1814.	Thomas and Jane.	Catharine Sommers.
George Platz, June 24, 1814. Nov. 15, 1814.	Thomas and Jane.	Catharine Sommers.
Jacob Frees, Oct. 24, 1814. Nov. 17, 1814.	Jacob and Susanna.	The parents.

Church Records. 231

Name of Child and Date of Birth and Baptism.	Parents.	Sponsors.
John George Dean, Nov. 16, 1811. Nov. 24, 1814.	Samuel and Sarah.	John George Moser, Sarah.
John Metzger, Oct. 20, 1814. Nov. 24, 1814.	Philip and Margaret.	John Raub, Christina Messinger.
Margaret Deily, Nov. 27, 1814. Nov. 28, 1814.	Valentin and Elisabeth.	Maria Traxsell.
Philip Odenwaelder, Oct. 5, 1814. Nov. 20, 1814.	Philip and Elisabeth.	Michael Abel, Maria.
Ludwig Richard, Aug. 29, 1814. (Wanting.)	John and Susanna.	John Richard, Susanna.
Robert Oberly, Sept. 28. Nov. 11.	John and Catharine.	John Scheimer, Susanna.
Joseph Moser, Oct. 18, 1814. Nov. 20, 1814.	John and wife.	Jacob Richard, Suanne Odenwaelder.
Juliana Oberly, Oct. 23, 1814. Dec. 5, 1814.	George and Elisabeth.	Elisabeth Oberly.
Elisabeth Steinbach, Oct. 6, 1814. Dec. 18, 1814.	George and Maria.	Philip Odenwaelder, Anna Maria.
John Adam Schuman, Nov. 13, 1814. Dec. 18, 1814.	William and Christina.	John Adam Sand, Anna Maria.
Andrew Reuben Koechlein, Nov. 13, 1814. Dec. 18, 1814.	Andrew and Susanna.	William Schuman, Christina.
Benjamin Roth, March 21, 1814. Dec. 25, 1814.	Jacob and Susanna.	John Janson, Susanna.
Peter Walter, Oct. 11, 1814. Dec. 30, 1814.	Michael and Elisabeth.	The parents.

Name of Child and Date of Birth and Baptism.	Parents.	Sponsors.
Maria Belles, Nov. 13, 1814. Dec. 30, 1814.	George and Maria.	The parents.
Anna Maria Walter, March 30, 1814. Dec. 30, 1814.	John and Elisabeth.	The mother.

ANNO 1815.

Peter Walter, Oct. 23, 1812. Jan. 5, 1815.	John and Elisabeth.	The parents.
Catharine Walter, March 30, 1811. Jan. 5, 1815.	John and Elisabeth.	The parents.
Anna Maria Koch, Nov. 11, 1814. Jan. 8, 1815.	Abraham and Anna Maria.	Robert Titus, Maria Catharina.
Susanna Pfeiffer, Dec. 27, 1814. Jan. 10, 1815.	John and Sarah.	Philip Pfeiffer, Sarah.
Jacob Bishoph, Oct. 13, 1814. Jan. 15, 1815.	Peter and Barbara.	Abel Lamb, Susanna.
Jacob Cliffton, Dec. 15, 1811. Jan. 15, 1815.	John and Gertrude.	The parents.
Philip Emick, Nov. 10, 1813. Jan. 15, 1815.	Henry and Dorcas.	P. Hay, Barbara.
Alexander James Cliffton, Oct. 7, 1814. Jan. 15, 1815.	John and Gertrude.	The parents.
Joseph Rosebury, April 24, 1814. Jan. 19, 1815.	John and Hannah.	The parents.
Eliza Ann Arndt Mixsell, Oct. 15, 1814. Jan. 19, 1815.	John and Diana.	The parents.

Church Records. 233

Name of Child and Date of Birth and Baptism.	Parents.	Sponsors.
Christian Schaefer, Aug. 26, 1814. Jan. 24, 1815.	Samuel and Rosina.	Christian Schick, Maria.
Isaac Seipel, Dec. 12, 1814. Jan. 24, 1815.	John and Maria.	Peter Miller, Maria Christina.
Peter Pfeiffer, Dec. 17, 1814. Jan. 25, 1815.	John and Sarah.	Peter Kocher, Elisabeth.
Catharine Walter, Nov. 25, 1814. Jan. 27, 1815.	Lenhart and Sarah.	The parents.
Peter Ferdinand Snyder, Dec. 26, 1814. Jan. 27, 1815.	Peter and Elisabeth.	The parents.
John Osenbach, Dec. 18, 1814. Jan. 28, 1815.	Jacob and Magdalena.	George Jacoby, Christina.
Peter Seipel, Nov. 28, 1814. Feb. 3, 1815.	Conrad and Elisabeth.	Peter Miller, Maria Christina.
John Herlinger, Aug. 30, 1814. Feb. 11, 1815.	Francis and Feronica.	John Schweitzer, Catharine Butz.
Leonora Heckman, Aug. 20, 1814. Feb. 12, 1815.	John and Maria.	The parents.
Elenora Bittenbender, Jan. 3, 1815. Feb. 12, 1815.	William and Anna.	The parents.
Eliz. Cath. Snyder, Jan. 8, 1815. Feb. 12, 1815.	Samuel and Susanna.	The parents.
Carl Kessler, Jan. 8, 1815. Feb. 16, 1815.	Andrew and Catharine.	The mother.
Christina Hay, Dec. 13, 1814. Feb. 28, 1815.	Melchior and Elisabeth.	Jacob Seip, Susanna.

234   *The First Reformed Church of Easton, Pa.*

Name of Child and Date of Birth and Baptism.	Parents.	Sponsors.
Ann Lumbert, Sept. 25, 1814. March 12, 1815.	Charles and Ann.	The parents.
Jackson Arndt, Feb. 12, 1815. March 12, 1815.	George and Henrietta.	The parents.
Sarah Ann Nungesser, Jan. 15, 1815. March 12, 1815.	Peter and Sarah.	The parents.
George Jackson Everitt, Jan. 20, 1815. March 12, 1815.	John A. and Elisabeth.	The parents.
Sarah Lantz, Feb. 10, 1815. March 23, 1815.	George and Margaret.	Jacob Lantz, Dorothea Ohnangst.
John and William Fengel, Jan. 20, 1815. March 26, 1815.	George and Elisabeth.	George Smith and wife Elisabeth, William Eichman and Magd. Smith.
Louisa Catharina (wanting), Feb. 7, 1815. March 26, 1815.	George and Sarah.	Daniel Herster and Catharine.
Catharina Fisher, March 13, 1815. March 27, 1815.	Jacob and Julia.	The parents.
George Snyder Fisher, Aug. 5, 1813. March 27, 1815.	Jacob and Julia.	The parents.
Joseph Edelman, Dec. 15, 1814. April 7, 1815.	Peter and Elisabeth.	Abraham Kocher and Susanna.
Sarah Abel, Feb. 17, 1815. April 7, 1815.	Jacob and Catharine.	Peter Edelman and Elisabeth.

Name of Child and Date of Birth and Baptism.	Parents.	Sponsors.
Christian Young, adult. Baptized April 7, 1815.		
Juliana Seipel, July 16, 1815. April 9, 1815.	Henry and Sarah.	Abraham Kocher and wife Susanna.
Abraham Moser, March 2, 1815. April 9, 1815.	Jacob and Magdalena.	Abraham Kocher and wife Susanna.
Thomas Rieser, Jan. 18, 1815. April 9, 1815.	Conrad and Christina.	Peter Koechlein and Catharina.
Rebecca Schaerer, Feb. 2, 1815. April 9, 1815.	Henry and Maria.	Adam Schaerer and Margaretha.
Ann Eliza Perry, May 3, 1814. April 12, 1815. "Schwartz."	John and Lucy.	Samuel Patterson and Maria.
John Franciscus Shoch, Jan. 15, 1815. Apr. 9, 1815.	Jacob E. and Rebecca.	Sabina Michler.
Jacob Shumacher, Jan. 24, 1815. Apr. 13, 1815.	John and Catharina.	The parents.
Rosina Berry, Jan. 22, 1815. April 13, 1815.	George and Susanna.	John Woodring and Elisabeth.
Mary Ann Werkhaeuser, Jan. 5, 1815. Apr. 13, 1815.	Valentine and Sarah.	The parents.
Catharine Scheierman, March 7, 1815. Apr. 28, 1815.	Ludwig and Christina.	Ludwig Wilhelm and Sabina.

Name of Child and Date of Birth and Baptism.	Parents.	Sponsors.
Benjamin Franklin Laddig, Apr. 6, 1815. May 4, 1815.	Jacob and Sarah.	The parents.
John Radenbach, March 8, 1815. May 7, 1815.	John and Elisabeth.	John Knobel and Margaretha.
Jacob Woodring, March 22, 1815. May 7, 1815.	Nicholas and Catharine.	Jacob Steinbach and Elisabeth.
Elisabeth Bond, Jan. 1, 1815. May 10, 1815.	Thomas and Maria.	George Steinbach and Maria.
Elisabeth Gangenwer, Feb. 10, 1815. May 10, 1815.	Anthony and Sarah.	Thomas Richard and Susanna.
Aaron Brown, Feb. 12, 1815. May 10, 1815.	Jonathan and Elisabeth.	Jacob Frauenfelder and Catharine.
Elisabeth Moser, Nov. 30, 1814. May 19, 1815.	Andrew and Catharine.	Jacob Moser and Elisabeth.
Elisabeth Huhm, July 24, 1814. May 19, 1815.	Daniel and Elisabeth.	George Kessler, Margaret Laubach.
John Rees Gray, May 2, 1815. May 21, 1815.	William and Christina.	The grandfather, Jacob Rees.
Daniel Wagner, Dec. 16, 1814. Feb. 12, 1815.	Peter and Elisabeth.	Adam Wagner and Regina.
Assanias Abel, June 7, 1808. May 5, 1815.	Henry and Maria.	The parents.
Frederick Fitz Randolph, Feb. 8, 1814. May 25, 1815.	William and Susanna.	Elisabeth Barthold.

Church Records.

Name of Child and Date of Birth and Baptism.	Parents.	Sponsors.
John Philip Wolf, July 18, 1814. May 29, 1815.	George and Maria.	Philip Wolf and Susanna.
John Henry Dewitt, Oct. 9, 1814. June 8, 1815.	Jacob and Catharine.	John Doering and Elisabeth Pomp.
Jeremiah Kotz, March 27, 1815. June 18, 1815.	Henry and Charity.	The parents.
Rosanna Ward, Dec. 9, 1814. June 23, 1815.	Adam and Susanna.	The parents.
Sabina Christina Sheip, May 14, 1815. June 25, 1815.	Jacob and Magdalena.	John Sheip, Maria Miller.
Christian Kaemrer, April 27, 1815. July 16, 1815.	George and Elisabeth.	The parents.
Daniel Edelman, April 27, 1815. July 16, 1815.	Conrad and Maria.	Abraham Kocher and Susanna.
Susanna Odenwelder, May 24, 1815. July 30, 1815.	John and Anna Margaret.	Jacob Richard and Susanna.
Sarah Ann Bauers, May 14, 1814. Aug. 2, 1815.	Henry and Margaret.	The parents.
Susanna Cath. Dengler, April 22, 1815. Aug. 9, 1815.	Jacob and Maria.	Catharine Sommers.
Catharine Bess, July 6, 1815. Aug. 10, 1815.	Jacob and Catharine.	George Knecht and Catharine.
Peter Lantz, July 21, 1815. Aug. 27, 1815.	Peter and Maria.	Peter Lantz and Catharine.
Margaret Kraemer, May 2, 1815. Sept. 7, 1815.	William and Susanna.	Margaret Jacoby.

Name of Child and Date of Birth and Baptism.	Parents.	Sponsors.
Andrew Dengler, March 5, 1815. Sept. 9, 1815.	George and Margaret.	The mother.
Henrietta Bruch, June 20, 1815. Sept. 13, 1815.	Jacob and Catharine.	William Yates and Maria.
Henry Pike Baldy, July 8, 1815. Sept. 14, 1815.	John and Elisabeth.	Susanna Weygandt.
Mary Ann Jumper, March 13, 1815. Sept. 22, 1815.	Conrad and Magdalena.	George Kuhn, Elisabeth Kotz.
Peter Dietz, May 23, 1815. Oct. 20, 1815.	Nicholas and Margaret.	The parents.
George William Woodring, Aug. 25, 1815. Oct. 22, 1815.	John and Elisabeth.	George Coleman and Catharine.
Eleanora Pomp, Oct. 16, 1815. Oct. 27, 1815.	Thomas and Catharina.	The parents.
Steven Decatur Dietrich, Aug. 4, 1815. Nov. 4, 1815.	Jacob and Salome.	The parents.
Elisabeth Weiss, Sept. 21. Nov. 5.	Solomon and Maria.	Jacob Kotz, Rebecca Frankenfield.
Rosina Woodring, Sept. 19, 1815. Nov. 19, 1815.	William and Rosina.	Jacob Steinbach and Elisabeth.
Daniel Feit, Sept. 27, 1815. Nov. 19, 1815.	Paul and Catharine.	The parents.
Mary Ann Deily, Nov. 12, 1815. Nov. 19, 1815.	Valentine and Elisabeth.	Joseph Traxsell, Mary Rayer.
Anna Maria Wagner, Sept. 12, 1815. Nov. 20, 1815.	George and Elisabeth.	Frederick Wagner and Catharine.

Church Records.

Name of Child and Date of Birth and Baptism.	Parents.	Sponsors.
Elisabeth Matilda Seip, May 28, 1815. Nov. 26, 1815.	Jacob and Susanna.	George Hilliart and Margaret.
Daniel Keller, Nov. 16, 1815. Nov. 29, 1815.	Jacob and Elisabeth.	Jacob Keller and Elisabeth.
Sally Hollart, May 7, 1815. Nov. 30, 1815.	David and Mary.	Catharine Erich.
George Adam Yeisley, Oct. 10, 1815. Dec. 25, 1815.	Nicholas and Sarah.	Abraham Herzell, Christina.

Anno 1816.

Name of Child and Date of Birth and Baptism.	Parents.	Sponsors.
Joseph Koch, Sept. 15, 1815. Jan. 1, 1816.	Jacob and Elisabeth.	Abraham Koch, Anna Maria.
Isaiah Stocker, Sept. 6, 1815. Jan. 1, 1816.	John and Susanna.	Peter Koechlein, Elisabeth.
Lydia Transue, —— 1815. Jan. 27, 1816.	Jacob and Lydia.	Maria Bond.
Maria White, July 26, 1814. Feb. 10, 1816.	William and Susan.	Frederick Barthold, Elisabeth.
Easter Krahn, Feb. 19, 1815. Feb. 11, 1816.	Abraham and Sarah.	The parents.
Anna Maria Stem, Sept. 1, 1815. Feb. 11, 1816.	John and Anna.	Henry Schaerer, Anna Maria.
William Heller, Sept. 20, 1815. Feb. 11, 1816.	Jacob and Susanna.	Daniel Reichard, Dorothea.
Zirus Dengler, Jan. 1, 1815. March 9, 1816.	John and Catharine.	John Messinger, Catharine.

Name of Child and Date of Birth and Baptism.	Parents.	Sponsors.
Adam Lewis Horn, Dec. 21, 1815. March 10, 1816.	John and Elisabeth.	The parents.
Peter Young, Nov. 8, 1814. March 10, 1816.	Peter and Anna.	The parents.
Catharine Feit, Feb. 11, 1816. March 10, 1816.	John and Catharine.	The mother.
John Oberly, Feb. 2, 1816. March 23, 1816.	John and Eva.	The parents.
James Neigh, Aug. 8, 1813. March 25, 1816.	Samuel and Catharine.	The parents.
Matilda and Malessa Barnes, March 19, 1816. April 1, 1816.	Stephen and Anna.	Henry Doeringer, Lewis Castner.
William Ross, Nov. 11, 1815. April 5, 1816.	Joseph and Susanna.	The parents.
Simon Koehler, Jan. 8, 1816. April 7, 1816.	Peter and Magdalena.	Conrad Kocher, Elisabeth.
Matthew Herzell, Sept. 21, 1815. April 7, 1816.	Peter and Christina.	The parents.
Catharine Lerch, March 28, 1816. April 7, 1816.	Anthony and Catharine.	John Lerch, Rosina.
Lusianna Kind, March 14, 1816. May 2, 1816.	Isaac and Elisabeth.	The parents.
Ann Elisabeth Nicholas, Dec. 25, 1815. May 2, 1816.	William and Elisabeth.	Daniel Weber, Hannah.
Rebecca Hackman, Nov. 11, 1815. May 5, 1816.	Jacob and Elisabeth.	The parents.

Name of Child and Date of Birth and Baptism.	Parents.	Sponsors.
Sarah Ann Miller, Nov. 26, 1815. May 5, 1816.	William and Maria.	Christina Laddig.
Anna Matilda Loescher, Oct. 24, 1815. May 5, 1816.	George and Elisabeth.	David Stocker, Christina Uhler.
Elisabeth Metzgar, Jan. 30, 1816. May 5, 1816.	Christian and Elisabeth.	The parents.
William Meixsell Burke, March 26, 1816. May 8, 1816.	Joseph and Susan.	The parents.
Sarah Siegly, April 1, 1816. May 9, 1816.	George and Susanna.	John Koch, Maria.
Anna Maria Eliz. Shnyder, Jan. 17, 1816. May 12, 1816.	Peter and Elisabeth.	The parents.
Susanna Eliz. Bittenbender, Jan. 19, 1816. May 12, 1816.	William and Ann.	The parents.
William Ferdinand Shnyder, Dec. 1, 1815. May 12, 1816.	William and Sarah.	Susan Young.
Mary Ann Shick, Oct. 7, 1815. May 15, 1816.	John and Jane.	The parents.
Anna Maria Lerch, Apr. 13, 1816. May 23, 1816.	George and Anna Maria.	Frederick Lerch, Elisabeth.
Elisabeth Riegel, Nov. 18, 1815. May 30, 1816.	George and Catharine.	Elisabeth Gehres.
Charles Kutzler, Nov. 13, 1815. June 1, 1816.	Christian and Susanna.	George Walter, Sarah.

Name of Child and Date of Birth and Baptism.	Parents.	Sponsors.
Abraham Coleman, Apr. 1, 1816. May 2, 1816.	Samuel and Maria.	Abraham Klauss, Barbara.
Sophia Frauenfelder, Dec. 28, 1815. May 2, 1816.	Jacob and Catharine.	Conrad Kocher, Elisabeth.
Catharine Pfeiffer, Apr. 24, 1816. June 9, 1816.	Philip and Sarah.	John Bess, Magdalena.
Christina Traxsell, Dec. 25, 1814. June 16, 1816.	Jacob and Maria.	Christina Gehry.
Mary Ann Gehry, Oct. 14, 1815. June 16, 1816.	John and Christina.	Maria Traxsell.
Susanna Wilhelmina Traxsell, May 5, 1816. June 23, 1816.	John and Elisabeth.	John Bishop, Anna.
Anna Elisabeth Bishop, March 17, 1816. June 23, 1816.	John, Anna.	Jacob Reichard, Elisabeth.
Anna Maria Coleman, Apr. 18, 1816. June 30, 1816.	Joseph, Maria Magdalena.	Frederick Boyer, Elisabeth.
Eliza Ann Transue, July 9, 1816. July 12, 1816.	Abraham, Elisabeth.	Thomas Reichard, Susanna.
John Geo. M. Stansbury, Feb. 3, 1816. July 16, 1816.	Jacob, Christina.	George Moser, Elisabeth Raub.
Joseph Koechlein, June 22, 1816. July 28, 1816.	Peter, Maria.	Peter Edelman, Elisabeth.
Cath. Ann Schumacher, Jan. 14, 1816. July 30, 1816.	Samuel, Maria.	Daniel Raub, Catharine.

Church Records. 243

Name of Child and Date of Birth and Baptism.	Parents.	Sponsors.
David Moser, May 31, 1816. Aug. 11, 1816.	Jacob, Elisabeth.	John Odenwaelder, Ann Margaret.
Christina Herzel, June 1, 1816. Aug. 11, 1816.	John, Elisabeth.	Abraham Herzel, Christina.
Daniel Brinker, April 15, 1816. Aug. 13, 1816.	George Elisabeth.	The parents.
Elias Musselman, March 20, 1816. Aug. 25, 1816.	Elias, Susanna.	The parents.
Reuben S. Lamb, July 22, 1816. Aug. 25, 1816.	Abel, Susanna.	Michael Seip, Catharine.
Mary Ann Traxsell, May 17, 1816. Aug. 25, 1816.	Michael, Catharine.	George Weinberg, Susanna.
Elisabeth Young, Aug. 5, 1816. Sept. 26, 1816.	Peter, Amy.	The parents.
Lorenzo Worman, Jan. 24, 1816. Oct. 6, 1816.	John, Jane.	Jacob Heller, Susanna.
John Shumacher, Aug. 7, 1816. Oct. 20, 1816.	John, Catharine.	The parents.
John Herzell, Aug. 22, 1816. Oct. 20, 1816.	Samuel, Susanna.	Christian Herzell, Anna Maria.
Henry Heckman, March 27, 1811. Oct. 20, 1816.	George, Mary.	Henry Shnyder, Catharine.
Catharine Heckman, Feb. 22, 1815. Oct. 20, 1816.	George, Mary.	Henry Shnyder, Catharine.
Mary Shnyder, Aug. 25, 1816. Oct. 20, 1816.	Samuel, Susanna.	The parents.

244 *The First Reformed Church of Easton, Pa.*

Name of Child and Date of Birth and Baptism.	Parents.	Sponsors.
Sarah Ann Steinbach, Sept. 26, 1816. Nov. 17, 1816.	George, Maria.	Anna Maria Bond.
Henry Jacob Young, Nov. 24, 1816. Dec. 15, 1816.	Peter, Ann.	The parents.
Henrietta Louisa Young, Nov. 24, 1816. Dec. 15, 1816.	Peter, Ann.	The parents.
Lisetta Cath. Sheip, Nov. 8, 1816. Dec. 15, 1816.	Jacob, Maria Magdalena.	John Sheip, Maria Christina.
John William Jacob Schlaugh, Oct. 27, 1816. Dec. 15, 1816.	John, Susanna.	The parents.

Anno 1817.

George Miller, Oct. 16, 1816. Jan. 1, 1817.	John and Rachel.	The father, Margaret Miller.
Christian Butz, Oct. 13, 1814. Jan. 1, 1817.	David and Susanna.	The parents.
Susanna Butz, Nov. 27, 1816. Jan. 1, 1817.	David and Susanna.	The parents.
Christian Keiper, Dec. 4, 1816. Jan. 1, 1817.	Peter and Maria.	The parents.
Samuel Kinsey Mixsell, July 20, 1816. Jan. 3, 1817.	Philip and Maria.	The father, Eva Wagner.
George Walter, Oct. 12, 1816. Jan. 21, 1817.	Michael and Elisabeth.	George Hilliart, Margaret.

Name of Child and Date of Birth and Baptism.	Parents.	Sponsors.
John Transue, Dec. 12, 1816. Jan. 23, 1817.	Anthony and Maria.	John Koch, Maria.
Susanna Roth, Sept. 3, 1816. Feb. 23, 1817.	Jacob and Susanna.	Jacob Seip, Susanna.
Sarah Seipel, March 8, 1816. Feb. 26, 1817.	Henry and Sarah.	The parents
Elisabeth Seip, Jan. 15, 1817. March 31, 1817.	Jacob and Susanna.	The parents
Jacob Arndt Meixsell, Feb. 17, 1817. April 3, 1817.	John and Diana.	The parents.
David Appel, Dec. 27, 1816. April 6, 1817.	Andrew and Elisabeth.	The parents.
Jacob Moser, Dec. 30, 1816. April 7, 1817.	Andrew and Catharine.	John Frutschman, Margaret.
Isaac Moser, Dec. 30, 1816. April 7, 1817.	Andrew and Catharine.	Samuel Nickum, Elisabeth.
Sarah Ann Walter, Nov. 6, 1816. April 19, 1817.	William and Maria.	Bernhart Walter, Maria.
Matilda Odenwaelder, Dec. 13, 1815. April 19, 1817.	Jacob and Maria.	The parents.
Sally Ann Weinland, Sept. 14, 1816. April 19, 1817.	Christian and Elisabeth.	Michael Odenwaelder, Margaret.
William Hackman, March 9, 1817. April 27, 1817.	Jacob and Elisabeth.	The parents.
Susanna Kieffer, Feb. 14, 1817. April 27, 1817.	Andrew and Elisabeth.	John Odenwaelder Margaret.

246   *The First Reformed Church of Easton, Pa.*

Name of Child and Date of Birth and Baptism.	Parents.	Sponsors.
Susanna Biers, Sept. 25, 1817.[1] April 27, 1817.	George and Elisabeth.	Frederick Moser, Rosina.
Edward Kaemrer, Feb. 25, 1817. March 19, 1817.	George and Elisabeth.	Nicholas Roth.
William Smith, Sept. 23, 1815. May 4, 1817.	John and Mary.	Frederick Barthold, Eva Maria Erb.
Henry Gustavus Wolf, Feb. 3, 1817. May 4, 1817.	George and Maria.	Frederick Barthold, Elisabeth.
Elisabeth Gulick, Jan. 12, 1814. May 4, 1817.	Nathan and Elisabeth.	Frederick Barthold, Elisabeth.
Margaret Gulick, April 7, 1816. May 4, 1817.	Nathan and Elisabeth.	Frederick Barthold, Mary Wolf.
John Henry Essert, May 3, 1816. May 4, 1817.	John and Hannah.	Frederick Wagner, Anna.
Peter Koch, Feb. 18, 1817. May 4, 1817.	Abraham and Anna.	Jacob Koch, Elisabeth.
Sabina Schade, Feb. 8, 1817. May 4, 1817.	John and Susanna.	Henry Klauss, Elisabeth.
John Bess, May 4, 1817. June 1, 1817,	Jacob and Catharine.	Philip Odenwaelder, Elisabeth.
Andrew Krotz, Oct. 31, 1816. June 1, 1817.	John and Catharine.	George Lerch, Maria.
Catharine Odenwaelder, April 4, 1817. June 1, 1817.	Philip and Elisabeth.	Jacob Bess, Catharine.

[1] Evidently a mistake.

Church Records. 247

Name of Child and Date of Birth and Baptism.	Parents.	Sponsors.
Louisa Kraemer, March 23, 1817. June 2, 1817.	William and Susanna.	Jacob Shimer, Elisabeth.
William Fehr, Feb. 14, 1817. June 8, 1817.	George and Susanna.	Michael Fehr, Elisabeth.
Anna Maria Moser, July 19, 1815. July 21, 1817.	George and Maria.	The parents.
William Ettinger, Oct. 18, 1812. July 31, 1817.	Abraham and Veronica.	The parents.
Daniel Ettinger, May 8, 1817. July 31, 1817.	Abraham and Veronica.	Daniel Raub, Catharine.
George William Raub, May 20, 1817. Aug. 2, 1817.	William and Elisabeth.	Peter Seiler, Margaret.
Peter Berry, June 12, 1817. Aug. 10, 1817.	George, Susanna.	Philip Peiffer, Sarah.
Evelina Faber Susan Rose Arndt, Oct. 16, 1816. July 1, 1817.	George, Henrietta.	Eva Faber, Maria Hayes.
William Bixler Reiss, March 9, 1817. July 13, 1817.	Peter and Susanna.	The parents.
Rosina Herzell, April 7, 1817. July 13, 1817.	Abraham and Christina.	Samuel Herzell, Susanna.
Caroline Simon, Jan. 8, 1816. Aug. 31, 1817.	Michael and Maria.	The parents.
Elisabeth Walter, May 27, 1817. Aug. 24, 1817.	Frederick and Elisabeth.	Elisabeth Schumacher.
Andrew Simon, April 12, 1817. Aug. 24, 1817.	John and Susanna.	Andrew Hay, Elisabeth.

Name of Child and Date of Birth and Baptism.	Parents.	Sponsors.
Henry S. Carey, Jan. 30, 1817. Aug. 24, 1817.	John and Christina.	Henry Shnyder, Catharine.
Susan Seagreaves, Oct. 22, 1815. Nov. 24, 1817.	Henry and Eva.	John Shuck, Mary Lucker.
Joseph Lewis Sculy, April 1, 1813. Sept. 3, 1817.	William and Margaret.	The parents.
Steven Decatur Sculy, May 14, 1815. Sept. 3, 1817.	William and Margaret.	The parents.
David Sculy, June 1, 1817. Sept. 3, 1817.	William and Margaret.	The parents.
Mary Annanetta Snyder, July 24, 1816. Sept. 3, 1817.	Joseph and Susanna.	The parents.
Edmund Odenwaelder, Sept. 25, 1816. Sept. 3, 1816.	Philip and Elisabeth.	Christian Butz, Magdalena.
John William Loesher, May 23, 1817. Sept. 4, 1817.	George and Elisabeth.	Jacob Kaemrer, Magdalena.
Rosanna Traxsell, Feb. 4, 1817. Sept. 14, 1817.	George and Rosina.	Andrew Hay, Elisabeth.
Sarah Ann Arner, Feb. 24, 1817. May 3, 1817.	Henry and Catharine.	Jacob Schnabel, Elisabeth.
Abraham Brotzman, Aug. 29, 1817. Sept. 13, 1817.	Joseph and Elisabeth.	Maria Brotzman.
Malvina Fierer, Sept. 1, 1811. Oct. 3, 1817.	John and Elisabeth.	The mother.

Name of Child and Date of Birth and Baptism.	Parents.	Sponsors.
Eva Fierer, Jan. 23, 1812. Oct. 3, 1817.	John and Elisabeth.	The mother.
Maria Fierer, July 4, 1815. Oct. 3, 1817.	John and Elisabeth.	The mother.
John McClaughin. Dec. 15, 1814. Oct. 3, 1817.	Anthony and Anna.	The mother.
William Valentine Deyli, Sept. 23, 1817. Oct. 5, 1817.	Valentine and Elisabeth.	Philip Deily, Anna Maria.
Anna Maria Traxsell, Apr. 13, 1817. Oct. 5, 1817.	Jacob and Maria.	Valentine Deily, Elisabeth.
Catharine Woodring, Sept. 10, 1817. Oct. 19, 1817.	Nicholas and Catharine.	Jacob Bess, Catharine.
John Ervin, Feb. 11, 1817. Oct. 24, 1817.	Hannah Robbins.	Joseph Traxsell, Maria Bishop.
Samuel Ward, Sept. 8, 1817. Nov. 16, 1817.	Adam and Susanna.	The parents.
Nicholas Lantz, Nov. 16, 1817. Dec. 23, 1817.	Peter and Maria.	Nicholas Klein, Margaret.
Anna Eliz. Knauss, Oct. 1, 1815. Dec. 30, 1817.	John and Regina.	The parents.
ANNO 1818.		
Elisabeth Bishop, Oct. 30, 1817. Jan. 11, 1818.	Peter and Barbara.	Charles Hay, Elisabeth.
Edmond Keller, Oct. 3, 1817. Jan. 11, 1818.	Jacob and Elisabeth.	Peter Odenwaelder, Veronica.

250   *The First Reformed Church of Easton, Pa.*

Name of Child and Date of Birth and Baptism.	Parents.	Sponsors.
Simon Laddig, Oct. 7, 1817. Jan. 16, 1818.	Jacob and Maria.	The parents.
Lewis Seip, Oct. 20, 1817. Jan. 25, 1818.	John and Salome.	Conrad Haas, Hannah.
Maria Ohnangst, Dec. 13, 1817. Jan. 31, 1818.	Philip and Ann Margaret.	The parents.
Edmond Herzell, Oct. 6, 1814. Feb. 8, 1818.	Jacob and Catharine.	Christopher Herzell.
Phoebe Ann Herzell, April 13, 1817. Feb. 8, 1818.	Jacob and Catharine.	Benjamin Medler, Margaret.
Sarah Ann Weiss, Sept. 19, 1817. Feb. 21, 1818.	Solomon and Maria.	The parents.
Sarah Ann Edelman, Oct. 7, 1817. March 6, 1818.	Conrad and Maria.	Philip Odenwaelder, Elisabeth.
Maria Eckart, Sept. 28, 1816. March 8, 1818.	John and Sarah.	Michael Frankenfeld, Susanna Eckart.
Joseph Shnyder, Feb. 13, 1818. March 9, 1818.	John and Elisabeth.	The parents.
Adam Heckman, Apr. 25, 1817. March 31, 1818.	George and Maria.	The mother.
Hannah Walter, Jan. 10, 1818. Apr. 11, 1818.	Jacob and Elisabeth.	The parents.
Thos. Richard Pomp, March 7, 1818. Apr. 8, 1818.	Thomas and Catharine.	Thomas Richard, Susanna.
Joseph Broeder, Feb. 12, 1818. Apr. 18, 1818.	John and Elisabeth.	Joseph Coleman, Magdalena.

Name of Child and Date of Birth and Baptism.	Parents.	Sponsors.
Anna Matilda Coleman. Feb. 2, 1818. Apr. 21, 1818.	Samuel and Mary.	George Shade, Elisabeth.
Samuel Belles, June 8, 1817. Apr. 26, 1818.	John and Elisabeth.	The parents.
Susanna Belles, Jan. 19, 1818. Apr. 26, 1818.	Joseph and Sarah.	Joseph Wolbach, Rachel.
Catharine Odenwaelder, Feb. 21, 1818. May 3, 1818.	John and Margaret.	Philip Odenwaelder, Elisabeth.
Susanna Odenwaelder, Nov. 27, 1817. May 3, 1818.	Bernhart and Sarah.	Henry Yaeger, Susanna.
George Kutzler, Jan. 11, 1818. May 3, 1818.	Christian and Susanna.	Henry Messinger, Sarah.
Anthony Lerch, Feb. 16, 1818. May 3, 1818.	Anthony and Elisabeth.	Michael Fraess, Gertrude.
Rosina Shumacher, Jan. 11, 1818. May 3, 1818.	John and Catharine.	The parents.
Jennetta Leidig, Sept. 3, 1809. May 12, 1818.	John and Juliana.	The parents.
Thomas Leidig, Dec. 15, 1814. May 12, 1818.	John and Juliana.	The parents.
Juliana Leidig, Feb. 13, 1818. May 12, 1818.	John and Juliana.	The parents.
Sarah Ann Dengler, July 22, 1816. May 18, 1818.	Jacob and Maria.	Cath. Sommer.

Name of Child and Date of Birth and Baptism.	Parents.	Sponsors.
Peter Thomas Miller, May 13, 1818. May 22, 1818.	Peter and Hester.	John Sheip, Elisabeth Pomp.
Catharine Koechlein, March 26, 1818. May 30, 1818.	Peter and Maria.	Catharine Edelman.
Samuel Kocher, Jan. 12, 1818. May 31, 1818.	Jonas and Catharine.	Samuel Neigh, Eva.
Hanna Eliz. Dreisbach, Jan. 7, 1818. May 31, 1818.	Adam and Eliza.	John Neiss, Cath. Dreisbach.
Elisabeth Bruch, April 7, 1818. June 28, 1818.	George and Catharine.	Jacob Lantz, Elisabeth Schaerer.
John Richard, April 15, 1818. June 28, 1818.	Jacob and Susanna.	John Odenwaelder, Sr., Eliz. Margaretha.
Mary Ann Wilhelm, May 12, 1818. June 28, 1818.	Henry and Susan.	Andrew Appel, Elisabeth.
Eliza Oberly, May 20, 1818. July 7, 1818.	George and Elisabeth.	John Schweitzer, Magdalena.
Elisabeth Young, June 25, 1818. July 11, 1818.	Peter and Margaret.	Eva Schower.
Conrad Seipel, Dec. 19, 1817. July 12, 1818.	Henry and Sarah.	George Dewalt, Elisabeth Wagner.
Susanna Herzell, May 30, 1818. July 12, 1818.	Samuel and Susanna.	Abraham Herzell, Christina.
Daniel Butz, July 13, 1818. Aug. 12, 1818.	David and Maria.	The parents.
John Woodring, April 2, 1818. Aug. 23, 1818.	John and Elisabeth.	John Bess, Magdalena.

Church Records. 253

Name of Child and Date of Birth and Baptism.	Parents.	Sponsors.
Isaac Yeisley, July 3, 1818. Aug. 23, 1818.	Nicholas and Sarah.	Jacob Spangenberg, Susanna.
Marietta Salzig, March 7, 1818. Aug. 23, 1818.	John and Maria.	John Coleman, Jane Salzig.
George Peter Essert, Aug. 11, 1818. Aug. 29, 1818.	John and Hannah.	Peter Miller Junr., Hetty.
Thomas Stem, Nov. 6, 1817. Aug. 31, 1818.	John and Anna.	The parents.
Eliza Ann Hackman, June 28, 1818. Sept. 20, 1818.	Jacob and Elisabeth.	The parents.
Susanna Cath. Shnyder, June 17, 1818. Sept. 24, 1818.	Joseph and Susanna.	The parents.
Wilhelmina Eliz. West. Sept. 7, 1817. Sept. 24, 1818.	George and Catharine.	The parents.
David Steitinger, Oct. 4, 1805. Sept. 24, 1818.	John and Christina.	The mother.
Ellenora Worman, Sept. 8, 1811. Sept. 24, 1818.	Andrew and Maria.	Christina Steitinger.
Caroline Worman, March 7, 1815. Sept. 24, 1818.	Andrew and Maria.	Margaret Purlees.
Andrew Worman, Nov. 8, 1817. Sept. 24, 1818.	Andrew and Maria.	Elisabeth Schmidt.
Catharine Bachman, Nov. 26, 1815. Sept. 24, 1818.	Abraham and Anna.	Andrew Worman, Maria.
Elisabeth Bachman, Feb. 10, 1818. Sept. 24, 1818.	Abraham and Anna.	Elisabeth Schmidt.

254   *The First Reformed Church of Easton, Pa.*

Name of Child and Date of Birth and Baptism.	Parents.	Sponsors.
Henrietta Dietz, Sept. 17, 1818. Sept. 25, 1818.	Nicholas and Mary.	The mother.
Maria Diehl, Aug. 17, 1818. Sept. 28, 1818.	Maria Diehl.	Margaret Diehl.
Maria Ann Juliana Bittenbender, Feb. 1, 1818. Nov. 15, 1818.	William and Ann.	Conrad Bittenbender, Elisabeth.
Sophia Sabina Snyder, Oct. 7, 1818. Nov. 5, 1818.	Samuel and Susanna.	The father and Cath. Snyder.
Susanna H. Odenwaelder, Sept. 25, 1818. Nov. 15, 1818.	Michael and Sarah.	The parents.
Christopher Nicholas, Feb. 25, 1818. Nov. 16, 1818.	William and Elisabeth.	Christoph Engel, Susanna.
(Wanting) O'daniel, May 30, 1818. Oct. 17, 1818.	Dennis and Elisabeth.	Joseph Gehres, Susanna.
Lewis Nicholas, July 6, 1818. Oct. 18, 1818.	Joseph and Elisabeth.	John Roeder, Sophia.
Margaret Lerch, Sept. 1, 1818. Oct. 18, 1818.	George and Maria.	John Lerch, Rosina.
William Henry Sheip, Aug. 27, 1818. Oct. 18, 188 .	Jacob and Maria Magd.	The parents.
Sophia Cath. Shnyder, March 16, 1818. Oct. 27, 1818.	Peter and Elisabeth.	The parents.
Elisabeth Stocker, July 30, 1818. Nov. 15, 1818.	George and Rosina.	Robert Ewing, Susanna Diehl.

Name of Child and Date of Birth and Baptism.	Parents.	Sponsors.
Jacob Young, Apr. 29, 1818. Nov. 18, 1818.	Peter and Amy.	The parents.
Emelia Eliz. Philips, Aug. 13, 1818. Dec. 1, 1818.	John and Maria.	Jacob Sheip, Maria Christina.
Eliza Ann Coleman, Oct. 13, 1818. Nov. 13, 1818.	Benjamin and Catharine.	George Oberly, Elisabath.
Rosina Brotzman, Sept. 6, 1818. Dec. 14, 1818.	Peter and Sarah Ann.	Frederick Moser, Rosina.
ANNO 1819.		
William R. Grotz, Sept. 21, 1818. Jan. 6, 1819.	Henry and Sarah.	Robert Miller and Catharine.
Sarah Young, Nov. 21, 1818. Jan. 22, 1819.	Adam and Margaret.	John Bess, Magdalena.
Solomon Walter, Dec. 25, 1818. Jan. 24, 1819.	Peter and Abigail.	The parents.
Christina Walter, Dec. 20, 1818. Jan. 24, 1819.	Michael and Elisabeth.	Solomon Walter, Christina Seip.
Matilda Gaehres, Nov. 30, 1818. Jan. 27, 1819.	George and Catharine.	Samuel Herzell, Susanna.
William H. Seagreaves, July 20, 1818. Feb. 7, 1819.	Henry and Eva.	John Shuck, Catharine Shnyder.
George Gangenwehr, Jan. 20, 1819. Feb. 7, 1819.	Jacob and Maria.	John Kessler, Elisabeth Hay.
Charles Heinlein, Aug. 16, 1816. March 8, 1819.	George and Elisabeth.	Frederick Moser, Rosina.

The First Reformed Church of Easton, Pa.

Name of Child and Date of Birth and Baptism.	Parents.	Sponsors.
Anna Maria Heinlein, Jan. 7, 1819. March 8, 1819.	George and Elisabeth.	John Kessler, Maria Shuel.
Regina Brotzman, Feb. 17, 1819. March 11, 1819.	Joseph and Elisabeth.	Andrew Kieffer, Elisabeth.
Alexander Young, Feb. 27, 1819. March 12, 1819.	Peter and Amy.	The parents.
Daniel Black, Oct. 30, 1818. March 12, 1819.	James and Mary.	The parents.
Abraham Transue, March 13, 1819. March 22, 1819.	Anthony and Ann Maria.	John Koch, Ann Maria.
Matilda Woodring, Feb. 17, 1819. March 25, 1819.	Philip and Elisabeth.	Nicholas Woodring, Catharine.
Lisetta Weiss, July 24, 1818. April 2, 1819.	Matthias and Christina.	Susanna Conrad.
Charles Hay, Dec. 14, 1818. April 2, 1819.	The mother is Maria Froelich.	George Lerch, Maria.
Eva Odenwaelder, March 13, 1818. April 8, 1819.	Jacob and Mary.	The parents.
Margaret Weinland, Jan. 24, 1819. April 8, 1819.	Christian B. and Elisabeth.	Jacob Odenwaelder, Mary.
Anna Matilda Scherer, Feb. 8, 1819. April 9, 1819.	Henry and Anna Maria.	John Stemm, Anna.
Samuel Gehres, March 17, 1819. April 20, 1819.	Joseph and Susanna.	Samuel Herzell, Susanna.
Catharine Janson, Adult—bap. May 28, 1819.	Daniel and Margaret.	

Church Records. 257

Name of Child and Date of Birth and Baptism.	Parents.	Sponsors.
Rebecca Ackerman, Nov. 20, 1818. May 29, 1819.	Jacob and Elisabeth.	Peter Edelman, Elisabeth.
Andrew Brinker, Dec. 20, 1818. May 30, 1819.	George and Elisabeth.	Andrew Schmidt, Margaret.
Susanna Peiffer, Feb. 14, 1819. May 30, 1819.	Philip and Sarah.	Sam¹ Wollenschlaeger, Dorothea.
Samuel Coleman, March 21, 1819. May 30, 1819.	Joseph and Magdalena.	Henry Derr, Rebecca.
Abraham Backaw, Oct. 26, 1818. May 30, 1819.	William and Elisabeth.	George Sickman, Sarah.
Catharine Bess, May 8, 1819. May 31, 1819.	Jacob and Catharine.	John Scheively, Elisabeth.
John Peter Jacoby, May 28, 1819. May 31, 1819.	Peter and Maria.	Margaret Jacoby.
Susanna Loesher, Feb. 28, 1819. June 13, 1819.	John and Elisabeth.	Harry Messinger, Sarah.
Catharine Eckart, April 11, 1819. June 13, 1819.	John and Sarah.	William Wayn (?), Elisabeth.
Lydia Moser, March 6, 1819. June 27, 1819.	George and Maria.	Jacob Bess, Lydia Klein.
William Zimmerman, May 2, 1819. June 20, 1819.	Joseph and Maria.	Isaac Scheimer, Elisabeth.
Wilhelmina Laddig, March 31, 1819. July 25, 1819.	Jacob and Maria.	The parents.
Caroline Maria Weygandt, Aug. 3, 1819. Aug. 22, 1819.	Peter and Barbara.	Nicholas Klein, Maria Ohl.

Name of Child and Date of Birth and Baptism.	Parents.	Sponsors.
Susanna Koch, June 10, 1819. Aug. 22, 1819.	Abraham and Anna Maria.	Leonard Frankenfield, Susanna.
Samuel Miller, March 13, 1819. Aug. 22, 1819.	John and Rachael.	The parents.
Isaac Hayney, July 13, 1819. Aug. 22, 1819.	John and Catharine.	Henry Ohnangsh, Elisabeth Taylor.
Sarah Ann Dennis, June 15, 1819. Sept. 19, 1819.	Peter and Maria.	John Hoffman, Maria Sarah.
Andrew Appel, May 23, 1819. Oct. 3, 1819.	Andrew and Elisabeth.	Peter Odenwaelder, Veronica.
William Odenwaelder, Jan. 2, 1819. Oct. 17, 1819.	Philip and Elisabeth.	The parents.
William Keller, July 17, 1819. Oct. 17, 1819.	Jacob and Elisabeth.	Joseph Richard, Elisabeth.
John Jacob Carey, April 1, 1819. Oct. 17, 1819.	John and Christina.	John Schuck, Rosina Pence.
Sophia Heckman, March 15, 1819. Oct. 24, 1819.	George and Maria.	Charles Shnyder, Elisabeth Pomp.
Maria Trahn, July 7, 1819. Oct. 28, 1819.	Matthew and Anna.	Catharine Smith.
Margaret Walter, Oct. 31, 1819. Nov. 7, 1819.	Frederick and Elisabeth.	Andrew Schmidt, Margaret.
Susanna Belles, March 21, 1819. Nov. 10, 1819.	John and Elisabeth.	The parents.
Nicholas Traxsell, Aug. 13, 1819. Nov. 14, 1819.	Jacob and Maria.	Nicholas Traxsell.

Church Records.

Name of Child and Date of Birth and Baptism.	Parents.	Sponsors.
Margaret Deily, Sept. 13, 1819. Nov. 14, 1819.	Valentine and Elisabeth.	Maria Traxsell.
Henry Steinbach, Oct. 2, 1819. Nov. 14, 1819.	George and Maria.	Nicholas Bess, Elisabeth Sheively.
Philip Meixsell, May 12, 1819. Nov. 19, 1819.	Philip and Maria.	The father and grandmother, Eva Wagoner.
John Stocker, Sept. 7, 1819. Dec. 2, 1819.	The mother is Margaret Koechlein.	Peter Koechlein, Sr., Anna Elisabeth.
John Young, Oct. 6, 1819. Dec. 12, 1819.	Daniel and Catharine.	Adam Young, Elisabeth.
Sarah Herzell, Oct. 3, 1819. Dec. 25, 1819.	Abraham and Christina.	Nicholas Yeisley, Sarah.
Anna Maria Eichman, Oct. 24, 1819. Dec. 25, 1819.	Henry and Elisabeth.	Jacob Scheip, Maria Magdalena.
Anna Maria Weygandt, April 9, 1819. Dec. 25, 1819.	Catharine Weygandt, widow.	Henry Eichman, Elisabeth.
ANNO 1820.		
Maria Kocher, July 4, 1819, Jan. 1, 1820.	John and Maria.	George Lerch, Maria.
William Koechlein, Dec. 4, 1819. Jan. 1, 1820.	Peter and Maria.	Peter Maurer, Ann Margaret.
Christina Shnyder, Nov. 23, 1819. Jan. 5, 1820.	John and Elisabeth.	George Hilliart, Margaret.
Elisabeth Keiper, Nov. 12, 1819. Jan. 9, 1820.	Peter and Mary.	The parents.

Name of Child and Date of Birth and Baptism.	Parents.	Sponsors.
David Edelman, Aug. 31, 1819. Jan. 10, 1820.	Peter and Elisabeth.	The parents.
Ann Maria Broeder, Dec. 15, 1819. Jan. 23, 1820.	John and Elisabeth.	Adam Schlecht, Susanna.
Henry Raub, Nov. 9, 1819. Jan. 27, 1820.	Bernhart and Maria.	Henry Krotz, Sarah.
Sophia Messinger, Nov. 21, 1819. Feb. 6, 1820.	Henry and Sarah.	John Roeder, Sophia.
Eva Bishop, Dec. 15, 1819. Feb. 6, 1820.	Peter and Barbara.	The parents.
Anna Maria Long, Nov. 27, 1819. Feb. 8, 1820.	Jacob and Elisabeth.	John Laubach, Susanna.
Mary Ann Russell, Sept. 5, 1819. March 5, 1820.	Robert and Elisabeth.	Jacob Moser, Elisabeth.
Jacob Ackerman, Feb. 9, 1820. March 5, 1820.	Jacob and Elisabeth.	Jacob Koechlein, Elisabeth.
John Bettinger, Dec. 21, 1819. March 5, 1820.	Maria Ward.	Adam Ward, Susanna.
Sarah Ann Transue, Jan. 8, 1820. April 2, 1820.	Abraham and Elisabeth.	Peter Wagner, Elisabeth.
Abraham Kiefer, March 3, 1820. April 19, 1820.	Andrew and Elisabeth.	Abraham Brotzman.
Mary Ann Lerch, March 13, 1820. April 30, 1820.	Anthony and Elisabeth.	George Lerch, Maria.
Daniel Young, March 10, 1820. May 6, 1820.	Peter and Margaret.	Daniel Young, Catharine.

Church Records. 261

Name of Child and Date of Birth and Baptism.	Parents.	Sponsors.
Jacob Loescher, April 8, 1820. May 16, 1820.	Melchoir and Elisabeth.	The parents.
Sophia Hackman, Nov. 11, 1819. May 28, 1820.	Jacob and Elisabeth.	The parents.
Anna Maria Seipel, Jan. 2, 1820. May 28, 1820.	Jacob and Elisabeth.	The parents.
Margaret Magd. Stem, Feb. 27, 1820. June 9, 1820.	John and Anna.	John Bess, Magdalena.
John Woodring, May 27, 1820. July 23, 1820.	Nicholas and Catharine.	John Bess, Magdalena.
William James Kelso, June 16, 1820. July 28, 1820.	James and Catharine.	Simon Butz, Elisabeth.
Elisabeth Plower, June 18, 1820, Aug. 8, 1820.	John and Catharine.	Peter Diehl, Elisabeth Schmidt.
Susanna Spangenberg, Dec. 19, 1819. Aug. 10, 1820.	Frederick and Anna.	Jacob Edelman, Susanna Richard.
Lewis Roth, April 14, 1820. Aug. 16, 1820.	Jacob and Susanna.	The parents.
Anna Rosina Woodring, July 23, 1820. Aug. 20, 1820.	Jacob and Sarah.	Rosina Woodring.
Elisabeth Shumacher, July 8, 1820. Aug. 20, 1820.	John and Catharine.	The parents.
Sophia Matilda Kinsey, July 4, 1820. Aug. 20, 1820.	Jonathon and Sarah.	The parents.

Name of Child and Date of Birth and Baptism.	Parents.	Sponsors.
Rebecca Hoffman, Nov. 13, 1808. Aug. 20, 1820.	Jacob and Maria Sarah.	Margaret Sheively.
Maria Sarah Hoffman, Dec. 1, 1817. Aug. 20, 1820.	Jacob and Maria Sarah.	Peter Sheively, Ann.
Rebecca C. Shnyder, March 16, 1820. Aug. 22, 1820.	Joseph and Susanna.	Aaron Shnyder, Rebecca Simon.
Maria Julian Sculy, Oct. 9, 1820. Aug. 22, 1820.	William and Margaret.	David Shnyder, Juliann Shnyder.
William Young, May 20, 1819. Aug. 28, 1820.	Peter and Amy.	The parents.
Selina Dietrich, Aug. 20, 1820. Aug. 28, 1820.	Joseph and Sarah.	Salome Dietrich.
Edward Lorentz, Nov. 19, 1819. Aug. 29, 1820.	George and Mary.	The parents.
Petter Laddig, June 5, 1820. Sept. 17, 1820.	George and Anna.	The parents.
Susanna Walter, Aug. 25, 1820. Oct. 26, 1820.	Leonhard and Sarah.	The parents.
Caroline Shnyder, March 25, 1820. Nov. 6, 1820.	Peter and Elisabeth.	The parents.
Anna Maria Black, Aug. 17, 1820. Nov. 27, 1820.	James and Mary.	The parents.
William Herzell, Sept. 12, 1820. Dec. 10, 1820.	Samuel and Susanna.	John Yeisley, Eliz. Herzell.
Mary Ann Steinbach, Nov. 3, 1820. Dec. 12, 1820.	Henry and Maria.	The parents.

Church Records. 263

Name of Child and Date of Birth and Baptism.	Parents.	Sponsors.
Margaret Koechlein, Oct. 23, 1820. Dec. 14, 1820.	Michael and Margaret.	The parents.
Mary B. Krotz, Nov. 21, 1817. Dec. 25, 1820.	Isaac and Hannah.	Samuel Bittenbender, Mary.
Eliza B. Krotz, Sept. 30, 1820. Dec. 25, 1820.	Isaac and Hannah.	William Bittenbender, Ann.
Aronetta S. Bittenbender, Sept. 28, 1819. Dec. 25, 1820.	William and Ann.	Aaron Shnyder, Juliann Shnyder.
ANNO 1821.		
Elisabeth Koechlein, Dec. 29, 1820. Jan. 10, 1821.	Jacob and Elisabeth.	The parents.
Cath. Frederica Hackman, Oct. 8, 1820. Jan. 12, 1821.	Jonas and Catharine.	Conrad Bender, Susanna.
Carl Wagner, Sept. 16, 1820. Jan. 26, 1821.	Peter and Elisabeth.	Jacob Roth, Susanna.
Eliza Coleman, Oct. 23, 1820. Feb. 4, 1821.	Joseph and Magdalena.	John Broeder, Elisabeth.
Josephina Gress, Dec. 19, 1820. Feb. 4, 1821.	John and Margaret.	Augustus Patier, Louisa.
Sophia Brotzman, Jan. 14, 1821. Feb. 4, 1821.	Joseph and Elisabeth.	Susanna Brotzman.
Thomas Koechlein, Jan. 20, 1821. Feb. 9, 1821.	Peter and Maria.	George Dech, Sarah.
Thomas Odenwaelder, Jan. 26, 1821. Feb. 21, 1821.	John and Ann Margaret.	The parents.

Name of Child and Date of Birth and Baptism.	Parents.	Sponsors.
Elisabeth Woodring, Dec. 27, 1820. March 4, 1821.	John and Elisabeth.	Jacob Steinbach, Elisabeth.
William Odenwaelder, Jan. 24, 1821. March 4, 1821.	Jacob and Elisabeth.	John Odenwaelder, Sr., Elisabeth.
Magdalena Binninger, Feb. 3, 1821. Feb. 17, 1821.	Jacob and Magdalena.	The parents.
Daniel Yeisley, Jan. 19, 1821. April 1, 1821.	Nicholas and Sarah.	John Richard, Susanna.
Sarah Derr, Dec. 16, 1820. April 1, 1821.	Henry and Rebecca.	John Coleman, Maria.
William Henry Swander, Feb. 28, 1821. April 1, 1821.	Daniel and Maria.	Jacob Keller, Jr., Elisabeth.
Charles Barnes, Aug. 14, 1819. April 13, 1821.	Stephen and Anna.	The parents.
Jacob Bess, March 31, 1821. April 14, 1821.	Jacob and Catharine.	Jacob Steinbach, Elisabeth.
Mary Ann Gehres, Nov. 27, 1820. April 15, 1821.	Joseph and Susanna.	Jacob Hasenfuss, Elisabeth Herzell.
Zacharias Simon, Aug. 12, 1819. May 10, 1821.	John and Susanna.	The mother.
Susanna Musselman, Jan. 2, 1821. May 24, 1821.	Elias and Susanna.	George Musselman.
Jacob Spangenberg, March 21, 1821. May 27, 1821.	Jacob and Susanna.	Jacob Richard, Susanna.

Name of Child and Date of Birth and Baptism.	Parents.	Sponsors.
William Spangenberg, March 21, 1821. May 27, 1821.	Jacob and Susanna.	Isaac Lantz, Elisabeth.
Sophia Woodring, April 8, 1821. May 27, 1821.	Philip and Elisabeth.	Philip Woodring, Catharine.
John Peter Beck, April 23, 1821. May 27, 1821.	Jacob and Susanna.	John Koch, Ann Maria.
Solomon Sterner, March 21, 1820. June 12, 1821.	Abraham and Elisabeth.	Peter Miller, Maria Christina.
Mary Eliz. Gehres, Dec. 2, 1820. June 24, 1821.	Peter and Molly.	Jacob Hasenfuss, Eliz. Herzell.
Lovina Osterstock, March 9, 1821. June 24, 1821.	John and Elisabeth.	Henry Kocher, Catharine.
Joseph Sewitz, March 11, 1820. June 24, 1821.	The mother, Eliz. Stocker.	John Osterstock, Elisabeth.
Caroline Matilda Swetland, Oct. 17, 1820. June 24, 1821.	William and Catharine.	Peter Seiler, Margaret.
Anna Marg. Osterstock, Feb. 17, 1821. June 24, 1821.	Peter and Christina.	Jacob Osterstock, Ann Frauenfeld
Sophia Lerch, May 6, 1821. June 24, 1821.	George and Maria.	Jacob Frees, Susanna.
Thomas Keller, June 5, 1821. July 8, 1821.	Jacob and Elisabeth.	Daniel Swander, Mary.
Joseph Seipel, Oct. 12, 1820. July 10, 1821.	Henry and Sarah.	John Wagner, Eva.

Name of Child and Date of Birth and Baptism.	Parents.	Sponsors.
George W. West, Feb. 22, 1820. July 14, 1821.	George and Catharine.	The parents.
George Gieser Barnet, Aug. 5, 1821. Aug. 10, 1821.	George and Catharine.	Joseph Herster.
Cath. Maria Lantz, July 22, 1821. Aug. 19, 1821.	George and Margaret.	Catharine Lantz.
John Seiffert, July 26, 1821. Aug. 28, 1821.	George and Elisabeth.	The parents.
John Seipel, Aug. 12, 1820. Sept. 3, 1820.	Jacob and Mary Magdalen.	The parents.
Jacob Young, Aug. 10, 1820. Sept. 24, 1820.	Adam and Elisabeth.	Peter Young, Margaret.
Matilda Nicholas, April 1, 1820. Oct. 11, 1820.	William and Elisabeth.	John Mayer, Elisabeth Ward.
John Ernst Willersdorf, Aug. 23, 1820. Oct. 15, 1820.	Peter and Catharine.	John Ernst Ort.
William Jacob Weygandt Simon, Oct. 24, 1820. Sept. 3, 1821.	Michael and Maria.	Jacob Weygandt, Elisabeth.
Maria Marg. Scherner, July 19, 1821. Sept. 30, 1821.	John Godfried and Elisabeth.	The parents.
Maria Magd. Frey, Aug. 4, 1821. Oct. 9, 1821.	Conrad and Maria.	The parents.
Sophia Coleman, Aug. 20, 1821. Oct. 21, 1821.	Benjamin and Catharine.	Michael Schmidt, Gertrude.

Name of Child and Date of Birth and Baptism.	Parents.	Sponsors.
Catharine Lantz, Oct. 21, 1821. Oct. 26, 1821.	Isaac and Elisabeth.	Catharine Lantz.
Daniel Diehl Stocker, June 5, 1821. Nov. 11, 1821.	George and Rosina.	The parents.
Catharine Knauss, Dec. 23, 1819. Nov. 17, 1821.	John and Regina.	Conrad Kroesge, Cath. Sax.
Catharine Arner, Sept. 2, 1821. Nov. 29, 1821.	Henry and Catharine.	Joseph Hutchin, Catharine.
George William Laddig, Oct. 1, 1821. Dec. 9, 1821.	George and Anna.	The parents.
Samuel Schumacher, Sept. 30, 1821. Dec. 9, 1821.	John and Catharine.	The parents.
Aaron Walter, Sept. 17, 1821. Dec. 23, 1821.	William and Maria.	Peter Heckman, Elisabeth.
William Bess, Nov. 26, 1821. Dec. 28, 1821.	Jacob and Susanna.	Jacob, Catharine.

ANNO 1822.

Daniel Nicholas Deily, Sept. 7, 1821. Jan. 6, 1822.	Valentine and Elisabeth.	Nicholas Traxsell.
Jacob Traxsell, Aug. 19, 1821. Jan. 6, 1822.	Jacob and Maria.	The parents.
John Johnson, Nov. 3, 1821. Jan. 7, 1822.	John and Susanna.	John Nicholas, Sarah.
Susanna Marg. Getter. Dec. 25, 1821. Feb. 3, 1822.	Matthias and Anna Barbara.	Margaret Weygandt.

Name of Child and Date of Birth and Baptism.	Parents.	Sponsors.
Ann Eliza Walter, Oct. 2, 1821. Feb. 8, 1822.	Michael and Elisabeth.	Christian Kutzler, Susanna.
Reuben Broeder, Jan. 21, 1822. March 3, 1822.	Jacob and Elisabeth.	Jacob Arner, Catharine.
Matilda Frey, March 8, 1820. March 3, 1822.	Adam and Maria Magd.	Jacob Broeder, Elisabeth.
Peter Maurer, July 24, 1821. March 11, 1822.	Peter and Barbara.	The parents.
Daniel Lewis Young, Aug. 12, 1821. March 11, 1822.	Peter and Anna.	The parents.
William Henry Ackerman, July 18, 1821. March 11, 1822.	Jacob and Elisabeth.	The parents.
Polly Oberly, Dec. 18, 1821. March 18, 1822.	John and Catharine.	George Oberly, Elisabeth.
Solomon Weiss, Dec. 2, 1821. March 21, 1822.	Solomon and Maria.	John Yeisley, Anna.
Ann Eliza Siegman, March 28, 1822. March 30, 1822.	John and Catharine.	Barbara Siegman.
Isaac Heckman Frees, Jan. 17, 1822. March 31, 1822.	John and Sarah.	The parents.
Peter Butz, Jan. 17, 1822. March 31, 1822.	Michael and Susanna.	The parents.
Sophia Smith, March 19, 1822. March 31, 1822.	Jacob and Elisbeth.	Elsie Lummerson.
William Lewis Appel, May 23, 1821. March 31, 1822.	Andrew and Elisabeth.	The parents.

Church Records. 269

Name of Child and Date of Birth and Baptism.	Parents.	Sponsors.
Jacob Zeller, Nov. 18, 1820. Apr. 6, 1822.	John and Margaret.	William Raub, Elisabeth.
Christian Eliz. Laddig, Jan. 26, 1821. April 28, 1822.	Jacob and Maria.	The parents.
Levina Walter, Feb. 16, 1822. April 28, 1822.	Frederick and Elisabeth.	George Lerch, Maria.
George Belles, Nov. 29, 1821. May 26, 1822.	George and Maria.	The parents.
Henry Koechlein, March 27, 1822. May 26, 1822.	Peter and Maria.	Henry Yaeger, Susanna.
Sophia Bess, April 10, 1822. May 26, 1822.	Jacob and Catharine.	Abraham Woodring, Margaret.
Philip Rudolph Brotzman, April 12, 1822. May 27, 1822.	Peter and Sarah Ann.	Philip Brotzman, Christina.
Susanna Baumgarten, Jan. 26, 1822. May 30, 1822.	Godfrey and Maria.	Catharine Wagner.
Robert Koch, March 13, 1822. June 10, 1822.	Abraham and Anna Maria.	Geo. Koch, Maria.
Anna Maria Lamb, May 6, 1822. June 13, 1822.	Abel and Susanna.	Catharine Sommer.
Daniel Boyer, Feb. 6, 1822. June 18, 1822.	Michael and Elisabeth.	Daniel Ritter, Rosina.
Juliana Frey, May 3, 1822. June 23, 1822.	Adam and Maria Magdalena.	John Arner, Elisabeth Schnabel.
John Schmidt, March 16, 1822. June 23, 1822.	Michael and Gertrude.	John Schmidt.

Name of Child and Date of Birth and Baptism.	Parents.	Sponsors.
Thomas Herzell, March 15, 1822. June 25, 1822.	Abraham and Christina.	George Laddig, Anna.
Rebecca Young, Nov. 26, 1820. June 25, 1822.	Peter and Amy.	The parents.
Maria Ann Miller, Nov. 16, 1821. July 7, 1822.	John and Rachel.	The parents.
Salina Eva Loescher, April 18, 1822. July 21, 1822.	John and Susanna.	John Roeder, Sophia.
Maria Folmer, March 11, 1822. Aug. 2, 1822.	Henry and Christina.	Bernhardt Odenwaelder, Sarah.
Charles Stephen Keiper, May 31, 1822. Aug. 4, 1822.	Peter and Mary.	The parents.
William Messinger, July 5, 1822. Aug. 18, 1822.	Henry and Sarah.	Philip Rieser, Christina.
Matilda Messinger, June 13, 1822. Aug. 18, 1822.	John and Elisabeth.	Henry Messinger, Sarah.
Margaret Schumacher, May 30, 1822. Aug. 22, 1822.	Jacob and Elisabeth.	Daniel Raub, Catharina.
Jacob Odenwaelder, March 11, 1822. Sept. 7, 1822.	Philip and Elisabeth.	The parents.
Maria Barnet Odenwaelder, July 28, 1821. Sept. 10, 1822.	Michael and Sarah.	The parents.
Matilda Magd. Heck, Sept. 2, 1822. Sept. 11, 1822.	Philip and Christina.	The parents.

Name of Child and Date of Birth and Baptism.	Parents.	Sponsors.
Maria Nicholas, April 28, 1822. Sept. 15, 1822.	Joseph and Elisabeth.	The parents.
Catharine Winter, July 2, 1822. Sept. 15, 1822.	Jacob and Sarah.	Isaac Lawall, Maria Froelig.
Mary Evans, Feb. 11, 1822. Sept. 26, 1822.	Evan L. Evans.	The parents.
Charity Moser, Jan. 10, 1822. Oct. 9, 1822.	John and Elisabeth.	The parents.
Sabina Kutzler, May 24, 1822. Oct. 13, 1822.	Christian and Susanna.	The parents.
Susanna Barbara Snyder, March 9, 1822. Oct. 16, 1822.	William and Susanna.	Valentine Albert, Barbara.
Susanna Oberly, April 10, 1822. Nov. 9, 1822.	John and Eva.	The parents.
Maria Ann Young, Sept. 4, 1822. Nov. 10, 1822.	Peter and Margaret.	John Odenwaelder, Margaret.
Amos Seip, Oct. 11, 1822. Nov. 10, 1822.	Michael and Catharine.	Charles Hay, Elisabeth.
Charles William Kinsey, Aug. 3, 1822. Nov. 10, 1822.	Jonathon and Sarah.	The parents.
Peter Lantz, Oct. 19, 1822. Nov. 22, 1822.	Jacob and Elisabeth.	Isaac Seiler, Susan Schaerer.
Jacob Walter, Aug. 24, 1822. Nov. 23, 1822.	Lenhart and Sarah.	The parents.

Name of Child and Date of Birth and Baptism.	Parents.	Sponsors.
Sophia Louisa Steinbrenner, Nov. 19, 1822. Dec. 8, 1822.	Gottleib and Elisabeth.	Michael Vally, Eliz. Steinbrenner.
Sarah Young, Sept. 29, 1822. Dec. 18, 1822.	Peter and Amy.	The parents.
William Kotz Snyder, Feb. 9, 1820. Dec. 25, 1822.	Samuel and Susan.	The parents.
Samuel Young, Sept. 29, 1822. Dec. 26, 1822.	Daniel and Catharine.	John Bess, Lena.
Elisabeth Young, Oct. 20, 1822. Dec. 26, 1822.	Adam and Elisabeth.	Philip Odenwaelder, Elisabeth.

ANNO 1823.

Charles A. Heckman, Dec. 3, 1822. Jan. 21, 1823.	John and Mary.	The parents.
Maria Cath. Bittenbender, Apr. 1, 1822. Jan. 21, 1823.	William and Ann.	The parents.
Ann Eliza Young, Sept. 12, 1822. Jan. 21, 1823.	John and Maria.	Jacob Edelman, Elisabeth.
Wm. Valentine Noll, Sept. 11, 1822. Jan. 26, 1823.	Jacob and Rebecca.	The parents.
Rebecca Bruch, Jan. 5, 1823. Jan. 30, 1823.	Peter and Mary Ann.	Adam Ward, Susanna.
Aaron.	"Uneheliches."	
Eliza Ann Keller, Jan. 3, 1823. Feb. 4, 1823.	Jacob and Elisabeth.	John Odenwaelder, Ann Margarett.

JOHN BECK, D. D.

Church Records.

Name of Child and Date of Birth and Baptism.	Parents.	Sponsors.
Nelly Raub, Nov. 14, 1822. Feb. 10, 1823.	Isaac and Nelly.	Cath. Ettinger.
Leonora Koechlein, Jan. 1, 1823. Feb. 19, 1823.	Michael and Margaret.	The parents.
Eliza Ann Gehres, Nov. 28, 1822. Feb. 21, 1823.	Joseph and Susanna.	Marie Steckel.
Rees Heckman Bruch, Oct. 30, 1822. March 2, 1823.	George and Catharine.	Rees Heckman Elisabeth.
Alexander Traxsell, Oct. 8, 1822. March 2, 1823.	Joseph and Susan.	Jacob Nicholas, Margaret.
Harriett Mixsell, March 29, 1820. March 5, 1823.	Daniel and Elisabeth.	The mother.
Mary Ackerman, Oct. 18, 1822. March 16, 1823.	Jacob and Elisabeth.	The parents.
Susanna Koechlein, Feb. 19, 1823. March 16, 1823.	Jacob and Elisabeth.	Jacob Ackerman, Elisabeth.
Maria Brotzman, Feb. 2, 1823. March 22, 1823.	Joseph and Elisabeth.	Thos. Richard, Susanna.
William Smith, Feb. 2, 1823. March 23, 1823.	Ludwig and Christina.	John Laubach, Susanna.
Phineas Kinsey, Aug. 9, 1823. Sept. 19, 1823.	Samuel and Elisabeth.	The parents.
Peter Wichelhauser, July 31, 1823. Oct. 3, 1823.	Jacob and Henrietta.	The parents.
John Philip Woodring, Aug. 22, 1823. Oct. 12, 1823.	Philip and Elisabeth.	Jacob Bess, Catharine.

Name of Child and Date of Birth and Baptism.	Parents.	Sponsors.
George Loesher, March 30, 1823. Oct. 12, 1823.	George and Elisabeth.	The parents.
Daniel Wagoner, Aug. 8, 1822. Oct. 26, 1823.	David D. and Maria.	Eva Wagner and the child's mother.
Samuel Rippel, June 17, 1823. Nov. 9, 1823.	Peter and Magdalena.	The parents.
Jesse Frutchman, March 23, 1823. Nov. 15, 1823.	Jacob and Elisabeth.	The parents.
Elisabeth Laddig, Sept. 3, 1823. Nov. 16, 1823.	George and Anna.	The parents.
John H. Leidig, Dec. 13, 1821. Nov. 16, 1823.	Henry and Hannah.	Jacob Lawall, Mary Worman.
Mary Leidig, Sept. 6, 1823. Nov. 16, 1823.	Henry and Hannah.	James Worton, Rosina Pentz.
John Bechtel, Oct. 24, 1823. Dec. 7, 1823.	John and Elisabeth.	John Scheively, Margaret.
David Kutzler, June 21, 1823. Dec. 16, 1823.	Henry and Elisabeth.	Jacob Frees, Susanna.
Sophia Weiss, Aug. 29, 1823. Dec. 17, 1823.	Solomon and Maria.	The parents.
Elisabeth Barthold, Sept. 23, 1822. April 15, 1823.	Alexander H. and Hannah.	Frederick Barthold, Elisabeth.
Mary Jane Ohnangst, Dec. 18, 1822. April 27, 1823.	Ludwig and Catharine.	Philip Christman, Maria Magdalena.
Jacob Stetler Sheip, March 28, 1823. April 27, 1823.	Jacob and Maria Magdalena.	Jacob Stetler, Catharine.

Name of Child and Date of Birth and Baptism.	Parents.	Sponsors.
Caroline Odenwelder, June 4, 1822. April 10, 1823.	Jacob and Mary.	John Bess, Lena.
Abraham Woodring, Jan. 14, 1823. March 31, 1823.	Nicholas and Catharine.	Abraham Woodring, Margaret.
Jacob Seip, Feb. 23, 1823. May 11, 1823.	Peter and Elisabeth.	Jacob Seip, Susanna.
Susanna Hagenbuch, March 8, 1823. May 11, 1823.	Joseph and Catharine.	Jacob Seip, Susanna.
Juliana Lawall, Feb. 22, 1823. May 20, 1823.	Abraham and Julian Salome.	Jacob Lechleiter, Margaret.
Matilda Lerch, March 8, 1823. May 25, 1823.	Jonas and Maria.	George Abel, Margaret Lerch.
Maria Anna Odenwaelder, April 17, 1823. May 25, 1823.	John and Anna Margaret.	John Riehl, Susanna.
Theodore Freeman Miller, April 28, 1823. May 25, 1823.	Peter and Esther.	Peter Miller, Maria Christina.
Isaac Bishop, April 1, 1823. June 1, 1823.	John and Ann.	Isaac Mais, Sallie Weller.
Aaron Odenwaelder, May 29, 1823. June 10, 1823.	Jacob and Elisabeth.	Philip Yaeger, Rosina.
Henry Worman, June 11, 1823. June 13, 1823.	Andrew and Maria.	Christina Steitinger.
Louisa Scheetz, May 22, 1823. July 6, 1823.	John and Catharine.	The parents.

Name of Child and Date of Birth and Baptism.	Parents.	Sponsors.
Abraham Woodring, May 25, 1823. July 13, 1823.	Philip and Catharine.	Abraham Woodring, Margaret.
Rachel Baty, Feb. 14, 1819. Aug. 27, 1823.	Benjamin and Margaret.	John Miller, mother.
Ann Eliza Baty, July 7, 1822. Aug. 27, 1823.	Benjamin and Margaret.	John Miller, mother.
Abraham Barnes, July 8, 1822. Aug. 27, 1823.	Stephen and Nancy.	The mother.
Susanna Arner, May 12, 1823. Sept. 3, 1823.	Nicholas and Susanna.	The parents.
William Folmer, April 8, 1823. Sept. 6, 1823.	Henry and Christina.	The parents.
Eliz. Marg. Klein, Nov. 18, 1823. Dec. 20, 1823.	Nicholas and Susanna.	Sam¹ Wollenschlaeger, Dorothea.
Anna Maria Kinsey, Dec. 3, 1823. Dec. 30, 1823.	Philip M. and Maria.	Susan Young.

[Having reached the beginning of the present living generation, it is thought well that the publication of the record of baptisms should cease at this point. It is to be understood, however, that the record runs on without a break to the present day. It would be impossible, within the limits of one volume, to continue the publication of all the baptisms and other entries.]

BOOK SECOND.

The title-page bears the following inscription:

"CHURCH-BOOK

"In which the affairs of the Four united Reformed Congregations shall be recorded, *viz :* Eastown, Greenwich, Dryland and Plainfield (Blaenfield). Eastown, August 1, 1767."

On the next page we read:

"A record in this Church-Book of transactions and occurrences that were especially noteworthy (*richt remarquabel*)."

"Anno, 1768, September 7. THE COETUS was held in Eastown."

[By the *Coetus* is meant the Synod of the Reformed Church. By this name it was known from 1747 to 1793, that is to say, so long as it was dependent upon the Church in Holland it was known as THE COETUS, but when, in 1793, the body separated from the Church in Holland and became independent, it was thereafter known as THE SYNOD.]

ANNO 1787.

May 30. It was resolved by the four united congregations, Eastown, Greenwich, Dryland and Plainfield, that the Elder of the congregation at Eastown, Mr. John Deichman, should be sent along with the minister as Deputy to the Coetus to be held at Lancaster, June 6, 1787.

FREDERICUS HERMAN, *Pfarrer*.

ANNO 1788.

April 5. It was resolved by the Elders and Deacons of the four united Christian congregations, Eastown, Blaenfield, Truckland and Greenwich, that the Elder of the church in Blaenfield, Mr. Frederick Hauser, shall be sent with the minister as Deputy to the Coetus, which will be held April 23, in Reading.   FREDERICK HERMANN, V.D.M.

Anno 1789.

June 10. The Coetus of Pennsylvania was held in Philadelphia to which, along with the minister, Mr. Jacob Arndt, Senior, Esquire, was sent as the Deputy of the four congregations.

FRID. HERMAN, *Prediger ibi*.

Anno 1794.

It was resolved by the four united congregations, Easton, Dryland, Greenwich and Plainfield, that the Elder of the congregation in Easton, Mr. Michael Odenwaelder, should be sent along with the minister as Deputy to the Synod which meets on the 18th of May in Reading.

[Note the change of name from *Coetus* to *Synod*.]

DR. C. L. BECKER, *Prediger*.

DEATHS AND BURIALS.

1786. Fredericus Hermann h. t. Pastor of the four united Reformed Congregations, Eastown, Greenwik, Trukland and Blaenfield, herewith records for you in this Church Book things noteworthy and according to law and order.

A Record of persons who died in the four congregations.

Anno 1786.

November 30. Died in Greenwitch the daughter of Mr. N. Gieser, Margaret by name, in the 19th year of her age. Buried Dec. 1.

December 19. Died in Blaenfield, a child of George Sewitz, Abraham by name, aged 3 years, 8 months.

Anno 1787.

January 1. Died in Greenwitch the wife of Adam Haag, Elisabeth, born Milich, in the 64th year of her life. The funeral text which had been chosen, was from the Song of Solomon, Chapter 2, verses 5 and 6.

Church Records. 279

January 16. Anna Maria, the daughter of George Sewitz, died in Plainfield, and was buried on the 17th. Aged 1 year, 3 months.

February 4. Christian Schmidt was buried in Dryland. Aged 77 years, 9 months.

February 11. Isaac, a son of John Rosenberg, died in Greenwich. Aged 9 months.

February 18. Eckhard Huettendorff died in Dryland. Aged 36 years, 2 months.

March 30. A child of Frederick Wilhelm was buried in Eastown. Aged 2 years, 9 months, 2 weeks and 2 days. The text assigned was Job 19: verses 25, 26, 27.

April 14. Died in Greenwich, the good wife of Michael Seiffert, Maria Elisabeth, born Huellers, in the 66th year of her age.

May 5. Died in Eastown, Helena, the wife of Mr. George Ernst Becker. Aged 67 years, 11 months, 4 days.

May 8. In Dryland, Mrs. Anna Catharine Koenig was buried. Born Illik. Age, 53 years.

May 30. Died in Plainfield, George Henry Young. Age, 63 years, 1 month.

June 11. In Dryland "ist ein Serrenbuebe begraben worden, in einem alter von 21 yahre."

June 12. Buried in Eastown, the daughter of the Schoolmaster, Mr. Christopher Schmidt, Maria Barbara. Age, 1 year, 7 days.

June 20. Died in Eastown, Anna Catharine, Mr. Daniel Schneider's child. Aged 1 year, 4 months, 5 days.

July 16. Conrad Schneider of Dryland was buried. Aged 27 years. Text, Psalm 90: 12.

August 17. A girl, named Susanna Beissel, of Dryland, was buried. Aged 14 years, 3 months, 3 weeks.

August 29. Buried in Greenwich, Peter, a son of Jacob Scherp. Aged 2 years, 1 month.

September 5. Buried in Plainfield, Philip, the son of Jacob Keller. Aged 3 years, 6 months.

September 24. In Eastown, the wife of Frederick Schaus was buried. Text, Job 27: 5, 6.

October 30. In Eastown was buried the wife of Thomas Terre (Terry?), Elisabeth. She died of consumption. The funeral text previously chosen was Job 19: 25, 26, 27. Her age was 35 years, 9 months.

December 26. In Eastown was buried the son of John Best, Andrew by name. Age, 10 years, 9 months, 1 week, 4 days.

ANNO 1788.

February 12. In Eastown was buried the son of John Steitinger.

February 20. In Eastown was buried the aged ("der alte") Frederick Schaus.

February 27. In Eastown was buried the daughter of Michael Odenwaelder.

March 11. In Greenwich was buried the wife of Philip Yeisley (?).

March 31. In Eastown, the daughter of Moritz Bischoff was buried.

June 2. John Mosch, a citizen of Eastown, died and was buried on the 4th.

June 27. Buried in Plainfield, Anna Catharine, born Knieriem. Text chosen, Psalm 57, verse 3.

July 18. Was buried in Greenwich, the wife of Gottfield Keins. Died of consumption.

August 24. Of the Easton congregation was buried a son of William Keller.

October 9. The child of John Kloeman was buried in Eastown.

October 10. Of the Easton congregation was buried a son of Christian Hertzell. The selected text was Job 14: 1, 2.

October 25. Born in Plainfield, the wife of Christian Engel, Elizabeth. Aged 34 years. She died of consumption. Funeral text, Psalm 39: 5, 6.

December 20. Buried in Greenwich, Michael Seiffert. Aged 88 years.

December 21. George Ernst Becker died, and on the 23d was buried in Eastown. Age, 82 years, 10 months. Selected funeral text, Psalm 47: 2, 3.

Church Records.

ANNO 1789.

January 4. Was buried a daughter of Frederick Barthold, named Elizabeth, who died on the 2d. Age, 6 months, 13 days.

January 3. Died in Eastown, the clockmaker, Moritz Bischoff, of consumption. Age, 33 years, less 1 day. His funeral text was from Ecclesiastes: Chapter 12, verse 1.

January 16. Died the wife of Christian Wolff, Maria Christina, and was buried the 18th, in Plainfield. Age, 48 years, 8 months.

February 6. John Henry Kegel (?) was buried. Age, 50 years, 1 month, 2 days.

February 7. A child of Philip Dotterer was buried in Eastown. Aged 1 year, 4 months, 2 weeks, 3 days.

March 1. Was buried in Plainfield John Conrad Hertzel. Age, 74 years, 2 weeks, 4 days.

March 11. Across the Lehigh ("uber der Lechau") the aged Jacob Best. Aged 67 years, 5 months, 1 week, 5 days. Text, Job 7: 1, 2, 3.

March 15. Buried in Eastown, Frederick Beyer's child. Aged 2 months.

March 31. Was buried in Dryland, the aged ("die alte") Apalora Fox. Aged 72 years.

April 29. Died in Eastown, a child of Andrew Stocker. Aged 2 years less 2 weeks.

April 30. Died in Williams Township, a child of John Knecht. Aged 1 year, 4 months, 1 week, 4 days.

May 10. In Dryland was buried a child of George Willhelm, named Anna Maria. Aged 4 weeks, less 1 day.

May 10. Likewise in Dryland was buried Elias, a son of John Blum. Aged 6 months, less 1 day.

May 24. In Dryland, was buried the daughter of Henry Ritter, Eva. Aged 12 years, less 3 months.

June 7. John Santy's child was buried in Dryland.

June 15. In Greenwich, the aged ("der alte") Gloessner was buried.

July 7. Was buried John Schneider's child, John George, of Dryland. Aged 4 years, 3 months, 2 days.

July 30. Of the congregation at Dryland, was buried the aged John Ulrich Schlepper. Aged 69 years, 1 month, 3 weeks.

August 23. Adam Hertzel's daughter, Maria, of Dryland, was buried. Aged 6 months, 2 weeks.

October 13. Lenhard Knect, of Dryland, was buried.

November 22. Across the Lehigh, Mr. Peter Laddig's daughter, Catharine, was buried. Aged 20 years, 10 months.

December 4. In the congregation at Plainfield a child was buried. The father is Conrad Germanton.

1789 (no month given). The wife of Mr. Lenhard Beyer was buried in Plainfield. Aged 72 years, 11 months, 1 day.

1789 (no month given). Jacob Oberdorf's grandson was buried in Dryland.

December 5. The wife of John Nicolaus Kloekner was buried in Upper Dryland. Aged 20 years.

December 25. Herman Kroch was buried in Eastown. Aged 33 years.

ANNO 1790.

January 13. Across the Lehigh was buried John George, a son of Mr. Peter Laddig. Aged 14 years, 10 months, 5 days.

February 24. In Plainfield Township was buried Michael, a child of Michael Glass. Aged 6 months, 3 weeks, 2 days.

March 7. Of the Plainfield congregation was buried the aged Barbara Witmer. Aged 83 years.

March 11. Of the Plainfield congregation was buried the aged Mother Germanton. Aged 81 years, 2 months.

April 14. In Dryland was buried Sarah Hertzel, a daughter of Adam Hertzel and his wife Clara. Aged 14 year, 3 months less 6 days. Text, II. Timothy, 2 : 19.

April 26. In Plainfield was buried Margaret Doll, th , good wife of Mr. Caspar Doll. Aged 66 years. Text (blank).

May 2. Buried in Easton, Mr. John Schuck's son, John Jacob. Aged 2 years, less 1 month. Text, Acts 17 : 31.

August 22. In Easton a child of Mr. John Koehler and his wife Anna Margaret was buried.

Church Records. 283

September 25. Was buried a child of Isaac Hertzel and his good wife Margaret, in the 1½ year of its age.

[Rev. Dr. Lebrecht Frederick Herman, who became pastor in 1786, resigned in October, 1790. There then followed a vacancy in the pastorate until August, 1793, when Rev. Dr. Christian Ludwig Becker became the pastor. He remained in charge for eighteen months, removing from Easton to Lancaster, Pa., March, 1795. These facts will help to explain the following statement in the handwriting of Dr. Becker.]

After September 25, anno 1790, this record was broken off owing to the absence, or want of a Reformed minister. After August 22, 1793, the record of the burials is resumed by Dr. Christian Ludwig Becker, sole pastor of the four united congregations, Easton, Greenwick, Trueckland (Dryland) and Plainfield.

EASTON. ANNO 1793.

August 28. Was buried the little daughter of Mr. Baedeker. Aged 1 year, less two days. There was a funeral address at the grave.

September 6. Entered into rest, Catharine, a daughter of the Rev. Mr. Frederick, the Evangelical Lutheran minister of Easton. Aged 7 years. Text, Psalm 103 : 15, 16.

October 15. Was buried Mr. James Baedeker, about 36 years of age. There was a funeral address on " The blessedness of those that die in the Lord."

November 18. Was buried Mrs. De Hasen, the wife of General De Hasen. Aged 51 years, less 1 month. Text, I. Peter, chapter I., verse 3.

ANNO 1794.

May 30. Was buried Marie Elisabeth Kaemmerer. Aged 82 years. Text, Luke 2 : 25.

June 5. Was buried Elisabeth Knauss, the wife of Mr. Ludwig Knauss. Aged 69 years, 7 months. Text, Luke 2 : 26.

August 13. John Peter Schuck. Aged 61 years. Luke 2: 29, 30.
August 26. Elisabeth Best, across the Lehigh. Aged 22 years. Text, Matthew 24:44.
September 14. Margaret Uly, the wife of John Uly. Aged 39 years.
September 23. Elisabeth, the little daughter of Mr. Debis. Aged 10 months, 6 days. Text, Romans 12:12.
October 26. Anna Margaret, the little daughter of Mr. Otto, across the Lehigh. Aged 6 months. Text, Hebrews 12:23.
October *30. Was buried in Easton Elizabeth Catharine, the wife of Mr. Richter. Aged 36 years, 4 months. Text, Luke 19:9.
November 9. Buried in Easton Anna Catharine, the wife of Mr. Eichelmeier. Aged 84 years. Text, I. John 2:1, 2.
November 22. Buried across the Lehigh, John Jacob, the young son of Mr. Peter Zeller. Aged 2 months, 8 days. Text, I. John 3:1.

BURIALS IN GREENWICH ("GRUENITZ").

ANNO 1793.

September 27. Buried in Greenwich, Mr. Jacob Menninger. Age, 56 years, 4 months, 1 week, 3 days. Text, Luke 12:37.
September 28. Buried in Greenwich, Catharine Fasbinder, born ("ins Haus geboren") Glasner. Age, 31 years. Text, Revelation 12:13.

ANNO 1794.

January 25. Was buried Maria Meier, the wife of Jacob Meier, in Greenwich. Aged 52 years, less 2 months. Text, Luke 10:20.
May 31. Was buried Christian Scherp in Greenwich. Aged 72 years, 2 months.
August 31. Was buried Frederick Mutschler in Greenwich. Aged 70 years.

BURIALS IN DRYLAND.

Anno 1793.

November 10. Was buried in Dryland, Mr. Sebastian Onangst. Aged 73 years. Text, Revelation 19 : 9.

Anno 1794.

March 8. Buried in Dryland the young son of Mr. Jacob Beier. Aged 3 weeks. Text, Revelation 22 : 7.

March 25. Buried in Dryland Maria Barbara, the wife of Mr. William Jansen (Johnson). Aged 48 years.

September 1. Was buried Dorothea, the wife of Mr. Kress. Aged 37 years, 8 months.

September 7. Was buried Thomas, the young son of Mr. Keringer. Aged 4 months, 3 weeks, 2 days. Text, Philippians 3 : 21.

September 7. Was buried Elisabeth, the young daughter of Mr. John Koenig. Aged 2 years. Text, Romans 8 : 1.

September 14. Was buried John Caspar Onangst. Aged 34 years. Text, Hebrews 2 : 14, 15.

October 17. Was buried Anna Maria, the wife of Mr. George Neihard. Aged 56 years. The text previously chosen, Revelation 14 : 13.

December 3. Philip, the young son of Mr. Schadi. Age, 10 weeks. Text, I. John 2 : 12.

December 29. Joseph Meier, a son of Jacob Meier. Age, 22 years. Text, Revelation 22 : 17.

BURIALS IN MOUNT BETHEL.

Anno 1794.

August 9. Was buried the wife of Mr. Correll. Age, 55 years, less 14 days.

August 18. Mr. Isaac Huebler. In the English churchyard. Age, 30 years. He was killed by lightning on the 16th. Text, Apocalypse 16 : 15.

September 2. Anna Maria, the wife of Mr. Guet. Age, 30 years, 6 months.
September 24. Jacob Weidman. Age, 47 years, 3 months, 2 weeks. Text, Romans 12 : 12.
September 29. Elisabeth, the wife of Henry Janson. Age, 30 years. Text, Luke 10 : 20.
October 14. Maria, the young daughter of Mr. Scherlach (Sherlock). Funeral address in the English burying-ground. Age, 2 years.

[In March, 1795, Rev. Dr. Becker resigned, and the charge was vacant until July, 1796, when the Rev. Thomas Pomp became the pastor, and remained in charge for more than a half-century. The new pastor seems at first to have followed the somewhat awkward method of his predecessors in grouping the burials according to locality, but afterwards reduced matters to a more orderly and convenient arrangement, as will be seen by what follows.]

BURIED AT EASTON.

ANNO 1797.

January 19. Was buried in Easton, Conrad Schilb, son of Peter Schilb. Aged 18 years, 11 months, 8 days.
April 4. Was buried in Mr. Jacob Arndt's church-yard (burying-ground) Mr. John Nicolaus Kaemer. Aged 84 years, 7 months, 9 days.
April 13. Buried in Mr. Jacob Arndt's burying-ground, Mr. Jacob Engelhart. Aged 29 years, 6 months, 24 days.
April 17. Buried in Arndt's graveyard, Anna Margaret Kaemrer, daughter of Mr. Jacob Kaemrer. Aged 1 year, 7 months, 8 days.
May 20. Buried in William's Township, William Woodring, son of Mr. William Woodring. Aged 2 years, 5 months, less 12 days.

May 30. Buried in William's Township, Matthias Bruch. Aged 88, 3 months, 16 days.

May 30. Buried in Easton, Mrs. Nauly. Aged 84 years, 6 months, 3 days.

May 30. Buried in Easton, Mrs. Meixell. Aged 58 years, 7 months, 16 days.

May 30. Buried in Easton, Henry Schnyder. Aged 9 months, 2 days.

May 30. Buried in Easton, Mrs. Catherine Gewinner. Aged 60 years, 1 month, 22 days.

Anno 1798.

April 24. Was buried, Maria Hess, Mr. Frederick Hess's wife. Age, 37 years.

No date. Magdalena Hertzel, wife of (undecipherable). Aged 85 years, 9 months.

No date. William Kessler. Aged 1 year, 7 months, 5 days.

August 5. Was buried, John George, the young son of Henry Ewald (?). Aged 14 months.

September 3. Elisha Howel, son of Eseck Howel. Aged 14 months, 3 weeks.

April 17. Catharine Beisher. Aged ———. (No entry.)

August 11. Anna Maria Schwartz. Aged 1 year, 9 months, 2 days.

October 2. Henry Laux ———. (Nothing more.)

October 25. Eva Eighorne ———. (Nothing more.)

Anno 1799.

No date. Maria Miller. Aged 73 years.

March 8. Maria Keller.

July 4. Michael Joseph Weber.

September 3. Daniel Buts, 1 year, 3 months, less 1 day.

October —. Eva Jumper, 24 years.

October 11. Samuel and Catharine Zoeller. 10 and 5.

October 28. Dorothea Wilhelmina Smidt. Aged 4 months.

October 31. Margaret Stem. William's Township.

September 17. Anna Margaret Christman. Aged 54 years, 8 months, 6 days.

Anno 1800.

March 21. Elisabeth Rambach. Aged 1 year, 7 months, 19 days.

June 24. Catharine Hertzel, Christoph Hertzel's wife. Aged 44 years, 9 days.

July 12. Peter, Philip Messinger's young son. Aged 1 year, 11 months.

September —. Christian Winter. Aged 34 years, 5 months.

October —. Jonathan Coleman's little daughter. Aged 1 year, 5 months.

December 28. Susanna Gress, Michael Gress's daughter, who was drowned in the Delaware. Aged 19 years, 6 months.

Anno 1801.

January 15. John Gruber's child. Aged 1 year, 4 months.
February 17. Sophia Ries. Aged 77 years, 3 months.
March 20. Joseph Harley (?). Aged 18 years.
August 27. —— Spangenberg's daughter. Aged 10 years.
August 27. Hay's child. Age, ——.
August 30. Jacob Moser's child. Aged 7 years, 9 months.
September 6. Susanna Kuhn, Isaac Kuhn's daughter. Aged 8 years, 11 months, 10 days.
September 30. John Philip Trumheller's child. Aged 1 year, 2 months.
September 30. Kaemrer's child. Aged 11 days.
September 21. Henry Bernd. Aged 67 years.
October 20. Elisabeth, Thomas Richard's child. Aged 5 years,
October 26. Abraham Vogt. Aged 41 years.
October 26. Catharine, John Otto's daughter. Aged 13 years.
November 1. Abraham Koch's (?) son. Aged 9 years.
November 6. Mrs. Baumgartner. Aged 80 years.
November 7. Valentine Koch's son. Aged 12 years, less 3 days.
November 11. John Peter Koch's son. Aged 7 years.
December 6. Susanna Yaeger (?). Aged 6 years, 6 months.

Anno 1802.

March 12. Elisabeth Stem. Aged 52 years.
March 28. Isaac Schumacher's daughter. Aged 1 year, 9 months.
May 24. William, Nicolaus Traxsell's son. Aged 7 years, 2 months, 29 days.
May 29. Another son of the same father. Aged 11 years.
June 8. Maria, John Simon's daughter. Aged 1 year, 9 months.
September 18. Susanna, John Traxsell's daughter. Aged 1 year, 2 months.

BURIED IN DRYLAND.

Anno 1796.

September 14. Mr. Michael Lawald. Aged 80 years, 3 months, 19 days.
September 19. Catharine Schmidt, daughter of John Schmidt. Aged 3 years, 9 months, 10 days.
December 13. Daniel Ziegenfuss, son of Andrew Ziegenfuss. Aged 5 months, 12 days.
———— Mr. John Geringer. Aged 29 (?) years.

Anno 1797.

April 7. Buried in Dryland, Simon Koenig, son of Matthias Koenig. Aged 11 months, 9 days.
June —. Buried in Dryland, Miss Susanna Arndt, a daughter of Mr. Bernhart Arndt. Aged 13 years, 4 months, 7 days.
———— Buried in Dryland, Miss Linishmidt. Aged 25 years, 8 months, 14 days.
June 24. Daniel, Peter Dornblaeser's son, was buried.
July 15. Wilhelmina Frederica Barbara Kittel. Aged 38 years, 10 months, 1 day.
February 13. Was buried John Somney (?). Aged 32 years.
February 20. Elisabeth Dornblaeser. Aged 87 years, 7 months 24 days.

May 19. Was buried Maria, Henry George's (?) daughter, Aged 1 year, 3 months, less 5 days.
May 28. Was buried Michael, Jacob Arndt's son. Aged 2 years, 2 months, 1 day.
February 13. Margaret, John Glass's daughter. Aged 7 months, 11 days.
February 17. Jacob Kraemer, N. Kraemer's son. Aged 10 months, 8 days.
August 29. Isaac, Walter (?) Miller's son. Aged 8 years, 1 month.
October 20. Susanna, Peter Beissel's daughter. Aged 2 years, 9 months, 5 days.
November 29. Elisabeth Doerr, Henry Doerr's daughter. Aged 10 years, 10 months, 2 days.
April 24.[1] Isaac Lawald. Aged 3 years, 8 months, 17 days.
August 16. Conrad George. Aged (no entry).
September 23. Anna Maria Boyer. Aged 5 years, 8 months, 3 days.
September 30. Christina Ginnard. Aged 1 year, 8 months, 11 days.
September 30. Jacob Boyer. Aged 8 years, 6 months, 16 days.
October 4. ——— George. Aged ———.
October 16. John George Boyer. Aged ———.
October 24. Susanna Roeder. Aged ———.
April 30. Magdalena Gross. Aged ———.
November 9. Daniel Balliet. Aged 2 years, 8 months, less 8 days.
November 26. Jacob Kaemrer. Aged 23 years, 10 months, 23 days.

Anno 1800.

January 30. Abraham Knecht. Aged 7 years, 5 weeks.
March 17. Mary Elis. Koehler. Aged 39 years, 6 months.
May 1. Daniel, John Malter's son. Aged 3 years, 2 months.

---

[1] The following eleven entries belong probably to the year 1799, although it is not so stated.

May 27. Henry, Thomas Hartman's son. Aged 8 years, 3 months.
June 21. Catharine, John Adam Willauer's daughter. Aged 5 years, 8 months, 6 days.
July 29. Catharine Ehreth (?), wife of Joseph Ehreth. Aged 40 years, 3 weeks, 2 days.
July 30. Peter, Philip Messinger's son. Aged 2 years, 2 months, 9 days.
October 29. J. George, George Heller's child. Aged 1 year, 9 months, 7 days.
November 5. George Heller himself. Aged 31 years, 7 months, 5 days.

Anno 1801.

September 1. Frederick Kern, Frederick Kern's son. Aged 4 years, 10 months, 17 days.
September 15. Catharine, Frederick Kern's daughter. Aged 6 years, 7 months, 11 days.

Anno 1802.

September 17. Henry Lahr. Aged 81 years.

BURIED IN PLAINFIELD.

Anno 1796.

October 16. Margaret Diel. Aged 39 years, 6 months, 20 days.
October 24, Conrad Riedy, son of Jacob Riedy. Aged 19 years, 6 months, 17 days.

Anno 1797.

June —. Joseph Heller, the son of Jacob Heller. Aged 1 year, 9 months, 18 days.
December —. Jacob Riedy. Aged 18 years, 6 months, 11 days.
December 28. Mrs. Jacob Heller. Aged 40 years, 6 months, 6 days.

ANNO 1798 and 1800.

July 17. Leonhard Boyer. Aged 84 years, 5 months, 12 days.
September 27. Anna Eliz. Metz.
October 3. George Frederick Siegel.
February 2, 1800. John Philip Achenbach. Aged 68 years, less 1 month.
April 8, 1800. Nicolaus Diel. Aged 62 years and 6 months.
August —. Maria Magdalena, Jacob Hess's(?) daughter. Aged 1 year, 7 months.
September 15, 1800. Peter Philip Hahn. Aged 84 years, 10 months.
Eodem, 1800. Three children — Henry Stofflets, George ——— and George Jansen.
December 23, 1800. George, John Dietz's son. Aged 5 years, 6 months, 10 days.

ANNO 1801.

May 29. Susanna Heller, Abraham Heller's daughter. Aged 8 years.
May 28. John, Andrew Bayer's (?) son. Aged 2 years.
August 25. Hannah, Frederick Faber's (?) child. Aged 2 years, 5 months.
September 13. John, George Warner's child. Aged 2 years, 3 weeks.
June 18, 1802. Anna Maria, Peter Best's daughter. Aged 10 weeks.
July 24. Sarah Kuessel, Samuel Kuessel's daughter. Aged 17 years, 2 weeks.
July 25. George, William Prutzman's son. Aged 10 months.
July 27. Jacob, Abraham Heller's son. Aged 14 years, 8 months.
July 28. Simon, William Prutzman's son. Aged 3 years, 9 months.
July 28. Michael Keiper's (?) child. Aged 3 months, 5 days.
August 15. Nicolaus Dietz's child.
September 11. John Henry, son of Henry Nicolas. Aged 6 years, 11 months.

BURIED IN MOUNT BETHEL.

Anno 1797 and 1798.

No date. Mr. John Frantz Hilliart. Aged 75 years, 6 months, 10 days.

February 13. Lena Janson. Mr. Henry Janson's wife. Aged 33 years, 10 months, 6 days.

March 25. Isaac Fritschie, Matthew Fritschie's son. Aged 1 year, 4 months, 10 days.

June 7. John Michael Eyer. Aged 25 years, 9 months, 13 days.

March 12. Henry Kratzer. Aged 1 year, 10 months, 18 days.

July 20. Maria Margaret Eyer. Aged 1 year, 2 months, 7 days.

Anno 1799.

March 10. Joseph Smith. Aged 71 years, 4 months.

March 10. Hannah Miller, *sive* Fenner.

November 5. John William Albert. Aged 72 years, 1 month, 5 days.

Anno 1800.

October —. Peter Hess, Christian Hess's son. Aged 21 years, 5 months.

Anno 1802.

May 29. William Schmidt, Peter Hilyart's hired boy ("Knecht"). Aged 10 years, 2 months.

September 9. Philip Preston (?). Aged 73 years.

September 8. Philip Appel. Aged 31 years, 3 months, 8 days.

The foregoing confused manner of keeping the Church Record, evidently becoming burdensome, the pastor, Rev. Thomas Pomp, now begins a more orderly and satisfactory method (somewhat confused at first), having the following heading:

BURIALS OF EASTON, PLAENFIELD, MOUNT BETHEL AND DRYLAND.

Date.		Names of Persons Buried.	Y.	M.	D.
		ANNO 1801.			
Jan.	14.	John Henry Happel, Plainfield.........	72	2	8
June	7.	John Kessler, Easton.......................	1	1	5
Oct.	3.	Anna Margaret Schwartz, Forks........	29	7	
"	5.	Gertrude Simon, Easton	72	3	16
"	12.	John Mueller, Dryland......................	13	5	5
"	14.	Catharine Richard, William's Township...	2	6	
Dec.	17.	Jacob Messinger, Forks....................	53	8	
Sept.	25.	Isaac Brotzman, William's Township..	2	4	
"	25.	Elisabeth Margaret Streuber.............	82	5	8
No date.		John Sterner (?), Plainfield..............	2		24
"		Maria Schleppe, "	4		
"		Abraham Schleppe, "	1	5	
1799.		Maria Eva Freiman, "	38	3	
"		Abraham Woodring, "	2		2
"		Maria Magd. Messinger, Greenwich...	57	8	20
1800, Sept.	9.	Anna Maria Rohn, Dryland........	4	4	15
July	22.	Sarah Bartolmei, Mount Bethel..........	8		
Aug.	10.	Solomon Koenig, Dryland................	4	7	2
"	20.	Elisabeth Miller, "	2	3	14
April	23.	Catharine Siwille, Plainfield.............	7	3	20
May	29.	Michael Koester, "	76		
1801, Apr.	22.	Conrad Heffelfinger, Indian Land	5	8	6
1800.		John Mase (?)...............................	56	5	
"		Caspar Engler, More Township.........	28	5	
"		John Roeder, Plainfield...................	3		
Sept.	20.	John Keller, "	81	6	3
June	18.	Catharina Happel, Plainfield		7	13
Aug.	28.	Peter Warner, "	10	7	3
"	27.	Maria Heimer, "	1	8	13

Church Records.   295

Date.	Names of Persons Buried.	Y.	M.	D.
Aug. 24.	Nicolaus Best, Williams Township......	28	9	13
" 29.	Catharine Knecht, Dryland...............	4	3	21
" "	John Frankenfeld, "	3	1	15
July 7.	Jacob Neuhart, "	79	11	
Aug. 20.	Solomon Tutt, "	16	5	
1798.	George Bender, Plainfield.................	1	3	21
1801, Nov. 4.	Anna Maria Schaus, Easton.........	69	4	9
1798.	John Klaus, Dryland....................	2	10	3
1800.	Dennes Young, Greenwich	76	3	2
1799.	Frederick Riel, a child, Dryland.............	1	11	11
1801. Sept. 15.	Elisabeth Moser, Easton...........	5	9	
" " 17.	Jacob Sand, Forks Township ...	1	10	14
" " 17.	Susanna Ohnangst, Williams Township.......................	2	1	10
" " 28.	Samuel Warner, Plainfield........	6	2	18
1800.	Jacob Brotzman, Williams Township.......	12	6	18
Same day.	John Brotzman, Williams Township	7	10	
" "	John Richard, Williams Township....	3		15
1801.	Sarah Albert, Plainfield........................	5	3	3
"	Michael Kinner, Plainfield.....................	2	10	7
" April 20.	Sarah Kieffer, Dryland..............	3	6	2
" Aug. 7.	John Henry Roeder, Dryland......	80	2	15
" " 10.	Michael Ettinger, Williams Township................................	1	3	7
1802, Feb. 1.	Elisabeth Catharine Schuck, Mount Bethel.....................	81	6	4
1800, Oct. 10.	William Labar, Mount Bethel......	70	5	7
" " 7.	Susanna Hoffart, Dryland...........	32		
" " 7.	Joseph Metzgar, Plainfield.........	1	8	21
" Aug. 9.	Elisabeth Smith, Forks.............	7	7	
1798, Sept. 23.	Anna Maria Boyer...................	5	8	21
1800, March 21.	Elisabeth Rambach, Forks.......	1	7	19
" Oct. 14.	Elisabeth Keller, Williams Township................................	1	5	2

The First Reformed Church of Easton, Pa.

Date.	Names of Persons Buried.	Y.	M.	D.
1800, Oct. 17.	William Moyer.......	1	8	11
1801, May 6.	Rosina Odenwaelder, Forks	1		

Anno 1802.

Date.	Names of Persons Buried.	Y.	M.	D.
March 4.	Elizabeth Ackerman, Plainfield.........	12	2	11
" 5.	Anna Marg. Cratz, Hamilton............	82		
" 14.	Agnes Yuncker, Dryland................	88		
" 21.	Maria Elisabeth Wacker, Dryland......		2	
April 25.	Maria Engel Keller, Plainfield.........	23	7	7
June 21.	Maria Eva Mueller, Easton.............	77	9	
July 9.	Joseph Yuncker, Plainfield		1	
Aug. 8.	Daniel Braun, Dryland..................		3	
" 11.	John Dreisbach, Plainfield..............	1	6	9
" 12.	John Moser "	2	2	5
" 19.	Dorothea Dehli, Dryland...............	46	7	
" 19.	Elisabeth Metz, Plainfield.............	82	2	
" 19.	Frederick Dietz, Plainfield	1	8	6
" 22.	Frederick Sober, Plainfield	1	8	6
" 26.	Karl Heimer, Plainfield..................		9	17
Sept. 2.	Peter Transu..............................	2	11	
" 20.	John Neuhardt, Dryland................	34	9	
Dec. 19.	William Henry Lawall, Dryland........	62	10	16
" 21.	James Baynes, Mount Bethel	27	4	

Anno 1803.

Date.	Names of Persons Buried.	Y.	M.	D.
Jan. 9.	Joseph Koenig, Dryland..................		4	2
" 11.	Adam Dreisbach, Easton................	80	2	
" 13.	Christian Labach, Mount Bethel........	8		
April 12.	Susanna Allen, Easton, Williams Twp.	13	3	11
" 23.	William, Son of William, Plainfield...		6	3
July 20.	George Derhammer, Dryland............	63	3	
Nov. 13.	Maria Gress, Isaac Gress' daughter.....		6	10
March 11.	Catharine Lerch, Forks Township......	2	6	15
" 15.	Elizabeth Mutshler, Greenwich.........	35	3	28
" 17.	Andrew Lerch, Forks		9	15

Church Records. 297

Date.		Names of Persons Buried.	Y.	M.	D
April	8.	Philip Correll, Stocker's Burying Ground...	67		22
"	21.	Maria Daniel, Dryland	47		
June	10.	John Hain, Williams Township.........	63		
"	13.	Henry Althous, Easton.......................	77	8	8
July	3.	Sarah Riedy, Plainfield........................	1	3	2
"	5.	Maria Magdalena, Forks.....................	88	3	16
Aug.	9.	Franciscus Hilliart, Mount Bethel......	10		4
Sept.	4.	Michael Hilliart, Mount Bethel.........	2	5	5
"	4.	Abraham Weidman, Mount Bethel.....	3	8	2

ANNO 1804.

Jan.	8.	Barnhart Fenner, Hamilton	47	4	17
"	19.	William Janson, Dryland..................	72	10	4
"	21.	Maria Correll, Stockers......................			19
March	19.	Anna Maria Gross, Dryland...............	70	2	4
"	27.	Sarah Borein (?), Dryland		5	17
May	11.	Catharine Hertzel, Dryland	58	2	2
"	12.	William Kellwich, Easton..			
"	13.	William Knauss, Easton	8	5	3
June	12.	Mrs. Withers, Easton	56	3	
"	13.	John Nicolaus Hoffman, Nokenixon...	55	3	14
"	30.	Adam Keller, Plainfield	13	8	1
Aug.	1.	Jacob Mueller, Mount Bethel.............	7	4	2
"	19.	Catharine McMurray, Easton.............	50		
Sept.	11.	Margaret Emrich, Mount Bethel.........	1	7	
"	16.	George Henry Ohnangst, Williams Township..................................	8	11	2
Aug.	10.	Barbara Batt, Easton........................	57	9	7
"	24.	Christian Eylenberger, Mount Bethel..	73	7	16
"	31.	Frederick Daely, Dryland................	68		
Nov.	24.	Elisabeth Metzgar...........................	60		
"	27.	Margaret Suehn, Nancy's Run..........	86	2	6
Dec.	1.	Dewald Frantz, Hamilton................	15	11	4
"	3.	George Mueller................................	1	8	

Date.		Names of Persons Buried.	Y.	M.	D.
Dec.	5.	Daniel Fiet, Greenwich......	59	10	11
"	6.	Elisabeth Yaeger, Easton......	76	8	6
"	21.	Anna Margaret Schwartz, Forks	37	3	18

Anno 1805.

Jan.	15.	Thomas Delong, Plainfield......		5	10
Feb.	4.	Jacob Schuck, Plainfield......			25
March	25.	George Christopher Heller, Mount Bethel......	74		
"	28.	Jacob Wilhelm, Dryland......	84	7	1
April	9.	Susanna Dreisbach, Easton......	81		
"	17.	William Freeman, Plainfield......	52		
"	18.	Jacob Opp, Easton......	64	4	
"	30.	John Adam Eschbach, Dryland......	27	5	25
May	4.	Eva Seipel, Easton......	86	7	
"	23.	Catharine Keller, Williams Township,	78		
June	17.	Simon Dengler, Hamilton......	12		9
"	11.	Jacob Odenwaelder, Williams Township	1	11	26
May	31.	Eva Hess, Mount Bethel......	1	8	28
July	14.	Susanna Lerch, Easton......	6	3	15
"	"	William Neise, Greenwich......	67		
"	17.	Maria Elisabeth Woodring, Williams Township......	2	5	7
"	19.	Anna Maria Hertzel, Williams Township......	6	2	
"	20.	Jacob Laehr, Dryland	74		
"	23.	Isaac Klaus (?), Dryland......	2		
"	24.	Maria Magdalena Stocker, Forks Township	64	4	18
"	30.	John Philip Mann, Mount Bethel	2		18
Aug.	4.	Jacob Arndt, Sr., Arndt's Mill......	80	4	10
"	5.	James Mackey's child, Mount Bethel..	1	5	11
"	7.	Maria Siegfried, Siegfried's Mill......	51	10	
"	7.	Caspar Happel, Plainfield	42		

Church Records. 299

Date.		Names of Persons Buried.	Y.	M.	D.
Aug.	8.	Jacob Woodring, Williams Township	2	10	27
"	10.	Daniel Eritt, Dryland	1	2	3
"	10.	Regina Nagel, Dryland			11
"	12.	Anna Margaretha Muffly, Plainfield	55	8	
"	13.	Conrad Willauer, Plainfield	1	2	16
"	14.	Margaretha Batt, Easton	11	6	
"	16.	Margaretha Dengler, Easton	5	11	4
"	21.	John Oberly, Easton	59	2	
"	25.	Elisabeth Hess, Williams Township	12		
"	29.	Elisabeth Lauer, Plainfield	25	2	11
Sept.	11.	Sarah Heller, Hamilton	8	4	29
Oct.	2.	George Heinlein, Durham	63		
"	18.	Margaret Spanomer, Plainfield	75	3	3
"	21.	Anna Maria Schuck, Forks Township	67	2	
"	27.	John Yost Keller, Williams Township	78		
"	30.	Leah Margaret Stofflet, Plainfield		4	20
Nov.	24.	A son of Robert Ennes, Easton		2	17
"	26.	Sebastian Dietrich, Dryland	35	8	15
"	12.	Anna Margaret Metz, Plainfield	22		6
July	10.	Sarah Koester, Mount Bethel	2		

Anno 1806.

Jan.	31.	Charlotte Kern, Plainfield	79	4	8
March	7.	Henry Fors, Easton		2	
"	23.	Catharine Barnett, Mount Bethel	26	3	1
April	22.	Frederica Elisabetha Bald, Plainfield	68	1	10
"	27.	Anna Maria Odenwaelder, Easton	17	4	5
Aug.	8.	Jacob Arndt, Arndt's Mill	21	3	10
Sept.	15.	Elisabeth Hulteman, Schweitzer's Burying Ground		3	4
"	23.	John Preis, Forks Township	24	5	15
"	28.	Charlotte Altemus, Hamilton	59		
Dec.	11.	Elisabeth Catharine Moser, Saucon Township	34	9	2

Anno 1807.

Date.		Names of Persons Buried.	Y.	M.	D.
Jan.	15.	Sarah Jacoby, Springfield	9	10	2
"	12.	Catharine Berge (?), Saucon	72	3	
"	30.	Andrew Ries, Dryland			17
Feb.	5.	Susanna Stecher, Stocker's Burying Ground	24		16
"	15.	George Butz, Dryland		1	1
"	21.	John Ulrich Schleppe, Plainfield	48	5	4
"	26.	Ludwig Heller, Hamilton	78	1	26
March	2.	John Kocher, Schweitzer's Burying Ground		6	8
May	10.	Daniel Reichardt, Easton	17	2	10
"	22.	Maria Gertrude Schaeffer, Greenwich	81	1	4
"	26.	John Andrew Daeling, Easton	26	3	20
June	13.	Frans Leidig, Noconixon	3	4	1
July	7.	Peter Frauenfelder, Stocker's Burying Ground	3	3	11
"	21.	Jacob Abel, Arndt's Burying Ground	88	6	
Aug.	31.	Carl Bishoff, Easton	1	2	27
Sept.	1.	Jacob Labach, Saucon	1	5	19
"	12.	Anthon Rose, Easton	83		
"	15.	Bernhardt Stocker, Stocker's Burying Ground	1	11	4
"	28.	Jacob Striebe, Plainfield	53	3	16
"	30.	Sarah Ann Ward, Easton		2	21
Oct.	22.	John Daniel Kocher, Arndt's Burying Ground	33	3	19
Dec.	10.	Barbara Hertzel, Dryland	86	7	19
"	10.	Elisabeth Meixsell, Easton	12	7	3

Anno 1808.

Jan.	17.	Elisabeth Repscher, Plainfield	38	4	
"	20.	John Blumen, Dryland	49	4	
March	7.	Sarah Engel, Plainfield	62	7	

Date.		Names of Persons Buried.	Y.	M.	D.
March	14.	George Gieser, Greenwich...............	77	5	19
"	25.	Jacob Linn, Saucon........................	1	7	6
April	10.	Michael Gress, Easton....................	81	3	
"	21.	Lorentz Erb, Easton.......................	49	4	6
"	23.	Catharine Happel, Plainfield............	74	5	13
May	2.	Sarah Roth, Saucon........................		11	3
"	11.	John Messinger, Stocker's...............	62	1	
"	24.	Elisabeth Kooper, Upper Saucon.......	50	3	21
"	29.	Andrew Opp, Saucon.....................	75	9	9
"	30.	Juliann Schuck, Easton...................	63	9	
June	17.	George Tobias Saetzer, Hamilton......	76	1	5
"	21.	Peter Maurer, Easton	5	2	
July	10.	Elmira Lucker, Easton....................	1	1	10
Aug.	13.	Peter Messinger, Arndt's................	6	6	
"	14.	Hannah Dietz, Williams.................	34	11	13
"	16.	Michael Traxsell, Easton................	42	9	
Sept.	3.	Rebecca Ohl, Saucon.....................	21	2	21
"	11.	John Meyer, Easton.......................	32	4	
Oct.	13.	Anna Diemer, Raub's....................	1	7	7
"	21.	Elis. Barnett, Easton......................	41	7	
"	31.	Anna Diemer, Raub's.....................		9	11
Nov.	10.	Frederick Hoenig, Plainfield.............	4	7	
"	20.	Levan Stocker, Stocker's.................	3	8	
Dec.	1.	Catharine Berry, Williams	33	6	
"	9.	Anna Maria Hufschmidt, Hamilton....	72		
"	12.	Catharine Gum, Plainfield	61	8	
"	17.	Joseph Sendee, Dryland	6	3	
"	30.	Carolina Herter, Saucon	6	7	

ANNO 1809.

Jan.	7.	Andrew Koechlein, Forks...............		8	19
"	11.	John Felix Lynn, Saucon................	68		
"	12.	Maria Ward, Plainfield...................	28	1	15
Feb.	11.	Regina Hess, Dryland....................	1	2	

Date.		Names of Persons Buried.	Y.	M.	D.
March	14.	Jacob Schaefer, Stocker's..............	2	5	
"	24.	John George Yunker, Dryland..........	79	4	12
"	29.	Marg. Grubb, Easton	39	4	18
April	14.	Simon Schaeffer, Stocker's..............		3	
May	8.	Peter Sendee, Dryland.....................	1	2	15
"	23.	Ludwig Fritz, Plainfield..................	22	6	7
June	4.	John Ludwig Knaus, Easton.............	79	3	19
July	27.	John Schaum, Plainfield	1		16
Aug.	3.	John Fellenser, Hamilton................	86	8	14
"	14.	Maria Osterstock, Dryland...............	1	2	2
"	15.	Henry Bishoph, Easton...................	1	3	12
"	29.	Conrad Arnold, Hamilton	28		
Sept.	1.	Michael Messinger, Messinger's	22	5	7
"	5.	John Fehr, Plainfield......................	1	4	22
"	9.	Frederick William Bruch, Plainfield...		10	21
"	29.	Albertina Dillinger, Dryland............	65	6	6
Oct.	3.	Caspar Metzger, Hamilton...............	17	8	26
"	6.	Jacob Rohr, Dryland.......................	59	7	4
"	23.	Margaret Lerch, Saucon..................	1		7
"	23.	George Adam Weber, Saucon...........	57	5	9
"	31.	Feronica Bossart, Hamilton.............	62	3	24
Nov.	4.	Thomas Buss, Dryland.....................	16	2	10
Dec.	19.	Margaret Moyer, Plainfield	66		
"	21.	Catharine Becker, Williams	70		

Anno 1810.

Jan.	1.	Catharine Altemus, Hamilton............	24	7	24
"	3.	Catharine Hirte, Williams................	29	5	26
"	4.	Jacob Lynn, Saucon........................	2	4	
"	5.	Barbara Fehr, Saucon	81		
"	12.	Anna Maria Seip, Easton	68		8
"	15.	Catharine Boyer, Dryland................	1	1	
March	16.	Anna Elis. Diel, Plainfield...............	70	2	3
"	23.	Barbara Sober, Plainfield.................	77	1	5
"	31.	David Odenwaelder, Williams..........	1	7	28

Date.		Names of Persons Buried.	Y.	M.	D.
April	9.	Maria Lantz, Williams	3	4	15
"	17.	Magdalena Transue, Williams	78		
"	19.	John Lenhart Kern, Plainfield	86	8	4
"	20.	Maria Margaret Knecht, Dryland	71		
"	21.	Susanna Williams, Plainfield	38	8	11
"	23.	Anna Maria Hertzel, Williams	15	6	14
"	25.	John Boorem, Dryland	39	1	18
May	24.	Jacob Emmerich, Mount Bethel	45	7	8
"	27.	Mrs. Ghent, Plainfield	92	4	7
June	17.	Abraham Traxsell, Easton	1	7	
"	21.	Benjamin Coleman, Easton	21	4	2
July	—.	Henry Moeller, Dryland	50	3	9
"	14.	Maria Muench, New Dryland		7	8
"	25.	Maria Heller, Hamilton	1	2	
"	27.	Mrs. Siegfried, Siegfried's	51	4	16
Aug.	1.	Peter Werkhaeuser, Hamilton	9	7	7
"	1.	Henry Werkhaeuser, Hamilton	3	2	22
"	4.	Margaretha Werkhaeuser,[1] Hamilton	33		
"	4.	Carl Werkhaeuser,[1] Hamilton	7	6	
"	4.	Susanna Werkhaeuser,[1] Hamilton	5	5	
"	4.	Henry (Werkhaeuser),[1] Hamilton	1	9	13
"	4.	Adam Murffy, Hamilton	3	3	
"	5.	Elisabeth Hafner, Hamilton	3	5	8
"	5.	Maria Magdalena Fenner, Hamilton	5		2
"	7.	Peter Gerhardt, Hamilton	1	1	23
"	10.	Anna Maria Opp, Easton	38	7	16
"	12.	Anna Catharine Wagner, Easton	66	5	4
"	13.	Susanna Woodring, Hamilton	1	2	21
"	14.	Salome Gauer, Hamilton	1	11	4
"	14.	Henry Hauser, Hamilton	61	4	19
"	18.	Anna Maria Frey, Dryland	14	3	14
"	18.	John Peter Dreisbach, Dryland	52	9	15
Sept.	5.	Abraham, illegitimate, Dryland	8		4

[1] All in one grave.

Date.		Names of Persons Buried.	Y.	M.	D.
Sept.	9.	Elisabeth Heller, Plainfield.............	18	3	2
"	24.	Elisabeth Kaemrer, Hamilton............	14	10	
"	30.	Mrs. Rath, Saucon.........................	26	9	
Oct.	7.	Jacob Schumacher, Arndt's...............	66		
"	13.	Jesse Rath, Saucon........................		1	
"	15.	Jacob Rippel, Easton.....................	1	10	
"	29.	Adam Butz, Hamilton.....................	50		
"	30.	John Wolfinger, Hamilton...............	6		26
Nov.	9.	Rebecca Dreisbach, Plainfield...........		2	1
"	25.	Jacob Seipel, Mount Bethel.............	60	3	13
Dec.	14.	Maria Magdalena Mersch, Hamilton...	21	2	
"	21.	Henry Schaum, Plainfield................	30	2	10
"	30.	Susanna Dietrich, Dryland...............	5	11	17
"	31.	George Diets, Easton......................	4	9	3

Anno 1811.

Jan.	15.	Margaret Herster, Easton................	48		
Feb.	6.	Christina Roth, Dryland..................	36	9	
"	7.	Sarah Kotz, Williams.....................	2		14
"	24.	John Reis, Easton..........................	5	6	20
"	24.	Christina Schaup, Easton................	76	6	
"	25.	Liddia Oberly, Saucon.....................	2	4	4
"	26.	Charlotte Schmidt, Dryland.............	81		
March	6.	Sarah Sponheimer, Plainfield............			16
"	10.	Jacob Hahn, Plainfield....................	1		10
"	13.	Anna Maria Nicholas, Easton............	67		
"	24.	Joseph Borum, Dryland	1	3	9
"	22.	Salome Gruber, Mount Bethel...........	75	6	
"	25.	George Schaum, Plainfield...............		9	7
May	3.	Benjamin Lerch, Saucon..................	5	8	18
"	18.	Maria Simon, Easton......................	1	1	
"	24.	Isaac Mayer, Mount Bethel..............	40	2	
June	2.	John H. Derr, Dryland...................	69	5	22
July	3.	Jacob Heller, Plainfield	1	3	23
"	3.	Rosina Heller, Hamilton..................	21	8	5

Date.		Names of Persons Buried.	Y.	M.	D.
July	15.	Elisabeth Kreidler, Dryland.............	27	6	11
"	26.	Catharine Wasser, Saucon................	1	7	17
Aug.	31.	Joseph Kind, Plainfield....................		1	
Sept.	4.	George Koch, Settlement................	67	1	6
"	4.	Maria Magdalena Lesch, Williams.....	41		5
"	26.	Simon Koch, Easton......................		1	25
Nov.	4.	John A. Laubach, Saucon................	36	4	
"	13.	Jacob Christman, Saucon...............	67	2	10
"	19.	John Mill's child			25
Dec.	16.	Thos. Roth, Dryland	4	2	2

Anno 1812.

Jan.	6.	John George Leibenguth, Lecha Twp..	74	10	
"	10.	Elisabeth Gruber, Moretown............	19		14
"	23.	Susanna E. Steiner, Plainfield...........	3	10	20
Feb.	2.	Isaac Gross, Dryland.......................	53	5	21
"	27.	Peter Oberly, Sheimer's...................	20	2	5
"	28.	John Laubach, Saucon.....................	1	7	21
March	9.	John Klericker, Hamilton................	57	10	20
"	12.	Elis. Beisell, Dryland........		6	
April	4.	John William Mill, Hamilton...........	34	10	15
"	5.	Henry Engel, Plainfield................	81	8	21
"	10.	Henrietta Boem, Saucon.................	1	3	25
"	16.	Susanna Sendy, Dryland...............		2	3
May	20.	John Melchior Edinger, Mount Bethel.	70	9	2
"	30.	Susanna Pfeiffer, Williams	47		
June	2.	Anna Maria Opp, Easton...............	41		2
"	3.	Susanna Shaefer, Forks........	2	2	9
"	10.	Anna Maria Miller, Williams	29	4	10
"	14.	Thomas Germanton, Plainfield...	1	9	8
"	29.	Maria Kreidler, Dryland...................		5	9
Sept.	6.	Magdalena Heller, Saucon..............	24	4	12
"	6.	Solomon, her child "			17
"	18.	Sarah Weis, Williams.....	1	1	
"	22.	William Mayer, Plainfield...............	45	6	10

Date.		Names of Persons Buried.	Y.	M.	D.
Sept.	26.	George Peter Kind, Plainfield............	17	3	13
Oct.	24.	Magdalena Voelke, Hamilton...........	25	4	24
"	29.	Jacob Arndt, Junior, Easton...........	56	5	14
Nov.	12.	Anna Dietz, Easton......................	81	10	11
Dec.	1.	John Henry Sieman, Williams.........	20	6	10
"	13.	Eleanor Lesch, Williams................	1	8	2
"	15.	Daniel Wever, Plainfield.................	79	5	12

Anno 1813.

Jan.	19.	Frederick Diehl, Plainfield..............	90	2	11
"	28.	Reuben Heinly, Dryland.................		1	13
Feb.	13.	John Young, Easton......................	31	4	1
"	14.	Anna Maria Knecht, Williams.........	60	4	13
"	25.	John Kratzer, Mount Bethel............	24	10	7
"	27.	Peter Lauer, Saucon......................	49		
April	3.	Jonathon Beisel, Dryland...............		1	10
"	5.	Benjamin Beisel, Dryland...............		1	12
"	6.	Herman Peter Young, Easton..........	1		8
"	7.	John Conrad, Germanton...............	75	5	18
"	26.	John Wilhelm, Dryland.................	28	7	5
"	30.	Abraham Transue, Williams...........	81	7	4
May	20.	Maria Kocher, Forks.....................	69	2	4
"	21.	Maria Gutzel, Forks.....................	72		
"	6.	John Young, Easton......................	62	5	16
June	13.	Catharine Riecher (?), Williams.......	71		
"	17.	Maria Elisabeth Getter, Williams......	52	2	
July	28.	Maria Young, Easton.....................	63	2	10
Oct.	2.	Peter Schick, Easton.....................	3		16
"	24.	John Henry Miller, Plainfield...........	59		19
Nov.	22.	Mr. Neuhart, Dryland....................	26	10	8
"	30.	Christian Bess, Williams.................	67	6	
Dec.	11.	Joseph Schuch, Forks....................	20	10	
"	29.	Sarah Cole, Dryland.....................	61	10	22
"	31.	Margaret Traxsell, Easton...............	56	1	12

Anno 1814.

Date.		Names of Persons Buried.	Y.	M.	D.
Jan.	16.	Elisabeth Walter, Williams...............		7	12
"	25.	Anna Maria Dietrich, Dryland...........	73	4	
"	29.	Maria Buss, Dryland......................	28	5	9
"	31.	Elisabeth Christina Sand, Easton.......	80	11	10
Feb.	7.	Verena Paulus, Dryland..................	89	5	15
"	8.	Joseph Schurtz, Dryland.................		1	10
"	17.	Joseph Nagel, Dryland...................	4	1	
March	16.	Sophia Dietz, Easton......................	6		
April	2.	Eliza Broeder, Dryland...................	3	5	
"	8.	Baltazer Reich, Saucon..................	84	4	
"	5.	John Joseph Keller, Plainfield...........	26	4	3
"	3.	John Deichman, Dryland................	66	7	3
"	21.	David Bender, Plainfield.................	5	5	
"	29.	Elisabeth Fehr, Williams	1		
May	24.	Caroline Hoffeditz, Dryland.............		4	11
"	28.	Susanna Rath, Dryland..................	48	2	
June	1.	Peter Heller, Plainfeld...................	29	1	18
"	11.	Joseph Beil, Saucon......................	13	4	15
"	28.	Eleonora Dengler, Easton................		1	18
"	29.	John Gangenwere, Williams	1	3	23
July	7.	Juliana Meixsell, Easton..................	21	3	3
"	12.	Anna Eve McCarty, Easton.............	32	10	17
"	24.	Joanna Elisabeth Kochert, Easton......	84	2	8
Aug.	19.	Reuben Hay, Easton.......................		11	
Oct.	1.	Henry Frauenfelder.........................		4	17
"	6.	Reuben Heckman...........................		6	12
"	8.	John, a child at whose baptism F. Ackerman was sponsor................	1	5	13
Nov.	4.	Maria Romage...............................	69	2	3
"	14.	Elisabeth Shnyder...........................	19	9	10
"	27.	John Metzger, Easton		1	5
"	28.	Lidia Nagel, Dryland	3		2
"	30.	Jacob Jacoby, Williams	90	3	

Date.		Names of Persons Buried.	Y.	M.	D.
Dec.	11.	Peter Siegfried, Settlement...............	33	3	4
"	22.	Catharine Arndt, Dryland		1	7
"	23.	Hanna Janson, Dryland	3	3	21
"	30.	A child of Martin Janson, Dryland.....		1	13

Anno 1815.

Jan.	8.	Thomas Traxsell, Easton	1	8	9
"	19.	Maria Elisabeth Bittenbender, Easton..	85	5	10
"	22.	Catharine Derr, Saucon	1	2	13
"	30.	John Seip, Easton........................	54	2	23
Feb.	9.	Anna Julianna Weis, Easton	11		
"	13.	Sarah Hauck, Plainfield		5	8
"	20.	Maria Eva Hoffman, Easton	91		7
"	28.	Regina Knecht, Dryland..................	48	4	3
March	10.	Wilhelmina Simon, Easton..............	1	9	21
"	10.	Anna Eliz. Snyder, Easton	81	2	10
"	14.	Salome Kleder, Dryland.................	9	10	22
"	15.	Elisabeth Bundstein, Dryland		9	2
"	19.	Nathaniel Kreidler, Dryland		10	
"	23.	Nicholas Lantz, Williams....	93	1	17
"	25.	Frederick Gehres, Williams.............	24	8	
April	1.	Christopher Raub, Williams	24	9	15
"	9.	Maria Hackman, Williams................	4	9	2
"	17.	Elisabeth Bess, Williams.................	61		22
"	26.	William Philips, Easton..................		4	10
May	5.	John Benner, Saucon		5	13
"	10.	Maria Spangenberg, Williams...........	26	6	
"	15.	Maria Barbara Ettinger, Williams......	52	1	19
"	19.	Elisabeth Moser, Williams...............	1	2	6
July	18.	Rev. Peter Frederick Niemayer,[1] Plainfield..	81	5	
"	19.	Sarah Kern, Hamilton.....................	18	3	
"	20.	George Peter Kessler, Hamilton		5	3

[1] The Lutheran minister at Plainfield.

Church Records.

Date.		Names of Persons Buried.	Y.	M.	D.
Aug.	2.	Peter Wilhelm, Easton............	6	7	22
"	14.	Dorothea Dech, Dryland...........		7	8
"	17.	Margaret Dech, Dryland...........		7	11
Sept.	16.	Jacob Brotzman, Williams.........	37	9	7
"	17.	Elisabeth Heller, Hamilton........	2	6	3
"	18.	Thos. Fehr, Plainfield............		3	20
"	19.	Andrew Dengler, Easton		6	12
"	22.	Elisabeth Koester, Plainfield......	50	6	23
"	26.	Sarah Kind, Plainfield	1	10	13
Oct.	20.	Susanna Dietz, Easton......	5	6	13
Nov.	2.	Maria Kocher, Greenwich.........	20		10
"	5.	Joseph Schleppi, Plainfield........	20	9	15
"	9.	Barbara Staut, Williams	63	4	1
"	10.	Anna Maria Nonnemacher, Easton..	94		7
"	15.	Michael Gies, Hamilton	61	5	
"	20.	Christina Frey, Hamilton.........	72		
"	23.	Samuel Kroner, Plainfield.........	27	9	28
"	24.	John George Hartman, Plainfield...	46		17
"	27.	John Frederick Hahn, Plainfield....	68		9
Dec.	1.	Sarah Weber, Plainfield...........	33	9	19
"	9.	Anna Margaret Engel, Plainfield...	93	1	18
"	17.	Peter Miller, Easton.............		1	16

Anno 1816.

Jan.	21.	Joseph Ritter, Dryland............	4	5	3
"	21.	William Augustus Wolf, Easton....	3	8	4
"	27.	Peter Lantz, Williams.............	58	4	
Feb.	2.	Maria Catharine Seipel, Easton....	62	11	1
"	6.	John Jacob Laddig, Williams.......	36	5	4
"	11.	Sarah Krahn, Williams	15	2	11
"	13.	Anthony Kind, Plainfield	28	11	3
"	28.	John Miller, Easton..............	1	10	22
March	5.	Carl Lawall, Dryland.............		1	8
"	9.	Sarah Snyder, Easton.............	21	3	21
"	13.	Sarah Weber, Plainfield...........		3	17

The First Reformed Church of Easton, Pa.

Date.		Names of Persons Buried.	Y.	M.	D.
March	20.	Anna Catharine Bess, Williams	91	3	4
"	21.	Anna Catharine Reichart, Williams...	60	4	12
April	4.	Michael Heller, Saucon	39		27
"	7.	Catharine Lerch, Greenwich	29	8	19
"	20.	Jacob Lynn, Saucon		3	6
"	27.	A daughter of John Belles and wife Elisabeth, Saucon		1	
May	6.	John Schweishaupt, Dryland	60		
"	15.	Elisabeth Hahn, Plainfield	30		2
"	30.	Valentine Gehres, Williams	72	5	
June	16.	Hannah Hornecker, Dryland	64		
"	23.	Maria Niemeyer,[1] Plainfield	72	9	28
Aug.	2.	Robert Traill, Easton	72	3	2
"	3.	Maria Streber, Saucon	24	7	21
"	10.	Samuel Ekart, Saucon	3	7	14
"	13.	Maria Kocher, Forks	18	6	7
"	27.	Susanna Rippel, Easton		1	10
Sept.	28.	Elisabeth Bauer, Plainfield			25
Oct.	18.	Jane Trach, Williams	22		
"	23.	George Ziegenfuss, Williams	1	6	4
		Peter Teiss, Bethlehem Township	46		
Jan.	1.	Sarah Peiffer, Plainfield	33	3	25
"	8.	Magdalina Grass, Plainfield	79	4	25
"	8.	A child of John Wasser (also baptized), Saucon		3	8
Feb.	1.	Catharine Laubach, Saucon	69	5	16
"	11.	Margaret Schwartz, Plainfield	74	2	
"	15.	Philip Boehm, Saucon	69	2	
"	17.	Jane Sively (?), Plainfield	67	3	
March	5.	Joseph Richard, Williams	82	6	27
"	11.	Henry Transue, Saucon	21		4
"	13.	Susanna Stocker, Easton	22	2	7
"	18.	Adam Frantz, Plainfield	18	8	27

[1] The wife of Rev. Peter Frederick Niemeyer.

Church Records. 311

Date.		Names of Persons Buried.	Y.	M.	D.
March	29.	Regina Wilhelm, Dryland................	29	6	14
April	1.	Catharine Schlecht, Plainfield...........	66	6	20
"	21.	Eliz. Margaret Hahn, Plainfield.........	57		29
"	24.	Margaret Hertzell, Plainfield............	69	4	26
May	—.	Joseph Stumpf, Dryland............	86	8	
"	13.	Philip Mixsell, Easton.....................	85	5	20
"	10.	Susanna Buss, Dryland	1	2	2
June	11.	Magdalena Schmidt, Dryland............	23	6	13
July	1.	Samuel Hamilton Arndt, Easton........	18	10	13
"	18.	Isaac Kocher, Dryland.....................		10	9
Aug.	8.	Barbara Michael, Dryland	59	11	29
"	11.	Elisabeth Lawall, Dryland	8	2	29
"	15.	Samuel Hoffert, Dryland	24		
"	16.	George Sauerbeck, Easton	72	9	29
"	16.	Joseph Russell, Plainfield...........		9	2
"	19.	Anna Maria Knecht, Plainfield	1	5	11
"	20.	John Boulsby, Easton	22		26
"	22.	John Jacob Wasser, Saucon..............	4	1	
"	24.	Levina Boyer, Dryland.....................	2	3	25
"	24.	Siadora, daughter of Catharine Hartman, Easton	3	7	28
"	30.	Rachael Frey, Plainfeld.....................		9	19
"	31.	Julius, a son of Cath. Hartman, Easton	3	8	4
June	2.	Eva Bader, Saucon........................	53	5	
Sept.	4.	George Lawall, Dryland............ ...	5	9	23
"	15.	Susanna Odenwaelder, Easton......... ..	2	3	20
"	16.	Hannah Neiss, Easton	49	10	2
"	16.	Samuel Kinsey Meixsell, Easton...	1	2	6
"	17.	John Reidenauer, Dryland...............	7	6	2
"	17.	Hester McHose, Saucon.................	3	3	6
"	22.	John Hertzell, Williams...................	1		28
"	24.	Maria Anna Sheip, Easton...............	3	11	22
"	25.	Frederick Royer, Dryland.................	8	4	5
"	26.	Catharine Freeman, Saucon.............		9	25
"	30.	William Kocher, Dryland................	3	11	22

Date.		Names of Persons Buried.	Y.	M.	D.
Oct.	1.	Catharine Buss, Dryland	9	10	4
"	3.	Child of Nicholas Dietz, Easton		6	
"	9.	Susanna Koemrer, Forks	14	7	24
"	23.	Conrad Ward, Plainfeld	45	2	19
"	24.	Maria Ann Traxsell, Easton	1	5	
Dec.	7.	John Jacob Appel, Easton	5	8	10

Anno 1818.

Date.		Names of Persons Buried.	Y.	M.	D.
Jan.	7.	Jacob Moser, Saucon	1		5
"	8.	Adam Heimer, Plainfield	56	8	18
"	17.	John Mond, Dryland	56		14
"	18.	John Bruch, Plainfield	46	2	15
"	21.	Thomas Weierman, Dryland	8		5
Feb.	6.	Maria Eliz. Beissell, Dryland	41	9	6
"	21.	Benedict Lutz, Saucon	82	3	24
"	21.	Joseph Kotz, Williams	1	5	20
"	23.	Gottlieb Faas, Dryland	42		23
March	1.	Ulrich Knecht, Dryland	82		8
"	3.	Samuel Kocher, Dryland	11	3	21
"	8.	Edward Daniel, Dryland	3	11	13
"	11.	Martin Kind, Plainfield	63	11	29
"	27.	Peter Stamm, Saucon	11	6	14
"	29.	Simon Ohl, Saucon	1	1	3
April	1.	Frederick Hoenig, Plainfield	48	7	2
"	5.	Henry Schnyder, Easton	50		2
"	8.	Maria Miller, Williams	27	3	27
"	8.	William Shyder, Easton	23	10	12
"	9.	Catharine Buss, Dryland	1	6	10
"	21.	Joseph Broeder, Easton		2	9
"	23.	Maria Magd. Kroner, Plainfield	38	3	25
"	28.	Susanna Gradwohl, Dryland	38	8	21
May	18.	George Adam Hay, Easton	82		24
"	20.	Caspar Roth, Dryland	47	2	7
"	22.	George Rieser, Dryland	11	4	15
June	3.	Eliza Heller, Plainfield	14	4	6

Date.		Names of Persons Buried.	Y.	M.	D.
July	9.	Cath. Eliz. Bauer, Plainfield............	73	6	16
"	14.	Christina Dreisbach, Plainfield..........	44	4	17
Aug.	19.	Adam Weber, Plainfield	1	6	25
"	21.	Juliana Leidig, Easton....................		6	3
"	27.	Carl Walter, Easton........................	9	9	22
Sept.	14.	Samuel Knecht, Dryland.................	9	10	29
"	19.	Juliana Siegfried, Dryland......	2	6	15
"	20.	Sarah Kind, Plainfield.	81	4	29
"	23.	Nicholas Koch, Easton..	81	4	29
"	28.	Maria Diehl, Plainfield.......	22	10	3
Oct.	9.	Susanna Nagel, Dryland.................	49		13
"	14.	Eliza Hahn, Plainfield....................	10	11	22
"	25.	Sarah Walter, Forks.......................	31	6	23
Nov.	16.	Catharine De Long, Plainfield...........	59	8	10
"	27.	Sarah Bodein, Forks......................	2		12
"	28.	Samuel Belles, Saucon...........	1	6	19

ANNO 1819.

Feb.	16.	George Frederick Faebel, Plainfield ...	49	10	
March	5.	Rebecca Laubach, Saucon................	24	10	3
"	8.	A son of Margaret Heinlein, Williams.		2	23
"	13.	Elisabeth Beitelman, Dryland..........	68	3	
"	19.	Leonard Beitelman, Dryland	78		
"	31.	Matthew Hertzell, Williams............	3	6	8
April	9.	Philip Woodring, Williams..............	78	2	28
"	10.	Lisetta Weis, Williams....................		8	14
"	11.	Elisabeth Derr, Saucon...................	45	11	5
"	13.	Simon Jacob Diehl, Plainfield..........	81		26
"	15.	Maria Magdalena Gehres, Williams...	1	5	24
"	21.	John Peter Kocher, Arndt's.............	77		21
"	22.	Susanna Odenwaelder, Easton..........	1	4	23
"	23.	Sarah Ann Weiss, Saucon...............	1	8	3
May	9.	Andrew Rippel, Easton	72	10	2
June	12.	John Peter Beissell, Dryland............	48	11	
July	10.	Rebecca Derr, Saucon.....................		5	8

Date.		Names of Persons Buried.	Y.	M.	D.
July	19.	John Jacob Scheip, Easton	59	8	1
"	31.	Henry McHose, Saucon		3	14
Aug.	9.	Catharine Derr, Dryland	71	3	21
"	19.	Michael Reeb, Plainfield	77	9	2
"	20.	A child of Jacob Woodring, Saucon		1	8
Sept.	1.	Conrad Haas, Dryland	64	6	15
Oct.	22.	Thomas Washington Laddig, Williams	7	0	4
"	9.	Rebecca Buss, Dryland			
"	30.	A son of Simon Butz, Dryland			4
Nov.	1.	Julius Keiser, Hamilton	2	5	25
"	6.	Jacob Frantz, Hamilton	64	3	10
"	7.	Juliana Walter, Easton	7	4	19
"	12.	Charles Poke, Williams	30	7	13
Dec.	4.	Edward Freeman, Saucon	64	6	3
"	25.	Peter Mayer, Saucon	59	9	1
"	28.	Anna Maria Steinbach, Saucon	23	7	24

ANNO 1820.

Date.		Names of Persons Buried.	Y.	M.	D.
Jan.	14.	Catharine Wagner, Dryland	75		19
"	16.	Manasseh Loehr, Plainfield	3	3	11
"	24.	John Carl Heimer, Plainfield	85	11	18
"	30.	Samuel Stein, Saucon	2	4	4
Feb.	9.	Maria Sarah Miller, Plainfield	25	5	6
"	14.	Maria Krotz, Williams	74	1	10
"	22.	Elisabeth Germanton, Plainfield	2	2	23
"	23.	Jacob Werner, Plainfield	78	8	9
"	25.	Salome Supper, Plainfield	16	11	1
March	1.	Susanna Engel, Easton	51	6	14
April	1.	Eliza Cath. Swander, Easton		7	2
May		William Boyer, Easton	25	4	17
"	15.	Sarah Kind, Plainfield	32	7	9
"	7.	Anna Margaret Fehr, Saucon	1	2	28
June	11.	Samuel Boyer, Saucon			21
"	22.	John Frederick Laubach, Saucon	4		18
July	20.	Eleanora Worman, Easton	8	10	11

Church Records. 315

Date.		Names of Persons Buried.	Y.	M.	D.
Aug.	5.	Aaron Kind, Plainfield....................		8	4
"	9.	John Kaemrer, Dryland	70	4	21
"	17.	Margaret Lerch, Saucon	66	1	17
"	19.	Susanna Cath. Shnyder, Easton.........	2	2	11
"	22.	Solomon Walter, Easton...................	21	4	
"	5.	Michael Boyer, Dryland	73	9	3
"	25.	Maria Sarah Hoffman, Williams	2	8	24
"	28.	Catharine Bess, Williams................	1	3	18
"	29.	Anna Sarah Transue, Williams.		7	19
Sept.	29.	A son of Peter Batt and wife Eliz., Easton	4	7	27
"	29.	Benjamin Roth, Dryland.	6	5	11
Oct.	31.	Susanna Frankenfield, Dryland	25	10	22
Nov.	6.	Susanna Shnyder, Easton	60	5	28
"	13.	David Shnyder, Easton	21	7	29
Dec.	9.	Christian Muffly, Plainfield	70	9	5
"	17.	Eliz. Ann Ward, Plainfield	5	7	15
"	28.	Peter Diehl, Plainfield....................	23	5	2

Anno 1821.

Jan.	22.	Elisabeth Gehres, Williams..............	75	1	
"	24.	Andrew Koechlein, Easton..............	68	2	4
March	5.	Michael Traxsell, Easton	39	4	28
"	11.	Maria Ziegler, Dryland	20	6	
"	22.	Lewis Worman, Easton	1	2	18
April	28.	Jacob Bess, Williams			27
May	8.	Lorentz Schwartz, Easton.................	66	7	11
"	12.	Jacob Lepper, Easton	48	5	5
"	12.	Maria Elisabeth Laddig, Williams	76		7
"	27.	Catharine Heck, Williams................	5	2	13
"	30.	Levi Bauer, Plainfield		9	4
June	3.	Jacob Belles, Plainfield...................	39	2	25
"	7.	John Buss, Dryland........................	85	11	13
"	8.	Anna Maria Steinbach, Williams........	26	1	13
"	19.	Abraham Miller, Saucon (?)............	66	1	27

Date.		Names of Persons Buried.	Y.	M.	D.
June	27.	Elisabeth Handshu, Dryland.............	25	9	27
July	2.	Margaret Koch, Saucon...................	1		9
"	10.	Susanna Conrad, Easton..................	77	8	25
Sept. 3, 1820		Jacob Edward Roth, Arndt's............	8	9	8
Oct. 15, 1820		John Adam Deschler, Easton	54	2	15
" 16, 1821		Margaret Haak, Easton..................	53	6	
Aug.	30.	John Freeman, Saucon.....................	27	11	
Sept.	11.	Jacob Lantz, Williams...................	1	1	17
"	15.	Marg. Elisabeth Klotz, Williams......	85		
"	16.	Catharine Ohnangst, Plainfield.........	22	11	
Oct.	3.	Christian Butz, Easton....................	64	10	13
"	12.	Margaret Riehl, Williams.................	69	9	7
"	13.	John Leonard Herzell, Williams.......	46	10	8
"	17.	Susanna Spangenberg, Williams........	1	9	29
"	23.	Thomas Nagel, Dryland..................	18	6	8
"	30.	Susanna Lerch, Saucon	62	8	7
Nov.	26.	John Beck, Dryland.......................	1	3	25
Dec.	2.	Sarah Kind, Plainfield....................	15	6	23
"	30.	Elisabeth Happel, Plainfield............	18		16
"	31.	Jacob Zimmerman, Greenwich.........	60	2	18

ANNO 1822.

Feb.	20.	Elisabeth Koehler, Dryland........	36	5	4
March	7.	Elisabeth Lynn, Saucon	39	1	16
"	9.	Felix Heckman, Dryland................	3	4	5
"	14.	John Simon, Easton......................	27	5	24
"	21.	Maria Brotzman, Williams..............	77	9	4
"	24.	Anna Marg. Eliz. Beisell, Dryland.....	79		14
"	27.	Anna Barbara Weygandt, Saucon	30	3	
"	31.	Sophia Hecht, Easton	82	11	
May	20.	Christian Wagner, Plainfield............	30	8	12
June	9.	Juliana Mann, Saucon	1	8	23
"	22.	George Washington Wolf, Easton......	17	7	29
"	23.	Anna Diehl, Plainfield.....................	19	7	28
"	27.	Rebecca Young, Easton...................	1	7	

THOMAS CONRAD PORTER, D.D., LL.D.

Date.		Names of Persons Buried.	Y.	M.	D.
June	30.	Hiob Heller, Saucon	42	5	6
July	13.	Susanna Eva Meixsell, Dryland	1		19
"	21.	Catharine Lawall, Dryland	1	2	7
"	22.	Catharine Kaemrer, Dryland	35	6	8
"	23.	Elisabeth Kraemer, Dryland	84	6	
Aug.	5.	Maria Schnabel, Dryland	51	10	13
"	7.	Margaret Schortz, Dryland	90		
"	26.	David Brown, Williams	21		6
Sept.	10.	John Coleman, Easton	21	11	26
"	29.	Sidny Kroner, Plainfield	71	5	21
Oct.	10.	Jacob Heller, Plainfield	72	7	2
"	22.	Elisabeth Beisher, Plainfield	85		
"	24.	Henrietta Schweitzer, Dryland.	3	5	19
"	31.	George Wagner, Dryland	18	5	19
Nov.	8.	Catharine Butz, Dryland			19
Dec.	17.	Anna Maria Broeder, Easton	3		

ANNO 1824.

Jan.	7.	Catharine Wagner, Saucon	73	10	
Feb.	5.	Conrad Schiffer, Plainfield	21	9	
"	9.	Elisabeth Scheively, Easton	36		8
"	17.	Isaac Heckman Frees, Easton	1		29
"	18.	Eliza Coleman, Easton	2	3	24
"	27.	Elisabeth Keller, Williams	31	4	15
March	1.	Susanna Townson, Dryland	79	3	
"	4.	John S. Young, Easton	19	9	1
"	13.	John Peter Harzel, Williams	40		
"	15.	Nicholas Kran, Williams	51	5	19
Sept.	15.	Jacob Derr, Saucon		1	24
"	19.	Jacob Wilhelm, Dryland	42	3	3
Oct.	30.	Anna Cath. Sommer, Easton	72	7	18
Nov.	1.	Philip Broeder, Dryland	29	2	19
"	21.	Peter Snyder, Easton	70	9	14
April	13.	Adam Hammel, Dryland	68	3	7

Date.		Names of Persons Buried.	Y.	M.	D.
April	15.	A child of John and Mary Engler, Plainfield		2	
"	26.	Anna Marg. Rippel, Easton	72	5	20
May	2.	Peter Engel, Easton	23	6	
"	13.	Eva Cath. Riegel, Williams	43	5	
"	3.	Peter Reiss, Easton	56		17
"	23.	Samuel Maurer, Easton	22	3	10
"	27.	Anna Maria Boyer, Easton	6	3	6
"	29.	Margaret Boyer, Dryland	75	11	4
June	10.	John George Wilhelm, Dryland	35	9	
"	16.	Elisabeth Ohnangst, Dryland	55	8	5
Aug.	30.	Martin Frey, Plainfield	5	7	
Sept.	1.	Elisabeth Schumacher, Easton	78		24
Dec.	20.	Carl Henry Lantz, Williams		7	17

Anno 1825.

Jan.	7.	Sarah Ann Woodring, Williams		7	
"	13.	Christina Imick, Plainfield	1	1	
"	26.	Jacob Miller, Williams	19	9	2
"	29.	Magdalena Eckel, of Saucon, in Springfield	75		
Feb.	23.	Fillemon Erich, Dryland		3	21
"	27.	George Miller, Easton	7	5	9
"	28.	Roselein Osburn, Easton		10	25
March	4.	Rebecca Hahn, Plainfield	17	10	9
"	7.	Wilhelm Werner, Plainfield		7	
"	11.	Thos. Kemrer, Forks			11
"	14.	Maria Weber, Plainfield	86	4	
"	29.	Christina Knecht, Plainfield	25	1	8
April	9.	Barbara Ward, Plainfield	82		
"	11.	James William Frey, Dryland	1	4	7
"	13.	Anna Taylor, Williams	17	6	2
"	16.	Elisabeth Germanton, Plainfield	75	1	7
May	19.	Anna Cath. Bess, Dryland	71	9	4
"	28.	Elisabeth Kind, Plainfield	1	5	

Date.		Names of Persons Buried.	Y.	M.	D.
May	29.	Edward Fridrich, Plainfield............		2	
June	9.	Hannah Hess, Saucon....................	10	1	16
"	14.	Sus. Siegley, Saucon....................	22		
"	15.	Sarah Ann Herster Rewalt, Easton...	2	2	
July	9.	Susanna Balliet, Dryland.................	8	2	13
"	16.	Sarah Young, Easton.........	1	10	
"	22.	Anthon Getter, Williams................	48	10	7
"	29.	Abraham Barnes, Easton.................	2		20
Aug.	2.	Peter Lattig, Williams..............	82	4	29
"	5.	John Traxsell, Easton.....................	46	3	23
"	16.	John Engel, Easton.......................	39	9	3
"	19.	Maria Snyder, Easton		10	2
"	22.	Edwin Koch, Plainfield...................			17
"	23.	Reuben Bauer, Plainfield...........	1	9	
"	31.	Carl Koechlein, Easton		8	
Sept.	3.	Jesse Frederick Loehr, Plainfield.	11	3	9
"	4.	John Shade, Easton........................	1	4	3
"	5.	Sophia Traxsell, Easton	1		29
"	6.	Catharine Roeder, Plainfield............	21	10	1
"	7.	A child of John and Cath. Otto, Williams........	2	6	13
"	9.	Elisabeth Bauer, Plainfield	6	10	7
"	13.	Frederick Barthold, Easton.............	64	5	
"	14.	Abraham Andre, Plainfield..............		11	4
"	18.	Peter Bauer, Plainfield.........	18	11	
Oct.	18.	Abraham Heller, Plainfield.............	73	5	8
"	21.	Nicholas Traxsell, Easton................	71	1	3
"	24.	Mary Brotzman, Williams...............	22	5	7
Feb.	11.	Harris Franklin Lock, Dryland.........			20
Dec.	1.	David Stern (Stem?), Williams.........	66	2	26
"	19.	Elisabeth Koch, Easton.	84	10	15

ANNO 1825.

Jan.	7.	John Boyer, Saucon.......................	82	4	21
"	9.	Jacob Bauer, Forks.......................	48		

Date.		Names of Persons Buried.	Y.	M.	D.
Jan.	10.	Maria Hardy, Forks	30		
"	13.	Maria Clara Loehr, Easton	58	2	7
"	14.	Elisabeth Wilhelm, Dryland	21	3	3
"	18.	Samuel Hilliart, Dryland	1		
"	20.	Christina Beissell, Dryland	40	5	6
"	24.	Sabilla Raub, Williams	45	3	
"	31.	Peter Jansen, Dryland	1	9	9
Feb.	4.	Salome Smidt, Dryland	5	3	11
"	6.	Frederick Boyer, Dryland	78	8	3
March	10.	Mary Arndt, Arndt's	1		7
"	19.	Sophia Hackman, Dryland		6	
"	21.	Anna Maria Boyer, Saucon	74	4	2
"	29.	Sophia Sus. Arndt, Dryland	1	3	14
April	19.	Jacob David Heller, Plainfield	1	8	
May	14.	Joseph Siegfried, Bath	76	1	6
"	18.	Matthias Wagner, Dryland	79	5	6
"	20.	John Siegfried, Bath	45	2	7
"	24.	Margaret Ohnangst, Williams	55	8	
"	25.	Elis. Ohnangst, Williams	70	7	
"	26.	Anthon Transue, Williams	1	5	14
June	3.	Catharine Frederica Hackman, Dryland	4	7	
"	7.	Hannah Loesch, Williams	6	6	6
"	26.	Cath. Boyer, Saucon	12	5	13
July	5.	Hannah McHose, Saucon	77		
Aug.	7.	Sophia Werner, Saucon	6	3	
"	12.	Joseph Andre, Plainfield	17	7	4
"	28.	Abraham Bachman, Easton	80	9	17
"	—.	Jacob Transue, Williams		7	8
Sept.	9.	Jacob Christman, Williams	44	11	21
"	—.	Simon Reiss, Saucon	47	10	
"	15.	Anna Maria Metz, Plainfield	30	2	14
"	26.	Sus. Schlecht, Plainfield	31	8	2
Oct.	5.	Eleonora Lawall, Dryland	6	3	19
"	10.	Fred. Ludwig Miller, Saucon	67	1	
"	—.	Maria Buss, Dryland	23	9	7

Date.		Names of Persons Buried.	Y.	M.	D.
Nov.	6.	Samuel Beil Hess, Saucon	1	9	
"	10.	Catharine Shaefer, Saucon	15	8	3
"	29.	Anna Welty, Saucon	2	4	2
Dec.	9.	John Roth, Plainfield	21	6	6
"	12.	John David Brinker, Forks	14	2	6
"	29.	Valentine Metz, Plainfield	75	1	15

ANNO 1826.

Jan.	10.	Sibilla Oberly, Forks		3	22
Feb.	8.	Sarah Christina Schlaug, Easton	1	6	18
"	15.	John Simons, Easton	52	11	3
"	16.	Ann Julina Steckel, Dryland		1	4
"	19.	Philip David Dinges, Easton	28	6	6
March	7.	Conrad Kocher, Dryland	86	2	
"	10.	Magdalena Odenwelder, Easton	42	11	3
"	17.	Jacob Lerch, Esq., Saucon	70	6	17
"	20.	Anna Margret Lerch, Saucon	60	7	2
"	28.	Henrietta Reich, Saucon	5	10	
April	3.	Dieterich Bauer, Plainfield	77		
"	8.	Catharine Kutsler, Forks	69		
"	20.	Eliz. Reich, Dryland	37	1	3
"	26.	John Stem, Williams	45	10	6
"	29.	Anna Margret Roeder, Dryland	64	9	13
May	9.	Juliana Schaefer, Dryland	24	10	
"	23.	Abraham Horn, Easton	69	4	22
July	20.	Reuben Vogel, Dryland	21	9	16
"	23.	John Andreas Koch, Easton	21	6	12
Aug.	20.	Reuben Butz, Forks	2	4	9
"	27.	Dina Hauer, Forks	1	3	2
"	28.	Maria Bassinger, Plainfield	62		
Sept.	9.	Anna Maria Laubach, Saucon	3		
"	25.	Conrad Bess, Dryland	80	10	
Oct.	3.	Samuel Franklin Scheip, Easton		6	5
"	19.	Mary Ann Handshue, Dryland		6	10
Nov.	6.	Christian Herzell, Williams	79	3	

Date.		Names of Persons Buried.	Y.	M.	D.
Nov.	14.	Eliz. Sabina Snyder, Easton	4	8	
"	17.	Benigna Eliz. Muffley, Plainfield	43	1	
"	26.	William Weaver, Saucon	2	9	5
Dec.	5.	Anna Maria Swander, Easton	2	11	5

Anno 1827.

Date.		Names of Persons Buried.	Y.	M.	D.
Jan.	14.	Cath. Clauss, Dryland	2	6	27
"	28.	A son of Christina Derr, Dryland	1	8	5
Feb.	10.	George Glass, Plainfield	6	11	
"	14.	Bernhart Arndt, Dryland	72	6	5
"	20.	David Butz, Easton	38		
"	24.	John Kind, Plainfield	48	5	11
"	27.	Abraham Traxsell, Easton	38	6	18
"	28.	John Jacob Weiss, Easton	30	5	1
March	11.	Christina Derr, Easton	1	4	7
"	12.	Henry Reiss, Saucon	23	4	14
"	17.	John Holl, Easton	1	2	9
April	8.	George Erich, Easton	36	6	
"	26.	John Wagner, Dryland	59	4	
May	8.	Sarah Kind, Plainfield	73	2	18
"	16.	Michael Simon, Easton	56	3	4
"	19.	Anna Maria Odenwelder, Easton	78	4	
"	20.	Eliz. Erich, Easton	52	6	24
"	24.	Liddia Reiss, Dryland	13	5	4
June	13.	Samuel Koenig, Dryland	19	2	10
"	30.	Susanna Horn, Easton	67	1	10
Aug.	6.	Thomas Nicum, Saucon	81	10	27
"	12.	A son of Peter Young and wife Anne, Easton		3	24
"	13.	Ebeneza Yodder, Easton		11	10
"	15.	Adam Koenig, Easton	65	3	4
"	28.	Isaac Koechlein, Easton		4	
"	30.	A daughter of Peter Young and wife Anne, Easton	1	2	14
Sept.	16.	Susanna Hauck, Plainfield	18	7	6

Date.		Names of Persons Buried.	Y.	M.	D.
Sept.	26.	Maria Koenig, Dryland.....................	1	1	28
"	28.	William Engel, Easton.....................	32		16
Oct.	12.	Eliz. Weber, Saucon........................	24	9	15
"	16.	Margret Young, Plainfield	9	4	17
Nov.	8.	John Hardy, Dryland	2	10	6
Dec.	4.	Christian Reich (?), Saucon	79	10	25
"	6.	John Weisgerber, Saucon..................	26	2	14
"	14.	Regina Knauss, Easton....................	18	11	10
"	30.	Susanna Derr, Saucon......................	43	11	27

ANNO 1828.

Jan.	18.	Eliz. Decker, Easton........................	45	11	25
"	19.	Rosanna Barns, Easton.....................	2	5	16
"	20.	Anthon Faas, Williams.....................	62	8	10
"	26.	Catharine Wagner, Plainfield............	24	11	4
March	11.	Michael Odenwelder, Easton............	78		
"	26.	Valentine Koehler, Saucon...............	79	2	22
April	11.	Maria Herger, Dryland.........	25	6	21
"	13.	Sarah Miller, Saucon................	10	7	9
May	4.	Matthias Weiss, Williams.................	64	10	26
"	22.	John Philip Odenwelder, Easton	79	8	18
June	2.	Eliza Ann Steckel, Dryland............	1	3	16
"	16.	John Messinger, Forks.....................	29	2	24
"	24.	Adam Stem, Williams......................	76	9	
"	25.	Anthon Oberly, Saucon....................	79	2	26
July	8.	Rosina Ritter, Dryland............	25	4	22
"	16.	Valentine Lewellen Canan, Plainfield.		5	28
"	26.	Francis Lynn, Saucon......................		11	7
"	27.	Joseph Sentee, Dryland...................	7	8	22
Aug.	12.	Sarah Ann Eliz. Heckman, Dryland...		1	
"	19.	Samuel Transue, Easton...................		9	22
"	21.	Julian Transue, Easton......	3	2	14
"	29.	Anna Maria Kerner, Easton............	19	3	26
Sept.	4.	George Adam Seipel, Easton............	50	1	26
"	5.	Samuel Coleman, Easton..................	67		

Date.		Names of Persons Buried.	Y.	M.	D.
Sept.	8.	Maria Eliz. Christman, Williams......	20	8	16
"	22.	Levina Koenig, Dryland.................			25
Oct.	2.	John Nolf, Dryland........................	22	4	25
"	4.	Carl Schreiver, Dryland.....	18	5	10
"	5.	Maria Cath. Daniel, Dryland...........	83	11	15
"	6.	Samuel Halteman, Dryland............		1	9
"	17.	William Ohl, Saucon...........	70	11	4
Nov.	8.	Catharine Keim, Forks...................	70	6	4
"	20.	Abraham Roeder, Dryland...............	30	7	12
"	21.	Peter Koechlein, Easton..................	78	7	12
"	14.	John Geiger, Dryland.....................	36	10	19
Dec.	1.	George Rodenberger, Dryland...........	30	2	26
"	3.	Maria Magdalena Lawall, Dryland.....	37	5	22
"	5.	Conrad Schwarz, Easton..................	47	6	13
"	7.	Rebecca Schiffer, Plainfield.............		2	5
"	10.	Sarah Ann Koechlein, Easton..........	2	7	23
"	28.	Margaret Stem, Williams................	65	4	25

ANNO 1829.

Jan.	2.	John William Kunckler.................	1		25
"	5.	Eliza Ann Roeder, Forks.............	16	6	25
"	6.	Francis Leidig, Easton.....................	28	4	4
"	11.	Luiza Swander, Easton..................	2	5	11
"	21.	George Elias Koch, Plainfield...........		5	17
"	25.	Adam Lewis Stem, Williams		6	11
"	28.	Catharine Stem, Williams................	27	4	2
Feb.	23.	Anna Barbara Oberly, Saucon..........	46	10	17
"	27.	John George Bruch, Williams..........	82	6	12
March	12.	Michael Walter, Forks......................	1	2	14
"	22.	Isaac Wilhelm, Dryland............	28	1	21
"	26.	Isaac Eckert, Williams....................	36	7	16
May	3.	Elisabeth Gardner, Saucon...............	2	2	17
"	19.	Frederick Frey, Dryland	65	8	2
June	5.	John Peter Herzel, Williams	11	9	23
"	11.	Eliz. Laubach, Saucon...................	63	2	1

Church Records.

Date.		Names of Persons Buried.	Y.	M.	D.
June	14.	Gottlieb Shnyder, Plainfield..............	52	2	28
July	16.	Ann Julina (family name not given), Dryland...................................		11	4
Aug.	21.	George W. Laddig, Williams............	7	10	19
Sept.	1.	Elisabeth Mesemer, Dryland.............		4	3
"	2.	Samuel Herzell, Williams................			14
"	2.	Decatur Washington Raub, Williams..	1	9	2
"	4.	Maria Isabella Rewalt, Easton		5	2
"	7.	Susanna Herzell, Williams.........	39	6	18
"	18.	Samuel Engel, Easton.....................	31	10	20
"	21.	John Peter Weygandt, Saucon......... ..	86	6	11
"	23.	Margaret Nauman, Dryland.............	59	11	26
"	26.	Daniel Dech, Dryland......	17	4	15
"	30.	Frederick Hahn, Plainfield.......	26	11	11
Oct.	4.	William Happel, Plainfield...............	1	4	12
"	8.	Anna Margaret Young, Williams	39	1	6
"	26.	Sarah Herzell, Williams..................	10		11
Nov.	6.	John George Brinker, Easton............	52	9	27
Dec.	13.	John Schuck, Easton.....................	75	4	12
"	13.	Levi Bess, Williams......................	2	6	10
"	27.	Eliz. Koechlein, Easton..................	11	7	9

Anno 1830.

Jan.	2.	George Hahn, Plainfield..................	71	0	3
"	12.	Elisabeth Musselman, Saucon............	23	11	2
"	11.	Catharine Herzell, Dryland..............	65	9	17
"	19.	Peter Bauer, Forks	1	8	23
"	11.	Hannah Engel, Dryland.................	13	1	23
"	20.	Sabina Kocher, Dryland.................	5	3	
Feb.	4.	A son of Maria Eliz. Woodring, Williams		6	5
"	5.	Maria Miller, Plainfield..................	40	10	23
"	16.	A daughter of John Ginnard and wife Eliz., Dryland			21
"	17.	A daughter of John Brinker, Easton...		1	24

The First Reformed Church of Easton, Pa.

Date.		Names of Persons Buried.	Y.	M.	D.
Feb.	19.	Maria William, Plainfield................	24	10	22
March	24.	Levi Augustus Taylor, Williams.........		8	28
"	28.	A daughter of Enoch Hoening, Plainfield...		3	5
April	6.	William H. Lynn, Saucon................	1	4	11
"	29.	Levi Levius Kind, Plainfield............	5	10	27
May	1.	Conrad Frey, Dryland.....................	40	6	20
"	13.	John Dieter Miller, Dryland............		8	9
"	17.	Anna Maria Erb, Easton.................	71	10	8
"	21.	Eliz. Getter, Dryland	81	4	23
"	25.	Eliz. Mayer, Plainfield..	4	2	23
June	10.	Anna Cath. Schroeder, Easton	3	3	25
"	13.	Cath. Oberley, Saucon.....................	75	6	21
"	17.	Michael Derrhammer, Dryland.........	54	9	
"	21.	Peter Neuhart, Dryland	56	6	20
July	18.	Catharine Rinker, Saucon................	59	10	1
Aug.	18.	Isaac Ginnart, Dryland.......			16
"	28.	Eliz. Cath. Lantz, Williams.............	72	8	14
Sept.	5.	Christopher Engle, Plainfield		10	
"	6.	Eliz. Philippi, Easton	28		4
"	9.	Ebenezer S. Fortner, Easton	61	6	
"	9.	Henry De Long, Plainfield...............	73	7	19
"	26.	John Stocker, Easton......................	11		18
"	28.	Barbara Loesch, Plainfield	21	9	23
Oct.	3.	Jacob Oberly, Saucon......................	75	5	14
"	13.	Samuel Eckert, Saucon..............	12		3
"	17.	Matthias Riegel, Saucon...................	66	9	18
"	18.	Anna Maria Ohl, Saucon	73	2	21
"	24.	Maria Magd. Canaan, Plainfield........	23	6	12
Nov.	1.	Cath. Riegel, Saucon.........	64	10	2
"	8.	Sus. Renner, Dryland	38	4	15
"	17.	David Heilman, Dryland	48	9	2
"	20.	Eliz. Hummel, Dryland...................	44	6	20
Dec.	16.	Cath. Anna Mann, Dryland	1	3	14

Anno 1831.

Date.		Names of Persons Buried.	Y.	M.	D.
Jan.	8.	John Odenwelder, Williams	53	6	25
"	9.	John Philip Faas, Dryland	80	11	14
"	22.	Margaret Gruber, Mount Bethel	44	8	10
"	25.	A son of Melchior Transue and wife Anna			22
"	26.	Edward Raub, Williams	4	11	6
Feb.	8.	John Shade, Easton	42	2	20
"	16.	Anna Maria Herzell, Williams	81	9	2
"	24.	Peter Weygandt, Williams		1	
March	7.	Gertraut Froelig, Dryland	87	11	18
"	20.	Maria Engel Ruth, Plainfield	65		23
April	6.	John Worman, Easton.			
"	8.	Susanna Christman, Saucon	19	7	25
"	9.	William Peiffer, Williams	4	10	22
"	19.	Susanna Nauman, Dryland	26	11	8
"	22.	George Dech, Dryland	2	9	11
May	1.	Philip Koester, Mount Bethel	88	8	29
"	5.	Sarah Ann Christina Weber, Easton		5	11
"	18.	Margaret Freeman, Plainfield	70	8	19
"	27.	Peter Mann, Saucon	36	8	8
June	3.	Rees Bruch, William	9	7	2
"	24.	Sarah Walter, Williams	44	4	23
"	27.	Jonas Ohnangst, Williams	2	1	12
July	4.	Anna Margreta Edelman, Easton	21	11	18
"	8.	Mary Keller, Williams	35	3	1
"	17.	Cath. Walter, Arndt's	52	10	19
"	25.	Rebecca Derr, Dryland		4	19
Aug.	6.	Andreas Dech, Dryland		6	21
"	18.	Anna Boyer, Easton	76	6	
Sept.	1.	Nicholas Dietz, Williams	38	3	28
Oct.	8.	Christina Uhler, Easton	67	7	14
"	13.	Maria Schick, Dryland	11	3	
Sept.	4.	William Reed, Easton	1	8	

328 The First Reformed Church of Easton, Pa.

Date.		Names of Persons Buried.	Y.	M.	D.
Oct.	16.	Jacob Kreidler, Dryland	51		
Nov.	6.	Francis Alsfeld (died Nov. 3d), Easton	41	6	
"	7.	Sophia Broeder, Easton	7	10	24
"	6.	Jacob Balliet, Dryland	80	4	
Dec.	1.	Peter Laddig, Williams	32	4	18
"	6.	William Henry Lawall, Dryland	50	11	3
"	15.	John Knobel, Williams	71		
"	15.	Christina Steitinger, Easton	72		

Anno 1832.

Date.		Names of Persons Buried.	Y.	M.	D.
Jan.	3.	Daniel Knauss, Easton	23	10	19
"	13.	Ellen Caroline Herzel, Williams		10	
"	16.	William August Heller, Plainfield		3	
"	26.	Henry Dilman Halteman, Dryland		10	1
"	27.	John Seipel, Easton	71	5	28
"	30.	John Bauer, Bushkil			19
Feb.	1.	Christian Holland, Plainfield	56	8	22
"	5.	George Lynn, Saucon	6	2	15
"	20.	George Peter Dreisbach, Plainfield	32	3	7
March	12.	Peter Dietz, Williams	70	7	2
"	14.	Anthonetta Transue, Saucon			16
"	16.	Thos. Wilhelm, Williams	16	6	29
"	31.	Washington Johannes Bauman, Williams		1	1
April	11.	Lydia Ann Dennis, Dryland	1		17
"	19.	Henrietta Shnyder, Forks		1	22
"	28.	John Peter Schmidt, Dryland	89		20
May	10.	John Schuck Neigh, Easton	2	4	29
"	22.	Mary Merz, Easton	2	8	1
June	8.	Anna Matilda Lehr, Easton	3		
"	14.	Henry Werkhaeuser, Forks	35	1	1
"	18.	Jacob Schaefer, Forks	60	8	28
"	28.	Andrew Weygandt, Williams	66	8	16
July	3.	Peter August Bauer, Plainfield		3	1
"	11.	Thomas Washington Lerch, Saucon	18	7	3

Date.		Names of Persons Buried.	Y.	M.	D.
July	19.	Catharine Lawall, Dryland...............	39	5	3
"	26.	Edward Henry Derr, Dryland...........	1	7	10
"	23.	Michael Lawall, Dryland.................	79	2	18
"	23.	Abraham Walten (Walter?) Dryland..	57	9	14
Aug.	13.	Ely Franklin Lerch, Saucon..............	3	10	4
"	15.	Sophia Transue, Saucon...................	64	9	3
"	18.	Anna Maria Lerch, Saucon..............		9	3
Sept.	7.	Anna Cath. Wasser, Saucon.............	85	5	18
"	13.	Sus. Oberly, Dryland.......................	7	9	26
"	15.	Lenora Sus. Lerch, Saucon...............	2	9	17
"	23.	Eliz. Bess, Dryland	59	1	27
Oct.	20.	Maria Eliza Leidy, Saucon..............	1	3	10
"	22.	Catharine Lucinda Jones, Saucon	8	7	25
"	23.	Peter Ginnard, Dryland...................	1	6	9
Nov.	1.	William Dech, Dryland	7	9	29
"	2.	Christian Wolf, Dryland.................	3		16
"	2.	Eliza. Ann Gerhart, Dryland............	3	2	
"	8.	Anna Luisa Coecilia Heckman, Dryland	2	7	18
"	15.	Sarah Ann Warrig, Saucon......		7	7
"	19.	Peter Lantz, Williams	4	1	27
"	23.	Cath. Kaemrer, Dryland.................	30	9	19
"	24.	Eliz. Young, Dryland	42	1	12
Dec.	4.	Maria Siegfried, Dryland............	61	7	13
Nov.	27.	Fayetta Laubach, Saucon.................	3	9	12
"	29.	Isabella Cecilia Frey, Dryland............,		8	5
Dec.	7.	Ellen Dorothea Hess, Saucon	1	8	11
"	11.	Lydia Rodenberger, Dryland............	27	3	
"	22.	Thos. Richard, Williams.................	61	10	
"	28.	John Hoeny, Arndt's......................	49		

ANNO 1833.

Jan.	12.	Benjamin Jansen, Dryland...............	4	9	
"	12.	John Henry Jansen, Dryland...........	2	6	5
"	20.	Maria Butz, Easton.......................	72		

Date.		Names of Persons Buried.	Y.	M.	D.
Jan.	20.	George Jacob Dietrich, Easton..........		2	
"	24.	Jacob Jansen, Dryland.....................	2	9	20
"	26.	Leonhart Tiel, Plainfield.................	27	4	2
Feb.	9.	William Jonathan Napp, Dryland......	3	3	
"	15.	Mary Wagner, Easton.....................	35	3	
"	16.	Simon Schrantz, Saucon.................	3	3	21
"	22.	Mary Ann Rosenberger, Easton.........	3	3	12
"	25.	Reuben Miller, Saucon....................	1	3	3
March	2.	Rebecca Lawall, Dryland.................	31	10	
"	3.	A very young child of Conrad Kocher and wife Sarah, Arndt's.			
"	6.	Absolon Messinger, Williams............	25	9	1
"	12.	Eliz. Koechlein, Easton...................	12	2	10
"	20.	Susanna Koechlein, Easton..............		3	20
"	21.	A son of Hannah Marg. Beisel, Dryland		3	3
April	5.	Sarah Ann Young, Dryland............		7	21
"	3.	Christina Ann Yoder, Dryland.........	4	10	24
"	12.	John Koechlein, Easton...................	1	9	12
"	15.	Maria Ruch, Saucon......................	8	7	29
"	19.	Susannah Heller, Plainfield..............	48	3	16
May	5.	Catharine Metz, Plainfield..............	80	3	20
"	8.	Susanna Sabina Stauffer, Plainfield.....	1	5	
"	12.	Susanna Messinger, Forks................	2		
"	21.	Salome Bauer, Forks......................	1	7	
June	3.	George Walter, Forks.			
"	24.	A son of Philip and Sarah Hahn, Plainfield.			
"	25.	Rosina Eliz. Odenwaelder, Forks.			
"	29.	George H. Dech, Dryland.			
July	1.	George Happel, Plainfield.			
"	11.	Martin Kind, Plainfield.			
"	13.	John Atherton Canaan, Plainfield.[1]			
"	25.	Elisabeth Oberly.[1]			

[1] A corner of the page being torn off, the record is wanting.

Church Records.

Date.		Names of Persons Buried.	Y.	M.	D.
Aug.	1.	Elisabeth Dech.[1]			
"	3.	Cath. Derr.[1]			
"	3.	A son of Mary Ann Nicholas.[1]			
"	3.	Elisabeth Mayers.[1]			
"	10.	Lydia Ruth, Plainfield............	wanting.		
"	15.	Elisabeth Kaemrer, Dryland......	wanting.		
"	24.	John Oberly, Easton............	51		
Oct.	10.	George P. Dreisbach, Plainfield......	65	9	2
"	27.	Susanna Bess, Williams...........	1	9	22
"	29.	Maria Eva Frankenfield, Dryland....	93	9	26
Nov.	3.	Daniel Heller, Plainfield...........	6		10
"	7.	Rebecca Traxsell, Easton..........	1	6	2
"	9.	Cath. Happel, Plainfield..........	3	3	20
"	15.	Maria Sarah Heller, Plainfield......	1	7	2
"	17.	John Hope, Dryland.............			3
"	17.	Samuel Wilt, Williams...........	46	5	23
"	27.	Sibilla Cath. Meyers, Dryland......	3	8	27
Dec.	2.	Simon Nauman, Dryland.........	28	8	15
"	6.	Henry Doeringer, Easton.........	77	4	
"	8.	George Washington Taylor, Williams..	1	8	17
"	12.	Eliza Ann Kogen, Williams........	1	4	22
"	31.	Captain John Dietz, Plainfield.......	70	6	2

Anno 1834.

Jan.	10.	Christian Wilhelm, Dryland........	30	11	23
"	23.	Michael Abel, Forks............	69	11	10
March	1.	Joseph Mixsell Roth, Forks........		1	3
"	11.	Sarah Rebecca Dewalt, Dryland.....		10	
"	14.	Coras Aaron Jansen, Dryland......		3	
"	16.	Eliza Ann Mixsell, Easton.........		3	7
"	17.	Caroline Siegel, Plainfield.........	4	8	14
"	18.	A son of Enoch Hoenig, Plainfield.....			21
April	3.	Abraham Heller, Plainfield.........	52	4	11

[1] A corner of the page being torn off, the record is wanting.

The First Reformed Church of Easton, Pa.

Date.		Names of Persons Buried.	Y.	M.	D.
April	7.	Mary Ann Schroeder, Easton	9	1	4
"	28.	Jacob Bess, Williams	2	1	28
May	1.	Conrad Schleppe, Dryland	67	5	
"	2.	Aaron Boyer, Saucon	1		9
"	9.	Sus. Bender, Plainfield	24	5	
"	16.	Miss Schaefer, Plainfield	16	6	3
"	18.	Jacob Ackerman, Plainfield	3	2	2
"	25.	Maria Magdalene Febel, Plainfield	64	1	26
"	25.	Anna Eliz. Hay, Forks	7		11
"	30.	Albert Henry Kraemer, Dryland		3	25
July	17.	Cath. Siegel, Plainfield	74	7	5
		(Five names are here wanting—the record being torn.)			
		Margaret Jansen, Dryland	28	1	5
Aug.	23.	John Peter Rohn, Dryland	71	7	17
"	24.	John Henry Wilhelm, Dryland	34	9	29
"	24.	Elias Hummel, Dryland	69	1	14
Sept.	11.	Jacob Werner, Dryland	1		19
Aug.	27.	Elisabeth Heller, Plainfield	82	3	18
"	29.	George Riegel, Plainfield	54	7	16
Sept.	18.	Maria Mayer, Dryland	12	5	17
"	20.	Luisa Sophia Malthaner, Dryland	1		5
"	26.	Edward Christian Herzel, Williams	1	10	12
"	29.	Maria Anna Weiss, Williams	22	1	7
Oct.	1.	Mrs. Eichman, Easton	66	4	4
"	10.	Anna Uhler, Easton	85	6	13
"	13.	Samuel Yiesley, Williams	22		
"	14.	Ely Bundstein, Easton	2	2	16
"	15.	Frederick Hahn, Plainfield	44	1	28
"	16.	Jacob Heller, Easton	52	5	21
"	23.	Feronica Diehl, Plainfield	29	6	7
"	24.	David Roth, Easton	51		
"	26.	Mary Ann Hahn, Williams		4	29
Nov.	8.	Elisabeth Lerch, Dryland	18	5	12
"	17.	John Paff, Dryland	1	5	6

Church Records.

Date.		Names of Persons Buried.	Y.	M.	D.
Nov.	19.	Peter Henrich, Dryland...............	31	8	
Dec.	5.	Daniel Schlabach, Dryland.............		1	23
"	19.	Cath. Weygandt, Easton..............	83	11	3

Anno 1835.

Jan.	1.	Jonathon Knecht, Plainfield.............	57	5	29
"	8.	Sarah Loehr, Plainfield.................	33	4	17
"	13.	David Oberley, Dryland................	42	5	29
"	31.	Cath. Frantz, Dryland.................	2	5	26
Feb.	5.	Jacob Albert, Plainfield	1		
"	9.	Caroline Ruth, Plainfield.			
"	13.	Fayetta Priscilla Koch, Dryland.........	1	9	7
"	27.	Anna Barbara Albert, Plainfield........	75	4	27
March	14.	Maria Brotzman, Williams..............	72	5	23
"	18.	Peter Siegel, Plainfield.................	79	5	12
"	20.	Eliz. Knauss, Williams	70	7	5
"	21.	Nicholas Dietz, Easton..................	63		16
April	5.	Michael Nieth, Forks......	10	5	24
March	9.	Anna Maria Herzell, Dryland...........	65	1	19
April	12.	Joseph Adam Weber, Easton...........		2	18
March	30.	Maria Matilda Kreidler, Plainfield	4	7	7
April	13.	Anna Maria Hahn, Williams............	2	11	7
"	15.	William Henry Koenig, Dryland.......	13	6	27
"	18.	Anna Maria Doffert, Dryland...........	2	8	18
"	23.	William Henry Wollbach, Dryland.....		5	
"	24.	Edmond Henry Schade, Dryland.......		2	7
May	8.	Charles Roth, Easton...................	34	1	2
"	21.	A son of David Metz, Plainfield			17
"	25.	Thos. Jacob Mohr, Plainfield...........		10	27
June	11.	Anna Luisa Schlecht, Plainfield.........	2	7	25
"	23.	John Schelly, Plainfield.................		2	3
July	15.	Cecilia Schlecht, Plainfield.............	1	2	16
"	26.	Jesse Ruth, Plainfield	6	2	1
"	27.	Michael Neuhart, Dryland	58	1	19
Aug.	1.	Eliz. Hutchins, Dryland	82	10	20

334   *The First Reformed Church of Easton, Pa.*

Date.		Names of Persons Buried.	Y.	M.	D.
Aug.	4.	Sus. Miller, Williams		2	
"	7.	Juliana Mohr, Plainfield	29	5	7
"	17.	George Michael Vierling, Williams	57	11	17
"	17.	Ludwig Carl Ellersiek, Williams	34	4	10
"	17.	Maria Magdalena Mehrwart, Williams	1		
"	17.	Ferdinand Seiler, Williams	14		
Sept.	1.	Samuel Roth, Bushkil	1		
"	8.	Simon Heller, Plainfield	82	6	25
"	9.	Sabina Fuhr, Williams		3	14
"	9.	Frederick Wilhelm, Easton	76	6	25
"	13.	John Werner, Easton		10	
"	15.	Eliz. Stecher, Easton	92		20
"	18.	Peter Jansen, Dryland	26	3	18
"	20.	Eliz. Kocher, Easton	48	11	9
Oct.	24.	William Diehl, Plainfield	4		22
Nov.	1.	Susanna Barron, Easton	33	2	29
"	10.	Abraham Bauer, Plainfield	52	8	27
"	16.	Maria Catharine Harris, Easton	54	8	6
Dec.	10.	John Roeder, Dryland	55	8	20
Nov.	30.	Joseph Balliett, Dryland	51	6	2
Dec.	20.	Eliz. Lock, Dryland	34	7	25
"	28.	William Hahn, Dryland	16	5	12

Anno 1836.

Jan.	5.	Sarah Young, Easton	45		
"	15.	Luisa Sophia Ginginger, Easton		6	3
"	18.	Jacob Young, Plainfield	1	2	8
Feb.	11.	Daniel Bauer, Plainfield	44	6	1
"	17.	Jonas Siegel, Plainfield	38	10	18
"	22.	Mary Ann Hauser, Easton	3	4	27
March	2.	Jonas Kreidler, Dryland	19	9	12
"	6.	Thomas Baumgarten, Bushkil	23	4	3
"	9.	Anna Maria Siegel, Plainfield	76	3	9
"	13.	Arminda Sus. Hahn, Plainfield	3	5	
"	19.	John Michael Hinkel, Dryland	72	4	5

Church Records. 335

Date.		Names of Persons Buried.	Y.	M.	D.
March	24.	Sarah Juliana Lawall, Dryland.........	46	5	13
April	3.	Leonhart Engler, Plainfield...............	80	4	28
"	9.	A daughter of Eliz. Nagel, Dryland...	1	3	1
"	13.	Michael Koehler, Dryland	82	6	15
"	18.	Stephen Leidy Oberley, Easton		3	12
"	19.	Eliz. Koechlein, Easton	30	7	22
June	17.	Philip William Geiger, Dryland........	11	4	22
"	21.	Fayetta Nagel, Dryland....................		5	
"	22.	Maria Christina Brotzman, Williams..	68	7	28
"	23.	Adam Beissell, Dryland	55	6	17
July	12.	Jacob Brotzman, Williams...............	5	6	14
Aug.	14.	Thos. Berry, Williams......	2		11
"	25.	Margaret Geiger, Dryland.................	66	8	24
Sept.	20.	Christian Daniel Koechlein, Easton	1		2
Oct.	4.	Sus. Eliz. Schwartz, Easton...............	1	9	16
Nov.	8.	John Schade, Dryland.....................	84	11	25
Dec.	27.	Adam Wilhelm, Dryland	42	6	9
Nov.	23.	Eliza Boyer, Dryland	2	6	19
Dec.	30.	Maria Eliz. Kaemrer, Arndt's............		11	23

Anno 1837.

Jan.	2.	Eva Walter, Dryland	35	1	25
"	8.	Christian Bender, Plainfield.............	61		16
"	30.	A daughter of John and Hetty Bundin, Arndt's		2	15
Feb.	2.	Mathias Wagner, Easton..................	49	4	17
"	6.	Simon Clauss, Dryland		11	2
"	26.	Marie Caroline Young, Dryland	3	8	4
March	2.	Ann Eliz. Moesner, Dryland.............	3	8	28
"	5.	John Huettinger, Bushkil..................	26	11	16
"	5.	A daughter of Geo. Hellick and wife, Eliz., Dryland.............................			15
"	6.	Anna Maria Dewalt, Dryland............	7	3	17
"	6.	Messiah Broeder, Easton..................	12	9	17
"	29.	John Warner, Arndt's.....................	68		

Date.		Names of Persons Buried.	Y.	M.	D.
April	2.	Magdalena Paff, Easton.................	72		
"	2.	Christoph. Werner, Easton.............		5	
"	14.	Sabina Herzel, Williams.................	1	10	
"	17.	William Reiher Stem, Easton..........	4	1	16
"	18.	Ann Eliza Rachael Lerch, Easton......		5	
"	25.	Aaron Lynn, Easton......................	3	8	2
May	5.	John Schiffer, Plainfield.................	68	2	19
"	5.	Jacob Moser, Easton......................	9		
"	12.	Isaiah Lynn, Easton......................	1	10	29
"	12.	Isaac Moser, Easton......................	1	5	24
"	15.	Elisabeth Sheimer, Saucon..............	80	10	14
"	18.	Diana Odenwaelder, Williams..........	1	3	11
"	19.	Hannah Maurer, Easton.................	9	1	15
"	21.	Feronica Appel, Easton	18		
"	23.	Rachael Sabella Laudenberg, Easton.	2	4	10
"	26.	John Ridenauer, Dryland................	29	5	20
June	3.	Abraham Bender, Forks.................		8	7
"	7.	Doctor J. F. A. Steckel, Dryland......	77	7	
July	3.	Isaiah Kind, Plainfield....................		2	3
"	23.	William Hinkle, Dryland	2	9	11
"	27.	Catharine Engel, Dryland...............	3		8
"	31.	George Hinkel, Dryland.................	1	6	6
Aug.	14.	Edward Koehler, Dryland	2		16
"	26.	John Frederick Stump, Easton	1	2	
Sept.	3.	Eliz. Heller, Plainfield...................	84	9	9
"	22.	Anna Matilda Hay, Forks...............		2	
Oct.	19.	Matilda Rebecca Koenig, Dryland......	2		
"	4.	Jacob Adam Schlecht, Plainfield.......		2	3
Nov.	4.	Aurelia Catharina Schlecht, Plainfield.	1	9	8
"	20.	Jacob Hohl, Easton......................		11	
"	21.	Johann Augustus Stout, Dryland.......	1	3	17
"	28.	Anna Maria Koch, Easton...............	39		1
"	29.	George Biers, Easton.....................	55	1	12
Dec.	8.	James Roth, Dryland.....................		1	27
"	9.	Susanna Eritt, Dryland	3	1	24

Date.		Names of Persons Buried.	Y.	M.	D.
Dec.	12.	John Ackerman, Mount Bethel	23	9	28
"	22.	Andrew Koechlein, Easton		3	
"	27.	Joseph Heller, Plainfield	19	1	2
"	28.	Maria Cath. Bender, Plainfield	67	4	28

ANNO 1838.

Jan.	8.	Edward Roeder, Williams	13	10	18
"	25.	A son of Karl Kunkler and wife Lyddia, Plainfield	1	2	10
Feb.	3.	Josiah Bunten, Arndt's			22
"	13.	Maria Magdalena Humes, Dryland	65		25
"	16.	John Eritt, Dryland	80	6	13
"	17.	William Henry Eritt, Dryland		1	2
"	18.	Jacob Philip Kaemrer, Arndt's		3	11
"	21.	Jacob Kaemrer, Arndt's	44	8	20
"	24.	Eliza Heckman, Easton	48	3	1
March	1.	Philippina Singer, Easton	6	11	23
"	2.	Elizabeth Cath. Schick, Plainfield	48	5	25
"	10.	Jacob Eritt, Dryland	10	3	1
"	19.	Maria Magd. Taylor, Easton	65	2	29
April	3.	Samuel Paul, Easton	1	11	16
March	29.	Jacob Diehl, Plainfield	32	8	12
April	9.	Jacob Schardt, Easton	10	3	4
"	12.	Christina Diehl, Lower Mt. Bethel	75		28
May	3.	Andrew Hay, Dryland	3	6	26
"	5.	Jacob Franklin Rothrock, Dryland	12	5	17
"	9.	Letitia Hess, Lower Saucon	21	5	13
"	14.	John Heimer, Plainfield	1		26
"	16.	Eliz. Hackman, Williams	55	4	19
"	22.	Henry Rieser, Dryland	26	4	
"	24.	Isaiah Weiss, Dryland	1	4	21
"	29.	William H. Samsel, Easton	1	1	22
June	11.	Sam¹ Weinberg, Forks	75	5	10
"	12.	Jacob Eritt, Dryland	10	3	1
"	16.	Carl Stocker, Forks	43	2	29

Date.		Names of Persons Buried.	Y.	M.	D.
June	19.	Cath. Koch, Easton....	75	7	8
"	29.	Eliz. Hahn, Plainfield.	84	1	11
"	29.	Eliz. Fritz, Plainfield	85		
July	15.	Anna Cath. Seip, Arndt's	69	10	9
"	7.	Eleonora Engel, Plainfield		9	19
"	22.	Eliz. Gradwohl, Dryland	12	11	23
"	26.	Joseph Brinker, Easton	2	11	22
"	27.	Deborah Werschel, Dryland	52		
"	29.	Sus. Wilhelm, Dryland	43	8	9
Aug.	30.	Cath. Moser, Dryland	38	4	
Sept.	9.	Jacob Henry Seipel Sheip, Easton	7	6	17
"	19.	Mary Ann Gum, Plainfield	3	1	4
Oct.	5.	Margaret Siegle, Plainfield	2	10	12
"	22.	Mrs. Hauser, Plainfield			
"	30.	Eliz. Kind, Plainfield	1	5	28
Nov.	1.	Michael Abel, Forks		5	15
"	13.	Mary Schmidt, Easton		15	
"	15.	Rebecca Young, Plainfield	2	1	2
"	29.	Maria Weber, Plainfield	45		
Dec.	2.	Wm. Henry Neigh, Easton	1	10	17
"	10.	Susanna Ohl, Easton	44	10	24
"	18.	Elenora Lerch, Easton	5		27
"	21.	Mary Matilda Broeder, Easton		10	12

ANNO 1839.

Jan.	14.	Ludwig Handshu, Dryland		4	3
"	16.	Tilman Flick, Dryland		8	20
"	27.	Jacob Ziegenfuss, Dryland	35	3	7
"	30.	William Maurer, Easton		4	10
Feb.	3.	Hannah Moritz, Easton	22	8	22
"	15.	A daughter of John Mayer, Plainfield			28
"	20.	Henry Hemsing, Easton	71		22
March	1.	Anna Breidinger, Plainfield	76	7	13
"	13.	Elisabeth Erritt, Dryland		2	6

Date.		Names of Persons Buried.	Y.	M.	D.
March	19.	George William Beck, Dryland.........		2	25
"	26.	John Casper Happel, Plainfield.........	1	11	5
April	7.	Henry Ruth, Plainfield	78	7	26
"	8.	Nicholas Arner, Dryland	58	6	13
"	29.	Catharine George, Dryland...............	35		
May	3.	Susanna Witman, Dryland...............	16	5	1
"	13.	Mary Ann Kaemrer, Arndt's	25	9	16
"	24.	Margaret Vogel, Dryland	52		
July	7.	Jacob Gross, Plainfield....................	45	2	12
"	13.	Carl Flick, Dryland.........................	4	9	22
"	27.	Barbara Heller, Plainfield.................	46	11	
"	17.	Leonhart Geiger, Schweizer's............	76	4	15
"	21.	William H. Heyl, Dryland...............		9	10
"	23.	Chrissy Ann Flick, Dryland.............	2	4	9
"	26.	George Adam Roth, Lower Saucon ...	3	8	14
"	29.	Charles H. Hauser, Dryland		8	26
Aug.	6.	John Henry Siegel, Plainfield............	84	6	27
"	16.	William Frederick Heller, Plainfield			
Sept.	4.	Owen Rudolph Mesemer, Dryland.....		9	15
"	14.	Ferdinand Schroeder, Easton............	33	3	11
"	16.	Elisabeth Koechlein, Easton...............	79	3	9
"	28.	Anna Regina Handshu, Dryland........	70	3	6
Oct.	7.	Sarah Laubenstein, Plainfield............	85	7	2
"	9.	John Fritz, Plainfield.......................	59	5	2
"	10.	Catharine Frankenfield, Dryland........	38	2	24
"	28.	Jacob Weinland, Easton	16		5
Nov.	15.	Susanna Derst, Williams..................	80	1	21
"	25.	William Gross, Plainfield	55	10	28
"	27.	Charles Kleder, Easton......................	23	8	24
Dec.	8.	Christina Seip, Easton......................	75	1	28
"	2.	Henry Heller, Plainfield...................	50	4	1

ANNO 1840.

Feb.	4.	Daniel Horn, Dryland......	34		26
"	2.	Edwin Samuel Heller, Plainfield........		7	17

340   *The First Reformed Church of Easton, Pa.*

Date.		Names of Persons Buried.	Y.	M.	D.
Feb.	22.	Aaron Bundstein, Dryland...............	27	3	17
March	7.	John Sentee, Dryland	81	6	27
"	18.	Edward Laudenberger, Dryland.........	1	11	11
April	5.	Anna Matilda Resch, Plainfield.........	5	3	24
"	14.	Jacob Bundstein, Dryland.................	85	2	
"	23.	John Kocher, Dryland.....................	50	3	26
"	30.	Jacob Wootring, Williams...............	47	2	3
May	19.	Catharine Feit, Greenwich...............	52	3	8
"	14.	John Henry Fuhr, Williams		2	
"	31.	Eliz. Hunter, Dryland.....................	29	11	2
June	22.	Mathias Koenig, Dryland................	13	1	7
"	23.	Joseph Kochler, Dryland.................	31	11	19
July	10.	—— Wolf, Dryland........................	53	2	
Aug.	5.	Violetta Koch, Dryland...................	2	11	8
"	19.	Maria Anna Kotz, Dryland...............	1	11	12
Sept.	4.	Margaret Frankenfield, Dryland.........	81	2	29
"	6.	Benjamin Kaemrer, Arndt's..............	13	6	
"	8.	John Jacob Derr, Easton..................	1	1	13
"	17.	William Miller, Easton	1	8	10
"	9.	Juliana Dech, Dryland.....................	35	6	26
"	13.	Henry George, Dryland	2	6	16
"	17.	Joseph Harrison Benjamin Koehler, Dryland.........		3	13
Oct.	8.	Sally Ann Koechlein, Easton............			21
"	12.	Henry Hohl, Easton.......................	1	10	21
"	23.	William Henry Hunter, Easton.........		5	
"	24.	Sarah Koch, Dryland.......................	31		24
Dec.	7.	Maria Christina Seip, Easton............	66		
"	8.	Joseph Dilford Dech, Dryland..........	1	3	32
"	11.	Maria Elisabeth Kretzler, Easton	1	9	7
"	27.	Eliza Jansen, Dryland..........	67	2	5
"	24.	Philip Drumheller, Dryland	47	6	19
		ANNO 1841.			
Jan.	21.	Barbara Rogers, Dryland.................	51	1	
Feb.	1.	John Kocher, Dryland.....................	59	4	27

Date.		Names of Persons Buried.	Y.	M.	D.
Feb.	1.	Maria Magd. Frey, Dryland.............	60		3
Jan.	30.	Maria Shnyder, Dryland.................	1	3	11
Feb.	17.	John Erett, Dryland........................	25	7	25
"	24.	Eliz. Gruber, Plainfield....................	32	9	25
June	3.	Alfred Transue, Dryland................	13		28
"	24.	Matilda Loehr, Easton....................	1		18
"	23.	Jacob Koester, Plainfield.................	87	7	25
July	27.	Mrs. Jacob Heller, Plainfield............	70	11	9
Aug.	20.	Thos. Kreidler, Dryland.................	12	6	14
"	26.	Daniel Jansen, Easton.....................	87		16
Sept.	1.	Valentine Gradwohl, Dryland...........	78	5	7
"	12.	Diana Parker, Williams....................		10	17
"	13.	Susanna Kohl, Dryland....................	68		
"	19.	Rebecca Stauffer, Plainfield.............		6	10
"	19.	Matilda Engel, Plainfield................	1	1	27
"	27.	Jos. Sponheimer, Plainfield.............	25		
Oct.	5.	Samuel Jacob Happel, Plainfield.......		4	17
"	15.	Christian Heiney, Dryland...............	86	9	5
"	29.	Eliz. Hauck, Plainfield....................	34	4	11
Nov.	3.	John Herzel, Williams.....................	85	5	9
"	29.	George Washington Rothrock, Dryland	20	2	23
Dec.	1.	Maria Koch, Dryland......................	52	8	28
"	3.	Thos. Boyer, Dryland.....................	26	11	3
"	17.	Anna Lynn, Easton	3	7	5
"	23.	Leah Happel, Plainfield...................	24	10	
"	27.	John H. Schwartz, Easton..................	2	1	13
"	30.	Margaret Miller, Dryland................	53	3	7

ANNO 1842.

Feb.	9.	Eliza Siegel, Dryland......................	14	4	16
"	14.	Margaret Messinger, Arndts	4		10
"	24.	Matilda Bossart, Dryland.................	12		
March	12.	John Odenwelder, Easton	86	1	4
"	27.	Lewis Mack, Dryland	16	9	18
"	29.	Polly Taylor, Easton........	7	9	6

The First Reformed Church of Easton, Pa.

Date.		Names of Persons Buried.	Y.	M.	D.
April	25.	Eliz. Sabina Dreisbach, Plainfield......		8	3
May	12.	Theodore David Deck, Dryland.........		3	
"	16.	Anna Eliz. Wootring, Williams........	3	11	1
"	20.	Jos. Hornecker, Dryland..................	85	3	22
"	21.	Sarah Ann Kreidler, Dryland............	1	1	5
"	22.	Thos. Wootring, Williams...............	2		4
"	27.	Zacharias Odenwelder, Williams......		5	2
June	2.	John David Hahn, Easton...............	1	2	18
"	5.	Sarah Rogers, Dryland....................	8	1	21
July	3.	Joseph Edward Kutzler (Kutsler), Arndt's...		2	24
"	4.	Sally Ann Gruber, Plainfield............	2	5	12
"	16.	Charles Miller, Plainfield.................	17	4	1
"	18.	Elonza Henry Lerch, Dryland...........			1
"	23.	Samuel Kutsler, Dryland		9	10
Aug.	1.	Magdalena Bender, Plainfield...........	63	1	9
"	22.	Alamanda Transue, Dryland.............	1	3	20
"	23.	Jacob Kaemrer, Arndt's....................	74	8	9
Sept.	15.	Simon Dreisbach, Dryland...............	57	7	22
"	25.	Elisabeth Odenwelder, Easton...........	60	6	20
"	7.	Aaron Kocher, Easton		2	16
Oct.	4.	Robert Laubach, Dryland.................	4	10	22
"	7.	Andalina Toleman, Dryland..............	1	7	13
"	10.	Peter Snyder, Forks........................	19	2	23
"	17.	Tilman Edwin Scheiocleine, Easton...		10	
Nov.	1.	Veronica Germanton, Plainfield.........	26	11	20
"	18.	David Dreisbach, Plainfield...............	37	9	9
Dec.	10.	Rebecca Hahn, Plainfield	58	5	
"	25.	Peter Nauman, Dryland...................	74	4	15

Anno 1843.

Jan.	10.	Michael Frey, Forks.............	50	4	30
"	13.	Jacob Buss, Dryland.............	76	3	21
"	23.	David Gruber, Plainfield.................	58	1	15
Feb.	5.	Samuel Rothrock, Dryland...............	27	5	7

Date.		Names of Persons Buried.	Y.	M.	D.
March	6.	George Knecht, Sr., Dryland............	68	6	22
May	26.	Liddia Metz, Plainfield..................	27	5	15
June	3.	Frederick Hahn, Plainfield......		4	2
"	19.	Anna Matilda Yundt, Easton............		4	3
July	26.	Sophia Dietz, Easton......................	73	1	1
Aug.	4.	Thomas Koenig, Dryland................	2		
"	8.	John Adam Metz, Plainfield.............		2	6
Sept.	12.	Edwin Henry Hendshu, Dryland........		3	6
"	18.	Frederick Herman, Dryland.............	78	4	20
Oct.	5.	Vayetta Lumbert, Dryland................		3	
"	20.	Sarah Stein, Plainfield.....................	48	1	10
"	24.	Peter Diehl, Plainfield.....................	60	2	5
"	31.	Hannah Salome Haas, Bushkil..........	83	3	5
Nov.	16.	Anna Maria Gradwohl, Dryland.........	87	7	9
Dec.	3.	Tunis Cohl, Dryland.......................	74	5	14
"	14.	Anna Maria Baumgart, Bushkil.........	52	3	

ANNO 1844.

Jan.	20.	Henry Rinker, Easton	85		
Feb.	23.	Maria Eliz. Herzel, Williams	65	6	17
March	1.	Caroline Dech, Dryland	20	7	13

MARRIAGES.

A record of the names of the persons who were united in marriage ("copuliert oder getraut worden") by me, Frederick Hermann, the pastor for the time being (" Zeittigen Pfarrer ") of the four united congregations.

ANNO 1787.

Jan. 9. Mr. N. Moessinger, Sr., with the widow Elizabeth Butz.

Feb. 20. John Bauer with Henry Young's daughter, Rosina.

" 25. John Thiel with Ludwig Klein's daughter, Anna Catharina.

Feb.   27.   John George Dengler with Catharine Eberhard.
May   17.   John Cowert with Maria Mueller in Greenwich.
July   9.   George Potz with Catharine Treisbach.
Aug.   12.   Henry Schneider with Catharina Busch.
"   19.   John Schneider with Peter Conrad's daughter, Louise.
Sept.   18.   Peter Hill with Elisabeth Flore.
Oct.   16.   Adam Heimer with Peter Bender's daughter, Margaretha.
Dec.   11.   Michael Potz with Catharina Keller.
"   18.   Michael Stuker with Ulrich Knecht's daughter, Catharina.

ANNO 1788.

Jan.   16.   Frederick Gewinner with Maria Mueller.
"   16.   George Nungester with Marie Plotz (?).
March   6.   Peter Rippel with Maria Dikenschidt.
"   27.   Peter Ladig with Anna Christina Brotzman.
May   25.   Adam Arnhold with Molly Saenty.
July   6.   John Keil with Maria Hess.
"   13.   Henry Winter with Catharine Thiel.
Aug.   10.   Samuel Mutschler with Maria Fischer.
"   12.   Conrad Schumacher with Maria Meixel.
Sept.   2.   Cornelius Bellesfield with Marg. Huffschmidt.
Dec.   2.   Elias Hummel with Dorothea Setzer.
"   2.   Jacob Romig with Catharine Knecht.
"   30.   John Frutschy with Sara Tildheimer.

ANNO 1789.

Feb.   3.   Jacob Princker with Adam Mahny's daughter, Anna Catharina.
"   8.   Abraham Muller with Maria Schick.
"   24.   Philip Watring and Anna Margaretha Flory.
March   10.   John William and Maria Catharine Busch.
April   9.   Jacob Schultz and Maria Keiper.
"   21.   John Knaus and Elisabeth Hay.
June   —.   Christoph Meixel and Elisabeth Schneider.

Sept. 8. John Kocher and Susanna Schneider.
Dec. 29. Peter Frich and Elisabeth Kuechlein.

ANNO CHRISTI 1790.

Jan. 17. Siegel Kohl with Elisabeth, William Hess' single daughter.
Feb. 25. John George Ebenreiter and Elisabeth Schordts.
March 28. John Abel and Christina Eva Stuehl (Steel ?).
April 12. Christoph Lanz and Catharine Loechner.
May 11. William Ellen and Lyna Young.
June 22. Thomas Ritscher and Susanna Ladig.
Aug. 15. John Michael and Elisabeth Billheimer.
" 17. George Hen. Koch and Anna Maria Paulus.
Sept. 28. Peter Beisel and Catharina Knecht.
Oct. 5. John Haul and Mary Giser.

[Here the record of Dr. Hermann ends, he having resigned the charge in October, 1790. His removal was followed by a vacancy which continued until August, 1793, when Rev. Dr. Christian Ludwig Becker became the Pastor, by whom the Marriage Record is continued as follows :]

A record of the names of the persons who were married by me, Dr. Ch. L. Becker, the Pastor of the four united Reformed congregations.

ANNO 1793.

Sept. 28. Adam Treisbach with Catharina Leidig.
Nov. 10. Mr. Sand with Miss Chorell.
" 10. Mr. Kessler with Gebe Schneider.
Dec. 25. Mr. John (?) Kintzig with Margaretha Meixsel.
" 29. Mr. John Leydig with Juliana Schneider.

ANNO 1794.

Jan. 9. Mr. Adam Willauer with Elisabeth Knecht, a daughter of Ulrich Knecht, of Dryland.

Feb.   11.   Mr. William Ward with the daughter of Mr. Heil, of Dryland.
March 16.   Mr. Peter Seiler with Margaretha Schumacher, daughter of Mr. Jacob Schumacher.
April   29.   Mr. Seib with Susanna Heller, daughter of Jacob Heller, Plainfield.
June   1.   Mr. Jonathon Herzel with Miss Klein, of Dryland.
July   27.   Mr. Knauss with Philip Achenbach's stepdaughter, of Plainfield.
Aug.   3.   Mr. George Gut (Good) with Catharina Brod, in Easton.
Oct.   12.   Mr. Jacob Meier with Catharine Young, daughter of Mr. Young in Greenwich.
"   14.   Mr. John Ward in Plainfield with Geba Lauer.
Nov.   23.   Mr. Cold, of Dryland, with Miss Ernst, daughter of Conrad Ernst.
Dec.   2.   Mr. Goetz with Maria Brog, across the Lehigh.
"   7.   Mr. Mutchler in Greenwich with Susanna Doffert.
"   16.   Mr. Anthon Kohl with Susanna Laball, a daughter of Henry William Laball, of Dryland.
"   22.   Mr. Kreiger with Rosina Vogel, a daughter of Mr. Vogel, of Dryland.

Anno 1795.

Jan.   27.   Mr. Kocher with Miss Bissecker, of Dryland.
Feb.   1.   Mr. Beuller with Elisabeth Moessinger, a daughter of Philip Moessinger.
"   24.   Mr. Nicholas Best with Rosina Odenwaelder, a daughter of Mr. Philip Odenwaelder.

Dr. Becker's pastorate terminated March, 1795. He was succeeded by the Rev. Thomas Pomp, who took charge in July, 1796, and by him the record is continued.]

Anno 1796.

Oct.   11.   Mr. John Cor. George with Miss Catharina Roth, Christian Roth's daughter, of Dryland.

Nov.   1.   Mr. Henry Bartholomew with Miss Barbara Happel.
"   6.   Mr. Bernt (Bernhart) Walder with Miss Mary Odenwaelder, daughter of Mr. Michael Odenwaelder.
Oct. 27.   Mr. Eseck Howell with Miss Gearer.
Nov. 29.   Mr. John Hess with Miss Catarina Knor.

ANNO 1797.

Jan.   3.   Jacob Roth with Catarina Bissecker, "*beide witt wenstandes.*"
"   10.   John Osterstock, of Dryland, with Margaretha Schmidt.
"   10.   John Hudchins, of Dryland, with Catarina Huber.
"   10.   Andrew Correll, of Mount Bettle, with Anna Maria Weidman.
March 7.   The Rev. Thomas Pomp, Minister in Easton, with Catarina Jonson.
April 6.   John Dech, of Dryland, with Elisabeth Overly.
"   25.   Mr. George Messinger with Elisabeth Kaemrer, Dryland.
May   30.   Mr. David Kaemrer with Miss Anna Dech, daughter of Mr. Jacob Dech of Dryland.
———   Mr. James Lucker with Maria Shook.
Nov. 19.   Mr. James Laumerson with Eliz. Yedistire.
Aug. 13.   John Flick with Cath. Boyer.
Sept. 25.   George Traxell with Rosina Seib.
Oct. 10.   Abraham Schmidt with Sibilla Frutschi.
Sept. 29.   Jacob Schumacher with Elisabeth Eberhard.
Dec. 10.   Christian Staut with Magdalena Hess.
"   10.   Peter Best with Margaret Billheimer.

ANNO 1798.

Jan. 12.   George Hauser with —— Metzger.
Feb. 20.   Jacob Borger with Maria Nagel.
May   28.   Nicholas Yeisley with Sara Knecht.
March 1.   Conrad Schumacher with Catarina Pershing.

May   28. John Krotz with Catarina Rippel.
July   29. Michael Messinger with Elisabeth Uhler.
Aug.   12. Jacob Hess with Maria Knor.
Sept. 18. John George Roeder with Sarah Hahn.
May   22. Doctor John Cooper, Mary Ervine.

Anno 1799.

Aug.   11. John Traxsel with Elisabeth Bishop.
April 16. John Reidenauer with Sarah Ann Townson.
May   13. Michael Rosenberry Peggy Macky.

Anno 1800.

Dec.   14. The previous year, John Spangenberg with Magdalena Gangwere.
April   6. Peter Holland with Susanna Correll.
"   6. John Meixel (?) with Margaret Oberle.
"   8. Jacob Roth with Christina Eritt.
"   27. Henry Vogt with Maria Spangenberg.
"   29. John Weber with Barbara Young.
July   18. Frederick Nicolaus with Catharine Willers.
Aug.   7. Abraham Force with Hanna Eyerman.
May   —. Michael Gum with Maria Barb. Muffley.
Oct.   7. Michael Koehler with Cornelia Frauenfeld.
Nov.   9. Christoph Miller with Maria Sorber.

Anno 1801.

Feb.   3. G—— Knecht with E—— Stocker.
"   17. Peter Schneider with Catharina Flory.
March 31. Frederick Miller with Catharina Prong.
April 10. Peter Hahn with Rebecca Freeman.
"   12. John Michael with Anna Elisabeth Hert.
Sept.   6. John Stam with Barbara Schleppy.
"   6. Isaac Grotz with Hanna Bittenbender.
Oct.   20. John Kind with Rosina Knecht.
"   22. John Medag with Margaret ———.
"   22. Philip Siegler with Margaret Lucas.

Nov. 8. Henry Frey with Elisabeth Roeder.
" 21. Jacob ——— with Anna Hess.

ANNO 1802.

Jan. 17. Henry Zoeller with Magdalena Beck.
Feb. 7. N. Moss (?) with Elisabeth Deringer.
June 27. John Remalie with Catharine Brader.
(Sept. 20, 1798. Nicholas Dietz and Sophia Flory.)
Jan. 20 (1801). Philip Rieser and Christina Stecher.
" 18. William Freeman and Margaret Andre.

ANNO 1802.

Aug. 29. Jacob (undecipherable) with Sarah Roth.
" 24. Anthony Dech with Magdalena Schug.
Sept. 5. Andrew Koechlein with Elisabeth Braun.
Nov. 21. ——— Koester with Christina Glass.

ANNO 1800.

June 24. Frederick Nagel with Elis. Kress (?).

ANNO 1801.

Aug. 27. Henry Kraemer with Barbara Kleider.

ANNO 1799.

Nov. 3. Philip Steinmetz with Elisabeth Obitz.
Aug. 13. John Elick with Catharine Boyer.

ANNO 1800.

Nov. 23. Jacob Rosengrautz with Elisabeth Martin.

ANNO 1801.

Nov. 8. Thomas Quick with Catharina Schuck.
Sept. 4. John Boyer with Margaret Frutschy.
" 4. Frederick Stein with Margaret Boyer.
" 4. John H. Smith and Anna Mott.
Dec. 8. Samuel Ervine and Rachael Heckman.
" 27. William Britton and Maria Jacoby.

350   *The First Reformed Church of Easton, Pa.*

May	3.	John Hauck and Elis. Miller.
Dec.	8.	Rudolph Oberly and Barbara Mann.
March	24.	Daniel Ginginger and Sophia Happel.
"	26.	John Roeder and Sophia Fluck.
"	31.	George Krotz and Maria Stecher.
"	31.	Jeremiah Hess and Catharine Butz.
May	10.	Henry Hoffart and Catharine Summy.
June	7.	Jacob Schaeffer and Elisabeth Freewell.
Dec.	13.	Nicholas Krau and Rosina Best.
"	13.	John Brown and Margaret Smith.
June	31.	Andrew Worman and Maria Sauerbeck.
Oct.	4.	Gotfried Moikley (?) and Hannah Stemm.

Anno 1800.

Oct.	7.	James Edmiston and Elisabeth Meddag.
March	30.	Valentine Matz and Elisabeth Schuck.
"	30.	John Smith and Elisabeth Woodley.
"	30.	Christian Singer and Susanna Woodley.
Apr.	12.	Peter Stauffer and Magdalena Weber.
"	18.	Frederick Reichart and Sarah Gross.
June	9.	Daniel Lawar and Elisabeth Menges.
"	1.	Philip Odenwaelder and Elisabeth Koch.
May	27.	Larentz Wartman and Ester Scheetz.

Anno 1803.

Jan. 16. John Stem with Anna Kellar.

Anno 1800.

Dec.	—.	Jacob Wentz and Maria Magdalena Kieffer.
Jan.	28.	Jacob Schabel and Elisabeth Arner.
May	6.	Benjamin Riehl with Magdalena Yohe.
March	4.	Conrad Schweitzer with Catharine Stecher.
"	4.	Jacob Janson with Cath. Erit.
"	4.	Michael Butz with Marg. Rippel.
May	14.	Joseph Raesley with Anna Maria ———.
"	14.	Jacob Messinger with Anna Maria Michael.

Church Records. 351

March	20.	Andrew Stiehl with Cath. Schwenk.
Jan.	4.	Jacob Dech with Elisabeth Geringer.
Nov.	11.	David Workman with Elisabeth Kleinman.
Aug.	17.	Abraham Krotz with Anna Maria Kuhn.
July	16.	John Fenner with Cath. Ward.
Oct.	12.	Philip Koester with Elisabeth Fox.
Dec.	9.	Henry Bartolmai with Cath. Labar.
Aug.	15.	Joseph Leimberg (?) with Christina Ehrit.

Anno 1801.

Feb.	22.	Bernhard Raub and Maria Krotz.
March	3.	Philip Person and Sarah Beck.
"	3.	George Happel and Elisabeth Koster.
"	12.	George Kreidler and Marg. Hertzel.
April	2.	Christian Yaeger and Eva Eritt.
"	5.	Philip Roth and Susanna Warton.
"	7.	Henry Mimmich and Anna Maria Hauck.
"	21.	Henry Oblinger and Elisabeth Braun.
May	10.	Abraham Hess and Maria Hahn.
June	14.	John Young and Susanna Schneyder.
July	7.	Abraham Kocher and Susanna Edelman.
"	12.	William Ennes and Elisabeth Arndt.
Aug.	30.	Henry Keller and Susanna Rothrock.
Dec.	13.	Jacob Fraes and Susanna Kaemrer.
"	31.	John Snyder and Elsy Barnes.

Anno 1802.

Jan.	3.	David Rundle and Magdalena Dietrich.
"	7.	Jacob Woodring and Elisabeth Odenwaelder.
"	7.	Daniel Weber and Sarah Schlecht.
"	19.	Paul Wolf and Catharina Moser.
Feb.	7.	Jacob Nauman and Maria Roth.
"	7.	John Paul Flick and Maria Marg. Roeder.
"	7.	Daniel Dreisbach and Catharine Gradwohl.
"	21.	Philip Odenwaelder and Elisabeth Butz.
"	21.	George Diemer and Margaretha Ohnangst.

March 16. Anthony Kleppinger and Maria Barbara Hess.
" 16. Philip Apel and Susanna Beitelman.
May 9. William Keller and Elisabeth Basler (?).
" 11. George Hauck and Sarah Yohe.
" 11. Peter Best and Maria Magdalena Hauer.
June 6. Philip Achenbach and Susanna Kahn.
" 8. John Heller and Elisabeth Beitelman.
" 13. John Frey and Margaret Glass.
" 28. John Schweitzer and Margaret Stecher.
July 11. Christian Kesler and Elisabeth Ruth.
Oct. 24. William Fits Randolf and Susan Barthold.
" 31. Henry Seagreaves and Eva Schuk.
Nov. 7. Michael Traxsel and Catharine Bishoph.
" 14. Jacob Kreidler and Elisabeth Hertzel.
Dec. 9. Christopher Flick and Susanna Brod.
" 9. John Christman and Christina Flick.
" 19. Jacob Wilhelm and Anna M. Hummel.
" 23. William Miller and Catharine Roseberry.
" 26. John B. Miles and Susanna Arndt.

Anno 1803.

Jan. 2. Christian Kocher and Susanna Schumacher.
" 16. John Stein and Anna Keller.
" 9. Adam Beisel and Christina Bauman.
March 30. John Yost ———[1] and Elisabeth Braeder (?)
May 24. Henry Riegel and Margaret Flick.
June 5. Christian Stocker and Susanna Stecher.
July 17. Christian Kemrer and Maria Kuder.
Aug. 7. Abraham Stemm and Charlotta Yeisley.
Dec. 4. George Adam and Christina Vollmer.
" 8. Andrew Correll and Christina Gross.
Jan. 15. George Knecht and Sara Willauer.
" 27. William Bier and Magdalena Kesler (?).
" 31. John Kohl and Barbara Lambert.
Feb. 26. John Rothrock and Maria Magdalena Lawal(?).

[1] The handwriting defies decipherment.

Church Records. 353

March 20. Henry Rohn and Maria Sleppi.
April 15. John Wilhelm and Sibilla Charlotta Lawal.
" 22. Conrad Kocher and Elisabeth Seitz.
July 1. Michael Boyer and Regina Sentry (?).
Aug. 19. Jacob Dech and Maria Oberle.
Sept. 4. Christian Gressman and Charlotta Messinger.
Nov. 25. Jacob Butz and Christina Arnold.

ANNO 1805.

Jan. 30. Jacob Kerner and Elizabeth Moyer.
April 7. John Kern and Marg. Young.
" 11. Peter Koechlein and Catharina Deichman.
Jan. 25. Peter Reis and Susanna Batt.
" 25. Michael Odenwaelder and Magd. Kercher (?).
" 25. William Sitgreaves and Ursula Beilman.
March 17. Conrad Raesly and Sarah Catharina Hertzel.
April 5. Conrad Frauenfelder and Maria Kotz.
" 17. Jacob Straus and Catharina Neuhardt.
" 10. Adam Labach and Catharina Odenwaelder.
" 11. Peter Anglemeyer and Susanna Nicolaus.
" 21. John Fellis and Catharine Bachman.
June 12. Richard Maccky and Mary Dewitt.
" 8. Christian Braun and Maria Catharina Koenig.
July 17. John Gerey, Jun., and Christina Shuck.
" 24. Mr. Trucks and Catharina Nicolaus.
" 31. Matthias Stecher and Elisabeth Anglemoyer.
Aug. 14. Jonathan Berger and Maria Butz.
June 26. John Kocher and Maria Ramstein.
" 26. Jacob Laddig and Sarah Krotz.
Sept. 27. Abraham Hertzel and Christina Yeisley.
Oct. 30. George Favi and Elisabeth Hertzel.
Nov. 16. David Richard and Margaret Lockard.
" 23. John Feit and Susanna Young.
" 20. Jonathon Knecht and Margaretha Hauser.
Dec. 4. John Lantz and Hanna Stemm.
" 27. Alexander Hayslett and Sarah Macky.

Anno 1804.

Feb.	26.	John Nicolaus Reimer and Elisabeth Gruber.
"	28.	Christian Kern and Catharine Gruber.
March	11.	John Knerr and Susanna Hess.
"	18.	Jacob Heller and Susanna Butz.
May	27.	John Geringer and Magdalena Hess.
Aug.	21.	Jacob Ziegler and Elisabeth Sewitz.
"	26.	George Stichdernoth and Rebecca Keller.
Sept.	23.	Lehnhart Nagel and Marg. Hertzel.
Oct.	10.	Isaac Kind and Elisabeth Messinger.
"	14.	George Hahn and Margaretha Schaum.
"	30.	John Brown and Rosina Roth.
Nov.	11.	John Frederick and Christina Nagel.
"	11.	Samuel Neigh and Catharine Metzger.
Dec.	2.	Henry Metz and Margaretha Riedy.
"	2.	John Barnes and Sara Casebier.
"	2.	Jacob Hertzel and Catharina Dietrich.

16 couples.

Anno 1805.

Jan.	6.	Peter Hauch and Margaret Winters.
Feb.	26.	Michael Ritter and Margaretha Arner.
March	5.	Lehnhart Nicolaus and Margaretha Reimer.
April	4.	Jacob Hauch and Magdalena Schlecht.
"	7.	John Bauer and Feronica Hahn.
"	4.	Isaac Hayden and Margaretha Schlauch.
"	7.	Henry Ettinger and Eva Schlecht.
"	7.	John Bishoff and Anna Maus (?).
"	9.	George William Raub and Elisabeth Saylor.
May	5.	John Achenbach and Elisabeth Fuhr.
"	5.	Conrad Hahn and Miss Freeman.
"	5.	Jacob Traxsel and Maria Gery.
"	14.	Matthias Thron and Anna Schmidt.
Aug.	4.	Peter Wagner and Elisabeth Transu.
June	16.	Christian Schick and Margaretha Mueller.
Aug.	11.	John Schweitzer and Elisabeth Butz.
"	18.	John Beysell and Elisabeth Kern.

Church Records.

Aug. 22. Philip Rees and Mary Barnes.
" 25. Abraham Kind and Sarah Lawall.
Sept. 1. William Lawall and Elisabeth Koenig.
" 5. Jacob Steinbach and Elisabeth Woodring.
" 5. Jacob Weber and Elisabeth Schreder.
" 15. William Weinel (?) and Catharina Frey.
" 29. Christian Hummel and Margaretha Schmidt.
Oct. 20. Abraham Osterstock and Scharlotta Schehrer.
" 27. John Best and Magdalena Stemm.
Nov. 3. Jacob Reimer and Elisabeth Hilliart.
" 10. John Halteman and Barbara (?).
Dec. 15. John George Walter and Sarah Schumacher.
"29 Paar."

Anno 1806.

Jan. 5. Conrad Best and Salome Kratzer.
" 5. John Best and Elisabeth Schnyder.
" 7. Abraham Stemm and Anna Margaretha Best.
" 28. John Schlough and Susanna Conrad.
Feb. 7. Abraham Ruth and Sophia Koch.
" 7. John Bundstein and Susanna Billheimer.
March 2. John Woodring and Eliz. Laddig.
" 22. John Baker and Barbara Schick.
" 24. Daniel Gruber and Christina Hauck.
" 30. Anthony Lerch and Catharina Dreisbach.
" 30. Peter Schuck and Susanna Messinger.
" 30. John Horn and Elis. Leidig.
" 30. John Huber and Margaretha Ritter.
April 22. Peter Steinmetz and Susanna Bauer.
" 22. Henry Schaum and Hannah Metz.
May 4. George Heller and Susanna Appel.
April 27. Daniel Achenbach and Elis. Hahn.
May 4. Jacob Frey and Maria Stocker.
June 1. John Keim and Maria Wagner.
" 1. Joseph Burke and Susan Wagener.
" 26. Henry Anthony and Sarah Schuck.
Aug. 3. Peter Mechlin and Sarah Riesler.

Aug. 19. Henry Fenner and Regina Rundis.
" 19. Seneca Duer and Elenor Baker.
" 19. George Schade and Salome Rumfeld.
" 31. Edward Lacky and Sarah Barthold.
Sept. 7. Henry Metz and Elisabeth Andon.
Oct. 5. John Gruber and Margaretha Hauck.
" 19. Mathias Buss and Elisabeth Eritt.
Nov. 30. John Kaemrer and Catharina Riegel.
Dec. 2. Henry Schreiber and Maria Margaretha Gruber.
" 7. Ludwig Scheuerman and Christina Wilhelm.
Nov. 2. Jacob Penz and Rosina Schuck.
" 23. George Beck and Catharina Fackenthal.
" 23. John Hagenbuch and Philipina Coleman.
" 25. John Oberly and Catharina Schweitzer.
" 30. John Broeder and Elis. Cohlman.
Dec. 9. Carl Frederick Philips and Hanna Tschudy.
" 14. Philip Miller and Barbara Riedy.
" 18. Abraham Young and Elis. Zimmerman.
" 25. John Miller and Rachael Bachman.
"41 Paar."

ANNO 1807.

Jan. 20. Daniel Folmer and Margaretha Boyer.
" 25. James McCracky and Ann Vanhorn.
" 27. Frederick Leinbach and Maria Batt.
Feb. 10. Philip Bartelmai and Elisabeth Hess.
" 28. Peter Siegfried and Margaretha Billheimer.
March 1. Frederick Kreidler and Susanna Eritt.
" 1. Abraham Messinger and Margaretha Kaemrer.
" 1. Barnhart Odenwelder and Sarah Boyer.
" 1. Andreas Appel and Elis. Gilmor.
April 5. John Lerch and Rosina Messinger.
" 12. Alexander Brown and Sarah Frauenfelder.
" 14. John Hilliardt and Maria Hess.
" 19. Jacob Rundis and Molly Grotz.
" 21. George Franckenfield and Maria Koch.
May 12. Mathias Wagner and Margaret Seipel.

May	18.	Elias Decker and Elisabeth Bishoph.
"	19.	Robert Moore and Maria Folmer.
"	21.	John Worman and Jane Armstrong.
"	24.	Charles Horn and Elisabeth Deshlar.
"	31.	Jacob Smith and Elisabeth Weber.
June	21.	Peter Kocher and Elisabeth Saylor.
"	21.	Joseph Kieffer and Sarah Klein.
Aug.	2.	Peter Kotz and Maria Haas.
"	16.	John Merrill and Ann Sites (?).
"	30.	John Rippel and Susanna Young.
Oct.	6.	John Overbeck and Sarah Buskirk.
"	11.	John Lawald and Maria Bundstein.
"	18.	William Moffett and Sharlotte Dily.
Nov.	22.	Jonas Hackman and Cath. Broeder.
Dec.	6.	Philip Erwine and Elisabeth Lauderbach.
"	8.	John Seibert and Magdalena Narrengang.
"	25.	John Slaytor and Sarah Arndt.

"32 Paar."

ANNO 1808.

Jan.	3.	Peter Wilhelm and Regina Sendii.
"	7.	Frederick Hess and Cath. Banes.
"	7.	Henry Shaerer and Maria Keller.
Feb.	2.	George Correll and Elisabeth Beck.
"	14.	Lehnhardt Kocher and Cath. Gross.
"	14.	Anthony McCluen and Ann Dietz.
"	16.	Peter Ohnangst and Christina Koch.
"	28.	Jacob Helick and Elisabeth Schmidt.
"	28.	John Kocher and Sarah Schmidt.
"	28.	Jacob Fehr and Elisabeth Heimer.
March	6.	Peter Siegel and Catharine Uhler.
April	7.	John Wasser and Barbara Anglemeyer.
"	18.	John Dengler and Catharina Sauerbeck.
"	24.	Henry Weitzel and Juliana Correll.
May	3.	Christian Nagel and Sarah Steckel.
"	8.	Peter Gruber and Elisabeth Diel.
June	5.	Paul Feit and Catharina Owerly.

July	3.	John Frutschman and Maria Nickum.
"	10.	Jacob Balliet and Cath. Hohenschild.
"	31.	Peter Yunken and Sarah Ginnard.
Aug.	7.	Jacob Miller and Cath. Riecher.
"	28.	Frans Herlinger and Feronica Kind.
Sept.	11.	Francis Miller and Rachael Metz.
"	13.	John Siegfried and Elisabeth Dreisbach.
"	18.	William Reis and Anna Maria Wilhelm.
Oct.	2.	Simon Dreisbach and Elisabeth Lerch.
"	30.	Conrad Fuhr and Marg. Reich.
Nov.	29.	Abraham Schlecht and Elisabeth Ohnangst.
Dec.	4.	Michael Lawald and Maria Magdalena Hertzel.
"	18.	John Roth and Elisabeth Schuck.

"30 Paar."

Anno 1809.

Jan.	24.	Carl Stauffer and Marg. Schmidt.
"	29.	Anthony Kind and Sarah Frieman.
Feb.	16.	John Melech and Sarah Melech.
"	19.	Jacob Dornblaeser and Cath. Dennis.
"	20.	John Gruber and Eliz. Bess.
"	20.	Isaac Hoe and Elisabeth Laubach.
"	26.	Henry Janson and Christina Frauenfelder.
March	26.	John Pfeiffer and Sarah Kocher.
April	11.	Jacob Heil and Susanna Butz.
"	18.	David Hess and Sarah Kohler.
May	21.	Jacob Hertzel and Magdalena Nagel.
"	30.	Frederick Fachnueth (?) and Susanna Buch.
June	4.	John Wind and Elisabeth Weldy.
"	4.	Frederick Bauer and Susanna Hohenschild.
"	11.	Jacob Miller and Elisabeth Boehm.
"	25.	Henry Schiffer and Elisabeth Frey.
July	2.	Conrad Rieser and Christina Hartendorf.
"	2.	Peter Schumacher and Elisabeth Dornblaeser.
"	9.	George Obitz and Magdalena Mill.
"	11.	Jacob Abel and Patty Arnold.
"	16.	Jacob Huber and Sarah Dewald.
"	30.	John Wolf and Maria Sendy.

Church Records.

Aug.	6.	Peter Bieber and Rachael Hoe.
"	22.	Conrad Seipel and Elisabeth Schaade.
Sept.	3.	Elias Heller and Hanna Wasser.
"	9.	Joachim Zopfy and Cath. Wilkins.
"	17.	David Butz and Maria Heister.
Oct.	1.	Jacob Spinner and Cath. Ochs.
"	24.	Joseph Jones and Maria Butz.
"	29.	Tobias Wasser and Magd. Haas.
"	31.	Charles Hauser and Cath. Hauck.
Nov.	5.	Peter Ochs and Cath. Zeigenfuss.
"	5.	William Garrison and Elis. Dehart.
"	12.	John Heller and Elis. Sober.
"	12.	Frederick Germanton and Elis. Frantz.
Dec.	24.	Samuel Leidig and Elis. Scheimer.
"	25.	Jacob Nagel and Regina Halteman.

"37 Paar."

Anno 1810.

Jan.	23.	Frederick Kerny and Cath. Roeder.
Feb.	1.	Lehnhart Andre and Jennet Ross.
"	6.	John Lehnhart Geiger and Maria Marg. Dornblaeser.
"	13.	John Moser and Elis. Bachman.
"	13.	George Berry and Susanna Hertzel.
"	13.	Peter Eberhardt and Susanna Bachman.
"	27.	John Taylor and Ann McCan.
"	25.	Daniel Walter and Cath. Siegfried.
"	25.	John Batt and Sarah Doan.
March	10.	John Robbins and Abbegal Calling.
"	18.	Jacob Laubach and Elisabeth Rinker.
"	18.	Jacob Rothrock and Susanna Brunner.
"	24.	Daniel Applebach and ——— Johnson.
"	27.	Peter Roeder and Cath. Fried.
"	31.	Francis Don Levy and Sarah Long.
April	8.	Peter Belles and Elisabeth Taylor.
"	8.	John Trittenbach and Cath. Barnett.
"	15.	George Dornblaeser and Maria M. Lawall.
"	17.	Lehnhardt Walter and Sarah Laddig.
May	6.	John Straus and Susanna Arner.

May 15. Jacob Lerch and Catharine Richard.
" 16. John Solomon and Camilla Jetester.
" 27. John Flick and Barbara Koester.
June 17. Solomon Weis and Maria Kotz.
" 17. Abraham Hay and Catharine Nicolaus.
Aug. 19. Daniel Bauer and Catharine Michael.
Sept. 11. John Young and Maria Dornblaeser.
" 23. Christian Otto and Mary Daniel.
Oct. 7. William Lerch and Maria Messinger.
" 21. William Miller and Maria Laddig.
Nov. 11. Isaac Stenger and Susan Deily.
" 11. John Kessler and Sarah Stocker.
" 18. David Miller and Barbara Richner.
" 18. Michael Roth and Cath. Riegel.
" 18. George Herzel and Cath. Young.
" 18. Peter Keiper and Molly Butz.
Dec. 2. John Herzel and Cath. Schweitzer.
" 2. Jonathan Ritter and Scharlotte Kaemrer.
" 30. Jacob Ziegenfuss and Cath. Hertzel.
" 30. Conrad Frey and Hanna Grimes.

— 40.

Anno 1811.

Jan. 5. John Koester and Elis. Schelly.
" 13. Jacob Dengler and Maria Traxsell.
" 14. David Demott and Sarah Abel.
" 22. Jacob Babb and Margaretha Young.
" 24. Jacob Kolver and Susanna Buss.
" 29. Malan Godley and Mary Taylor.
March 3. Henry Werkhaeuser and Cath. Arnold.
" 19. Abraham Roeder and Hannah Steckel.
" 31. Christian Muffley and Cath. De Long.
April 4. Jacob Reesly and Elisabeth Schwartz.
May 7. Joseph George and Maria Eva.
" 26. Henry Schumacher and Susanna Fenner.
June 2. Joseph Derrhammer and Rachael Doll.
" 2. Jacob Transue and Liddia Sterner.
" 5. William Gray and Christina Rees.

Church Records.

June	23.	Jacob Kaemrer and Regina Frantz.
"	30.	George Broeder and Elisabeth Kocher.
July	14.	John Welsh and Elisabeth Frutschman.
"	21.	James Hackett and Catharine Deshler.
"	28.	Joseph Norton and Barbara Hackman.
Aug.	8.	Joseph Ross and Susanna Fox.
"	25.	Frederick Hahn and Cath. Heimer.
"	25.	Henry Woolever and Maria Connard.
"	27.	Joseph Keller and Sus. Roeder.
Sept.	1.	John Kocher and Mary Hunt.
"	6.	Philip Kiebler and Rosina Washborn.
"	6.	Peter Heckman and Elis. Bundstein.
"	10.	George Steinbach and Maria Bess.
"	15.	Jonathan Knappenberger and Sus. Stout.
"	17.	Valentin Deily and Elis. Traxsell.
"	18.	Peter Herzel and Christ. Lahr.
"	27.	George Ochs and Maria Gress.
Dec.	8.	Michael Gress and Sarah Schneyder.
"	8.	Jacob Miller and Maria Metz.
"	22.	Valentine Keim and Maria Mertz.

— 35.

Anno 1812.

Jan.	15.	John Shnyder and Elis. Rinker.
"	16.	Jacob Hess and Marg. Heil.
"	28.	Jacob Frantz and Sarah Lerner.
March	17.	Joseph Dewald and Elis. Arndt.
"	22.	John Dornblaeser and Cath. Lawall.
April	14.	John Eritt and Cath. Willhelm.
"	14.	George Bundstein and Rosina Billheimer.
"	17.	Heath Hall and Cath. Trucks.
May	7.	Joseph Rothrock and Marg. Roth.
"	17.	George Knecht and Cath. Bess.
"	17.	Jacob Beck and Sus. Haas.
"	17.	Conrad Erich and Maria Ward.
"	18.	George Engel and Elis. Kreidler.
"	24.	John Fulkinson and Elisabeth Stenger.
"	26.	Tobias Heller and Susanna Rensheimer.

May	26.	Jacob Osterstock and Anna Maria Price.
"	31.	Jacob Mayer and Elisabeth Romig.
June	14.	Jacob Bess and Catharine Stem.
"	16.	Jacob Rees and Elisabeth Siegel.
"	28.	Peter Taylor and Margaret Mayer.
July	9.	William Swerer and Polly Richart.
"	26.	Paul Heller and Cath. Owen.
Aug.	16.	Joseph Frey and Sarah Otto.
Sept.	20.	Jacob Kreidler and Anna Transue.
"	27.	Rees Heckman and Eliza Simson.
Oct.	1.	Christian Keiser and Christina Mehrwein.
"	4.	Samuel Shnyder and Susan Bittenbenner.
"	6.	Peter Siegel and Hannah Kratzer.
"	18.	Peter Freeman and Maria Greiling.
"	18.	Richard Freeman and Catharine Laubach.
Nov.	1.	John Arndt and Susanna Roeder.
"	7.	Henry Wolf and Susanna Sendy.
"	15.	Peter Altemos and Maria Silfuss.
"	22.	Henry Reis and Elisabeth Falstich.
Dec.	20.	George Lerch and Maria Andre.
"	22.	John Heller and Elisabeth Siegel.

—36.

Anno 1813.

Jan.	24.	Jacob Ackerman and Elisabeth Koechlein.
"	31.	Jacob Hahn and Catharina Andre.
Feb.	28.	Lewis Micky and Maria Hoffman.
March	7.	George Oberly and Elisabeth Schweitzer.
"	7.	Tobias Gruber and Susanna Weber.
"	9.	Christoph Heller and Susanna Lantz.
"	16.	Peter Lantz and Maria Klein.
"	21.	Daniel Yost and Feronica Hess.
"	24.	George Greiling and Eva Cath. Moebus.
April	6.	Joseph Narrengang and Elisabeth Nolf.
"	11.	Jacob Gish and Sarah Henjon.
"	13.	Jacob Keller and Elisabeth Odenwaelder.
"	18.	George Schurtz and Cath. Schmidt.
"	25.	Daniel Koehler and Barbara Gross.

May	6.	Jonathon Heil and Catharine Haak.
"	23.	William Nicholas and Elisabeth Engel.
"	25.	Jacob Handshu and Elisabeth Beisel.
"	29.	George W. Arndt and Henrietta Byllesby.
"	30.	Simon Butz and Elisabeth Freeman.
Aug.	1.	John Miller and Gertrude Kotz.
"	10.	Frederick Fenner and Elizabeth Rundio (Rundis?).
"	29.	John Mann and Elisabeth Reich.
"	29.	Michael Frees and Sarah Schwartz.
Sept.	9.	Abraham Schurtz and Catharine Kaemrer.
Oct.	19.	George Loesher and Catharine Kaemrer.
"	24.	Adam Bugelly and Anna Maria Leidig.
"	31.	Jacob Freeman and Susanna Butz.
Nov.	1.	George Hahn and Maria Magd. Sewitz.
"	14.	Simon Mayer and Susanna Scharley.
June	13.	George Stecher and Elisabeth Jones.
Aug.	15.	William McCaw and Elisabeth Winters.
Dec.	17.	Frederick Imich and Catharine Diel.
"	19.	Solomon Nungesser and Catharine Nolf.
"	19.	Daniel Huhn and Elisabeth Kessler.

—34.

Anno 1814.

Jan.	11.	Peter Beisell and Barbara Koenig.
"	13.	Paul Higgins and Maria Luisa Sidman.
"	15.	Jacob Dewitt and Catharine Doering.
"	16.	Jacob Warner and Catharine Schwartz.
Feb.	20.	Jacob Eritt and Elisabeth Beck.
"	20.	John Hertzel and Elisabeth Claus.
"	22.	David Lerch and Mary Stout.
"	26.	Frederick Bodine and Christina Deily.
March	15.	George Lantz and Anna Marg. Ohnangst.
"	20.	Paul Siegfried and Johanna M. Clewell.
"	29.	Christian Miller and Elisabeth Ziegler.
April	19.	John Schumacher and Catharine Lambert.
"	19.	John Riegel and Maria Kauffman.
"	23.	John Edmonds and Elisabeth Hoenig.
"	23.	Frederick Demuth and Elisabeth Thompson.

April	23.	Jonathon Laycock and Mary Allen.
"	25.	John Streiker and Mary Sickman.
May	1.	Rudolph Laubach and Maria Huber.
"	15.	Adam Metz and Maria Breidinger.
"	29.	Peter Correll and Catharine Mill.
"	29.	William Bittenbenner and Ann Shnyder.
"	31.	Abraham Fehr and Elisabeth Klein.
June	5.	George Seiffert and Elisabeth Bachman.
"	5.	Nicholas Werckhaeuser and Elisabeth Sand.
"	7.	Abraham Scherer and Elisabeth Carpenter.
"	12.	John Huthmacher and Maria Obitz.
July	3.	Jacob Cramm and Susanna Frankenfield.
"	3.	John Reiman and Margaret Hauck.
"	3.	Henry Stofflet and Elisabeth Beitelman.
"	3.	George Weber and Anna Vogel.
"	10.	Joseph Moser and Susanna Lawall.
"	31.	William Demuth and Elisabeth Kind.
"	31.	John Washborn and Maria Pink.
"	31.	John Hinckel and Margaret Spengler.
"	31.	Jonathon Stocker and Christina Stecher.
"	31.	John Yohe and Eva Fehr.
Aug.	7.	John Lesher and Susanna Helick.
"	7.	William Laudenbach and Catharine Buss.
"	23.	George P. Kessler and Magdalena Frees.
"	23.	George Engler and Sarah Sterner.
"	27.	Capt. John Baldy and Elisabeth Weygandt.
"	28.	Abraham Buss and Maria Claus.
"	28.	Isaac Gross and Christina Wilhelm.
"	28.	Christian Weinland and Elisabeth Odenwaelder.
Oct.	9.	Isaac Freeman and Ann Maria Andre.
"	18.	Peter Dehmer and Maria Kerch.
Nov.	22.	Jacob Zimmerman and Anna Sheimer.
"	24.	William Dalton and Christina Huber.
Dec.	18.	John Dewitt and Elisabeth Mutschler.

ANNO 1815.

Jan.	15.	Philip Imich and Margaret Erl.
"	19.	Peter Miller and Hetty Freeman.

Church Records. 365

Feb.	5.	John Oberly and Eva Christman.
"	11.	Conrad Boas and Martha Arnold.
"	18.	William Barnett and Juliana Winters.
"	19.	Christian Young and Elisabeth Broeder.
"	19.	George Schade and Elisabeth Buss.
"	21.	Peter Sand and Maria Werckhaeuser.
March	26.	John Carr and Emelia Nicholas.
Apr.	4.	Frederick Gehres and Susanna Sterner.
"	9.	Joseph Huber and Maria Weiss.
"	9.	Charles Frey and Maria Daley.
"	13.	William Denson and Hannah Kennedy.
May	4.	Joseph Sterner and Catharine Transue.
"	4.	Jacob Demond and Charlotte Ginthar.
"	7.	Peter Hess and Margaret Saylor.
"	7.	Jacob Richard and Susanna Odenwaelder.
"	13.	Joseph Schnyder and Susanna Simon.
"	28.	Peter Lerch and Catharine Lerch.
June	11.	Jacob Walker and Elisabeth Roeder.
"	18.	Henry Winters and Mary Ann Ferrill.
"	25.	—— Knecht and —— Freeman.
Aug.	1.	Samuel Herzell and Susanna Gehres.
"	6.	Joseph Coleman and Magdalena Leidig.
"	6.	James Kelsoph and Catharine Eichman.
"	13.	Jacob Bachman and Maria Frey.
"	17.	Charles Miller and Catharine Fetterman.
"	20.	Mathias Transue and Catharine Heckman.
"	27.	John Koenig and Sabina Yodder.
Sept.	10.	Philip Jacoby and Ann Queer.
"	10.	Joseph Schick and Susanna Laubach.
"	10.	David Hanke and Elisabeth Haak.
"	15.	Peter Walter and Abbe Belles.
Oct.	15.	Christian Laubach and Rebecca Lutz.
Nov.	26.	Peter Young and Margaret Laubach.
Dec.	5.	Conrad Metz and Catharine Keim.
"	17.	Frederick Vogel and Susanna Seip.
May	15.	Michael Stecher and Margaret Leidig.

—38.

Anno 1816.

Jan.	9.	Peter Steckel and Catharine Arndt.
"	25.	Jacob Transue and Sarah Boehm.
Feb.	1.	Jacob Keller and Elisabeth Schuck.
"	6.	David Deschler and Catharine Mertz.
March	19.	John Ache and Maria Ochs.
"	31.	George Mack and Magdalena Kramm.
"	31.	John Zeller and Anna Marg. Saylor.
April	9.	Jacob Brotzman and Maria Christina Hess.
"	11.	Adam Schlecht and Susanna Bender.
"	13.	John Kerkenthal and Sarah Sendy.
"	13.	Philip Ohl and Maria Klees.
"	13.	Henry Wilhelm and Susanna Eichman.
"	26.	John Shade and Susanna Klauss.
"	23.	Henry Anthony and Eva Danner.
May	2.	Daniel Weber and Hannah Schaum.
"	5.	John Hoffman and Sarah Brotzman.
"	5.	George Hensel and Elisabeth Ohl.
"	7.	Samuel Moyer and Elisabeth Steckel.
"	9.	Adam Jumper and Christina Miller.
"	26.	Joseph Gehres and Margaret Moser.
June	2.	Adam Young and Elisabeth Mann.
"	9.	Jacob Walter and Elisabeth Dewalt.
"	9.	Michael Smith and Gertrude Rothrock.
"	16.	Christian Wagner and Magdalena Faebel.
"	16.	Anthony Transue and Maria Koch.
"	16.	Ludwig Reichard and Mary Rayer.
"	30.	Philip Knecht and Catharine Brotzman.
July	7.	Daniel Stapp and Catharine Flick.
"	3.	Lewis A. Hayden and Mary Rees.
Aug.	18.	Andrew Emrich and Magdalena Knobel.
"	25.	Joseph Brotsman and Elisabeth Knecht.
Sept.	8.	Isaac Eckart and Maria Brown.
"	15.	Samuel Emrich and Maria Laubach.
"	15.	George Andre and Susanna Dietz.
"	15.	Joseph Belles and Sarah Fox.
"	22.	Samuel Hoffart and Margaret Froelig.

Oct. 13. John Philip Clewell and Maria Roth.
" 15. David Frey and Catharine Vogel.
" 15. John Hess and Maria Koehler.
" 27. Henry Messinger and Sarah Buchannan.
" 27. John Jones and Catharine Schiffer.
Nov. 5. Peter Lerch and Catharine Correll.
" 10. Jacob Mengel and Salome Hohenschild.
" 17. Isaac Raub and Elenor Sterner.
" 17. John Seip and Salome Haas.
Dec. 15. Jacob Henn and Susanna Moser.
—46.

ANNO 1817.

Jan. 5. Jacob Klees and Elisabeth Jacobina Lynn.
" 10. Joseph Werner and Ann Hahn.
" 14. Henry Gruber and Magdalena Bess.
" 21. John Shnyder and Elisabeth Hilliard.
" 30. Conrad Hahn and Sarah Heller.
" 23. John Handshu and Elisabeth George.
March 2. Adam Ohl and Catharine Ohl.
" 9. Daniel Gehringer and Sarah Roth.
" 20. Anthon Lerch and Elisabeth Frees.
" 23. Jacob Hess and Elisabeth (wanting).
April 17. Jesse Worly and Magdalena Hering.
" 20. Leonard Derr and Maria Curry.
" 20. George Herzel and Susanna George.
" 22. Philip Eberts and Salome De Long.
" 24. Conrad Broeker and Elisabeth Germanton.
June 8. Philip Hahn and Sarah Franz.
" 10. John Buss and Susanna Clauss.
" 15. Stephen Winn and Catharine Coleman.
" 17. Henry Keller and Maria Engler.
" 17. Philip Haupt and Susanna Arndt.
July 6. Peter Holland and Margaret Miller.
Aug. 21. Charles Sculy (Schooley (?) and Catharine Sampson.
" 31. Benjamin Riegel and Elisabeth Leidy.
Sept. 21. William Major and Sarah Snyder.

Sept.	27.	Jonas Rothrock and Eliza Hinkel.
Oct.	2.	Joseph B. Carpenter and Maria Sheimer.
"	12.	John Koch and Eva Weber.
Nov.	4.	Samuel Butz and Maria Transue.
"	30.	Joseph Weber and Rosina Sheimer.
Dec.	9.	Rudolph Funck and Anna Kauffman.
"	11.	Henry Steinbach and Maria Eckart.
"	16.	Joseph Lerch and Susanna Oberly.
"	27.	Daniel Jansen and Magdalena Transue.
"	28.	Daniel Derr and Rebecca Coleman.

— 34.

Anno 1818.

March	1.	Zacharias Neiss and Maria Hilliart.
"	8.	John Dietz and Anna Breitinger.
"	19.	Michael Diehl and Margaret Emrod.
"	22.	Jacob Stofflet and Sarah Reinheimer.
April	5.	David Oberly and Susanna Seip.
"	9.	Jacob Morgan and Maria Doeringer.
"	19.	Anthon Oberly and Rebecca Schweizer.
"	26.	George Laubach and Rebecca Laubach.
May	10.	John Schiffer and Eliz. Kratzer.
"	12.	David Seiler and Maria Osburn.
"	12.	Jacob Hauck and Christina Hilliart.
"	24.	John Nolf and Susanna Schmidt.
June	14.	Philip Woodring and Elisabeth Brotsman.
Aug.	2.	George Mayer and Sarah Happel.
"	12.	George Renner and Susanna Keller.
Sept.	13.	Jacob Anglemayer and Catharine Brown.
"	20.	Michael Mayer and Catharine Vogel.
"	27.	John Kloeckner and Elisabeth Bender.
Oct.	6.	Conrad Siegel and Elisabeth Rilpert.
Dec.	6.	Jacob Schumacher and Hannah Trach.
Oct.	27.	Jacob Seiler and Margaret Dickson.
Nov.	14.	Bartholomew Huber and Margaret Raub.
"	15.	John Freeman and Margaret Jarrett.

— 23.

Church Records.

ANNO 1819.

Jan.	5.	John Rentsheimer and Catharine Lerch.
Feb.	21.	Samuel Weber and Elisabeth Buss.
March	13.	William Stevenson and Elisabeth Thomas.
April	25.	Samuel Laubach and Rebecca Ruch.
May	30.	Jacob Hahn and Elisabeth Miller.
Aug.	8.	William Daniel and Susanna Shnyder.
Oct.	3.	Jacob Bluhm and Margaret Schmit.
"	3.	Henry Wilhelm and Maria Koenig.
Nov.	16.	John Frankenfield and Catharine Happel.
"	21.	Jonathon Kinsey and Sarah Dietz.
Oct.	21.	William Henry Kocher and Catharine Fox.
"	10.	John Kreidler and Catharine Schleppi.
"	30.	Joseph Hilliart and Elisabeth Dech.
Sept.	28.	William Swetling and Catharine Seiler.

— 14.

ANNO 1820.

Jan.	4.	Jonas Frankenfield and Susanna Maurer.
Feb.	20.	Adam Brown and Sarah Ohl.
"	24.	John Schelly and Maria Schuck.
"	29.	Jacob Odenwaelder and Elisabeth Yaeger.
March	5.	Jacob Koechlein and Elisabeth Handschu.
"	14.	John Ohnangst and Catharine Bender.
"	19.	George Nagel and Rosina Danner.
"	21.	Simon Heller and Elisabeth Ruth.
"	25.	Henry Riegel and Elisabeth Transue.
"	28.	David Roth and Catharine Biers.
April	2.	Andrew Lynn and Catharine Schade.
"	16.	Henry Beck and Elisabeth Jansen.
"	25.	Anthon Koch and Susanna Lynn.
May	4.	Peter Brown and Liddy Carl.
"	20.	Peter Horrace and Susanna Roth.
"	28.	Abraham Stauffer and Susanna Ruth.
June	4.	George Bender and Catharine Mersch.
"	6.	John Schnabel and Catharine Walter.
"	17.	Francis Alsfeld and Christina Castner.
Aug.	8.	Peter Diehl and Elisabeth Schmidt.

Oct.   31.   Samuel Koechlein and Sarah Snyder.
Nov.   16.   George Febel and Elisabeth Reeb.
  "   19.   Isaac Lantz and Eliz. Richard.
Dec.   19.   Daniel Derr and Sus. Wittemer.

—24.

Anno 1821.

Jan.   14.   Thomas Happel and Sarah Voelker.
  "   23.   Charles Willauer and Christina Hess.
  "   25.   David Boyer and Maria Lutz.
Feb.   8.   Henry Schuck and Catharine Ackerman.
  "   25.   John Kunsman and Catharine Woodring.
March   6.   Philip Woodring and Catharine Kunsman.
  "   11.   Enoch Hoenig and Elisabeth Dreisbach.
  "   13.   John Coleman and Maria Bender.
  "   20.   Jacob Bess and Susanna Ohnangst.
  "   25.   Abraham Gross and Maria Lerch.
  "   27.   John Yeisley and Anna Reinheimer.
April   8.   John Ward and Elisabeth Schleppi.
  "   12.   George Warner and Susanna Siegel.
  "   12.   Peter Metzger and Catharine Metz.
  "   15.   David Koenig and Maria Schurtz.
  "   17.   John Edelman and Elisabeth Bess.
  "   18.   Joseph Hagenbach and Catharine Seip.
  "   22.   James Kincaid and Catharine Reich.
May   13.   Peter Meixsell and Catharine Scheid.
June   5.   John Michael and Maria Werner.
July   1.   Andrew Diehl and Maria Ehrguth.
  "   29.   Isaac Buss and Anna Halteman.
  "   31.   George Metzger and Christina Gross.
Aug.   19.   Daniel Ritter and Rosina Oberly.
Sept. 14, 1820. Jacob Hess and Christina Giltner.
Oct.   1,   "   William Janson and Elisabeth Young.
Sept.   6, 1821. George Steinbach and Maria Ward.
Dec.   2.   John Dewalt and Elisabeth McKinney.
Oct.   22.   Alexander H. Barthold and Hannah Kill Patrick.
  "   23.   Peter Buss and Elisabeth Rosenberger.
  "   30.   Michael Hinkel and Catharine Wagener.

A CONFIRMATION SERVICE IN THE OLDEN TIME.

Nov. 20. Henry Siegfried and Abigail Romig.
" 25. William Levers and Magdalena Kaemrer.
Dec. 9. Jacob Smith and Eliz. Lummerson.
" 20. William Siebring and Eliz. Davis.
" 23. Jacob Bohrum and Catharine Bundstein.
—36.

ANNO 1822.

Jan. 13. Jacob Hahn and Elisabeth Diehl.
" 20. Abraham Keiper and Catharine Lawall.
" 27. George Bachman and Sarah Laubach.
Feb. 11. Christian Hoenig and Catharine Traxsell.
" 12. Jacob Ohnangst and Elenora Gerhardt.
" 13. Thomas Gold and Ann Christina Knecht.
" 28. Jacob Edelman and Elisabeth Young.
March 10. Robert Browers and Sarah Moser.
" 12. Joseph Roth and Maria Riegel.
" 26. Jacob Lantz and Elisabeth Schaerer.
" 28. Jacob Winter and Sarah Froelich.
" 31. Jacob Stocker and Margaret Reesly.
April 2. William Miller and Catharine Laubach.
" 2. Joseph Koempfer and Maria Gottschall.
" 4. Joachim Schill and Anna Maria Boatz.
" 21. John Yost and Maria Rosina Stuben.
" 13. Henry Stem and Margaret Knauss.
" 25. John Kressler and Maria Seitel.
" 25. John Broeder and Jane Salzig.
June 25. Frederick Faebel and Christina Kaemper.
" 25. Jacob Hassenfuss and Eliza Herzell.
July 2. Ludwig Schmidt and Christina Weiss.
" 7. George Frantz and Catharine Kreidler.
Sept. 3. Henry Steinbach and Margaret Eckart.
" 5. Jacob Everitt and Elisabeth Hoenig.
" 15. Thomas Sendy and Susanna Rosenberger.
Oct. 6. Henry Weiss and Catharine Riehl.
" 13. Isaac Lawall and Maria Froelich.
" 20. Anthon Lerch and Susanna Weber.

Oct.   27.   Joseph Yodder and Ann Eliz. Beisell.
Nov.   21.   Aaron Snyder and Rebecca Simon.
"   24.   John Kaemrer and Magdalena Gruber.
"   24.   Samuel Schwartz and Polly Transue.
"   24.   George Helick and Eliz. Brown.
Dec.   1.   Peter Wasser and Elisabeth Heller.
"   8.   Jacob Ziegler and Margaret Willhelm.
"   17.   David Lerch and Eliz. Bachman.
"   24.   John Ackerman and Sus. Metz.
"   28.   William Miller and Kazia Laddig.

ANNO 1823.

Jan.   5.   George Taylor and Anna Hoffman.
"   21.   Philip M. Kinsey and Maria Young.
"   26.   Joseph Keller and Liddia Butz.
Feb.   16.   Peter Yaeger and Christina Wilhelm.
"   20.   John Menninger and Margaret Yaerger.
March   31.   Christian Laubach and Susanna Beyl.
Sept.   18.   George Schuck and Eliz. Ackerman.
"   20.   John Brotzman and Anna Maria Lock.
"   21.   Charles Heimer and Elisabeth Ruth.
Oct.   28.   Charles Mehrwein and Cath. Willauer,
(Wanting)   Daniel Butz and Elvina Barnett.
Nov.   16.   Samuel Snyder and Cath. Leidy.
"   23.   John Handshu and Elisabeth Kerkenthal.
Dec.   7.   Anthony Transue and Eliz. Henn.
"   7.   Melchoir Meixsell and Margaret Messinger.
April   22.   Henry Young and Margaret Andre.
May   4.   Isaac Miller and Sarah Cowley.
"   24.   John Transue and Elisabeth Wasser.
"   24.   John Michael and Elisabeth Stocker.
June   2.   Charles Ward and Catharine Shewel.
Aug.   12.   Henry Broeder and Cath. Borum.
April   5.   John Tilton and Sarah Seip.
"   3.   Henry Young and Cath. Berry.
"   5.   Jacob Smith and Sarah Reich.

Anno 1824.

Jan.	11.	John Sculey and Nancy Eckert.
"	27.	Philip Ruth and Cath. Ettinger.
Feb.	15.	Israel Muffly and Rachael Marjarum.
March	27.	Jacob Keiper and Julian Odenwelder.
"	27.	Jacob Reichart and Susanna Randel.
April	6.	Christian Bess and Maria Rieser.
"	10.	Lewis Singer and Christina Leidig.
"	18.	Jacob Heller and Sarah Belles.
May	18.	Anthon Dech and Julian Koenig.
June	13.	William Henry Cole and Cath. Froelig.
July	4.	Jacob Huber and Rebecca Moser.
"	4.	John Herzel and Maria Andreas.
"	10.	John Smith and Charlotte Barthold.
"	27.	Isaac Laubach and Elisabeth Kieffer.
Aug.	8.	John Gundt and Elisabeth Appel.
"	8.	John Koch and Rosina Krahn.
"	10.	John Davis and Julian Snyder.
"	15.	George Weber and Hannah Reinheimer.
"	29.	Jacob Wetsel and Rosina Wilhelm.
Sept.	12.	William (wanting) and Sus. Bundstein.
"	14.	Joseph Bender and Eliz. Hahn.
Oct.	28.	Charles Snyder and Sophia Schick.
Nov.	28.	Samuel Right and Cath. Schall.
Dec.	19.	Peter Kaemrer and Maria Magd. Odenwelder.

Anno 1825.

Jan.	30.	William Transue and Elisabeth Schnabel.
March	22.	Jonas Sand and Elisabeth Bender.
"	24.	Philip Kessler and Catharine Kind.
"	27.	Peter Lynn and Elisabeth Schmidt
April	3.	John Odenwelder and Margaret Heller.
"	4.	Jacob Keller and Marg. Arndt.
"	5.	Henry Keller and Sophia Snyder.
"	7.	Adam Sand and Cath. Snyder.
"	17.	John Koechlein and Eva Gross.

April	19.	Samuel Baron and Sus. Mixsell.
May	22.	Jacob Bauer and Sus. Hay.
"	26.	John Laubach and Mary Huber.
June	28.	John Hoffman and Maria Siegfried.
Aug.	14.	Joseph Musselman and Eliz. Belles.
"	23.	George Stuber and Maria Boehm.
Sept.	1.	William Cunningham and Emelia McMichael.
"	18.	Henry Mack and Ann Batt.
"	20.	John Bachman and Elsy Belles.
"	25.	Isaac Transue and Sally Call.
Oct.	9.	Jacob Woodring and Hannah Moore.
"	11.	Dan'l Kreidler and Marg. Boyer.
Nov.	13.	John Heller and Cath. Appel.
"	20.	Daniel Schurz and Maria Gradwohl.
"	27.	John Bergstraeser and Maria Lynn.
Dec.	11.	Daniel Walter and Eve Freeman.
"	11.	John Berstler and Maria Esch.
"	25.	Isaac Oberly and Maria Heller.
"	25.	Daniel Laubach and Hannah Reich.
"	27.	George Miller and Maria Diehl.
Feb.	12.	Jacob Correll and Phebe Reidenauer.
"	21.	Adam Bruch and Sarah Maurer.
April	9.	Thomas Snabel and Salome Buss.
"	11.	John Bender and Elisabeth Shaum.
"	16.	Samuel Richard and Mary Worman.
"	27.	Peter Nauman and Susan Oberly.
May	1.	William Hoe and Maria Miller.
June	10.	Anthon Lehr and Cath. Swesey.
"	18.	Abraham Dewalt and Maria George.
"	18.	Thomas Bachman and Elisabeth Heller.
July	2.	Jacob Sterner and Margaret Wasser.
"	16.	Joseph Doffert and Sarah Kelly.
Aug.	27.	George Lynn and Anna Moser.
Nov.	5.	John Brinker and Anna Werkhaeuser.
"	5.	George Mixsell and Elisabeth Rieser.
Dec.	17.	Jacob Buss and Sarah Cole.

Church Records. 375

Dec.	31.	Jacob Saylor and Maria Walter.
"	23.	William Philips and Cath. Moyer.
"	24.	John Seipel and Susan Ohnangst.
"	25.	David Woodring and Liddia Correll.
"	25.	Jacob Stiles (colored people) and Phillis Shipman.

ANNO 1827.

Feb.	27.	Jesse Lynn and Maria Lynn.
May	8.	Samuel Yohe and Maria Heller.
"	25.	William Woodring and Cath. Brotsman.
"	25.	Joseph Koechlein and Maria Brinker.
"	25.	Jacob Riegel and Eliz. Lutz.
"	25.	Frederick Schaefer and Eliz. Paul.
April	8.	Joseph Hess and Sarah Stump.
"	29.	Thos. Kessler and Cath. Heller.
May	1.	John Gehres and Eliz. Reiss.
"	1.	William Engel and Sus. Jansen.
"	3.	Andrew Neigh and Sarah Pence.
"	6.	Philip Koch and Cath. Lynn.
"	6.	Lehnhart Schnyder and Cath. Werkhaeuser.
"	19.	Isaac R. Richard and Hannah Christein.
"	22.	Charles Innes and Matilda Mixsell.
June	2.	Christian Speer and Eliz. Frees.
"	3.	Adam Roth and Eliz. Lumbert.
"	10.	David Koenig and Maria Schnabel.
"	17.	Abraham Transue aud Eliz. Klauss.
"	17.	John A. Canaan and Maria Magd. Heller.
"	28.	Henry Heberling and Maria Hildebrand.
July	22.	John Kostenbader and Sarah Keller.
"	22.	John Reicheldoerfer and Sus. Sponheimer.
Aug.	4.	Joseph Algert and Elisa Riemer.
"	4.	John Berry and Eliz. Stem.
"	9.	Abraham Kind and Sus. Queer.
"	26.	Joseph Heller and Eliz. Odenwelder.
"	26.	John Taubert and Sus. Moser.
Sept.	9.	Jonas Trumbor and Eliz. Stapp.

Sept.	23.	David Koechlein and Eliz. Maurer.
"	23.	Henry George and Hannah Dewalt.
Oct.	4.	John Laubach and Anna Walter.
"	7.	Joseph Sand and Rebecca Bauer.
"	7.	Charles Nicholas and Mary Transue.
"	14.	Michael Dech and Cath. Herz.
"	21.	Samuel Bergtraesser and Eliz. Transue.
"	30.	John Steinmetz and Rebecca Metz.
Nov.	1.	Charles Roth and Sophia Eichman.
Dec.	13.	Thomas Richard and Eliz. Reel.
"	16.	John Halteman and Cath. Neuhart.
"	16.	Isaac Sendee and Cath. Hayden.
"	16.	Bernet Arndt and Ann Rowland.
"	16.	Adam Metz and Maria Coleman.
"	18.	Jacob Hardiemer (?) and Eliz. Herzell.

Anno 1828.

Jan.	6.	Philip Berstler and Maria Hahn.
"	6.	Joseph Riess and Sarah Heller.
"	13.	Jacob Hagenbuch and Cath. Heckman.
"	20.	David Gausner and Molly Kleder.
"	22.	Gidion Haupt and Eliz. Uhler.
Feb.	3.	Jacob Everitt and Eliz. Heller.
"	3.	Isaac Ackerman and Sarah Hahn.
"	14.	Samuel Stocker and Rebecca Heller.
March	23.	Thomas Ritter and Rebecca Correll.
April	6.	Simon Belles and Judith Snyder.
"	6.	Thomas Koenig and Lea George.
"	13.	Andrew Keller and Eliz. Fitz Randolph.
"	24.	Wernhart Mesmer and Cath. Nauman.
May	4.	Simon Kaemrer and Eliz. Abel.
"	25.	Joseph Loesher and Sabina Roth.
"	25.	Isaac Walter and Ann Odenwelder.
"	31.	Samuel Trockenmiller and Hannah Snyder.
July	27.	Peter Henrich and Lydia Sommer.
Aug.	21.	Charles Simon and Rachael Loehr.

Sept. 10. William Leidig and Martha Kennedy.
" 21. David Roth and Anna Hartman.
" 23. Valentin Wagner and Annet Rodgers.
Oct. 12. John Metz and Ann Hahn.
" 12. Charles Bauer and Eliz. Weber.
" 19. John Willauer and Margaret Reesley.
Nov. 18. Thomas Murfey and Maria Coleman.
Dec. 7. Frederick Hahn and Caroline Koch.
" 7. Conrad Bender and Ann Bauer.
" 7. Jacob Roth and Hannah Werkhaeuser.
" 14. William Lawall and Christina Kreidler.

ANNO 1829.

Jan. 3. Abraham Gaston and Lydia Metzger.
" 3. George Herman and Mary Ann Steinmetz.
" 22. Jacob Taylor and Jane Kennedy.
" 25. Conrad Kocher and Sarah Buntin.
Feb. 15. George Vogel and Julian Koch.
March 15. Thomas Oberly and Anna Maria Fredrick.
" 15. Peter Rohn and Sabina Seip.
" 19. Peter Resch and Eliz. Engel.
" 17. Anthon Laubach and Eliz. Hess.
" 21. William J. Harmaney and Ebezena Butz.
" 22. Samuel Engel and Mary Daniel.
" 24. Joseph Engler and Hannah Hahn.
" 24. George Stadler and Feronica Kind.
April 5. Charles Miller and Sarah Herzel.
" 5. Peter Shnyder and Sus. Jacoby.
" 9. Michael Long and Cath. Nauman.
" 12. Samuel Riegel and Sus. Lerch.
May 12. George Teel and Eliz. Bowers.
June 7. Abram Miller and Dina Eichelberger.
" 7. Jacob Abel and Eliz. Stecher.
" 13. Benjamin Dech and Hannah Kreidler.
Aug. 2. Charles Radenbach and Sarah Rodenberger.
" 2. Jacob Transue and Maria Ruth.

Aug.   9. David Knobel and Susanna Christein.
"   23. Christian Yaeger and Elisabeth Walter.
"   30. Peter Handshu and Ann Kloeckner.
"   30. Thomas Kessler and Lydia Kind.
Sept. 6. Christian Wilhelm and Maria Christina Wagner.
"   6. John W. Kessler and Luisa Snyder.
"   9. Henry Horning and Maria Weiss, *sive* Hilliart.
"   12. John Kinney and Sally Ann Gardner.
"   20. John Long and Maria Schlegel.
"   27. Abraham Moyer and Catharine Roesley.
"   27. Isaac Koch and Maria Frey.
Oct. 18. Christian George and Catharine Herzell.
"   20. Franklin Frey and Susanna Engelman.
Nov. 10. Peter Ohnangst and Anna Maria Feeman.
"   15. George Yost and Maria Kocher.
"   29. Isaac Lee and Elisabeth Miller.
Dec.   6. David Metz and Anna Bruch.
"   26. Samuel Woodring and Susanna Yeisley.

Anno 1830.

Feb.   8. Reuben Nolf and Elisabeth Heckman.
March   2. Charles Brown and Christina Heller.
Feb.   23. Jesse Beitelman and Susanna Walter.
March   7. Henry Moser and Susanna Frederick.
"   16. John Fuhr and Maria Boyer.
April   3. George Sheivley and Sarah Abel.
"   4. Jacob Brinker and Susanna Wilhelm.
"   18. John Hackman and Rebecca Kieffer.
"   18. David Knauss and Christina Kleder.
"   20. Levi Barber and Maria Hering.
May   18. Peter Diehl and Teresia Walter.
"   29. Henry Schwartz and finnetta Leidig.
June   1. Doctor John Deichman and Cath. Stocker.
"   10. Charles Fehr and Julian Winters.
"   15. Charles Transue and Maria Weber.
"   19. Jacob Reineck and Maria Bundstein.

Church Records.

June	20.	Ulrich Knecht and Sus. Roeder.
"	28.	Caspar Simon and Eliz. Seip.
July	3.	Thos. C. Major and Mary V. Sholl.
"	27.	Abraham Sewitz and Hannah Carl.
Sept,	28.	Adam Happel and Elisabeth Neiss.
Oct.	5.	Paul Miller and Hannah Bess.
"	14.	Charles W. Down and Elisabeth Heck.
"	16.	George Correll and Cecelia McHose.
"	17.	Henry Schnabel and Sarah Koch.
"	19,	Joseph Sand and Susanna Koechlein.
"	16.	Ebenezer Cord and Ann Leidig.
"	24.	Hugh Barr and Lydia Stock.
"	31.	Thos. Kunsman and Cath. Woodring.
Nov.	7.	Daniel Koch and Susanna Schnabel.
"	9.	Joseph Riegel and Maria Neukomer.
"	27.	John Bender and Ann Fortner.
Dec.	7.	David Abel and Cath. Rieser.
"	9.	John Kern and Mary Bess.
"	12.	Joseph Kerzell and Sarah Young.
"	26.	Enoch Kaemrer and Julian Arner.

Anno 1831.

Jan.	13.	Charles Woodring and Elisabeth Radenbach.
"	13.	Andrew Reiss and Hannah Reichart.
"	20.	Frederick Maurer and Anna Maria Schaerer.
"	22.	Joseph Balliett and Louisa Herzel.
"	23.	George Heller and Sus. Odenwelder.
Feb.	20.	Joseph Schlabach and Eliz. Reiss.
"	20.	Joseph Lynn and Maria Moser.
"	27.	Jacob Stauffer and Ann Hahn.
March	17.	Jacob Cane and Eliz. Myers.
"	20.	Timothy Stotz and Eliz. Herzel.
"	22.	Daniel Knauss and Rachael Jacoby.
April	3.	Jonas Roeder and Mahila Walter.
"	3.	Charles Walter and Lea Kramm.
May	3.	Jacob Weber and Margaret Mackel.

May 15. John Kind and Sally Ann Coleman.
" 19. Ely Riegel and Anna Maria Ohnangst.
" 22. Michael Kind and Maria Diehl.
June 9. Charles Koch and Lucinda DeWitt.
July 3. Thomas Broeder and Mary Ann Froelig.
Aug. 4. Jacob Biery and Susanna Reiss.
" 7. John Bosch and Eliz. Lynn.
" 18. John Bowers and Cath. Weber.
" 21. George Reidenauer and Eliz. Weber.
" 21. Danl George and Juliana Gross.
" 27. William Straub and Margaret Harlacher.
" 28. Jesse Lynn and Eliz. Oberly.
" 28. Jacob Wimmer (?) and Eliz. Heller.
Sept. 3. John Mayers and Rebecca Zellers.
" 4. Philip Woodring and Henrietta Heller.
" 4. Samuel Ruth and Rebecca Lynn.
" 15. Jonas Lehr and Sarah Shuman.
" 24. Matthias Brown and Walberga Joseph.
Oct. 9. John Schuler and Rebecca Reiss.
" 6. John A. Innes and Sus. Heller.
Nov. 6. Charles Knauss and Ann Fuhr.
" 10. William Schultz and Sarah Hay.
" 13. Jacob Batt and Mary Walter.
Dec. 2. Jacob Rose and Sarah Metzger.
" 4. William Steiner and Levina Brown.
" 4. John Lehn and Eliz. Schnyder.
" 11. John Barley and Maria Riley.
" 24. Peter Herzel and Margaret Lambert.
" 25. Gidion Staut and Maria Merkenthal.
" 25. Reuben Drein and Susanna Kaemrer.

Anno 1832.

Jan. 7. George Guth and Anna Maria Schmidt.
" 21. William Kogan and Mary Loesch.
Feb. 7. Jesse Dech and Eliz. Ritter.
" 2. Peter Alt and Cath. Biesecker.

Church Records. 381

Feb.	26.	Hieronimus Wunderling and Eliz. Staut.
March	4.	John Wilhelm and Rachael Hepler.
"	13.	George Herzel and Fanny Odenwelder.
"	13.	Aaron Traxel and Eliz. Cooper.
"	13.	Samuel Samsel and Margaret Weiss.
"	27.	Abram Heller and Susanna Bauer.
"	29.	Edward Seib and Mary Ann Odenwelder.
"	31.	Joseph Clewer and Eva Hartman.
April	8.	Charles Hackman and Sophia Koenig.
"	8.	Charles Fehr and Eva Fuhr.
"	10.	Jacob Heller and Cath. Keller.
May	1.	Herman S. Heckman and Mary Butz.
"	3.	Abram Eckert and Cath. Stapp.
"	8.	Benjamin Broeder and Eliz. Hyle.
June	9.	Thomas Leidy and Hannah Schaefer.
"	10.	John Wagner and Sus. Jansen.
"	10.	Abram Walter and Eliz. Uhler.
"	20.	Jacob Butz and Cath. Hagenbuch.
"	3.	John Belles and Cath. Kleder.
July	22.	John Mehrwaeh and Barbara Blaar.
"	31.	Henry Kostenbader and Caroline Hahn.
Aug.	11.	Philip Becker and Sarah Price.
"	19.	Frank Roth and Dina Barber.
"	19.	Benjamin Dietrich and Maria Lerch.
Sept.	2.	Daniel Warrich and Fredericka Bender.
"	9.	Jacob Bauer and Florentina Bender.
"	23.	Edward Kreidler and Maria Boyer.
Oct.	2.	John Nolf and Rebecca Woodring.
"	7.	Simon Frankenfield and Eliz. Herzel.
"	11.	Samuel Ruth and Eliz. Metz.
"	19.	John Keller and Maria Keim.
"	30.	Michael Maurer and Rosina Woodring.
Nov.	1.	Jacob Young and Anna Maria Schill.
"	15.	John Price and Catharine Miller.
"	18.	Jacob Yeisley and Susanna Maurer.
"	20.	Joseph Keller and Lydia Fried.

Nov. 22. John Lantz and Cath. Clauss.
" 26. Alexander Stanton and Mary Gebhardt.
Dec. 2. Frederick Wagner and Anna Julina Stenger.
" 6. Horace Wolf and Sabina Simon.
" 9. Jacob Kunsman and Julian Huber.
" 23. Charles Nicholas and Rebecca Wilhelm.
" 25. Charles Messinger and Nancy Buntin.
" 25. Jonathon Riegel and Eliz. Herzel.
" 25. Jacob Miller and Eliz. Schlecht.

Anno 1833.

Jan. 7. David Young and Jane Andrews.
" 8. Samuel Herzel and Cath. Hoe.
" 31. Jesse Laubach and Maria Eliz. Walter.
Feb. 10. Samuel Seymour and Sarah Ann Stem.
" 17. Jacob Jansen and Eliz. Young.
" 19. John Taylor and Mary Steinmetz.
" 24. Jacob Bender and Sabina Hahn.
" 28. John Merz and Eliz. Faust.
March 8. Charles Siegley and Hannah Roth.
" 10. Christian Paff and Hannah Kerchenthal.
" 24. George Moser and Maria Frey.
" 21. George Jansen and Mary Steinmetz.
April 2. Kraft Weber and Christina Fierling.
" 2. John Andre and Charity Hartendorf.
" 7. Ulrich Knecht and Sarah Girt.
" 7. William Werner and Margaret Arner.
" 7. John Lawall and Sabina Lawall.
" 20. George Andrews and Sarah Ann Miller.
May 8. Felix Herzel and Sarah Messinger.
June 4. Enos Lehr and Susanna Hahn.
Aug. 6. David Seaward and Rebecca Schaum.
" 13. George Kocher and Eliza Lerch.
" 17. Richard Smith and Anna Maria Fraess.
" 25. Peter Koechlein and Eliz. Reinhart.
" 25. William Abbit and Sarah Transue.

Church Records.

Aug.	27.	Adam Hahn and Rosina Lombert.
Sept.	7.	William F. Randolph and Cath. Derr.
Oct.	3.	Jos. Beisher and Margaret Edmonds.
"	27.	Rudolph Stocker and Juliana Dieter.
"	27.	Frederick Reiss and Eliz. Odenwaelder.
Nov.	17.	Charles Edelman and Sus. Walter.
"	17.	Matthias Hahn and Christina Alsfeld.
Dec.	1.	Jesse Kaemrer and Sarah Abel.
"	3.	David Kotz and Ann Neiss.
"	5.	Daniel Dech and Cath. Stem.
"	8.	Tobias Lynn and Hetty Wimmer.
"	15.	Abram Gruber and Ann Cath. Snyder.
"	15.	Jacob Haak and Cath. Wilhelm.
"	22.	Daniel Vogel and Eliz. Odenwelder.
"	22.	George Krotz and Cath. Ackerman.
"	31.	Capt. Jacob Wilt and Cath. Freeman.
"	31.	John J. Herster and Susan Nicholas.

Anno 1834.

Jan.	5.	Peter Paff and Sarah Bundstein.
"	5.	John Schitz and Lena Walter.
"	6.	Gottlieb Scheibely and Christina Schwartz.
"	8.	William Diehl and Maria Otto.
"	12.	Jacob Sholl and Mary Ann Hagenbuch.
"	13.	George Sherr and Ottilla Yaekel.
"	17.	John Ross and Mary Ann Roberts.
"	21.	Charles Dech and Lydia Koehler.
"	26.	George Knecht and Philipina Uhler.
Feb.	2.	Chorles Roeder and Maria Bess.
"	8.	John Miller and Sophia Stem.
"	9.	Simon Koehler and Eva Wagner.
"	18.	David Dech and Liddia Beidler.
"	18.	Joseph Keller and Sally Ann Mitman.
"	23.	Daniel Nolf and Sarah Kern.
"	25.	Jacob Gerhardt and Anna Christine.
"	25.	Philip Ox and Sus. Schick.

Feb.	25.	Benjamin McQuaw and Christina Clauss.
March	2.	Samuel Lerch and Sus. Kocher.
"	9.	Joseph Fritz and Salome Wilhelm.
"	18.	Peter Weber and Mary Ann Bowers.
"	27.	Michael Jansen and Eva Ward.
April	6.	Jonas Buss and Eliz. Wagner.
"	20.	Gidion Basler and Mary Ann Heller.
"	20.	David Jansen and Sus. Deichman.
"	22.	Abr. Woodring and Cath. Ruth.
"	22.	John Barley and Floriana Miller.
"	27.	George Schwetizer and Cath. Walter.
May	4.	Daniel Frutschman and Mary Emig.
"	11.	Samuel Oliver and Anna Maria Appel.
"	15.	David Schiffer and Mary Nice.
June	8.	Jacob Jacoby and Mary Ann Belles.
"	8.	Paul Flick and Cath. Rieser.
"	14.	Joseph Heid and Mary Wilhelm.
"	15.	Joseph Van Lear and Luisa Rogers.
"	18.	James Wubler and Mary Piatt.
"	19.	Thomas Barber and Mary Ann Romig.
"	22.	John Folmer and Eliz. Riegel.
"	24.	Jacob Driesbach and Matilda Germanton.
July	10.	Peter Transue and Eliz. Beaver.
"	10.	John Gruber and Eliz. Hahn.
"	20.	Robert Staetler and Liddia Schaefer.
Aug.	17.	Ludwig Mayer and Eliz. Berry.
"	17.	Adam Miller and Maria Mayer.
"	26.	Simon Wilhelm and Mary Schmidt.
"	31.	Abr. Reich and Cath. Miller.
Oct.	4.	Christian Fierbach and Maria Hackney.
"	7.	David Gehris and Sarah Kocher.
"	12.	Peter Metz and Anna Happel.
"	12.	Tobias Schmidt and Eliz. Ackerman.
"	15.	John Kleder and Maria Gross.
"	26.	John Heckman and Luisa Kaemrer.
Nov.	4.	Samuel Albert and Rebena Shuck.

Church Records. 385

Nov.	8.	Ludwig Decas and Eliz. Reisner.
"	9.	Samuel Odenwelder and Maria Ohnangst.
"	14.	Thos. George and Mary Ann Bassinger.
"	18.	John Fritz and Sus. Reib.
Dec.	2.	Edward Bauer and Ann Stoehr.
"	14.	Samuel Adams and Polly Knecht.
"	16.	Jacob Odenwaelder and Mary Ann Gradwohl.
"	21.	Charles Abel and Cath. Nicholas.

ANNO 1835.

Jan.	5.	Conrad Boeckel and Cath. Steinhelfer.
"	13.	Jonas Lichtenwalter and Liddia Gradwohl.
"	18.	Michael Frauenfelder and Mary Ann Koechlein.
"	18.	John Reesley and Ebe Hortendorf.
"	18.	Thos. Baumgarten and Matilda Odenwelder.
"	29.	Edward Lightcap and Susanna Ruth.
Feb.	10.	Xapherius Loeb and Anna Maria Ziegenfuss.
March	1.	Samuel Shuck and Sarah Shuhman.
"	8.	Peter Lynn and Hannah Dech.
May	17.	John Herzel and Levina Werkhaeuser.
"	26.	Philip Ohnangst and Lea Hahn.
"	28.	Michael Schmike and Cath. Heller.
June	2.	Adam Mayer and Luisa Germanton.
"	21.	John Bousch and Rachael Berry.
July	28.	Peter Young and Cath. Deichman.
Aug.	2.	John Osterstock and Rachael Lawall.
"	4.	John Diehl and Eliz. Fehr.
"	4.	Enos Heller and Sarah Mufley.
"	11.	George William Ziegenthal and Cath. Jansen.
"	15.	John Fred. Bietze and Rosina Stump.
"	30.	Daniel Balliett and Cath. Dreisbach.
Sept.	6.	William Miller and Margaret Hahn.
"	6.	John Schnyder and Rosanna Berry.
"	13.	Elias Trumbore and Cath. Vocht.
"	15.	Charles Happel and Lea Kotz.
"	16.	Frederick Stump and Cath. Schnerr.

Sept. 20. Simon George and Cath. Scheuerman.
Oct. 6. George Kessler and Sarah Gratwohl.
" 12. John Frederick Schoenthal and Wilhelmina Reiter.
Nov. 5. Benjamin F. Laddig and Maria Messinger.
" 7. Joseph Derr and Lena Shnyder.
" 15. John B. Beisell and Christina Nolf.
" 24. Washington Hellick and Sarah Beisel.
" 28. Christian Kreider and Anna Maria Zeller.
Dec. 1. Thomas Roeder and Rebecca Knecht.
" 20. Mannass Koemrer and Mary Ann Gross.
" 29. Timotheus Miller and Mary Hoffert.

Anno 1836.

Jan. 2. Jacob Keiper and Polly Hare.
" 3. Paul Wunderling and Christina Kerkenthal.
" 21. Andrew Frankenfield and Sarah Odenwelder.
" 28. Jacob Hauser and Eliz. Heller.
" 31. John Jacoby and Violetta Coleman.
" 31. Simon Jansen and Sarah Seipel.
" 31. John Mack and Sarah Barnes.
Feb. 9. Nathan Koch and Sus. Reich.
" 18. Daniel Gross and Eliz. Koch.
" 21. Charles Hoenig and —— Storm.
" 23. Jacob Happel and Eliz. Sandt.
" 25. Adam Heimer and Sarah Hahn.
March 1. John Riegel and Cath. Steel.
" 10. David Koehler and Levina Schortz.
" 17. Jacob Michael and Cath. Keim.
" 20. Jacob Keiser and Luisa Bruch.
" 22. Jacob Reeser and Eliz. Weber.
April 10. Daniel Woodring and Cath. Zeller.
" 12. Peter Miller and Maria Jansen.
" 26. John Sentee and Lea Steinmetz.
May 3. Jacob Hope and Sarah Seiler.
" 3. Jacob Frey and Margaret Jumper.
" 8. John Scheively and Cath. Rieser.

Church Records. 387

May	15.	John Siegel and Sus. Seiler.
"	24.	Thomas Kind and Maria Werkhaeuser.
June	14.	William Moser and Cath. Diehl.
July	14.	Levi Barber and Eliza Herst.
"	30.	John Zieger and Cath. Roetz.
"	31.	Joseph Lehr and Maria Hessinger.
Sept.	25.	Reuben L. Seip and Sarah Ann Hemsing.
"	25.	Stephen Balliett and Ann Lowrey.
"	29.	John Deichman and Sarah Kuntz.
Oct.	16.	Joseph Lahr and Sus. Nickum.
Nov.	20.	Frederick Dietz and Nancy Kotz.
"	22.	Samuel Roeder and Eliza Heller.
"	27.	Peter Lantz and Abbe Belles.
Dec.	11.	Daniel Edelman and Mary Wolfinger.
"	13.	Joseph Mitman and Sarah Roser.
"	15.	John Schaefer and Eliza Ann Frey.

Anno 1837.

Jan.	3.	Abr. Koenig and Caroline Helick.
"	7.	Peter Weber and Agnes Hess.
"	15.	Isaac Balliett and Cath. Koechlem.
"	17.	Philip Odenwelder and Eliza Heller.
"	24.	Charles Weber and Caroline Heyl.
"	15.	John Wagner and Matilda Smith.
Feb.	2.	John Leidy and Sarah Heckman.
"	9.	Nicholas Dewalt and Judith Mayer.
"	11.	Reuben Junkin and Eliza Arner.
"	12.	Charles Hauser and Mary Seifert.
"	14.	Jacob Schneider and Sarah Duglas.
"	15.	Nathan Junt and Sophia Walter.
March	9.	George Bassinger and Mary Ann Bauer.
"	22.	John Henry Heintz and Cath. Stump.
"	28.	Simon Janson and Henrietta Theodora Seifried.
"	30.	Richard Prawl and Ann Juline Kutzler.
April	18.	Samuel Buntin and Diana Stoflet.
May	2.	Peter Nauman and Eliz. Roth.

May   23. Simon Heller and Sophia Dreisbach.
"   25. Philip Kaeyser and Ann Juline Osterstock.
June   15. Joseph Seider and Eliz. Rohn.
"   22. Edward Werkhaeuser and Lydia Kind.
"   29. Reuben Koep and Cath. Koch.
July   30. Herman Shnyder and Sus. Gogen.
Sept.   5. James Stackhouse and Cath. Schiffer.
"   10. Henry Shnyder and Maria Martin.
"   10. George Woodring and Sarah Ann Rodenbach.
"   17. William Wilhelm and Sarah Jansen.
"   22. Franklin Niles and Henrietta Innes.
Oct.   1. John Heller and Mary Ann Seifriedt.
"   14. Philip Beisher and Eliz. Smith.
"   15. Aaron Koep and Mary Ann Ricks.
"   29. Joseph Kaemrer and Matilda Jansen.
Nov.   19. Peter Koenig and Maria Helick.
"   30. Christian Butz and Sarah Vogel.
Dec.   5. Thos. Dech and Eliz. Dewalt.
"   6. Courtland Bell and Serina Osterstock.
"   12. Christian Stump and Glory Herzel.
Oct.   8. Simon Junkin and Ann Bishop.
Dec.   21. Anthon Pohl and Elisabeth Blum.
"   26. Simon Kleder and Cath. Roth.
"   31. David Bauer and Sus. Schnabel.

Anno 1838.

Jan.   4. John Stump and Elisabeth Walter.
"   7. Nicholas Lantz and Sarah Ann Edelman.
"   16. Jacob Best and Juliana Schweitzer.
Feb.   11. John Kocher and Margaret Buntin.
"   24. Daniel Gorr and Charity Andre.
March   25. Xerxes Helick and Sarah Handlein.
"   25. John Herzel and Elisabeth Rogers.
"   27. Thos. Lawall and Cath. Geiger.
April   8. John Ruth and Ann Mayer.
May   1. Michael Abel and Anna Seipel.

May	15.	John Reed and Cath. Haupt.
June	7.	John Schnyder and Sus. Kiefer.
"	12.	Samuel Heller and Margaret Gold.
July	3.	David Ackerman and Cath. Flick.
Sept.	9.	Isaac Mitman and Cath. Sliewer (?).
"	29.	Dan¹. Reichard and Mary Ann Scheivley.
"	29.	Dr. Evan Schlaugh and Mary Innes.
Nov.	12.	Solomon Blotz and Mary Sponheimer.
"	13.	Jacob Miller and Polly Mill.
"	18.	Daniel Queer and Sus. Kohl.
Dec.	9.	Jeremiah Hope and Lyddy Ann Frey.
"	18.	Daniel Rohn and Levina Ritter.
"	25.	Bernhart Kind and Cath. Bellesfield.
"	27.	John George Riedeser and Anna Cath. Riedeser.
"	27.	George Hackman and Julian Derr.

Anno 1839.

Jan.	1.	Frederick Leitling and Luzetta Leisner.
"	1.	Edward Lamb and Lyddia Schminck.
Feb.	14.	Abr. Fitz Randolph and Mary May.
"	24.	Peter Hackman and Rebecca Hess.
March	24.	Jacob Herzel and Sus. Rothrock.
April	7.	Daniel Brinker and Caroline Frederick.
May	4.	Adam Gottschall and Lyddia Ackerman.
"	9.	Ehrhart Nees and Francisca Yaeger.
"	9.	Jacob Andrews and Christina Herzel.
"	14.	Ernst Rissmiller and Luisa Heller.
"	18.	Dan¹. Ohl and Sully Fritz.
July	7.	Charles Handshu and Cath. Stocker.
"	25.	Jacob Weber and Hannah Dreibley.
"	30.	Aaron Dreisbach and Mary Ann Stocker.
Aug.	25.	Samuel Keim and Caroline Jacoby.
Sept.	1.	George Peter Werkhaeuser and Eliz. Stocker.
"	10.	George Heller and Hannah Swarthwood.
"	17.	Peter Diehl and Mary Ann Sand.
"	21.	Israel Kiefer and Sibilla Shuck.

Sept. 21. Jacob Kutzler and Eliza Fritz.
" 21. Francis Edward Reed and Susan Stem.
Oct. 13. Reuben Hummel and Mary Ann Roth.
" 15. Joseph Mill and Sibilla Bartelmei.
Nov. 2. Samuel Hahn and Sally Ann Dech.
" 3. Jacob Dech and Eva Rieser.
" 7. John Rodenbach and Mary Kunsman.
Dec. 10. Samuel Bauer and Maria Russel.
" 10. Peter Coal and Lea Lawall.
" 10. Charles Heller and Elisabeth Breidinger.
" 19. John B. Heinlein and Rosanna Hartzel.
" 26. David Butz and Maria Iderly.

Anno 1840.

Jan. 12. Christian Odenwelder and Maria Uhler.
" 23. Abraham Abel and Elisabeth Diehl.
" 25. J. H. B. Mertz and Lyddia Flick.
" 28. Michael Ache and Luisa Farling.
" 29. Peter Lerch and Lucy Ann Ritter.
Feb. 4. William H. Shouse and Ann Arndt.
" 8. Solomon Hummel and Levina Jansen.
" 16. Jesse Drasbach and Diana Herzel.
" 29. Samuel Fengel and Feronica Schmidt.
March 6. Peter Liebenguth and Elisabeth Best.
" 14. Christian Bender and Susanna Sand.
" 24. Daniel Weber and Matilda Stecher.
" 24. Charles Young and Regina Knecht.
" 29. John Young and Mary Elliot.
" 17. Daniel W. Davis and Mary Ann Sleter.
April 1. Peter Reichard and Charlotte Smith.
" 31. George Moser and Cath. Schroeder.
" 12. Jacob Ackerman and Lyddia Hahn.
" 19. Thos. Seiler and Eliza Koenig.
" 26. Jesse Bergstraeser and Julian Fuhr.
" 28. Jacob Hauser and Lucinda Clewell.
May 17. Jacob Handshu and Sus. Young.

Church Records. 391

June	8.	Thomas Buss and Eliza Ann Hackman.
"	28.	George Findley and Julia Kind.
Aug.	4.	George Werner and Lyddia Metz.
"	21.	Samuel Fabion and Ester Sassaman.
Sept.	1.	Stephen Hess and Emma Aurelia Clewell.
"	6.	Samuel Carl and Cath. Lawall.
"	6.	Levi Ruth and Nancy Bachman.
"	8.	Aaron Roeder and Sabina Bauer.
"	10.	Amlin Lake and Rosina Ohnangst.
"	26.	Abraham Bauer and Sarah Keller.
"	29.	Samuel Reit and Eliza Kelly.
Oct.	4.	Isaac Moser and Ellen Weber.
"	25.	Samuel Scheivley and Caroline Roeller.
"	30.	Nicholas Arner and Eliz. Ecker.
"	31.	David Appel and Anna Matilda Loescher.
"	31.	John Scheuerman and Cecilia Haas.
Nov.	14.	George Dietz and Eliz. Jones.
"	28.	John Wootring and Mary Ann Koechlein.
"	29.	Geo. Dengler, Sr., and Eliz. Bender.
Dec.	1.	Enoch Wootring and Mary Ann Peiffer.
"	13.	Christian Schlam and Lena Seipel.
"	15.	Peter Engel and Ann Engler.

ANNO 1841.

Jan.	5.	Peter Ohnangst and Sophia Lerch.
"	5.	Gidion Leigh and Sus Lawall.
"	24.	Edward Kocher and Levina Beck.
"	24.	Susanna Peiffer and Hannah Adams.
Feb.	2.	Benjamin Nolf and Maria Wootring.
"	2.	John Herzel and Rebecca Sanders.
"	18.	Jacob Shock and Eliz. Butz.
March	7.	Jacob Werner and Anna Eliz. Correll.
"	9.	Jacob Ackerman and Luisa Fraess.
"	18.	Christopher Koenig and Levi Rothrock.
April	4.	John Jacoby and Eliz. Koenig.
"	8.	Daniel Miller and Sus. Herzel.

April 20. Philip Fauerbach and Eliz. Pleck (?).
May 18. Aaron Happel and Mary Ann Iderley.
" 30. Daniel Hornecker and Eliz. Haas.
" 30. Samuel Scheuerman and Susan Walter.
" 30. Peter Walter and Williamina Laddig.
June 4. William Fengel and Sarah Hellman.
" 29. Lewis Appel and Ann Rohn.
July 11. Abr. Hackman and Luisa Kremer.
Aug. 7. Benjamin Eckert and Cath. Frankenfield.
" 13. John Flory and P. Ann Gruber.
" 28. John Werkheuser and Deborah Hahn.
Sept. 9. George Reiss and Mary Lamb.
Oct. 3. Samuel Lawall and Eliza Reiss.
" 10. William Wensel and Sus. Engel.
" 17. David Bergstraeser and Maria Cawley.
" 17. John Kraemer and Hannah Getter.
Nov. 10. Robert G. Heiss and Eliza Gray.
" 21. Jacob Stofflet and Lydia Weber.
" 23. Jacob Kreidler and Ann Messinger.
" 27. Jacob Ruch and Isabella Keller.
Dec. 5. Wm. Noll and Cath. Bundstein.
" 9. John F. W. Stocker and Eliza Riegel.
" 14. Aaron Frey and Sus. Miller.
" 14. Henry Ueberroth and Ann Oberley.
" 24. John Gehres and Matilda Hoffman.
" 25. Peter Cunningham and Juliana Carey.
" 25. Jacob Sheip and Mary Ann Frey.

Anno 1842.

Jan. 12. Jos. Koechlein and Cath. Wagner.
" 18. George Ruch and Margaret McCrackin.
" 25. Thos Hahn and Cath. Buss.
March 5. Henry Roeder and Eliz. Keller.
" 12. David Schnabel and Eliz. Schnabel (widow).
" 15. Jos. Hahn and Ann Frauenfelder.
" 24. Abr. Moyer and Lucy Ann Young.

Church Records.

March	31.	Dan¹ Ball and Camilla Moser.
April	2.	John Martendorf and Mary Rieser.
"	10.	Solomon Walter and Levina Walter.
"	16.	Jacob Barnes and Catharine Steinmetz.
May	29.	Daniel Heister and Caroline Odenwelder.
July	26.	Henry Broeder and Lusetta Lynn.
Aug.	9.	Barnet Wagner and Maria Young.
"	16.	Peter Herz and Sophia Kreidler.
"	19.	Jacob Matz and Christina Ganzel.
"	21.	Cyrus Frees and Levina Zerfass.
Sept.	7.	Isaiah Moser and Sarah Biegly.
Oct.	8.	Edward Hahn and Caroline Metz.
"	11.	Samuel Taylor and Peggy Ann Engler.
"	15.	Joseph Ernst and Cath. Schnerr.
"	23.	Simon Sentee and Caroline Koenig.
"	29.	Jacob Shuck and Rebecca Berger.
"	30.	Joseph Wilhelm and Levina Kelchner.
"	30.	Samuel Krotz and Margaret Heitsman.
Nov.	7.	George Nolf and Eliz. Lechliter.
"	11.	Richard Hahn and Sophia Bender.
"	24.	William Hoeny and Margaret Siegel.
"	26.	Samuel Kressman and Cath. Croferty.
"	27.	Andrew Price and Ann Kreidler.
"	27.	William Herzel and Matilda Messinger.
Dec.	11.	Reuben Dech and Sarah Koehler.
"	15.	Samuel Schurtz and Maria Schweitzer.
"	31.	Francis Roth and Hannah Barber.

Anno 1843.

Jan.	7.	Ephraim Ohl and Juliana Stofflet.
"	21.	Joseph Keller and Maria Klein.
March	4.	George Fritz and Ann Roeder.
"	19.	John Leibert and Sally Ann Bellesfield.
"	23.	Reuben Eckert and Margaret Arnold.
April	4.	Samuel Peiffer and Sophia Wootring.
"	4.	James Shnyder and Christina Fox.

April 29. George Yeisley and Susan Herzel.
" 4. Stephen D. Roeder and Ellen Flick.
June 13. Charles Michael and Elisabeth Mack.
" 13. Philip Engel and Catharine Heller.
" 23. Peter Berry and Polly Ohnangst.
" 31. Edward Walter and Matilda Odenwelder.
Sept. 7. Jacob Keller and Mary Vogel.
" 10. William Kotz and Sarah Ann Zimmerman.
Oct. 3. Henry Gruber and Charlotte Burke.
" 3. Benjamin Herzel and Matilda Oberley.
" 17. Daniel Kaemrer and Mary Ann Dewalt.
" 26. Aaron Dech and Eliz. Amanda Schreiber.
" 28. Peter Roeder and Levina Dunbar.
" 28. William Mack and Susan Rosen.
" 29. Peter Hess and Hannah Gehres.
Nov. 14. William Odenwelder and Anna Wootring.
" 26. William Erich and Matilda Baumgardt.
Dec. 2. Michael Resch and Cath. Stackhaus.
" 10. Charles Rieser and Eliza Bauer.
" 12. Aaron Koch and Mary Koch.
" 31. Levi Kogen and Matilda Fengel.

Anno 1844.

Jan. 2. Peter Andree and Nancy Hahn.
" 14. William Walter and Mary Walter.
" 27. Andrew Metzger and Sophia Matilda Kinsey.
" 26. Henry Werner and Mary Bender.
" 18. Peter Herzel and Eliz. Carwell.
" 27. Stephen Derrhammer and Eliz. Lerch.
" 29. Solomon Koehler and Mary Ann Ehrit.
March 2. Thomas Metz and Rebecca Andre.
" 2. Herman Kemper and Susan Shelly.

NOTE.—It is to be observed that the record of marriages, made in the handwriting of the Rev. Thomas Pomp, ceases at this point, 1844. He was now an aged and venerable man, having continued in office as pastor for forty-eight years. In the year 1845 the Rev. J. H. A. Bomberger became the Englist assistant pastor. In another book will be found his record of marriages, the first entry being made April 4, 1847. These records it is not our purpose to publish, our aim being merely to publish the records from the earliest entry down to the close of the ministry of the Rev. Thomas Pomp.

It is further to be observed that "Father Pomp's" relation to the congregation still continued in a regular manner, even after the coming of Rev. Mr. Bomberger as the assistant pastor. Father Pomp was still the regular German minister, and Rev. Mr. Bomberger the English pastor. This arrangement continued from 1845 to April 19, 1850, when, owing to the increasing infirmities of age, Father Pomp retired from the active service of the church, still retaining, however, his official relation as pastor with salary. "Four years later in the early morning of April 22, 1852, death gently released him from all his earthly labors and trials, in the eightieth year of his age, the sixtieth of his ministry, and the fifty-seventh of his pastorate in Easton."

During the latter years of his ministry he seems not to have made any entries of marriages, baptisms, etc., in the church books. From what I have learned from members of his family I am persuaded that he kept such records in a private memorandum book, his son William as occasion afforded, copying them into a book which was afterward used as an "Account Book." Some years ago, prior to the death of the sole survivors of his immediate family, the Misses Susan and Mary Pomp, I secured from them the privilege of cutting out the leaves of this account book which contained such records, and inserted them in the Church Register at the people place. I can find only the record of the marriages — which here follows:

ANNO 1846.

Oct.	4.	Samuel Blum and Catharine Frey.
"	4.	Simon Arndt and Rebecca Dech.
"	22.	William Dech and Eliza Heller.
Nov.	3.	Charles Hay and Maria Babb.
"	12.	Joseph Emmerich and Ella Melinda Derhamer.

ANNO 1847.

Jan.	2.	Jacob Mufley and Eliz. Weitman.
"	5.	Conrad Miller and Sophia Stocker.
"	5.	Henry Milton and Cath. Rodenbach.
"	19.	Anthony Kochler and Lydia Buss.
"	20.	Frederick Schmidt and Maria Margaret Lauber.
"	27.	Jacob Howard and Eliz. Weaver.
"	31.	Stephen Smith and Susan Johnson.
Feb.	13.	Elias Iderle and Eliz. Immick.
"	13.	Amandus Paul and Camilla Koechlein.
"	14.	Michael Hensel and Christiana Picht.
March	21.	John Picht and Cath. Newmayer.
"	27.	David Steinmetz and Sarah Stein (Stem?).
April	10.	Michael Ruf and Rebecca Resh.
July	4.	Jacob Fenstermaker and Eliz. Rohn.
"	15.	Thomas H. Leary and Eliz. K. Wagener.
Aug.	5.	John Handshue and Eliz. Transue.
Sept.	12.	Enoch Arndt and Sarah Kreidler.
"	12.	Reuben Kessler and Cath. Lichliter.
Oct.	2.	John Helwick and Luiza Holl.
"	9.	Stephen Hahn and Caroline Hortendorf.

ANNO 1848.

May	2.	Peter Kochler and Margaret Wagner.
"	21.	John Oberhoner and Levina Moebus.

Jan. 25. Aaron Best and Mary Ann Young.
" 30. John Reinbolt and Mille ———.
Feb. 17. Thomas Reigel and Sarah Ann Lutz.
April 1. Michael Iderle and Elisabeth Fortner.
" 15. Jacob Wootring and Sibella Unangst.
Nov. 27. David Ritter[1] and Levina Seipel.
" 30. Cornelius Unangst[1] and Caroline Heller.
Dec. 4. George Schenk[1] and Eliz. Bossart.
" 16. George Ernst[1] and Sarah Koch.
Jan. 25. Aaron Best[1] and Mary Ann Young.
March 4. Jonathan Hahn and Angelisa Stotz.
" 12. Jacob Lerch and Liddy Ann Lerch.
Nov. 2. Alfred Rouch and Maria Penton.
Dec. 2. Peter Young and Eliza Heimer.
" 4. James Schmidt and Belinda Fluk.
" 24. George Bieler and Sabina Willauer.
" 26. John Riesser and Susanna Arner.
" 30. Saphane Bulleing and Ann Shup.

Anno 1849.

Jan. 13. Nicholas Fishler and Cath. Broeder.
Feb. 22. William Ohnangst and Rebecca Matilda Kemrer.
May 6. Richard Kachlein and Ann Matilda Coleman.
" 7. Martin Reinhamer and Anna Picht.
" 13. Lewis Group (?) and Maria Snyder.
Jan. 16. Levi Dahn and Lucetta Abel.
" 23. David Dahn and Maria Stocker.
July 10. Joseph Radenbach and Caroline Werkhouser.
" 29. Stephen Eritt and Eliz. Franz.
Aug. 4. Charles Bolsappel and Sarah Davenport.
" 11. Charles Andre and Caroline Bahn.

Anno 1850.

March 12. William Stocker and Sally Ann Laubach.
May 28. John Fluck and Cath. Rockel.

[1] These entries have been crossed with pencil marks — I know not why.

May   28. John Jonlus and Diana Shade.
July   6. Isaac Shuck and Sarah Gottshal.
"   14. John Justice Carty and Mary Fishler.
Aug.   3. George Iderle and Eliza Metzger.
Sept. 14. George Rinker and Peggy Ann Kocher.
Nov.   2. Daniel Heller and Luisa Schiffler.
"   8. Samuel Knecht and Eliza Gruber.
Dec.   20. Philip Miller and Levina Derr.
"   26. Philip Adam Yob and Sarah Dech.
"   28. Jacob Dietz and Julian Heller.

Anno 1851.

Jan.   5. John Jansen and Susanna Jansen.
"   14. John Stephen Dech and Anna Maria Heller.
Feb.   2. George Erich and Cath. Erich.
March 22. Isaac Dietz and Eleanora Peiffer.
"   23. Anton Knap and Eliz. Linn.
April 19. Reuben Hahn and Sarah Hahn.
"   20. Amandus Daubert and Sarah Fishler.
May   17. Peter Siegel and Eliz. Caroline Koenig.
"   18. John Carling and Sarah Mosier.
"   26. Anthon Boyer and Caroline Schnyder.
"   27. Thomas Apple and Emma Miller.
Oct.   4. William Koch and Juliann Stocker.
"   5. Gottlieb Scheivly and Emeline Brunner.
"   29. John Huber and Eliza Weber.
Nov.   8. Edward Apple and Elisabeth Heller.
"   22. George Stonebach and Cornelia S. Hinsey
Dec.   21. Christian Collmar and Mary Dillinger.
"   24. John Nise and Sarah Caroline Vogel.

Anno 1852.

Jan.   22. Martin Simon and Elisabeth Laub.
Feb.   17. John Nagel and Cath. Nolf.
"   19. John Schall and Luisa Mittenberger.
March   7. George Wilhelm and Cath. Stansbury .

Church Records. 399

ANNO 1849.

Dec. 10. Peter Class and Margaret Bauer.

ANNO 1786.

In the congregation at Greenwich the following persons were in the Consistory ("Kirchen-Rath"): *Elders*, Jacob Welsh, Jacob Meyer; *Deacons*, John Winter, Herman Schubman.

ANNO 1787.

April 15. As a deacon of the congregation, Herman Schubman passed out of office, and in his stead William Henry Haentz was elected and installed.

ANNO 1788.

In the month of May, two additional persons were elected by the Christian Congregation for service in the Consistory, viz.: Peter Scherp and William Passinger.

ANNO 1790.

May 16. Two members of the Christian Reformed Congregation at Greenwich, namely, Mr. Baltzer Zimmerman and Peter Young were ordained as elders, the term of Mr. William Henry Haentz, Jacob Winter and John Meyer having expired.

ANNO 1793.

There was chosen for the Consistory at Greenwich, as elders, Jacob Welsch, Peter Scharp; and as deacons, William Passinger, Balthasser Zimmerman, Peter Young.

ANNO 1794.

In this year William Passinger and Balthasser Zimmerman went out of office as deacons, and in their stead were chosen Abraham Zimmerman and Peter Winter, who on the 23d of November were duly presented to the congregation and ordained to their offices.

THE CHURCH AT DRYLAND.

ANNO 1786.

The Consistory of the Church at Dryland consisted of the following persons, to wit: *Elders*, Lenhard Knecht, William Jansen, Jacob Meyer; *Deacons*, Nicholas Koemmerer, John Ehrit, George Hertzel.

ANNO 1788.

In the Christian Congregation at Dryland, the term of office of the following persons expired, *viz.*, as Elder, Jacob Meyer, and as Deacon, Nicholas Koemmerer, and in their stead were chosen and duly obligated by the congregation, Michael Lawald and as Deacon, Frederick Lerch.

ANNO 1789.

April 26. In the congregation at Dryland the two elders, Lenhard Knecht and William Jansen went out of office, and in their stead were chosen as Elders in the Congregation, Jonas Hertzel and Ulrich Knecht.

ANNO 1790.

January 31. In the Christian Reformed Congregation at Dryland the two deacons ("Almosen-pfleger"—almoners, overseers), Mr. John Ehrit and John Hertzel went out of office, and in their stead were chosen and duly obligated before the congregation as "Almonsen-pfleger," George Roether and John Schneider.

ANNO 1793.

The Consistory of the Church at Dryland was constituted as follows: *Elders*, Ulrich Knecht, Philip Faas; *Deacons*, George Roether, John Schneider.

ANNO 1793.

December 25. Ulrich Knecht, the elder to this time of the Reformed Dryland Congregation ("bisheriger aeltister") went out of office, and in his stead as elder was chosen, and on the 29th December was presented to the Christian Congregation and to his office duly obligated as elder—Bernhardt Arndt.

Church Records. 401

ANNO 1794.

November 30. Philip Faas, elder to date ("bisheriger aeltister") laid down his office, and in his stead was chosen George Rhoeder, thus far a deacon; and in his stead John Erit. Both were installed in their several offices, December 28.

Elder, GEORGE RHOEDER.
Deacon, JOHN ERIT.

THE CONGREGATION AT PLAINFIELD.

ANNO 1786.

The following persons constituted the consistory in the Christian congregation at "Blaenfield" (Plainfield): *Elders*, Caspar Doll, George Henry Young; *Deacons*, Henry Hauser, Philip Fendt.

ANNO 1787.

In the month of September, Caspar Doll and George Henry Young went out of office as Elders, and in their stead were chosen and installed Valentine Metz and Joseph Keller, both as deacons (?) of the congregation.

ANNO 1788.

After a due Church settlement Henry Hauser and Philip Fendt went out of office, and in their stead were chosen and obligated as elders—George Trumbauer (?) and Peter Pender.

ANNO 1789.

In the fall of the year Mr. Valentine Metz and Joseph Keller went out of office, and in their stead were chosen and obligated Philip Achenbach and Jacob Keller.

ANNO 1793.

The consistory at Plainfield consisted of the following persons: *Elders*, Philip Achenbach, Henry Happel; *Deacons*, Diedrich Bauer, Frederick Hahn.

Anno 1794.

In this year the two elders, Philp Achenbach and Henry Happel, laid down their offices, and in their places as elders were elected " die bisherigen vorsteher " — the deacons, Diedrich Bauer and Frederick Hahn, and as deacons Abraham Heller and Philip Keller. These were, on the 16th of November, 1794, brought before the congregation and consecrated to their several offices. *Elders*, Diedrich Bauer, Frederick Hahn; *Deacons*, Abraham Heller, Philip Keller.

CONCLUSION.

It may be worth while to call the reader's attention to the fact that the above meager extracts from the proceedings of the consistories of these several churches show that it was not customary, in that day, and in the Reformed Church, for the same persons to succeed themselves in office as elders as deacons. When their terms of office expired, others were elected in their stead.

Here the editor lays down his pen and brings his long and interesting work to a conclusion. His purpose originally was simply to translate and publish the contents of the two oldest of the church books in the possession of the congregation. This he has now done. There are besides these two church books three others of a more recent date. These future pastors may care for. The editor's purpose was merely to put the oldest and most valuable records of the congregation in such a form that they could be neither lost nor destroyed by fire. It is really a wonder that these old books were not long since destroyed by fire or lost by careless handling. When they are once printed and distributed no carelessness and no fire can ever destroy a lose *all* of the copies published. That these precious records may be preserved is the hope of the editor, and that every one who turns over the pages of these records of Christian people, long since gone to the better world, may have his name written in the Lamb's Book of Life is his most earnest prayer.

"Then they that feared the Lord spake often to one another; and the Lord hearkened, and heard it, and a book

of remembrance was written before Him for them that feared the Lord, and that thought upon His name.

"And they shall be mine, saith the Lord of Hosts, in that day when I make up my jewels, and I will spare him as a man spareth his own son that serveth him. Then shall ye return and discern between the righteous and the wicked, between him that serveth God and him that serveth Him not." *Malachi III., 16–18.*

"And I saw the dead, small and great, stand before God; and the books were opened; and another book was opened which is the book of life; and the dead were judged out of those things which were written in the books, according to their works." *Rev. XX., 12.*

FINIS.

INDEX OF SURNAMES

ABBIT, 382
ABEL, 90 98 104 139 143 149 162 179 180 188 201 210 231 234 236 275 300 331 338 345 358 360 376-379 383 385 388 390 397
ABLE, 176
ACHE, 366 390
ACHENBACH, 44 77 78 96 101 105 110 127 292 346 352 354 355 401 402
ACKERMAN, 224 257 260 268 273 296 307 332 337 362 370 372 376 383 384 389-391
ADAM, 352
ADAMS, 48 385 391
ALBERT, 271 293 295 333 384
ALBRECHT, 109
ALGERT, 375
ALLEN, 296 364
ALSFELD, 328 369 383
ALSHOUSE, 6 7
ALT, 380
ALTEMOS, 362
ALTEMUS, 299 302
ALTHOUS, 297
AMATINCKA, 28

ANBERGER, 85
ANDERSON, 6
ANDON, 356
ANDRE, 319 320 349 359 362 364 366 372 382 388 394 397
ANDREAS, 373
ANDREE, 394
ANDREWS, 68 382 389
ANGLEMAYER, 368
ANGLEMEYER, 353 357
ANNEWALT, 90 91
ANTHONY, 190 355 366
APEL, 352
APLONA, 127
APPEL, 166 195 202 208 228 245 252 258 293 312 336 355 356 373 374 384 391 392
APPLE, 67 68 398
APPLEBACH, 359
ARENDT, 92
ARMSTRONG, 357
ARND, 107 112 114 116 117
ARNDT, 8 9 57 84 88 92 93 100 120 122 126 129 130 149 165 177 185 192 234 247 278 286 289 290 298 299 306 308 311 320 322 351 352 357 361-363

ARNDT (Continued)
  366 367 373 376 390 396 400
ARNER, 154 161 182 198 218 248
  267-269 276 339 350 354 359
  379 382 387 391 397
ARNHOLD, 344
ARNOLD, 112 302 353 358 365
  393
ASHEIER, 84
AUBER, 90
AYER, 17 200
BAB, 136 147
BABB, 160 203 360 396
BACHMAN, 7 63 86 114 129 253
  320 353 356 359 364 365 371
  372 374 391
BACKAW, 257
BADER, 311
BAEDEKER, 283
BAEYSHER, 186
BAHN, 397
BAIER, 133
BAKER, 355 356
BALD, 299
BALDY, 238 364
BALL, 393
BALLIET, 290 319 328 358
BALLIETT, 334 379 385 387
BANES, 357
BARBER, 378 381 384 387 393
BARLEY, 380 384
BARNES, 17 224 229 240 264 276
  319 351 354 355 386 393
BARNET, 172 266
BARNETT, 184 299 301 359 365
  372
BARNS, 216 323
BARON, 374

BARR, 379
BARRON, 334
BARTEL, 158
BARTELMAI, 356
BARTELMEI, 390
BARTHOLD, 44 79 123 124 133
  176 203 236 239 246 274 281
  319 352 356 370 373
BARTHOLOMEW, 347
BARTOLMAI, 351
BARTOLMEI, 294
BASLER, 352 384
BASSINGER, 321 385 387
BASSLER, 166
BATT, 172 173 297 299 315 353
  356 359 374 380
BATY, 276
BAUER, 104 310 313 315 319 321
  325 328 330 334 343 354 355
  358 360 374 376 377 381 385
  387 388 390 391 394 399 401
  402
BAUERS, 220 237
BAUMAN, 328 352
BAUMGARDT, 394
BAUMGART, 343
BAUMGARTEN, 218 269 334
  385
BAUMGARTNER, 288
BAYER, 196 292
BAYNES, 296
BEARD, 220
BEAVER, 384
BECHTEL, 274
BECK, 29 34 58 61 62 67 69 72
  139 201 265 316 339 349 351
  356 357 361 363 369 391
BECKER, 6 7 44 52 56 69 77 78

BECKER (Continued)
  87 89 93 95 103 130 134 278-
  280 283 286 302 345 346 381
BEIDLER, 383
BEIER, 285
BEIL, 307
BEILMAN, 353
BEISCHER, 178
BEISEL, 306 330 345 352 363 386
BEISELL, 305 316 363 372 386
BEISHER, 87 154 287 317 383
  388
BEISSEL, 279 290
BEISSELL, 312 313 320 335
BEITELMAN, 148 150 152 153
  156 161 185 190 195 201 203
  207 313 352 364 378
BEITZE, 385
BEKER, 50
BELELS, 204 315
BELL, 388
BELLES, 191 232 251 258 269 310
  313 359 365 366 373 374 376
  381 384 387
BELLESFIELD, 344 389 393
BELLING, 196
BENDER, 9 109 118 142 208 263
  295 307 332 335 336 337 342
  344 366 368-370 373 374 377
  379 381 382 390 391 393 394
BENNER, 308
BERGE, 300
BERGER, 353 393
BERGSTRAESER, 374 390 392
BERGTRAESSER, 376
BERLIN, 6 28 85 86 97 98 99 117
  119
BERND, 109 143 160 190 288

BERNDT, 217
BERNHARD, 97
BERNTZ, 105
BERRY, 17 212 223 235 247 301
  335 359 372 375 384 385 394
BERSTLER, 374 376
BERTHOLD, 78 115 117 155
BESS, 205 208 218 221 224 237
  242 246 249 252 255 257 259
  261 264 267 269 272 273 275
  306 308 310 315 318 321 325
  329 331 332 358 361 362 367
  370 373 379 383
BEST, 44 50 78-80 83 87 90 91 92
  98 99 103 105 107 111 115 116
  118 120 124-126 131 132 135
  140 144 150 170 190 198 213
  280 281 284 292 295 346 347
  350 352 355 388 390 397
BETTINGER, 260
BETZERBACHER, 85
BEULLER, 346
BEUTELMAN, 100
BEUTELMANN, 108
BEYER, 120 128 144 281 282
BEYL, 372
BEYSELL, 354
BEYTELMAN, 171
BIBIGHAUS, 56 76
BIEBER, 359
BIEGLY, 393
BIELER, 397
BIER, 207 352
BIERS, 191 230 246 336 369
BIERY, 380
BIESECKER, 177 380
BIJI, 102
BILLHEIMER, 345 347 355 356

BILLHEIMER (Continued)
  361
BINNINGER, 264
BISCHOF, 121
BISCHOFF, 111 280 281
BISEKER, 110
BISHOFF, 196 300 354
BISHOP, 202 242 249 260 275
  348 388
BISHOPH, 184 211 225 232 302
  352 357
BISSECKER, 346 347
BITTENBENDER, 44 233 241
  254 263 272 308 348
BITTENBENNER, 362 364
BLAAR, 381
BLACK, 66 76 256 262
BLAECKLEY, 176
BLATZ, 94
BLOTZ, 389
BLUHM, 369
BLUM, 83 88 92 281 388 396
BLUMEN, 300
BOAS, 365
BOATZ, 371
BODEIN, 313
BODINE, 363
BOECKEL, 385
BOEHLER, 122
BOEHM, 310 358 366 374
BOEM, 305
BOHRUM, 371
BOLSAPPEL, 397
BOMBERGER, 56-58 69 395
BOND, 236 239 244
BONSTEIN, 9
BOOREM, 303
BOP, 172

BOREIN, 297
BORGER, 347
BORUM, 304 372
BOSCH, 380
BOSSART, 302 341 397
BOTZER, 93
BOULSBY, 311
BOUSCH, 385
BOWERS, 377 380 384
BOYER, 98 114 155 162 170 180
  227 242 269 290 292 295 302
  311 314 315 318-320 327 332
  335 341 347 349 353 356 370
  374 378 381 398
BRADER, 349
BRAEDER, 352
BRAUCKER, 177
BRAUN, 131 140 296 349 351
  353
BRECHT, 145
BREIDINGER, 338 364 390
BREING, 93
BREINIG, 93
BREITER, 93
BREITINGER, 368
BRINKER, 201 215 225 243 257
  321 325 338 374 375 378 389
BRITTON, 349
BROD, 346 352
BROEDER, 140 151 164 179 195
  208 210 217 219 230 250 260
  263 268 307 312 317 328 335
  338 356 357 361 365 371 372
  380 381 393 397
BROEKER, 367
BROG, 346
BRONCE, 212
BROTSMAN, 138 177 366 368

BROTSMAN (Continued)
 375
BROTZMAN, 87 99 102 121 130
 132-135 137 141 151 159 160
 162 163 168 191 216 217 224
 248 255 256 260 263 269 273
 294 295 309 316 319 333 335
 344 366 372
BROTZMANN, 88 109
BROWERS, 371
BROWN, 142 195 236 317 350
 354 356 366 368 369 372 378
 380
BRUCH, 83 86 96 115 118 147
 151 156 158 173 179 203 204
 210 217 238 252 272 287 302
 312 324 327 374 378 386
BRUG, 86 111 144 148 150
BRUNNER, 359 398
BRUTSMAN, 206
BUCH, 358
BUCHANNAN, 367
BUGELLY, 363
BULL, 22-27
BULLEING, 397
BUNDIN, 335
BUNDSTEIN, 308 332 340 355
 357 361 371 373 378 383 392
BUNSTON, 9
BUNTEN, 337
BUNTIN, 377 382 387 388
BURKE, 17 199 355 394
BURNSIDES, 16 206 219
BUSCH, 50 92 103 109-111 119
 121 344
BUSH, 7 96
BUSKIRK, 357
BUSS, 106 177 302 307 311 312

BUSS (Continued)
 314 315 320 342 356 364 365
 367 369 370 374 384 391 392
 396
BUTS, 287
BUTZ, 9 44 53 76 78-80 83-85 87
 90 91 93 94 100 101 103 105
 112 114 124 126 127 139 142
 147 152 163 165 171 194 205
 213 216 223 233 244 248 252
 261 268 300 304 314 316 317
 321 322 329 343 350 351 353
 354 358-360 363 368 372 377
 381 388 390 391
BYLLESBY, 363
CALL, 374
CALLING, 359
CANAAN, 326 330 375
CANAN, 323
CANE, 379
CAREY, 17 191 214 222 230 248
 258 392
CARL, 369 379 391
CARLING, 398
CARLSON, 13
CARPENTER, 364 368
CARR, 365
CARTY, 398
CARWELL, 394
CASEBIER, 354
CASTNER, 240 369
CAWLEY, 392
CHAPMAN, 7
CHIDSEY, 75 76
CHOREL, 79 80
CHORELL, 345
CHRISTEIN, 375 378
CHRISTINE, 383

CHRISTMAN, 274 288 305 320 324 327 352 365
CLASS, 399
CLAUS, 192 209 363 364
CLAUSS, 214 322 335 367 382 384
CLEMENS, 17 165
CLEWELL, 363 367 390 391
CLEWER, 381
CLIFFTON, 232
CLIFTON, 17 199
COAL, 390
COHL, 343
COHLMAN, 356
COLD, 346
COLE, 306 373 374
COLEMAN, 142 145 150 152 178 201 202 223 238 242 250 251 253 255 257 263 264 266 288 303 317 323 356 365 367 368 370 376 377 380 386 397
COLLMAN, 141
COLLMAR, 398
CONNARD, 361
CONRAD, 137 153 176 256 306 316 344 355
CONWAY, 29
COOPER, 348 381
CORD, 379
COREL, 127 133
CORELL, 107 116 127 133
CORREL, 164 173 182 186
CORRELL, 131 146 149 169 178 179 189 193 197 198 200 201 203 205 206 208 214 219 285 297 347 348 352 357 364 367 374-376 379 391
COWERT, 344

COWLEY, 372
CRAIG, 6
CRAMER, 87
CRAMM, 364
CRATZ, 296
CROFERTY, 393
CUMINGS, 76
CUNNINGHAM, 27 374 392
CURRY, 367
DAELING, 300
DAELY, 297
DAHN, 397
DALEY, 365
DALLI, 108
DALTON, 364
DANIEL, 93 228 297 312 324 360 369 377
DANN, 109
DANNAKER, 45 70
DANNER, 366 369
DAUBERT, 398
DAVENPORT, 397
DAVIS, 17 159 204 371 373 390
DEAN, 22 25 28 226 231
DEANE, 23
DEBINDER, 143
DEBIS, 284
DECAS, 385
DECH, 92 111 112 139 155 161 167 180 202 263 309 325 327 329-331 340 343 347 349 351 353 369 373 376 377 380 383 385 388 390 393 394 396 398
DECHANT, 220
DECHART, 184
DECHET, 106
DECK, 342
DECKER, 323 357

DEHART, 359
DEHASEN, 283
DEHLI, 296
DEHMER, 364
DEICHER, 110
DEICHMAN, 44 78 79 95 104
    114 116 119 125 211 224 277
    307 353 378 384 385 387
DEIGMAN, 77 78
DEIGMANN, 77
DEILY, 197 231 238 249 259 267
    360 361 363
DELACOUR, 105
DELLIKER, 105
DELONG, 298 313 326 360 367
DELPHERTZ, 103
DEMOND, 365
DEMOTT, 360
DEMUTH, 363 364
DENGLER, 85 89 95 104 105 121
    124 128 133 211 215 217 228
    229 237-239 251 298 299 307
    309 344 357 360 391
DENLER, 50
DENNIS, 258 328 358
DENSON, 365
DEPU, 17
DEPUE, 197
DERHAMER, 396
DERHAMMER, 296
DERINGER, 113 119 124 349
DERR, 153 257 264 304 308 313
    314 317 322 323 327 329 331
    340 367 368 370 383 386 389
    398
DERRHAMMER, 326 360 394
DERST, 339
DESCHLER, 316 366

DESHLAR, 357
DESHLER, 182 361
DEWALD, 358 361
DEWALT, 252 331 335 366 370
    374 376 387 388 394
DEWITT, 237 353 363 364 380
DEYLI, 249
DICKSON, 368
DIEDER, 140
DIEDRICH, 149
DIEHL, 156 254 261 306 313 315
    316 332 334 337 343 368-371
    374 378 380 383 385 387 389
    390
DIEL, 106 291 292 302 357 363
DIEMER, 197 202 210 214 301
    351
DIETER, 383
DIETERICH, 178
DIETRICH, 211 238 262 299 304
    307 330 351 354 381
DIETS, 184 304
DIETZ, 84 86 132 141 143 145
    151 153 157 166 167 169 191
    195 196 206 216 221 238 254
    292 296 301 307 309 312 327
    328 331 333 343 349 357 366
    368 369 387 391 398
DIGEMAN, 190
DIKENSCHIDT, 344
DILCHER, 131
DILLINGER, 302 398
DILY, 357
DINGES, 321
DIWLER, 98
DOAN, 359
DODENDORF, 192
DOERING, 136 219 237 363

DOERINGER, 132 240 331 368
DOERR, 290
DOFFARD, 160
DOFFERT, 333 346 374
DOFFT, 150
DOLL, 84 89 282 360 401
DOPHARD, 103
DOPHART, 112
DORINGER, 129
DORNBLAESER, 289 358-361
DORSHEIMER, 94
DOTTERER, 126 183 184 281
DOWN, 379
DRACHEL, 130
DRACHSEL, 77 78 102 112
DRAHN, 205
DRASBACH, 390
DREIN, 380
DREISBACH, 112 115 138 155 176 193 252 296 298 303 304 313 328 331 342 351 355 358 370 385 388
DRIESBACH, 115 384
DRITTENBURG, 152
DROEHL, 110
DRUM, 120
DRUMHELLER, 50 111 138 141 146 340
DRUMMHELLER, 113 114
DUER, 356
DUFFART, 96
DUGLAS, 387
DULL, 84
DUMI, 103
DUNBAR, 394
DUPPER, 314
DURSCHHEIMER, 105
EBBEL, 9
EBENREITER, 345
EBERHARD, 104 123 131 133 344 347
EBERHARDT, 359
EBERHART, 229
EBERTS, 367
ECKART, 195 250 257 366 368 371
ECKEL, 318
ECKER, 219 223 391
ECKERT, 324 326 373 381 392 393
EDELMAN, 178 194 234 237 242 250 252 257 260 261 272 327 351 370 371 383 387 388
EDINGER, 305
EDMISTON, 350
EDMONDS, 363 383
EHLER, 99 112
EHRENFIELD, 102
EHRETH, 291
EHRGUTH, 370
EHRICH, 15 95 105
EHRIG, 15 111 112
EHRIT, 351 394 400
EICHELBERGER, 377
EICHELMEIER, 284
EICHMAN, 234 259 332 365 366 376
EIERMAN, 226
EIGHORNE, 287
EIPPEL, 313
EKART, 310
ELICK, 349
ELLEN, 97 345
ELLERSICK, 334
ELLIOT, 390
EMICK, 232

EMIG, 189 203 384
EMMERICH, 303 396
EMRICH, 126 132 297 366
EMROD, 368
ENGEL, 112 134 135 137 185 197 208 226 254 280 300 305 309 314 318 319 323 325 336 338 341 361 363 375 377 391 392 394
ENGELHART, 286
ENGELMAN, 378
ENGLE, 98 326
ENGLER, 294 318 335 364 367 377 391 393
ENNES, 165 187 211 299 351
ERB, 115 117 155 164 165 176 192 203 216 246 301 326
ERDMAN, 120
ERETT, 341
ERICH, 15 227 239 318 322 361 394 398
ERIG, 15 102-104
ERINGER, 186
ERIT, 350 401
ERITT, 139 211 216 299 336 337 348 351 356 361 363 397
ERL, 364
ERNDFRIED, 98
ERNST, 346 393 397
ERRITT, 338
ERVIN, 249
ERVINE, 348 349
ERWINE, 357
ESCH, 374
ESCHBACH, 298
ESSER, 6 7
ESSERT, 246 253
ESSIG, 114

ETTINGER, 181 186 197 247 273 295 308 354 373
EVA, 360
EVANS, 69 271
EVERIG, 50
EVERITT, 234 371 376
EWALD, 287
EWART, 157
EWERITT, 157
EWERITZ, 102
EWING, 50 193 254
EYER, 206 293
EYERMAN, 66 127 167 172 185 348
EYLENBERGER, 297
FAAS, 312 323 327 400 401
FABER, 247 292
FABION, 391
FACHNUETH, 358
FACKENTHAL, 356
FAEBEL, 313 366 371
FALKINSON, 17
FALSTICH, 362
FARLING, 390
FASBINDER, 284
FAUERBACH, 392
FAUST, 89 382
FAVI, 353
FEBEL, 332 370
FEEMAN, 378
FEHR, 147 166 247 302 307 309 314 364 378 381 385
FEIDT, 124 126
FEIT, 238 240 340 353 357
FEITH, 99
FELL, 112
FELLENSER, 302
FELLIS, 353

FENDT, 401
FENGEL, 234 390 392 394
FENNER, 78 79 122 128 297 303 351 356 360 363
FENSTERMAKER, 396
FERRILL, 365
FETTERMAN, 365
FIERBACH, 384
FIERER, 248 249
FIERLING, 382
FIET, 298
FINDLEY, 391
FINLEY, 6 7
FISCHER, 344
FISHER, 234
FISHLER, 397 398
FITZ-RANDOLPH, 17 188 197 213
FITZ RANDOLPH, 236 376 389
FLEMSING, 202
FLICK, 338 339 347 352 360 366 384 389 390 394
FLORE, 344
FLORI, 88 93 100 110 134
FLORIN, 93
FLORY, 124 136 344 348 349 392
FLUCK, 350 397
FLUK, 397
FOCHT, 172
FODREDT, 122
FOGEL, 161
FOLKINSON, 213
FOLMER, 205 270 276 356 357 384
FORCE, 17 172 348
FORRE, 89
FORS, 299
FORSE, 160 182 190

FORTNER, 326 379 397
FOX, 82 83 92 99 166 228 281 351 361 366 369 393
FRAES, 44 77 78 104 107 112 115 120 126 127 141 198 203 351
FRAESS, 116 156 157 163 251 382 391
FRANCKENFIELD, 356
FRANKENFELD, 210 250 295
FRANKENFIELD, 222 224 238 258 315 331 339 340 364 369 381 386 392
FRANTZ, 167 297 310 314 333 359 361 371
FRANZ, 136 367 397
FRAUENFELD, 178 348
FRAUENFELDER, 116 124 129 169 170 182 195 203 205 215 216 227 236 242 300 307 353 356 358 385 392
FRAUNFELDER, 112
FREDERICK, 84 153 283 354 378 389
FREDRICK, 377
FREEMAN, 133 298 311 314 316 327 348 349 354 362-365 368 374 383
FREES, 181 190 209 212 214 230 265 268 274 317 363 364 367 375 393
FREEWELL, 350
FREIMAN, 294
FRES, 113 121
FREY, 140 160 169 170 173 192 223 228 266 268 269 303 309 311 318 324 326 329 341 342 349 352 355 358 360 362 365 367 378 382 386-389 392 396

FRICH, 345
FRICKER, 7
FRIDRICH, 319
FRIED, 359 381
FRIEDERICH, 105
FRIEDRICH, 104
FRIEMAN, 358
FRIES, 150 167
FRITSCHIE, 293
FRITZ, 138 302 338 339 384 385 389 390 393
FROELICH, 371
FROELIG, 271 327 366 373 380
FRUTCHMAN, 274
FRUTSCHI, 104 114 347
FRUTSCHIE, 169
FRUTSCHMAN, 245 358 361 384
FRUTSCHY, 344 349
FRYTAG, 186
FUHR, 334 340 354 358 378 380 381 390
FULKINSON, 361
FULLER, 7
FULLERT, 28
FULMER, 76
FUNCK, 368
GAEHRES, 255
GANGENWEHR, 255
GANGENWER, 236
GANGENWERE, 307
GANGEWER, 82
GANGWER, 82
GANGWERE, 348
GANZEL, 393
GARDNER, 324 378
GARRISON, 359
GASTON, 17 215 377

GAUER, 303
GAUSNER, 376
GEARER, 347
GEBHARDT, 382
GEBHART, 50
GEHRES, 159 241 254 256 264 265 273 308 310 313 315 365 366 375 392 394
GEHRINGER, 367
GEHRIS, 384
GEHRY, 199 242
GEIDING, 181
GEIGER, 324 335 339 359 388
GEISHLE, 79
GEISLI, 134
GEISSLE, 78 79 80 121 124
GELLMAN, 152
GEORGE, 290 339 340 360 367 374 376 378 385 386
GEORGE III, KING OF ENGLAND 11
GEREY, 208 353
GERHARDT, 303 371 383
GERHART, 329
GERINGER, 289 351
GERMANTON, 282 305 314 318 342 359 367 384 385
GERN, 129
GERY, 179 190 208 354
GETTER, 167 267 306 319 326 392
GETTERT, 42 77
GETTHERT, 86
GEWINNER, 86 142 287 344
GHENT, 303
GIES, 7 309
GIESER, 92 278 301
GILMOR, 356

GILTNER, 370
GINGINGER, 334 350
GINNARD, 325 329 358
GINNART, 326
GINNERT, 115
GINTHAR, 365
GIRT, 382
GISER, 345
GISH, 362
GLAAS, 99
GLASNER, 284
GLASS, 282 290 322 349 352
GLOECKNER, 131
GLOESSNER, 281
GODLEY, 360
GOEBEL, 119
GOETZ, 346
GOGEN, 388
GOLD, 371 389
GOOD, 346
GORDON, 6 7
GOREL, 79 122 123
GORR, 388
GORRELL, 122
GOTTHARD, 118
GOTTSCHALL, 371 389
GOTTSHAL, 398
GRADWOHL, 312 338 341 343 351 374 385
GRAMER, 87
GRASS, 310
GRATWOHL, 386
GRAY, 17 54 216 236 360 392
GREBER, 210 215
GREEN, 17 28 157
GREILING, 362
GRESS, 9 41 44 50 78 82 84 93 96 102 106 108 112 113 115 116

GRESS (Continued)
119 124 128 263 288 296 301 361
GRESS(IE), 81
GRESSIG, 82
GRESSMAN, 353
GRIESEMER, 103
GRIMES, 360
GROOS, 90
GROSS, 93 139 149 154 168 185 216 290 297 305 339 350 352 357 362 364 370 373 380 384 386
GROTZ, 110 117 153 255 348 356
GROUP, 397
GROUSE, 9
GROVES, 186
GRUB, 83 89 102 104 109 148 167
GRUBB, 302
GRUBER, 152 199 213 288 304 305 327 341 342 354-358 362 367 372 383 384 392 394 398
GUENNERT, 114
GUET, 286
GULICK, 165 176 192 203 216 246
GUM, 301 338 348
GUNDT, 373
GUT, 346
GUTH, 139 380
GUTZEL, 306
HAACK, 179 227
HAAG, 105 119 224 278
HAAK, 316 363 365 383
HAAS, 217 221 250 314 343 357 359 361 367 391 392
HACH, 106
HACKETT, 361

HACKMAN, 132 140 150 177 192 200 206 215 227 240 245 253 261 263 308 320 337 357 361 378 381 389 391 392
HACKNEY, 384
HAENTZ, 399
HAFNER, 303
HAG, 99
HAGENBACH, 370
HAGENBUCH, 275 356 376 381 383
HAHN, 9 44 78 183 292 304 309-311 313 318 325 330 332-334 338 342 343 348 351 354 355 361-363 367 369 371 373 376 377 379 381-386 390 392-394 396-398 401 402
HAIN, 297
HAK, 97
HALL, 361
HALTEMAN, 324 328 355 359 370 376
HAMBERT, 154
HAMMEL, 317
HANDLEIN, 388
HANDSCHU, 369
HANDSHILL, 150
HANDSHU, 316 338 339 363 367 372 378 389 390
HANDSHUE, 321 396
HANKE, 365
HAPPEL, 294 298 301 316 325 330 331 339 341 347 350 351 368-370 379 384 385 386 392 401 402
HARBAUGH, 41 49
HARDIEMER, 376
HARDY, 320 323
HARE, 386
HARENDORF, 170
HARLACHER, 380
HARLEY, 288
HARMANEY, 377
HARRIS, 7 334
HART, 6 7
HARTENDORF, 223 358 382
HARTMAN, 142 215 291 309 311 377 381
HARTZEL, 140 390
HARTZELL, 9
HARZEL, 317
HASENFUSS, 264 265
HASSELBACH, 125
HASSENFUSS, 371
HAUCH, 153 161 176 189 208 322 354
HAUCK, 171 203 214 308 341 350 351 352 355 356 359 364 368
HAUER, 321 352
HAUL, 345
HAUPT, 367 376 389
HAUSER, 114 122 277 303 334 338 339 347 353 359 386 387 390 401
HAY, 9 83-88 90 94 96 97 101 107 108 124 137 138 146 147 151 152 171 173 186 189 190 200 224 232 233 247-249 255 256 271 288 307 312 332 336 337 344 360 374 380 396
HAYDEN, 17 199 354 366 376
HAYES, 247
HAYN, 207
HAYNEY, 258
HAYSLETT, 353

HEBERLING, 375
HECHT, 316
HECK, 270 315 379
HECKMAN, 134 156 157 159
  191 199 210 219 233 243 250
  258 267 272 273 307 316 323
  329 337 349 361 362 365 376
  378 381 384 387
HEFFELFINGER, 294
HEID, 384
HEIL, 147 185 208 346 358 361
  363
HEILMAN, 326
HEIMER, 294 296 312 314 337
  344 357 361 372 386 397
HEIMRICH, 87
HEINEY, 341
HEINLEIN, 190 255 256 299 313
  390
HEINLY, 306
HEINTZ, 387
HEISLER, 62 68
HEISS, 392
HEISTER, 359 393
HEITSMAN, 393
HELICK, 110 230 357 364 372
  387 388
HELLER, 66 96 127 138 182 190
  194 203 218 219 226 239 243
  291 292 298 299 300 303-305
  307 309 310 312 317 319 320
  328 330-332 334 336 337 339
  346 352 355 359 361 362 367
  369 372-375 376 378-381 384-
  389 390 394 396-398 402
HELLICK, 51 335 386
HELLMAN, 392
HELWICK, 396

HEMB, 105
HEMBD, 88
HEMP, 196 200 216 229
HEMSING, 220 224 338 387
HENDSHU, 343
HENJON, 362
HENN, 367 372
HENOP, 11 41-43 69 77 82 92
HENRICH, 333 376
HENRY, 100
HENSEL, 366 396
HENTZ, 100
HEPLER, 381
HEPP, 101 105
HERGER, 323
HERING, 90 367 378
HERLINGER, 233 358
HERMAN, 80 127 144 196 277
  278 283 343 377
HERMANN, 51 52 69 78 118 120
  124 277 278 343 345
HERR, 87
HERST, 387
HERSTER, 97 110 129 143 147
  159 172 185 234 266 304 383
HERT, 348
HERTER, 301
HERTZ, 106 139
HERTZEL, 110 118 123 124 129
  130 132 139 142 145 152 159
  160 163 179 180 187 193 212
  215 217 220 228 281-283 287
  288 297 298 300 303 351-354
  358-360 363 400
HERTZELL, 223 227-229 280 311
  313
HERTZLER, 114 162
HERZ, 376 393

HERZEL, 96 97 202 203 243 324 328 332 336 341 343 346 360 361 367 373 377 379 380-382 385 388-391 393 394
HERZELL, 239 240 243 247 250 252 255 256 259 262 264 265 270 316 321 325 327 333 365 371 376 378
HESS, 50 54 66 78 79 83 84 90 91 93 96 98 101 102 104 108-111 114 115 118 122 123 126 132 134 139 173 198 209 219 225 287 292 293 298 299 301 319 321 329 337 344 345 347-352 354 356-358 361 362 365-367 370 375 377 387 389 391 394
HESSINGER, 387
HEYL, 85 339 387
HEYMER, 88
HIGGINS, 363
HILDEBRAND, 375
HILGER, 133
HILL, 344
HILLE, 124
HILLGART, 202
HILLIARD, 91 367
HILLIARDT, 356
HILLIART, 239 244 259 293 297 320 355 368 369 378
HILLYARD, 17
HILYART, 293
HINCKEL, 364
HINKEL, 334 368 370
HINKLE, 336
HINNERLIN, 93
HINSEY, 398
HIPP, 111
HIRTE, 109 302
HOE, 358 359 374 382
HOENIG, 301 312 331 363 370 371 386
HOENING, 326
HOENY, 329 393
HOFFART, 295 350 366
HOFFEDITZ, 54 56 307
HOFFERT, 311 386
HOFFMAN, 7 258 262 297 308 315 362 366 372 374 392
HOFFMANN, 106
HOHENSCHILD, 358 367
HOHL, 336 340
HOLL, 87 322 396
HOLLAND, 99 149 186 198 208 328 348 367
HOLLART, 239
HOLLER, 341
HOPE, 331 386 389
HORN, 7 84 96 102 107 143 146 152 159 191 198 221 222 229 240 321 322 339 355 357
HORNBECK, 201
HORNECKER, 310 342 392
HORNING, 378
HORRACE, 369
HORTENDORF, 194 385 396
HORTI, 102
HOWARD, 396
HOWEL, 287
HOWELL, 16 154 177 347
HUBER, 75 76 198 347 355 358 364 365 368 373 374 382 398
HUBLER, 132
HUDCHINS, 136 347
HUEBLER, 285
HUELLERS, 279
HUERSTER, 110

HUETTENDORFF, 279
HUETTINGER, 335
HUFFSCHMIDT, 344
HUFSCHMIDT, 301
HUHM, 236
HULL, 87
HULTEMAN, 299
HUMES, 337
HUMMEL, 326 332 344 352 355 390
HUNT, 361
HUNTER, 340
HURTENDORF, 187
HUTCHIN, 267
HUTCHINS, 333
HUTCHINSON, 67
HUTH, 157
HUTHMACHER, 364
HUTTENDORF, 178
HYLE, 381
IDERLE, 396-398
IDERLEY, 392
IDERLY, 390
IHRICH, 94 128
IHRIE, 15 94 95 226
IHRIG, 83 116 129
ILLIK, 279
IMICH, 363 364
IMICK, 318
IMMICK, 396
INGOLD, 41 49 51 69 77 81 95 96 98 100 105 113 117 118 119
INNES, 375 380 388 389
IRVINE, 149
JACKSON, 17 157
JACOBS, 131 158
JACOBY, 233 237 257 300 307 349 365 377 379 384 386 389

JACOBY (Continued) 391
JAEGER, 9
JANSAN, 139
JANSEN, 285 292 320 329-332 334 340 341 368 369 375 381 382 384-386 388 390 398 400
JANSON, 142 213 231 256 286 293 297 308 350 358 370 387
JARRETT, 368
JETESTER, 360
JOHNSON, 230 267 285 359 396
JOHNSTON, 89
JONES, 222 329 359 363 367 391
JONLUS, 398
JONSON, 347
JOSEPH, 380
JUMPER, 15 147 158 167 168 187 205 230 238 287 366 386
JUNKER, 196
JUNKIN, 16 207 387 388
JUNT, 387
JUSTICE, 186
KACHLEIN, 397
KACHLINE, 50
KAEMER, 286
KAEMMERER, 90 138 181 192 194 283
KAEMPER, 371
KAEMRER, 142 145 152 159 161 163 166 184 188 204 205 214 223 237 246 248 288 290 304 315 317 329 331 335 337 339 340 342 347 351 356 360 361 363 371-373 376 379 380 383 384 388 394
KAEYSER, 388
KAHN, 352

KAKNAH, 28
KATZ, 194
KAUFFMAN, 363 368
KEDER, 173
KEEL, 84
KEGEL, 281
KEHL, 82
KEHLER, 100
KEIFER, 221
KEIL, 126 344
KEIM, 324 355 361 365 381 386 389
KEINS, 280
KEIPER, 211 223 244 259 270 292 344 360 371 373 386
KEISER, 314 362 386
KELCHNER, 393
KELER, 100
KELIDER, 197
KELLAR, 350
KELLER, 44 63 80 98 111 115 121 124 125 139 143 146 156 157 163 166 167 180 205 209 210 215 226 239 249 258 264 265 272 279 280 287 294-299 307 317 327 344 351 352 354 357 361 362 366-368 372 373 375 376 381 383 391-394 401 402
KELLWICH, 297
KELLY, 374 391
KELSO, 261
KELSOPH, 365
KEMMERER, 44 77 78 88 96 97 107 109
KEMPER, 394
KEMRER, 218 318 352 397
KENNEDY, 365 377
KERCH, 364

KERCHENTHAL, 382
KERCHER, 353
KERES, 122
KERINGER, 285
KERKENTHAL, 366 372 386
KERN, 44 127 155 159 291 299 303 308 353 354 379 383
KERNER, 323 353
KERNT, 96
KERNY, 359
KERSTER, 141
KERZELL, 379
KESLER, 133 345 352
KESLINN, 129
KESSELER, 151
KESSLER, 116 122 132 135 139 168 173 186 198 214 215 233 236 255 256 287 294 308 360 363 364 373 375 378 386 396
KESSLY, 207
KICHLINE, 7 68 69
KIEBLER, 361
KIEFER, 221 260 389
KIEFFER, 62 63 67 68 69 75 76 135 162 179 180 245 256 295 350 357 373 378
KIELER, 138
KIETZ, 306
KILLPATRICK, 370
KINCAID, 370
KIND, 122 125 131 137 179 188 207 240 305 306 309 312-316 318 322 326 330 336 338 348 354 355 358 364 373 375 377 378 380 387-389 391
KINDT, 125
KING, 98
KINNER, 295

KINNEY, 378
KINSEY, 261 271 273 276 369 372 394
KINTZIG, 345
KIRNSER, 91
KITTEL, 289
KLAUS, 139 161 168 295 298
KLAUSS, 169 242 246 366 375
KLEDER, 308 339 376 378 381 384 388
KLEES, 366 367
KLEHANS, 122
KLEIDER, 349
KLEIN, 100 158 190 204 212 221 249 257 276 343 346 357 362 364 393
KLEINHANS, 113
KLEINHAUS, 96
KLEINMAN, 351
KLEPPINGER, 352
KLERICKER, 305
KLESS, 99
KLOECKNER, 368 378
KLOEKNER, 282
KLOEMAN, 192 280
KLOEMANN, 124
KLOTZ, 7 316
KNAP, 398
KNAPPENBERGER, 361
KNAUS, 7 81 107 110 113 117 199 219 302 344
KNAUSS, 41 42 50 77 81 88 120 123 124 128 249 267 283 297 323 328 333 346 371 378-380
KNECHT, 90 162 180 201 209 210 223 237 281 290 293 295 303 306 308 311-313 318 333 343-345 347 348 352 353 361

KNECHT (Continued) 365 366 371 379 382 383 385 386 398 400
KNECT, 282
KNERR, 354
KNIERIEM, 280
KNOBEL, 236 328 366 378
KNOR, 347 348
KOCH, 87 91 93 94 96 99 102 104 109 110 118 143 149 151 162 163 170 177 181 182 188 204 212 216 218 222 223 225 232 239 241 245 246 256 258 265 269 288 305 313 316 319 321 324 333 336 338 340 341 345 350 355-357 366 368 369 373 375 377-380 386 388 394 397 398
KOCHER, 91 97 108 120 168 177 178 187 188 201 202 221 225 233-235 237 240 242 252 259 265 300 306 309-313 321 325 330 340 342 345 346 351-353 357 358 361 377 378 382 384 388 391 398
KOCHERT, 307
KOCHLEIN, 319
KOCHLER, 396
KOCKER, 221 334
KODHER, 369
KOECHLEIN, 94 128 165 183 195 198 207 209-211 224 230 231 235 239 242 252 259 260 263 269 273 301 315 322 324 325 330 335 337 339 340 349 353 362 369 370 373 375 376 379 382 385 391 392 396
KOECHLEM, 387

KOEHLER, 126 128 219 225 226 240 282 290 316 323 335 336 340 348 362 367 383 386 393 394
KOEMMERER, 126 400
KOEMPFER, 371
KOEMRER, 312 386
KOENIG, 94 143 153 177 181 195 205 279 285 289 294 296 322-324 333 336 340 343 353 355 363 365 369 370 373 375 376 381 387 388 390 391 393 398
KOEP, 388
KOESTER, 294 299 309 327 341 349 351 360
KOGAN, 380
KOGEN, 230 331 394
KOHL, 341 345 346 352 389
KOHLER, 207 358
KOHLMAN, 166 167 181
KOLEMAN, 178
KOOPER, 301
KORREL, 166
KORRELL, 142 144
KOSTENBADER, 375 381
KOSTER, 351
KOTZ, 158 178 188 210 237 238 304 312 340 353 357 360 363 383 385 387 394
KRAEMER, 220 237 247 290 317 349 392
KRAHN, 239 309 373
KRAMM, 366 379
KRAN, 317
KRATZ, 84 88 125 209
KRATZER, 158 293 306 355 362 368
KRAU, 350
KRAUSS, 134
KREAMER, 332
KREIDER, 156 178 386
KREIDLER, 305 308 328 333 334 341 342 351 352 356 361 362 369 371 374 377 381 392 393 396
KREIGER, 346
KREMER, 87 392
KREN, 81
KRESS, 200 285 349
KRESSLER, 371
KRESSMAN, 393
KRETZLER, 340
KROCH, 282
KROESGE, 267
KRONER, 309 312 317
KROTZ, 7 156 178 194 222 224 229 246 260 263 314 348 350 351 353 383 393
KUDER, 352
KUECHLEIN, 97 101 109 112 118 125 130 133 136 345
KUECHLINE, 121
KUESSEL, 292
KUHN, 100 108 118 159 177 238 288 351
KUNCKLER, 324
KUNKEL, 123
KUNKLER, 337
KUNSMAN, 370 379 382 390
KUNTZ, 387
KURTZ, 160
KUTSLER, 321 342
KUTZ, 203
KUTZLER, 215 241 251 268 271 274 342 387 390
LAABACH, 192

LABACH, 183 296 300 353
LABALL, 130 131 346
LABAR, 295 351
LABARRE, 86
LACKY, 188 213 356
LADDIG, 138 151 156 159 170
    184 188 196 208 210 218 224
    225 236 241 250 257 262 267
    269 270 274 282 309 314 315
    325 328 353 355 359 360 372
    386 392
LADICH, 87
LADIG, 79 80 83 123 125 344 345
LAEHR, 298
LAER, 50
LAHER, 126
LAHR, 137 212 291 361 387
LAKE, 391
LALOR, 66
LAMB, 202 213 219 232 243 269
    389 392
LAMBERT, 352 363 380
LANTZ, 158 162 166 171 187 200
    224 225 226 234 237 249 252
    265 266 267 271 303 308 309
    316 318 326 329 353 362 363
    370 371 382 387 388
LANZ, 345
LATTIG, 44 80 101 106 111 115
    121 130 132 134 135 143 168
    319
LAUB, 398
LAUBACH, 50 209 236 260 273
    305 310 313 314 321 324 329
    342 358 359 362 364-366 368
    369 371-374 376 377 382 397
LAUBENSTEIN, 339
LAUBER, 396
LAUCKS, 136
LAUDENBACH, 364
LAUDENBERG, 336
LAUDENBERGER, 340
LAUDERBACH, 119 357
LAUER, 299 306
LAUERBACH, 119
LAUMERSON, 347
LAUTZ, 177 200
LAUX, 99 103 108 132 287
LAVARE, 86
LAWAL, 352 353
LAWALD, 103 289 290 357 358
    400
LAWALL, 9 66 271 274 275 296
    309 311 317 320 324 328-330
    335 355 359 361 364 371 377
    382 385 388 390 391 392
LAWAR, 107 117 350
LAWRY, 27
LAYCOCK, 364
LEARY, 396
LECHLEITER, 275
LECHLITER, 393
LECHNER, 97
LEE, 378
LEFEBRE, 7
LEHN, 91 119 134 141 380
LEHR, 148 328 374 380 382 387
LEIBENGUTH, 305
LEIBERT, 197 393
LEIDI, 92
LEIDICH, 87 93 179
LEIDIG, 117 122 132 136 139-141
    159 166 190 251 274 300 313
    324 345 355 359 363 365 373
    377-379
LEIDY, 9 87 329 367 372 381 387

LEIGH, 391
LEIMBERG, 351
LEINBACH, 356
LEISNER, 389
LEITLING, 389
LEPPARD, 214
LEPPART, 219
LEPPER, 315
LERCH, 50 121 125 130 132 139
　　154 158 164 168 178 193 194
　　206 207 215-217 221 223 224
　　229 240 241 246 251 254 256
　　259 260 265 269 275 296 298
　　302 310 315 316 321 328 329
　　332 336 338 342 355 356 358
　　360 362 363 365-372 377 381
　　382 384 390 391 394 397 400
LERNER, 361
LESCH, 306
LESHER, 230 364
LEVAN, 209
LEVERS, 371
LEVITZ, 7
LEVY, 22 359
LEWERS, 102
LEWIS, 268
LEYDIG, 79 80 127 132 345
LICHLITER, 396
LICHT, 138
LICHTENWALTER, 385
LIEBENGUTH, 390
LIGHTCAP, 385
LIKFELD, 98 108
LINCOLN, 62
LINISHMIDT, 289
LINN, 301 398
LION, 93
LOCK, 319 334 372

LOCKARD, 353
LOEB, 385
LOECHNER, 345
LOEHR, 314 319 320 333 341 376
LOESCH, 320 326 380
LOESCHER, 241 261 270 391
LOESHER, 218 248 257 274 363
　　376
LOHR, 81
LOMBERT, 383
LONG, 260 359 377 378
LONGERSON, 17 138
LORENTZ, 262
LOSEY, 164
LOUDENBURG, 59
LOWAR, 114
LOWREY, 387
LOWRY, 53
LUCAS, 348
LUCKAR, 184
LUCKER, 142 158 180 191 216
　　248 301 347
LUDEWIG, 131
LUDWIG, 86 87 189 214
LUMBERT, 220 234 343 375
LUMERSON, 17 179
LUMMERSON, 268 371
LUTZ, 104 115 120 129 312 365
　　370 375 397
LYNN, 194 301 302 310 316 323
　　326 328 336 341 367 369 373-
　　375 379 380 383 385 393
MACCKY, 353
MACK, 341 366 374 386 394
MACKEL, 379
MACKEY, 298
MACKY, 348 353
MAGDALENA, 297

MAGRANN, 17
MAHNY, 344
MAIS, 275
MAJOR, 367 379
MALTER, 290
MALTHANER, 332
MANDEL, 137
MANN, 9 83 91 97 108 298 316 326 327 350 363 366
MARJARUM, 373
MARKS, 17 168 171 187 217
MARTENDORF, 393
MARTIN, 3 7 105 349 388
MASE, 294
MATTES, 183
MATZ, 350 393
MAUER, 92
MAUN, 85
MAURER, 85 197 205 259 268 301 318 336 338 369 374 376 379 381
MAUS, 354
MAY, 389
MAYER, 113 154 165 167 185 201 207 211 217 266 304 305 314 326 332 338 362 363 368 384 385 387 388
MAYERS, 331 380
MCCAN, 359
MCCARTY, 227 307
MCCAW, 363
MCCLAUGHIN, 249
MCCLEARY, 16 117
MCCLUEN, 357
MCCLUREY, 17
MCCLURY, 206
MCCRACKIN, 392
MCCRACKY, 356

MCDANIEL, 17 131 196
MCDANILL, 170
MCDANNOLD, 185
MCDAUNALD, 153
MCHOSE, 311 314 320 379
MCKINNEY, 370
MCMICHAEL, 374
MCMURRAY, 297
MCQUAW, 384
MECDANIEL, 16 131
MECHLIN, 180 355
MEDAG, 348
MEDDAG, 350
MEDLER, 250
MEHRWAEH, 381
MEHRWART, 334
MEHRWEIN, 362 372
MEIER, 94 132 284 285 346
MEIXEL, 44 50 58 81 82 98 102 119-121 126 129 130 134 148 163 344 348
MEIXELL, 48 50 135 222 287
MEIXSEL, 134 345
MEIXSELL, 178 190 199 204 220 226 229 241 245 259 300 307 311 317 370 372
MELECH, 227 358
MENGEL, 367
MENGES, 103 111 350
MENICH, 84 91
MENNER, 217
MENNIER, 126
MENNINGER, 82 284 372
MERKENTHAL, 380
MERRILL, 357
MERSCH, 304 369
MERTZ, 361 366 390
MERUNY, 134

MERZ, 328 382
MESEMER, 325 339
MESMER, 376
MESSINGER, 98 100 107 110 117
    121 131 140 146 149 150 156-
    158 162-164 169 171 178 179
    181 185 188 189 193-196 201
    203-205 207 211-214 218 219
    221 229 231 239 251 257 260
    270 288 291 294 301 302 323
    330 341 347 348 350 353-356
    360 367 372 382 386 392 393
METZ, 132 292 296 299 320 321
    330 333 343 354-356 358 361
    364 365 370 372 376-378 381
    384 391 393 394 401
METZGAR, 178 241 295 297
METZGER, 167 168 189 209 231
    302 307 347 354 370 377 380
    394 398
MEUXEL, 116
MEXEL, 127
MEYER, 81 94 116 122 127 301
    399 400
MEYERS, 331
MICHAEL, 98 311 345 348 350
    360 370 372 386 394
MICHEL, 90
MICHLER, 235
MICKY, 362
MILES, 206 227 352
MILICH, 278
MILL, 188 214 219 305 358 364
    389 390
MILLER, 6 7 9 58 84 89 94 101
    133 136 144 145 157 166 194
    196 200 202 212 216 221 227
    229 230 233 237 241 244 252

MILLER (Continued)
    255 258 265 270 275 287 290
    293 294 305 306 309 312 314
    315 318 320 323 325 326 330
    334 340 341 342 348 350 352
    356 358 360 361 363-367 369
    371 372 374 377-379 381-386
    389 391 392 396 398
MILTON, 396
MIMMICH, 351
MIMON, 106
MINER, 7
MINOR, 7
MITMAN, 383 387 389
MITTENBERGER, 398
MIXSEL, 80
MIXSELL, 66 232 244 273 311
    331 374 375
MOEBECK, 101
MOEBUS, 362 396
MOELLER, 303
MOESNER, 335
MOESSINER, 124
MOESSINGER, 79 80 128 343
    346
MOFFETT, 357
MOHR, 93 94 333 334
MOIKLEY, 350
MOKELERA, 126
MOKELEREI, 15 16 119
MOKELREI, 114
MOKLEREI, 117
MOND, 312
MONIG, 93
MOOR, 86 89
MOORE, 9 17 214 357 374
MORGAN, 368
MORITZ, 99 152 173 338

MORPHY, 99
MORRIS, 25
MORTON, 76
MOSCH, 96 280
MOSEN, 224
MOSER, 97 98 102 111 116 142
    163 181 192 197 198 224 227
    231 235 236 242 243 245-247
    255 257 260 271 288 295 296
    299 308 312 336 338 351 359
    364 366 367 371 373-375 378
    379 382 387 390 391 393
MOSIER, 398
MOSS, 349
MOSTEN, 102
MOTT, 349
MOYER, 108 145 156 198 211
    228 296 302 353 366 375 378
    392
MUELLER, 96 101 103 111-114
    116 123 127 128 159 171 181
    183 294 296 297 344 354
MUENCH, 303
MUFFLEY, 322 348 360
MUFFLY, 299 315 373
MUFLEY, 385 396
MUHALLON, 17
MULHALLON, 155
MULHOLLON, 173
MULLER, 344
MURFEY, 377
MURFFY, 303
MUSCH, 89 106 107 116
MUSSELMAN, 229 243 264 325
    374
MUTCHLER, 346
MUTSCHLER, 172 284 344 364
MUTSHLER, 296

MYERS, 379
MYTAKAWHA, 28
MZGER, 167
NAGEL, 7 299 307 313 316 335
    347 349 354 357-359 369 398
NAPP, 330
NARRENGANG, 357 362
NAUL, 111
NAULY, 287
NAUMAN, 325 327 331 342 351
    374 376 377 387
NEES, 389
NEIGH, 208 240 252 328 338 354
    375
NEIHARD, 285
NEISE, 298
NEISS, 252 311 368 379 383
NEUHARDT, 296 353
NEUHART, 83 88 306 326 333
    376
NEUKOMER, 379
NEWHARD, 91
NEWMAYER, 396
NICE, 384
NICHOLAS, 226 240 254 266
    267 271 273 304 331 363 365
    376 382 383 385
NICKUM, 227 245 358 387
NICLAC, 89
NICOLAS, 89 182 292
NICOLAUS, 102 151 348 353 354
    360
NICUM, 198 322
NIEMAYER, 308
NIEMEYER, 310
NIETH, 333
NILES, 388
NISE, 398

NITAUNIER, 88
NOLF, 324 362 363 368 378 381 383 386 391 393 398
NOLL, 272 392
NONNEMACHER, 309
NORTON, 361
NUEHART, 295
NULF, 122
NUNGESSER, 117 220 234 363
NUNGESTER, 127 344
NUSBICKEL, 195
O'DANIEL, 254
OBELRY, 329
OBERDORF, 282
OBERHONER, 396
OBERLE, 50 104 146 348 353
OBERLEY, 326 333 335 392 394
OBERLY, 161 166 178 196 202 214 231 240 252 255 268 271 299 304 305 321 323 324 326 330 331 350 356 362 365 368 370 374 377 380
OBITS, 205
OBITZ, 214 218 349 358 364
OBLINGER, 351
OCHS, 359 361 366
ODENWAELDER, 103-107 111 119 123 129-131 135 146 150 152 158-160 170-172 182 184 188 194 198 200-202 205 210 215 223 224 226 227 229 231 243 245 246 248-252 254 256 258 263 264 270-272 275 278 280 296 298 299 302 311 313 330 336 346 347 350 351 353 362 364 365 369 383 385
ODENWELDER, 9 42 44 50 53 77-80 83 84 93 97 99 100 150

ODENWELDER (Continued) 170 237 275 321-323 327 341 342 373 375 376 379 381 383 385-387 390 393 394
ODEWAELDER, 109 113 114 115 119
OEHLER, 83 87 89 187
OHL, 257 301 312 324 326 338 366 367 369 389 393
OHLANGST, 144
OHNANGSH, 258
OHNANGST, 148 234 250 274 295 297 316 318 320 327 351 357 358 363 369-371 375 378 380 385 391 394 397
OLIVER, 384
ONANGST, 285
OPP, 51 80 89 98 100 103 106 107 122 124 129 199 208 298 301 303 305
ORT, 266
OSBURN, 17 204 318 368
OSBURNE, 225
OSENBACH, 233
OSTERSTOCK, 91 111 119 167 185 211 215 265 302 347 355 362 385 388
OTTO, 141 170 193 206 284 288 319 360 362 383
OVERBECK, 357
OVERLY, 347
OWEN, 362
OWERLY, 357
OX, 383
PAFF, 332 336 382 383
PAINE, 29
PAINTER, 9
PALMER, 17 189 218

PAPP, 101
PARKER, 341
PARSONS, 3 4 6 7
PASSINGER, 133 399
PATIER, 263
PATTERSON, 17 235
PAUL, 87 337 375 396
PAULUS, 87 135 152 307 345
PAYNE, 22 24
PEIFFER, 247 257 310 327 391 393 398
PENCE, 258 375
PENDER, 401
PENN, 1 3 44
PENTON, 397
PENTZ, 189 274
PENZ, 356
PERRY, 235
PERSHING, 347
PERSIL, 188
PERSON, 351
PETERSEN, 100
PFAFF, 213
PFEIFFER, 9 90 97 101 201 205 218 232 233 242 305 358
PHILIP, 186
PHILIPPI, 326
PHILIPS, 17 94 154 165 255 308 356 375
PIATT, 384
PICHT, 396 397
PINK, 364
PITHAN, 43 49 69 92
PITTERBENDER, 98 106
PLATZ, 94 98 105 191 192 230
PLECK, 392
PLOWER, 261
POHL, 388

POKE, 314
POLEN, 172
POMFRET, 1
POMP, 13 52-57 67 69 72 135 142 144 183 195 200 208 220 237 238 250 252 258 286 293 346 347 394 395
PORTER, 61 62 68 69
POTTER, 17
POTZ, 344
PRAWL, 387
PREICE, 188
PREIS, 199 213 299
PRESTON, 293
PRICE, 362 381 393
PRINCKER, 344
PRONG, 348
PRUTZMAN, 292
PURLEES, 253
PUTZ, 123
QUEER, 365 375 389
QUERE, 219
QUICK, 349
RADDLER, 9
RADENBACH, 236 377 379 397
RADER, 63
RAESLEY, 197 350
RAESLY, 163 166 187 205 353
RALSTON, 17 157
RAMBACH, 97 102 121 126 138 142 156 164 169 179 288 295
RAMBERG, 161
RAMSTEIN, 353
RANDEL, 373
RANDOLF, 352
RANDOLPH, 383
RAPP, 162
RATH, 304 307

RAU, 101 164
RAUB, 91 98 106-108 113 117 140 168 182 200 203 215 229 242 247 260 269 270 273 308 320 325 327 351 354 367 368
RAUCH, 91
RAUP, 126
RAYER, 238 366
REBSCHER, 95 99 116
REEB, 314 370
REED, 327 389 390
REEDER, 7 17 193
REEL, 376
REES, 186 210 228 236 355 360 362 366
REESER, 7 386
REESLEY, 377 385
REESLY, 210 212 217 230 360 371
REIB, 385
REICH, 307 321 323 358 363 370 372 374 384 386
REICHARD, 219 239 242 366 389 390
REICHARDT, 9 300
REICHART, 7 310 350 373 379
REICHELDOERFER, 375
REICHERT, 167
REICHURT, 152
REIDENAUER, 192 311 348 374 380
REIGEL, 180 369 384 397
REILY, 68
REIMAN, 364
REIMER, 115 133 135 139 149 166 178 189 354 355 375
REINBOLT, 397
REINECK, 378
REINHAMER, 397
REINHART, 382
REINHEIMER, 368 370 373
REIS, 172 180 185 202 214 304 353 358 362
REISNER, 385
REISS, 247 318 320 322 375 379 380 383 392
REISSER, 144
REIT, 391
REITHER, 386
REMALIE, 349
REN, 171
RENNER, 326 368
RENSHEIMER, 361
RENTSHEIMER, 369
REPSCHER, 300
RESCH, 340 377 394
RESH, 396
RESSER, 149
RESSLY, 141 148
REUTEL, 99
REWALT, 319 325
RHOEDER, 401
RIBBEL, 143
RICHARD, 135 145 157 159 160 169 177 189 192 193 199 212 226 228 231 236 237 250 252 258 264 273 288 294 295 310 329 353 360 365 370 374 375 376
RICHARDS, 9
RICHART, 151 362
RICHARTS, 137
RICHERT, 143
RICHNER, 360
RICHTER, 126 284
RICKS, 388

RIDENAUER, 336
RIEBEL, 50 97 102 103
RIECHER, 306 358
RIEDESER, 389
RIEDY, 291 297 354 356
RIEGEL, 192 212 229 241 318 326 332 352 356 360 363 367 371 375 377 379 380 382 386 392
RIEGER, 113
RIEHL, 138 275 316 350 371
RIEL, 223 295
RIES, 81 93 97 100 120 128 134 143 288 300
RIESER, 81 83 86 92 100 107 161 181 188 217 235 270 312 337 349 358 373 374 379 384 386 390 393 394
RIESLER, 355
RIESS, 376
RIESSER, 143 144 397
RIGHT, 373
RILEY, 380
RILL, 143
RILPERT, 368
RINEK, 63 75
RINKER, 7 180 326 343 359 361 398
RIPPEL, 97 106 113 125 129 156 164 178 185 207 211 274 304 310 318 344 348 350 357
RIPPLE, 181 223
RISSMILLER, 389
RITSCHER, 345
RITTER, 123 182 269 281 309 323 354 355 360 370 376 380 389 390 397
ROADT, 131
ROBBINS, 225 359

ROBERTS, 383
ROCHEL, 103
ROCKEL, 397
RODENBACH, 181 388 390 396
RODENBERGER, 324 329 377
RODGERS, 377
ROEDER, 177 254 260 270 290 294 295 319 321 324 334 337 348-351 359 360-362 365 379 383 386 387 391-394
ROELLER, 391
ROESLEY, 378
ROESSLY, 152
ROETHER, 400
ROETZ, 387
ROGERS, 340 342 384 388
ROHN, 113 119 124 132 228 294 332 353 377 388 389 392 396
ROHR, 302
ROKEL, 97 108
ROMAGE, 307
ROMIG, 188 200 210 344 362 371 384
ROS, 106
ROSE, 300 380
ROSEBERRY, 352
ROSEBURRY, 162
ROSEBURY, 232
ROSEN, 394
ROSENBERG, 279
ROSENBERGER, 101 148 155 158 330 370 371
ROSENBERRY, 348
ROSENGRAUTZ, 349
ROSER, 387
ROSS, 17 98 214 220 225 240 359 361 383
ROTH, 151 231 245 246 261 263

ROTH (Continued)
    301 304 305 312 315 316 321
    331-334 336 339 346-349 351
    354 358 360 361 367 369 371
    375-377 381 382 387 388 390
    393
ROTHER, 125
ROTHROCK, 147 214 337 341
    342 351 352 359 361 366 368
    389 391
ROUCH, 397
ROUP, 44
ROWLAND, 376
ROWNIG, 9
ROYALL, 9
ROYER, 311
RUCH, 330 369 392
RUF, 396
RUMFELD, 356
RUNDIO, 363
RUNDIS, 356 363
RUNDLE, 351
RUP, 147
RUPP, 27
RUSSEL, 390
RUSSELL, 7 137 260 311
RUTH, 327 331 333 339 352 355
    369 372 373 377 380 381 384
    385 388 391
RUTHSTEIN, 88
SAAM, 84
SABEL, 102
SACKS, 190
SAENTY, 344
SAETZER, 301
SALSICH, 217
SALZICH, 230
SALZIG, 253 371

SAMPSON, 367
SAMSEL, 337 381
SAND, 109 116 136 139 141 148
    149 151 164 168 179 183 187
    195 198 201 225 231 295 307
    345 364 365 373 376 379 389
    390
SANDEL, 103
SANDERS, 391
SANDT, 386
SANDY, 9
SANTEE, 66
SANTY, 281
SARRELS, 213
SASSAMAN, 139 391
SAUBERTS, 101
SAUERBECK, 206 311 350 357
SAX, 103 267
SAYLOR, 17 66 165 197 198 200
    354 357 365 366 374
SCHAADE, 359
SCHABEL, 350
SCHADE, 219 246 333 335 356
    365 369
SCHADI, 285
SCHAEFER, 199 205 227 233 302
    321 328 332 375 381 384 387
SCHAEFFER, 111 168 300 302
    350
SCHAERER, 198 235 239 252
    271 371 379
SCHALL, 86 373 398
SCHARDT, 337
SCHARLEY, 363
SCHARP, 399
SCHAUB, 88 104 112 118 143
SCHAUM, 302 304 354 355 366
    382

SCHAUP, 207 304
SCHAUS, 106 110 113 119 123 279 280 295
SCHAUSE, 130
SCHAUSS, 92
SCHEETZ, 275 350
SCHEIB, 44 79 80 126 133 170 183
SCHEIBELY, 383
SCHEID, 370
SCHEIERMAN, 203 213 235
SCHEIMER, 231 257 359
SCHEIOCLEINE, 342
SCHEIP, 204 224 259 314 321
SCHEIPP, 130
SCHEIVELY, 257 274 386
SCHEIVLEY, 154 389 391
SCHEIVLY, 398
SCHEKRER, 103
SCHELLY, 333 360 369
SCHENEN, 112
SCHENK, 397
SCHERER, 148 158 228 256 364
SCHERLACH, 286
SCHERNER, 266
SCHERP, 279 284 399
SCHERRER, 222
SCHEUERMAN, 216 356 386 391 392
SCHEUERMANN, 102 108
SCHICK, 145 153 160 161 177 181-183 206 227 228 233 306 327 337 344 354 355 365 373 383
SCHIFFER, 192 204 317 324 336 358 367 368 384 388
SCHIFFLER, 398
SCHIK, 104

SCHIKLI, 109 110
SCHILB, 286
SCHILL, 371 381
SCHISTER, 177
SCHITZ, 383
SCHIVELY, 317
SCHLABACH, 333 379
SCHLAM, 391
SCHLATTER, 6 39 40
SCHLAUCH, 111 160 169 196 199 230 354
SCHLAUG, 321
SCHLAUGH, 244 389
SCHLECHT, 260 311 320 333 336 351 354 358 366 382
SCHLEGEL, 378
SCHLEPPE, 294 300 332
SCHLEPPER, 282
SCHLEPPI, 309 369 370
SCHLEPPY, 348
SCHLOUCH, 222
SCHLOUGH, 183 184 186 355
SCHMID, 122 140 147 169 171
SCHMIDT, 83 86 100 105 127 129 183 194 206 212 220 229 253 257 258 266 269 279 289 293 304 311 338 347 354 355 357 358 362 368 369 371 373 380 384 390 396 397
SCHMIKE, 385
SCHMINCK, 389
SCHMIT, 369
SCHNABEL, 131 161 167 248 269 317 369 373 375 379 388 392
SCHNADER, 148
SCHNECK, 54
SCHNEIDER, 42 77 83 86-91 93

SCHNEIDER (Continued)
   119 128 133 155 279 282 344
   345 348 387 400
SCHNERR, 385 393
SCHNEYDER, 98 99 108 110 112
   113 115 118 130 132 151 155
   157 159 179-181 351 361
SCHNYDER, 136 138 152 190
   191 222 287 312 355 365 375
   380 385 389 398
SCHOENTHAL, 386
SCHOLL, 101 109 126 169
SCHONZ, 151
SCHOOLEY, 367
SCHOOLY, 17 203
SCHORDTS, 345
SCHORTZ, 317 386
SCHOWER, 252
SCHRANTZ, 330
SCHREDER, 355
SCHREIBER, 356 394
SCHREIVER, 324
SCHROEDER, 326 332 339 390
SCHUBB, 181
SCHUBMAN, 399
SCHUCH, 306
SCHUCHARD, 154
SCHUCK, 77 78 110 112 117 119
   123 124 127 130 134 135 137
   141 147 157 158 164 180 182
   189 195 201 206 207 213 223
   258 282 284 295 298 299 301
   325 349 350 355 356 358 366
   369 370 372 389
SCHUESSER, 178
SCHUESSTER, 153 156
SCHUESTER, 161
SCHUG, 143 148 149 161 168 349

SCHUHMACHER, 77 116
SCHUK, 352
SCHULER, 380
SCHULTZ, 344 380
SCHUMACHER, 78 83 92 100
   107 108 111-113 120 126-128
   131 137 145 151 157 179 189
   207 228 242 247 261 267 270
   289 304 318 344 346 347 352
   355 358 360 363 368
SCHUMAN, 178 231
SCHUMPER, 165
SCHURTZ, 7 307 362 363 370
   393
SCHURZ, 374
SCHWARBACH, 49
SCHWARTZ, 104 107 116 121
   141 147 153 160 189 196 229
   235 287 294 298 310 315 335
   341 360 363 372 378 383
SCHWARZ, 129 324
SCHWEISHAUPT, 310
SCHWEITZER, 133 154 156 163
   187 188 195 207 210 213 217
   218 220 221 233 252 317 350
   352 354 356 360 362 388 393
SCHWEITZZER, 188
SCHWEIZER, 204 368
SCHWENK, 351
SCHWERTZER, 161
SCHWETIZER, 384
SCHYDER, 355
SCNABEL, 172
SCRIBNER, 223
SCULEY, 373
SCULL, 7
SCULY, 248 262 367
SEAGREAVES, 17 215 248 255

SEAGREAVES (Continued)
  352
SEARLES, 17
SEAWARD, 382
SEBRING, 136
SECHER, 110
SEHLER, 97
SEIB, 138 186 346 347 381
SEIBBEL, 133
SEIBEL, 118 121 133 144 170
SEIBERT, 357
SEIDER, 388
SEIFERT, 387
SEIFFERT, 266 279 280 364
SEIFRIED, 387
SEIFRIEDT, 388
SEILER, 117 122 137 145 151 247
  265 271 334 346 368 369 386
  387 390
SEIP, 9 185 191 211 224 225 233
  239 243 245 250 255 271 275
  302 308 338 339 340 365 367
  368 370 372 377 379 387
SEIPEL, 135 178 194 201 202 204
  214 216 233 235 245 252 261
  265 266 298 304 309 323 328
  356 375 386 388 391 397
SEITEL, 371
SEITZ, 353
SELER, 128
SELLER, 131 136
SENDEE, 301 302 376
SENDII, 357
SENDY, 305 358 362 366 371
SENTEE, 323 340 386 393
SENTRY, 353
SERRELS, 193 207
SETTEL, 104

SETZER, 344
SEWITZ, 116 215 265 278 279
  354 363 379
SEYERS, 149
SEYMOUR, 382
SHADE, 251 319 327 366 398
SHAEFER, 215 305 321
SHAEFFER, 187
SHAERER, 198 357
SHAUM, 374
SHEIMER, 336 364 368
SHEIP, 173 222 237 244 252 254
  255 274 311 338 392
SHEIVELY, 259 262
SHEIVLEY, 378
SHELLY, 394
SHERLOCK, 286
SHERR, 383
SHEUND, 9
SHEWEL, 372
SHICK, 241
SHIMER, 247
SHIPMAN, 375
SHNEYDER, 129
SHNYDER, 53 66 197 209 210-
  212 241 243 248 250 253-255
  258 259 262 263 307 315 325
  328 341 361 362 364 367 369
  377 386 388 393
SHOCH, 235
SHOCK, 391
SHOEMACHER, 202
SHOLL, 379 383
SHOOK, 9 347
SHOUP, 165
SHOUSE, 127 390
SHUCH, 214
SHUCK, 177 187 193 195 215 221

SHUCK (Continued)
   248 255 353 384 385 393 398
SHUHMAN, 385
SHUMACHER, 235 243 251
SHUMAKER, 44
SHUMAN, 187 380
SHUP, 397
SHYDER, 312
SIBELE, 147
SICHLIN, 111
SICKMAN, 131 141 180 257 364
SICKMANN, 117
SIDMAN, 28 363
SIDMANN, 117
SIEBRING, 371
SIEGEL, 105 209 292 331-334 339
   341 357 362 368 370 387 393
   398
SIEGFRIED, 298 303 308 313 320
   329 356 358 359 363 371 374
SIEGLE, 338
SIEGLER, 348
SIEGLEY, 319 382
SIEGLY, 241
SIEGMAN, 268
SIEMAN, 306
SIENTEOG, 9
SIEPEL, 359
SIFFART, 93
SIKLIN, 109
SIKMAN, 122
SIKMANN, 107
SILFUSS, 362
SIMON, 44 77 81 86 87 90 93 102
   108 111 132 135 155 159 160
   173 177 187 197 208 223 247
   262 264 266 289 294 304 308
   316 322 365 372 376 379 382

SIMON (Continued)
   398
SIMONS, 218 321
SIMSON, 362
SINGER, 337 373
SITES, 357
SITGREAVES, 17 189 353
SIVELY, 310
SIWILLE, 294
SLAUCH, 169
SLAYTOR, 227 357
SLEPPI, 353
SLETER, 390
SLIEWER, 389
SMIDT, 287 320
SMITH, 7 9 234 246 258 268 273
   293 295 349 350 357 366 371-
   373 382 387 388 390 396
SNABEL, 374
SNYDER, 44 122 123 201 204 210
   224 233 248 254 271 272 308
   309 317 319 322 342 351 367
   370 372 373 376 378 383 397
SOBER, 296 302 359
SOLOMON, 360
SOMER, 99
SOMMER, 195 197 222 251 269
   317 376
SOMMERS, 230 237
SOMNEY, 289
SORBER, 348
SOURBECK, 228
SPANGENBERG, 87 149 253 261
   264 265 288 308 316 348
SPANGENBERGER, 97
SPANGLER, 140
SPANOMER, 299
SPECHT, 101

SPEER, 375
SPENGLER, 364
SPENKLER, 140
SPINNER, 359
SPONHEIMER, 304 341 375 389
STACKHAUS, 394
STACKHOUSE, 388
STADLER, 377
STAETLER, 384
STAM, 348
STAMM, 312
STANSBURY, 242 398
STANTON, 382
STAPP, 366 375 381
STAUFFER, 330 341 350 358 379
STAUT, 309 347 380 381
STECHER, 88 90 94 98 102 107 108 111 114 124 133 138 149 156 158 182 185 188 197 198 212 213 221 224 300 334 349 350 352 353 363-365 377 390
STECKEL, 219 273 321 323 336 357 360 366
STECKER, 156
STEEL, 345 386
STEIN, 91 148 162 163 228 314 343 349 352 396
STEINBACH, 217 231 236 238 244 259 262 264 314 315 355 361 368 370 371
STEINBRENNER, 272
STEINER, 120 305 380
STEINHELFER, 385
STEINMETZ, 349 355 376 377 382 386 393 396
STEITINGER, 122 253 275 280 328
STEM, 62 68 169 170 193 203 206

STEM (Continued) 219 239 253 261 287 289 319 321 323 324 336 350 362 371 375 382 383 390 396
STEMM, 178 180 197 209 225 256 350 352 353 355
STENGER, 179 199 204 214 217 360 361 382
STERN, 319
STERNER, 265 294 360 364 365 367 374
STETLER, 274
STEVENS, 138
STEVENSON, 369
STEWART, 63
STICHDERNOTH, 354
STIEHL, 109 351
STILES, 375
STINE, 193
STOCK, 379
STOCKER, 141 144 146 149 162 164 166 172 185 187 188 190 197-201 204 207 211 218 239 241 254 259 265 267 281 298 300 301 310 326 337 352 355 360 364 371 372 376 378 383 389 392 396 397 398
STOEHR, 385
STOFFLET, 193 198 299 364 368 392 393
STOFFLETS, 292
STOFLET, 172 387
STOLTZ, 107
STONEBACH, 398
STORM, 89 91 386
STOTZ, 379 397
STOUT, 336 361 363
STRAUB, 380

STRAUS, 353 359
STREBER, 310
STREIKER, 364
STREUBER, 294
STRIEBE, 300
STRIET, 49
STUBEN, 371
STUBER, 374
STUCKER, 122 125
STUEHL, 345
STUKER, 344
STUMP, 336 375 385 387 388
STUMPF, 311
SUEHN, 297
SUMMY, 350
SWANDER, 264 265 314 322 324
SWARTHWOOD, 389
SWERER, 362
SWESEY, 374
SWETLAND, 265
SWETLING, 369
SYNG, 26
TAASQUAH 28, 31
TAUBERT, 375
TAWANAH, 28
TAYLOR, 17 21 22 24 27 50 228
    258 318 326 331 337 341 359
    360 362 372 377 382 393
TEEDYSCUNG, 4 24
TEEDYUSCUNG, 1 23
TEEL, 377
TEISS, 310
TERRE, 280
TERRY, 280
TETZT, 141
THIEL, 343 344
THOMAS, 172 369
THOMPSON, 63 363

THRON, 180 354
TIEL, 330
TILDHEIMER, 344
TILTON, 228 372
TITIUS, 144
TITUS, 232
TODDEN, 16 146
TOEPPLIN, 106
TOLEMAN, 342
TOWNSEND, 9 17
TOWNSON, 158 189 317 348
TRACH, 197 310 368
TRAHN, 258
TRAILL, 17 310
TRANSU, 161 296 354
TRANSUE, 213 219 220 229 239
    242 245 256 260 303 306 310
    315 320 323 327-329 341 342
    360 362 365 366 368 369 372-
    378 382 384 396
TRAUCH, 95
TRAXEL, 78 79 116 119 122 124
    127 129 132 134 140 142 147
    151 152 168 170 171 381
TRAXELL, 135 137 138 190 223
    238 347
TRAXSEL, 348 352 354
TRAXSELL, 129 184 185 186 188
    197 210 211 222 224 226 231
    242 243 248 249 258 259 267
    273 289 301 303 306 308 312
    315 319 322 331 360 361 371
TREISBACH, 344 345
TREXLER, 7
TRITTENBACH, 359
TROCKENMILLER, 376
TROXEL, 44 77 79 101 102 110
    130 141

TROXELL, 44 101
TRUCKS, 353 361
TRUM, 87
TRUMBAUER, 401
TRUMBOR, 375
TRUMBORE, 385
TRUMHELLER, 100 181 288
TSCHUDI, 186
TSCHUDY, 356
TSCHUMPER, 15
TUFFART, 87
TUTT, 295
UEBERROTH, 392
UHL, 114
UHLER, 141 163 164 181 193 194
   197 204 207 217 225 226 241
   327 332 348 357 376 381 383
   390
ULER, 98 100 108
ULY, 124 125 284
UNANGST, 397
VALLY, 272
VANDERSLOOT, 208
VANHORN, 356
VANLEAR, 384
VANNETTE, 92
VERNON, 3 6 7
VIERLING, 334
VOCHT, 385
VOELKE, 306
VOELKER, 370
VOGEL, 132 180 321 339 346 364
   365 367 368 377 383 388 394
   398
VOGT, 96 288 348
VOLLMER, 352
VULCAR, 143
WACKER, 296

WAGENER, 144 355 370 396
WAGLE, 7
WAGNER, 108 125 141 145 148
   149 156 157 165 186 191 194
   202 207 213 218 220 226 228
   236 238 244 246 252 260 263
   265 269 274 303 314 316 317
   320 322 323 330 335 354 355
   356 366 377 378 381-384 387
   392 393 396
WAGONER, 191 198 259 274
WAIED, 131
WALDER, 347
WALKER, 365
WALL, 184
WALSCH, 44
WALTEN, 329
WALTER, 96 100 103 123 136
   149 159 165 173 181 189 200
   207 222 228 231-233 241 244
   245 247 250 255 258 262 267
   268 269 271 307 313-315 324
   327 329 330 335 355 359 365
   366 369 374-376 378-384 387
   388 392-394
WALTON, 21 22 24 27 50
WARD, 16 82 85 137 209 212 227
   237 249 260 272 300 301 312
   315 318 346 351 361 370 372
   384
WARNER, 292 294 295 335 363
   370
WARRICH, 381
WARRIG, 329
WARTMAN, 350
WARTON, 351
WASHBORN, 361 364
WASHINGTON, 48

WASSER, 305 310 311 329 357 359 372 374
WATRING, 344
WATTRING, 78 114
WAYN, 257
WEAVER, 9 322 396
WEBER, 128 165 186 225 240 287 302 309 313 318 323 327 333 338 348 350 351 355 357 362 364 366 368 369 371 373 377-380 382 384 386 387 390-392 398
WEIBERG, 200
WEICHANT, 97 102
WEIDELICH, 98
WEIDMAN, 7 286 297 347
WEIERBACHER, 107
WEIERMAN, 312
WEINBERG, 243 337
WEINEL, 355
WEINLAND, 245 256 339 364
WEIS, 137 189 203 217 226 230 305 308 313 360
WEISER, 4 23
WEISGERBER, 323
WEISS, 176 212 217 238 250 256 268 274 313 322 323 332 337 365 371 378 381
WEITMAN, 396
WEITZEL, 217 357
WEIZEL, 200 204 206
WELDY, 358
WELLER, 275
WELSCH, 78 104 110 111 121 127
WELSH, 361 399
WELTY, 321
WENSEL, 392
WENTZ, 350
WERCKHAEUSER, 364 365
WERKHAEUSER, 182 195 196 203 209 221 230 235 303 328 360 374 375 377 385 387 388 389
WERKHAUSER, 128
WERKHEUSER, 392
WERKHOUSER, 397
WERNER, 90 314 318 320 332 334 336 367 370 382 391 394
WERSCHEL, 338
WESNER, 206
WEST, 218 253 266
WESTERMAN, 181
WETSEL, 373
WEVER, 306
WEYAND, 115
WEYANT, 114
WEYBERG, 11 41 42 69 81 82
WEYGAND, 44 120 133
WEYGANDT, 87 121 187 238 257 259 266 267 316 325 327 328 333 364
WEYGANT, 111
WHARTON, 25-27
WHITE, 16 165 182 208 239
WHITESELL, 76
WICHELHAUSER, 273
WILAKNKO, 28
WILHELM, 100 120 144 206 235 252 279 298 306 309 311 317 318 320 324 328 331 332 334 335 338 352 353 356-358 364 366 369 372 373 378 381-384 388 393 398
WILKINS, 359
WILLAUER, 148 158 162 166

WILLAUER (Continued)
  173 182 201 209 217 291 299
  345 352 370 372 377 397
WILLERS, 348
WILLERSDORF, 266
WILLHELM, 281 361 372
WILLIAM, 326 344
WILLIAMS, 303
WILT, 331 383
WIMMER, 380 383
WIND, 130 358
WINN, 367
WINTER, 17 44 78 79 80 113 121
  155 203 271 288 344 371 399
WINTERS, 142 146 163 172 183
  354 363 365 378
WITE, 165
WITHERS, 297
WITHUS, 182
WITMAN, 339
WITMER, 282
WITTEMER, 370
WOLBACH, 251
WOLF, 17 127 153 164 173 176
  192 203 215 237 246 309 316
  329 340 351 358 362 382
WOLFF, 54-56 67 69 72 154 168
  281
WOLFINGER, 304 387
WOLLBACH, 333
WOLLENSCHLAEGER, 257 276
WOODLEY, 350
WOODRING, 144 145 148 150
  163 166 171 177 183 184 188
  191 201 202 204 208 209 212
  221 224 235 236 238 249 252
  256 261 264 265 269 273 275
  276 286 294 298 299 303 313

WOODRING (Continued)
  314 318 325 351 355 368 370
  374 375 378-381 384 386 388
WOODRINGER, 137
WOOLEVER, 361
WOOTRING, 340 342 391 393
  394 397
WORKHAEUSER, 230
WORKMAN, 351
WORLY, 367
WORMAN, 195 206 207 224 243
  253 274 275 314 315 327 350
  357 374
WORTON, 274
WOTRING, 79 126 134
WOTTERING, 78
WOTTRING, 106 118 120
WOTTRINGET, 109
WUBLER, 384
WUDRING, 161
WUNDERLING, 381 386
WYKOFF, 66
YAEGER, 85 88 97 115 133 150
  158 251 269 275 288 298 351
  369 372 378 389
YAEKEL, 383
YAERGER, 372
YATES, 151 210 238
YEAGER, 183
YEDISTIRE, 347
YEISLE, 170
YEISLEY, 134 140 145 146 152
  157 160 162 163 167 177 189
  219 239 253 259 262 264 268
  280 347 352 353 370 378 381
  394
YETZ, 118
YIESLEY, 332

YOB, 398
YODDER, 322 365 372
YODER, 330
YOHE, 7 96 97 113 137 160 350 352 364 375
YOST, 103 362 371 378
YOST----, 352
YOUNG, 9 44 63 78 85 92 96 97 100 101 108 110 112 127 138 140 148 156 161 167 168 180 183 196 203 205 206 215 216 221 228 235 240 241 243 244 252 255 256 259 260 262 266 268 270-272 276 279 295 306 316 317 319 322 323 325 329 330 334 335 338 343 345 346 348 351 353 356 357 360 365 366 370-372 379 381 382 385 390 392 393 397 399 401
YUNCKER, 296
YUNDT, 343
YUNKEN, 358
YUNKER, 196 302
ZEIGENFUSS, 359
ZELLER, 125 134 186 269 284 366 386
ZELLERS, 380
ZERFASS, 185 393
ZETTEL, 120
ZIEGENFUSS, 289 310 338 360 385
ZIEGENTHAL, 385
ZIEGER, 387
ZIEGLER, 163 315 354 363 372
ZIMMERMAN, 98 109 116 162 186 211 257 316 356 364 394 399
ZOELLER, 287 349
ZOPFY, 359
ZUILCH, 76

www.ingramcontent.com/pod-product-compliance
Lightning Source LLC
Chambersburg PA
CBHW050829230426
43667CB00012B/1928